Fourth Edition

IN OUR TIMES

America Since World War II

Norman L. Rosenberg
Emily S. Rosenberg

Macalester College

NEW ENGLAND INSTITUTE OF TECHNOLOGY
LIBRARY

PRENTICE HALL, Englewood Cliffs, New Jersey 07632

Rosenberg, Norman L.,
    In our times : America since World War II / Norman L. Rosenberg,
Emily S. Rosenberg. -- 4th ed.
      p.   cm.
    Includes bibliographical references and index.
    ISBN 0-13-465899-X
    1. United States--History--1945-   I. Rosenberg, Emily S.,
. II. Title.
E741.R667 1991
973.92--dc20   90-44632
                                                       CIP

Editorial/production supervision and
    interior design: Michael R. Steinberg
Cover design: Diane Conner/Marianne Frasco
Prepress buyer: Debra Kesar
Manufacturing buyer: Mary Ann Gloriande
Acquisitions Editor: Steve Dalphin

 © 1991, 1987, 1982, 1976 by Prentice-Hall, Inc.
A Division of Simon & Schuster
Englewood Cliffs, New Jersey 07632

Printed in the United States of America

10 9 8 7 6 5 4 3 2 1

ISBN 0-13-465899-X

PRENTICE-HALL INTERNATIONAL (UK) LIMITED, *London*
PRENTICE-HALL OF AUSTRALIA PTY. LIMITED, *Sydney*
PRENTICE-HALL CANADA INC., *Toronto*
PRENTICE-HALL HISPANOAMERICANA, S.A., *Mexico*
PRENTICE-HALL OF INDIA PRIVATE LIMITED, *New Delhi*
PRENTICE-HALL OF JAPAN, INC., *Tokyo*
SIMON & SCHUSTER ASIA PTE. LTD. *Singapore*
EDITORA PRENTICE-HALL DO BRASIL, LTDA., *Rio de Janeiro*

To the memories of Joseph and Dorothea Rosenberg
and to Albert A. and Helen Griggs Schlaht,
and our children, Sarah, Molly, Ruth, Joseph

Contents

Chapter Eleven

Nostalgia and Nostrums: The United States in the 1980s   285

Preface

In preparing a fourth edition of *In Our Times*, we have tried to follow our initial goal: to provide students and instructors with a useful framework upon which they can expand their own views of the history of postwar United States. Heartened by the many positive responses and humbled by justified criticism, we have maintained the basic approach of the book, while continuing to modify the portions that seemed troublesome.

Every section of this edition has been revised and updated to reflect new scholarship, and many portions, including the final chapter, have been completely rewritten.

We wish, again, to thank our colleagues and students at Macalester College; Lee Allen Dew of Kentucky Wesleyan College and Melvin Small of Wayne State University, who reviewed the previous edition for purposes of this revision; Kimberlee Gunning, who expertly did the index; and our production editor, Michael Steinberg. Final special thanks go to Prentice Hall's History Editor, Steve Dalphin, for his encouragement and support over the past fifteen years.

This book, like our teaching career, is a joint production. For any errors that have slipped through, the traditional response offered to students and colleagues remains operative: "You must be looking for the other Professor Rosenberg."

Chapter One

The World's Superpower

COLLAPSE OF THE OLD ORDER, RISE OF THE NEW

The war was over! Japan had surrendered! At seven in the evening on August 14, 1945, President Harry S Truman made the official announcement. Across the country people began to celebrate the end of World War II. Outside the White House, a crowd that had been waiting all day struck up the chant, "We want Harry, we want Harry!" The president appeared, said a few words, and left, only to be called back twice more by repeated shouts. Finally, he sank into a chair and expressed the universal sentiment: "I'm glad that it's over."

However, pressing problems and hard decisions did not end with the war. Postwar reconstruction and the development of a cold war between the United States and the Soviet Union kept international affairs in a state of perpetual crisis.

Before World War II Europeans believed they occupied the center of progress, civilization, and world power. London and Paris set the trends in world culture, held the reins of government for colonial peoples throughout the globe, and provided financial institutions for the business of far-flung empires. But World War II, coming only two decades after the tremendous strain of World War I, dramatically altered Europe's position. The costs of the long struggle left the nations of Europe—both the victors and the vanquished—exhausted and bankrupt. As Europeans spent their military and economic strength in what some historians have called a European civil war, their grasp over colonial areas weakened. Worldwide fighting strengthened local nationalist movements and whetted tastes for independence and self-determination. Anticolonial revolutionary movements were poised to dismember the European empires and to create a host of new nations in Asia and Africa.

As the old order of European dominance and colonialism disintegrated after the war, few dared to predict what would happen. Cordell Hull, Franklin D. Roosevelt's secretary of state, warned that "the people of many countries will be starving . . . homeless . . . their factories and mines destroyed; their roads and transport wrecked. . . . Disease will lurk everywhere. In some countries confusion and chaos will follow the cessation of hostilities." Hull advised that "victory must be followed by swift and effective action to meet these pressing human needs."

It fell to America, Hull and other internationalists believed, to supply the blueprint for a postwar order. Untouched by battle, enriched by wartime profits, and free from scarcity and instability, the United States emerged as victor of the victors. With much of the world in its debt, America became the undisputed superpower. American leaders tried to devise ways of using this power in postwar diplomacy. The supposed folly of isolationism and the "lessons" of appeasement during the 1920s and 1930s had turned many American policymakers into internationalists. Throughout the war they planned for postwar reconstruction.

One of the architects of American policy, Undersecretary of State Dean Acheson (later Truman's secretary of state), entitled his memoirs of this period *Present at the Creation*. The title was revealing. It reflected the belief that Americans would have to construct a new world order. It also displayed confidence—even arrogance—in America's ability to shape events. To policymakers like Acheson, forming a postwar settlement would involve little give-and-take diplomacy; it would be primarily an act of creation, a monumental American-directed effort affecting the well-being of future generations.

The American Vision

How did American policymakers envision the postwar world? Two articles of internationalist faith—maintenance of open access for trade and investment and creation of an international organization—provided the cornerstones of America's plan for lasting peace.

A trading nation with a dynamic, expanding economy, America had always opposed restrictions to the free flow of its overseas trade and investment. During the Depression decade of the 1930s, Americans watched uneasily as economic restrictions threatened to close large parts of the world to their businesses. Great Britain moved toward an "imperial preference" system that placed nations outside the British Empire at a commercial disadvantage; Japan's expansionist leaders threatened to create a closed economic sphere in Asia; fascist Germany reached out to encompass new sources of raw materials. American leaders hoped to eliminate restrictionist trends in the postwar world. They believed that unhampered commerce brought peace, while economic restrictions—such as unequal tariffs, preferential commercial arrangements, and currency inconvertibility—bred jealousy and war. "If we could get a freer flow of trade," Cordell Hull wrote, "the living standards of all countries might rise, thereby eliminating the economic dissatisfaction that breeds war." While ushering in prosperity and peace, freer trade would, not incidentally, also enhance United States influence worldwide because of America's dominant financial position. In planning a postwar world, as in most other endeavors, ideology and self-interest dovetailed.

During World War II, Roosevelt also revived the Wilsonian dream of an international peacekeeping organization. The notion that a free exchange of ideas promoted understanding, compromise, and consensus had been a persistent American belief, and many influential Americans became convinced that an international body would serve, not undermine, national interests in the postwar world. Refusal to join the League of Nations after

V-J Day in Omaha. All across the country, people were celebrating victory over Japan. Source: *Nebraska State Historical Society.*

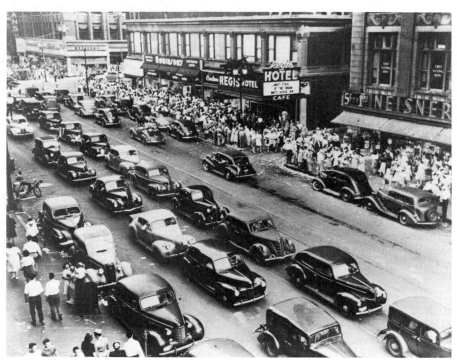

World War I, policymakers believed, had contributed to the breakdown of peace in 1939. Behind their convictions lay certain assumptions: that international conflicts often stemmed from breakdowns in communication, that free debate would produce a consensus in support of the most convincing argument, and that the American point of view would invariably triumph in an open forum. A representative world assembly, policymakers believed, would provide a means of moderating tensions and building a world community under the aegis of the United States, Britain, France, and the Soviet Union. These powers would become the collective guarantors of postwar peace.

American postwar plans sounded selfless and impartial. Nonrestrictive trade and investment policies and an open international forum for debate appeared to give everyone an equal chance and to set aside narrow nationalism. But critics of American policy claimed that those policies would inevitably advance the interests of the nation that was economically and politically the strongest—the United States. Americans used internationalist rhetoric, critics charged, only to camouflage self-interest and their own globalist designs.

Did American policy serve the world or itself? Could it do both? These questions have formed the basis for many of the debates on postwar American foreign policy. They have also been central to interpreting the cold war that developed between America and the Soviet Union. In the period immediately following the war few American observers doubted that their country's policy was righteous and benign. But a newer generation of analysts, writing mostly after the debacle of Vietnam, severely criticized an America that tended to identify the world's well-being with its own. The nature of America's role in the postwar world promises to remain a contentious issue in future historical debates.

Reconstructing an International Economic System

Secretary of State Hull made America's position on economic issues clear: It expected equal access to trade and raw materials in the postwar world. As a condition for receiving lend-lease assistance from the United States during the war, Allied nations had to promise to work toward the "elimination of all forms of discriminatory treatment in international commerce." And in July 1944 representatives from forty-four countries gathered at Bretton Woods, New Hampshire, to work out a postwar economic structure. The Soviet Union did not attend. Although the Bretton Woods delegates did not adopt every American proposal, they did formulate a system that generally reflected American goals.

Stable monetary exchange rates and full convertibility among the world's currencies seemed essential to free-flowing trade and investment. The delegates consequently created the International Monetary Fund (IMF) and charged it with maintaining a stable international system of exchange in which each national currency was convertible into any other at a fixed rate. A country could alter its exchange rate (that is, adjust the value of its money in relation to other currencies) only by agreement with the IMF. The architects of the IMF hoped that the system would combat the economic nationalism of the 1930s and believed that it would forge an interdependent world economy that would contribute to peace. The system of exchange rates did provide the foundation for unparalleled growth and prosperity in the developed nations of the Western world.

The delegates to Bretton Woods also created the International Bank for Reconstruction and Development, now called the World Bank. This institution was to encourage loans for postwar economic recovery. Loans would help restore war-ruined economies and bring resumption of normal trading patterns; financial stabilization, it was believed, would also help curb radical political movements that fed on economic discontent. Since its creation, the World Bank has been dominated by American capital and headed by an American director. It gained its most prestigious head when Robert McNamara, former secretary of defense under presidents Kennedy and Johnson, directed the bank between 1967 and 1981.

United States support for the World Bank stemmed not only from a desire to stabilize and assist needy nations, but also from the pragmatic realization that its own trade would suffer unless other countries possessed the money to buy its products. In addition, the World Bank advanced American interests by promising to foster private investment. The bank would participate in or guarantee private American loans made in foreign nations. America was by far the richest nation in the postwar world, and the bank helped many Americans invest their excess capital around the globe, particularly in the development of raw materials needed by American industry. The outflow of American investment reduced the pressures toward inflation at home and greatly increased America's financial holdings abroad. Americans believed that the World Bank served world reconstruction and America's domestic prosperity equally well.

The Bretton Woods agreements stabilized the international economy and helped revive trade and investment. They helped sustain America's postwar economic predominance, and the American dollar became the kingpin of international finance. Until 1971, when a system of floating exchange rates replaced the fixed system set forth at Bretton Woods, the economic agreements of 1944 remained the foundation for the world economy outside the Soviet bloc. For the developed nations, Bretton Woods provided a structure for nearly three decades of dynamic growth and global economic integration.

The Creation of the United Nations

During World War II, American officials revived Woodrow Wilson's idea of a League of Nations. They proposed an international body that would mediate disputes and create a multinational force to deter potential aggressors. They hoped to substitute collective security for old-style balance-of-power diplomacy.

At Dumbarton Oaks in Washington, D.C., in August 1944 and at San

Francisco in April 1945, the wartime Allies hammered out the structural details of the United Nations. They established a General Assembly, in which all member nations had one vote; a Security Council composed of five permanent members (the United States, Great Britain, France, the Soviet Union, and Nationalist China) and six rotating temporary members; a Secretariat to handle day-to-day business; and an Economic and Social Council comprising committees for worldwide social rehabilitation and economic development.

The Security Council, which according to the UN charter had the "primary responsibility for the maintenance of international peace and security," consisted of the major victors in World War II. The inclusion of China, at American insistence, always seemed incongruous. At the time of the UN charter, China possessed an unpopular and corrupt government led by Jiang Jie-shi (formerly spelled Chiang Kai-shek). Many observers doubted that Jiang could maintain control at home, much less play an active role in international affairs. But the inclusion of Jiang's China represented the Roosevelt administration's desire to turn China into a friendly Pacific power that would fill the vacuum left by Japan's defeat. In 1949, however, Jiang's Nationalist government fled to the small island of Formosa and a communist regime headed by Mao Zedong (formerly spelled Mao Tse-tung) came to power. Under Mao, China did become a major power, but the Nationalist regime continued to sit on the Security Council until 1971. This discrepancy between the realities of world power and Security Council membership proved to be a weakness of the United Nations.

The provision for veto power within the Security Council also undermined the UN's effectiveness. The charter provided that each permanent member of the Security Council could exercise an absolute veto over UN decisions. None of the great powers would have joined the UN without this means of safeguarding their national interests. But the veto provision meant that the United Nations could act only when all five permanent members agreed, and unanimity was rare in the postwar world. The UN's strongest action, sponsoring a military force to assist South Korea in 1950, was approved during the absence of the Soviet Union's delegate.

If the Security Council did not always fulfill the peace-keeping role that its founders envisioned, other UN bodies did serve useful functions. The humanitarian programs of the UN's various social and economic agencies boosted UN prestige. In addition, the General Assembly provided a forum in which nations could articulate their positions; it was a barometer of international tensions and a gauge of shifting views on various issues. It also provided a platform for smaller nations whose viewpoints might not otherwise be heard.

During the early years, the United States dominated UN votes and structures. However, as United States global policies became increasingly unpopular in Third World nations and as more and more new nations joined the body, the United States began to find itself isolated and embattled in UN forums. The UN did not fulfill the hopes of American globalists during the 1940s—but neither was it a failure.

THE ONSET OF THE COLD WAR

The political and economic order that American leaders had planned depended upon cooperation among the great powers. But divisions within the wartime Grand Alliance eventually undermined the kind of world that American policymakers hoped to create.

Mounting Distrust

Throughout the war, tensions had existed between the Soviet Union and the other Allies. The greatest disputes centered on the issue of wartime strategy. British planners, eventually supported by the United States, favored peripheral campaigns against Germany, first into French North Africa and then up through Sicily and Italy. Soviet Premier Joseph Stalin denounced these Anglo-American offensives because they delayed the opening of a second front to the west of Germany and forced the Soviet Union to bear the main thrust of German power. Stalin suspected that his allies were carving out spheres of influence in North Africa, Italy, and the Middle East while allowing Germany and the Soviet Union to exhaust each other. The long delay in opening a second front, Stalin reasoned, indicated that the wartime alliance against Nazism had not softened capitalist hostility toward Soviet communism.

The fierce fighting on the eastern front and the Soviet army's tremendous casualties helped shape Stalin's postwar policies. The Soviet leader wanted to eliminate the German menace that had repeatedly threatened his country. He viewed the creation of a pro-Soviet zone in neighboring Eastern Europe as vital to his country's national security.

During 1944 and 1945 Stalin believed he had some Allied support for his goal of creating a Soviet sphere of influence. At a meeting in 1944, Winston Churchill and Stalin reached an informal agreement: Churchill would grant Soviet predominance in Romania and Bulgaria in return for British preeminence in Greece. Roosevelt did not protest the agreement. Publicly, Americans talked of eliminating spheres of influence; privately, American policymakers seemed to understand their inevitability. At the Yalta Conference in February 1945, Allied harmony reached its high tide with the implicit recognition of spheres of influence: Germany was divided into four zones of occupation; the Soviet Union agreed to sign a treaty of friendship with America's ally in China, Jiang Jie-shi; the Allies agreed to a vague promise to hold "free elections" in liberated Europe, but Anglo-American negotiators implied their understanding of Stalin's need to have Poland as a friendly neighbor.

In the end, the course of battle largely determined the postwar power situation. Soviet troops marched into Berlin from the east as American forces advanced through Germany from the west, and the separate zones of occupation eventually hardened into a divided Germany. The nationality of occupation forces likewise helped determine the destiny of the countries surrounding Germany. Anglo-American influence was strong in France,

Italy, Greece, and the Middle East; Soviet power predominated in Eastern Europe. The United States assumed exclusive control of the Japanese-dominated Pacific islands and of defeated Japan itself.

Stalin largely ignored the Yalta declaration supporting free elections in Eastern Europe. Pro-Soviet governments came to power in Romania, Hungary, Bulgaria, Albania, and Poland; Latvia, Lithuania, and Estonia were absorbed completely by the Soviet Union. Stalin refused to include an Anglo-American-sponsored group in the new government of Poland, and some Americans cried that that country had been betrayed.

To Stalin, a Soviet-dominated zone in Eastern Europe represented a minimal guarantee of future security. It seemed a just reward for having borne the brunt of Germany's force and for having suffered staggering casualties. (The Soviet Union lost more than ten times as many soldiers as the United States.) Stalin also recalled that Anglo-American commanders had not allowed Soviet participation in governments under their military influence. In Italy after Benito Mussolini's overthrow, for example, Britain and the United States had installed a rightist regime committed to purging any leftist or pro-Soviet sentiment.

Stalin regarded his Eastern European policy as defensive, but to many people in the United States it appeared aggressive. Republicans blamed President Roosevelt especially for failing to obtain stronger guarantees for Eastern Europe at the Yalta Conference. They felt he had betrayed the cause of democracy. Americans of Eastern European descent and others who had expected the war to open all of Europe to American trade and ideas began to view the Soviet Union as a new threat to peace similar to Nazi Germany. Both Roosevelt and Truman had acknowledged the importance of the 6 million Polish-Americans to the Democratic party's strength. And Stalin's brutal, iron-handed suppression of domestic dissent made him a convincing villain. Accustomed to thinking in terms of an evil and aggressive enemy, a growing number of Americans substituted the Soviets for the Germans as the new archenemies. A former State Department official, William C. Bullitt, expressed this attitude: "The Soviet Union's assault upon the West is at about the stage of Hitler's maneuvering into Czechoslovakia." This analysis could have only one conclusion—that there could be no appeasement, no compromise with Soviet power.

American-Soviet relations thus degenerated from an atmosphere of cooperation at Yalta in early 1945 to one of deep distrust by the end of the same year. Stalin's Eastern European policies provided the backdrop to this cooling of relations, but events in the United States also contributed.

Harry S Truman, who had become president in April 1945 following the death of Roosevelt, lacked FDR's cool self-confidence, easy affability, and cosmopolitan world view. He had not been close to Roosevelt and knew little of his policies or intentions. In attempting to form guidelines for his new administration, Truman quickly sided with those advisers who advocated a harder line against the Soviet Union, and he rejected the notion of a Soviet sphere of influence in Eastern Europe. Setting a style for his successors, he began to talk tough to the Russians, especially at the Potsdam Conference of July 1945.

Truman and his advisers had two potent weapons in bargaining with Stalin. The first was atomic power. Even before Roosevelt's death, some advisers had suggested that the bomb might be an effective diplomatic lever. After demonstrating the horrible power of this weapon at Hiroshima and Nagasaki to bring about Japan's rapid surrender, some officials believed that Stalin could no longer ignore American demands to open Eastern Europe. Truman also hoped that the Soviet's need for postwar economic assistance would bring Stalin into line. After the termination of lend-lease, Stalin requested additional aid to help rebuild Russia's war-damaged economy. But Truman's tough tone indicated that assistance would be contingent upon a change in the Soviet Union's Eastern European policy. Possessing overwhelming nuclear and economic power, American leaders were in no mood to compromise.

Rather than forcing Stalin into accommodation, Truman's hard-line policy reinforced Stalin's apprehensions about Soviet security and Western hostility. Fearful of the strings America might attach to any economic aid

The A-Bomb, 1946. The tremendous power of the atom bomb created a terrible new military weapon; it also stimulated false hopes of a bountiful and cheap energy source in peacetime. Source: *National Archives*.

package, he eased his country's difficulties in other ways: a new Five-Year Plan to rebuild Soviet industry and an expropriation of materials from occupied territories, particularly East Germany. Just as the United States had removed thousands of tons of military materials and scientific documents from West Germany, so the Soviet Union carried away whatever it could use—in some cases whole factories. More and more, Stalin closed the Soviet zone to Anglo-American influence.

Some Americans believed that Truman's hard line was at least partially responsible for Stalin's growing hostility. Secretary of Commerce Henry A. Wallace, for example, advocated a more cooperative attitude toward the Soviet Union, warning that the United States had everything to lose by "beating the tom-toms against Russia." In a speech in 1946 he pleaded "[We] should recognize that we have no more business in the political affairs of Eastern Europe than Russia has in the political affairs of Latin America." Wallace argued that a secure and prosperous Russia would be more accommodating than a frightened and hungry one. But this view ran counter to Truman's foreign policy. Angered by the public display of disunity within his administration, the president asked for Wallace's resignation.

From allies in a hot war the United States and the Soviet Union became enemies in a "cold war." In 1946 Stalin publicly expressed distrust of his old capitalist allies. Their objections to Soviet policy in Eastern Europe, he believed, indicated their intention to crush socialism and isolate the Soviet regime. On the other side, Winston Churchill denounced Soviet actions, charging that Stalin had dropped an "iron curtain" across Europe. With the collapse of the wartime alliance, the world plunged into a period of bipolar politics in which America and the Soviet Union vied for worldwide influence.

Cold War Aid Programs

By 1947 the American government faced a dilemma. It had almost completed a period of rapid military demobilization, and the public longed for the "normalcy" of peace. At the same time, government policymakers perceived the Soviet Union as a new aggressor and decided to adopt a hard line. In 1946 Secretary of State James Byrnes wrote, "We must help our friends in every way and refain from assisting those who either through helplessness or for other reasons are opposing the principles for which we stand." But would the American Congress and public approve the appropriations that such "help" required?

By early 1947 the issue could no longer be postponed. A leftist revolution threatened the conservative regime in Greece, and Great Britain, which had previously considered Greece within its sphere of responsibility, announced that it could no longer provide economic and military assistance. The State Department wanted to grant extensive military aid to Greece and Turkey, a move that would have established a precedent for America's entry into other areas as a replacement for European power. But the chances that

Congress would support such a commitment seemed slim. Senator Arthur Vandenberg correctly assessed the situation: "If Truman wants it, he will have to go and scare hell out of the country."

Truman was equal to the task, and he set out to sell Congress and the public on both the aid program and his cold-war viewpoint. A leftist victory in Greece, he explained, would lead to communist takeovers in other parts of Europe. Before a joint session of Congress in March 1947, the president advanced the Truman Doctrine. He portrayed the struggle in Greece as a conflict between two ways of life, one "distinguished by free institutions, representative government, free elections, guarantees of individual liberty, freedom of speech and religion, and freedom from political oppression." The other system relied upon "terror and oppression, a controlled press and radio, fixed elections, and the suppression of personal freedoms." By failing to act, Truman concluded, "we may endanger the peace of the world—and we shall surely endanger the welfare of our own nation." These arguments helped cast anticommunism in global terms and brought a $400 million authorization to extend assistance, primarily military aid to Greece and Turkey, a neighboring country strategically located on the Dardanelles.

The rationale for the Truman Doctrine set the terms of Americans' analysis of foreign affairs for years to come and formed the core of a policy called *containment*. The classic and most sophisticated statement of containment came in a 1947 article in *Foreign Affairs* written by George Kennan, a respected foreign service officer. Writing under the pseudonym "Mr. X," Kennan analyzed the Soviet Union's "expansive tendencies" and advocated a "firm and vigilant" application of counterforce to meet Soviet maneuvers until internal change in Russia moderated the threat to the West. Kennan stressed the importance of ordering strategic priorities, concentrating strength only in the locations deemed truly critical to national interest, and of seeing the Soviet Union, not some vague ideology called international communism, as the threat to be "contained." But these crucial subtleties became lost as containment evolved into a global, ideological crusade.

In December 1947 the president again requested a strong commitment of economic aid—this time to European nations, including Germany. Initially Congress balked, but a pro-communist coup in neutralist Czechoslovakia convinced many people that Soviet aggression threatened Europe and that containment had to be implemented. The new aid program—the Marshall Plan—passed by an overwhelming margin.

The Marshall Plan sprang not only from a genuine desire to alleviate human suffering but also from a very practical assessment of America's national interests. The entire economic and political system that American policymakers had arduously constructed in postwar conferences depended upon the economic revival of European nations. But European economies were faltering, and West Germany remained a weak and defeated nation. American leaders recognized that their own country's prosperity ultimately required a prosperous and stable Europe. In addition, as hostility toward the Soviet Union mounted, it seemed increasingly necessary to counter Soviet power with a strong, industrialized West Germany. Germany, the Nazi enemy that had once united capitalists and communists, now became the focal point of the cold war, ominously divided between the two competing camps. As the Soviet Union changed from ally to enemy, West Germany changed from enemy to ally.

Following the enunciation of the Truman Doctrine and Marshall Plan, the United States government would continue to employ economic and military aid as instruments to advance its global power. Money often brought needed assistance to poverty-ridden areas and helped boost America's trade and investment abroad. American aid helped revitalize Europe. But the policy also frequently led to expensive or impossible commitments. While the Soviet Union sometimes took advantage of global postwar disruption by backing revolutionary and anticolonial movements, the United States tried to "contain" instability. Threats to the status quo became suspect, and nationalist movements in the Third World, even when they had little connection with Moscow, were too often viewed solely as part of a cohesive international communist conspiracy. At a time when Europe's empires were breaking down, the United States moved into these power vacuums and often continued to back unpopular regimes. The United States increasingly pitted its might against any change that it did not control.

COLD WAR CRISES

The cold war grew more menacing during Truman's second term, and Dean Acheson, who became secretary of state in 1949, confronted a series of foreign-policy crises. In each of these, Truman and Acheson nurtured a virulent anticommunist sentiment that then came to justify supression of dissent at home and new techniques for extending American control abroad. Acheson hoped that later generations would recognize the "truly heroic mold" of the Truman administration's cold war policies, but many subsequent historians have viewed these years as ones of lost opportunities, when complex global realities were forced into the simplistic mold of an ideological battle between Soviet "slavery" and United States "freedom."

The Berlin Crisis

By 1947, American policymakers had accepted the need to contain Soviet aggression by stabilizing Europe through economic assistance. The reestablishment of Germany as an industrial power and its reintegration into Europe's economy seemed essential for the continent's full recovery. Consequently, the United States, Great Britain, and France decided to merge their zones of occupation into one federal republic and to institute a program of economic rehabilitation. On June 18, 1948, the three powers announced a currency reform for what would become, in 1949, the Federal Republic of Germany.

The Soviet Union saw the strengthening of West Germany as a provocation. Stalin wanted Germany to remain weak and divided; he desired German reparations for war damage; and he sought to dismantle the country's industrial capacity, not to rebuild it. In retaliation for the West's actions, he formed the German Democratic Republic in East Germany and closed off West Berlin, an Anglo-American-controlled sector of the capital city that was wholly within the Soviet zone.

Only one way remained into the blockaded city—by airplane. Planes began flying around the clock to deliver food, fuel, and medicine to the 2.5 million people in West Berlin. In Montana pilots practiced landings at a flight-training center with an air corridor, runways, and navigational aids exactly duplicating those in Berlin. Assisted by the latest radar techniques, Operation Vittles, as the pilots dubbed the airlift, landed almost 13,000 tons of provisions during its peak day. By the spring of 1949 the airlift was bringing as much into Berlin as water and rail had provided before the blockade. To underscore how seriously he viewed the crisis, Truman also reinstated the draft and sent two squadrons of B-29s to Great Britain. In the face of this commitment, the Soviet Union backed off. In May 1949 Stalin reopened certain corridors of surface travel into West Berlin, and the city returned to its uneasy equilibrium. But the divided city would remain a symbol and point of tension throughout the cold war.

During the year-long Berlin crisis, which had closely followed the communist coup in Czechoslovakia, the nations of Western Europe grew increasingly anxious about cold war tensions. With United States encouragement, Britain, France, Belgium, the Netherlands, and Luxembourg signed the Brussels Pact, pledging cooperation in economic and military matters. They also appealed for a stronger United States commitment to their security. Finally, in the spring of 1949 twelve nations, including the United States and the Brussels Pact countries, established the North Atlantic Treaty Organization (NATO). This collective-security pact provided that an attack against one of the signatories would be considered an attack against all. Furthermore, the contracting nations promised to encourage economic ties with one another. NATO laid the groundwork for America's long-lasting military presence in Western Europe and formed a pattern for later collective-security pacts, CENTO and SEATO, in other parts of the world. NATO, together with the Marshall Plan, brought Western Europe under America's economic and military umbrella.

The Chinese Revolution

Throughout World War II, civil war plagued China. The United States consistently supported the Nationalist government of Jiang Jie-shi, providing it with arms, money, advisers, a prestigious position on the United Nations Security Council, and an assurance of Soviet support. Yet most American diplomats in Asia believed that Jiang's government could not last. Joseph Stilwell, who went to China in 1942 to organize its military effort against the Japanese, reported that Jiang was too corrupt and incompetent to gain wide support among the Chinese people. The communist forces under Mao Zedong were both more effective in fighting the Japanese and more popular with the peasants.

Statistical comparisons made Jiang's victory over the communists seem a sure thing: by 1947 he had twice the number of men under arms and three or four times the number of rifles. From 1945 through 1948 the United States extended him a billion dollars in military aid and another billion in economic assistance. Yet these figures only measured his incompetence and lack of support. Despite American help, Jiang's armies rapidly lost ground; Chinese peasants flocked to the communist side, which promised land reform and popular government. At the end of 1948 the director of the American military advisory group in China, Major-General David Barr, reported that "the military situation [had] deteriorated to the point where only the active participation of United States troops could effect a remedy." And this adviser "certainly [did] not recommend" allying with what he termed "the world's worst leadership" to attempt the impossible: regaining the enormous expanse of Chinese territory that Jiang had lost to the communists. Still, although many officials in China believed Jiang's downfall inevitable, both the Roosevelt and Truman administrations continued supporting Jiang and his corrupt clique.

Early in 1949 the Nationalist government was forced to withdraw to the island of Formosa (Taiwan), leaving Mao Zedong in complete control of the mainland. To Secretary Acheson the turn of events was disturbing, but in a white paper presented to the president he wrote that the situation in China was "beyond the control of the government of the United States." Still, the United States government was trapped by its previous attempt to strengthen Jiang. Not wishing to harm the Nationalist cause, American officials had failed publicly to acknowledge the full extent of Jiang's unpopularity and ineptness. What seemed inevitable to officials knowledgeable about China looked like a sell-out to communism by Americans who viewed Jiang as the strong and respected leader of "free" China. By the time Jiang retreated, it was too late to revise the public's view of him.

The news of China's "fall" hit the United States like a bombshell. The Truman administration's Republican opponents, especially members of a powerful "China lobby" financed by conservative Republican business leaders, began charging that Truman and his State Department were responsible for "losing" China. Both policymakers and their opponents pictured the uneasy and short-lived alliance between China and the Soviet Union of 1949 as an ideological bond that cemented an international communist conspiracy to conquer the world. For twenty years the United States refused to recognize or deal with the communist Chinese government, even after the Sino-Soviet split totally shattered myths about a monolithic threat called "international communism."

The Anticommunist Crusade

Following swiftly upon the news from China came word that the Soviet Union had exploded a nuclear device. America no longer had sole possession of the ultimate weapon. Publicly, the Truman administration issued reassuring comments that the announcement had been expected and necessitated no change in America's own policies. Privately, however, Truman tilted toward his hard-line advisers and made the fateful decision to escalate atomic competition by developing a hydrogen bomb, a device based upon the still-hypothetical concept of nuclear fusion.

The constant crises of 1949—Berlin, China, and Russia's new bomb—unsettled many Americans. The communist threat appeared to be everywhere; American power seemed in retreat. Many Republicans and some Democrats sought the source of America's problems not in the world at large but in traitors in their midst. The charge seemed to gain credibility when a former State Department officer, Alger Hiss, was accused of passing government papers to the Soviet Union. The search for Soviet spy rings became the order of the day; Republican Senator William E. Jenner of Indiana charged that the Truman administration consisted of a "crazy assortment of collectivist cutthroat crackpots and Communist fellow-traveling appeasers." Acheson's assessment regarding China—that America could not control all world events—sounded to some like a new doctrine of appeasement, and many Republicans demanded Acheson's resignation. The cry for an all-out crusade against communism, including suppression of dissent at home and of revolution abroad, would affect American life and policy for years to come.

The international shocks of 1949 and the fire from Republican leaders prompted senior officials in the State and Defense departments to draw up a paper outlining foreign-policy assumptions and future strategy. The report, called NSC 68, was approved by the National Security Council and the president. In 1950 Acheson traveled throughout the country trying to regain his credibility as a tough anticommunist by preaching the assumptions upon which NSC 68 was based. The report's logic eventually became the conventional wisdom of the cold war. According to NSC 68, the Soviet Union was determined to stamp out freedom and dominate the world. Negotiation with the communists was futile, for they did not bargain in good faith. And there could be no valid distinction between national and world security. The United States could not, as Acheson put it, "pull down the blinds and sit in the parlor with a loaded shotgun, waiting." The country had to embark upon a massive military buildup at home and create "situations of strength" abroad, regardless of cost. NSC 68 provided the blueprint for a "national security state": a leviathan with overwhelming military power, a wide variety of economic weapons, and an extensive capacity for covert operations.

In his cold war speeches Acheson argued that freedom meant simply anticommunism. Those people who wanted to go from ally to ally "with political litmus paper testing them for true-blue democracy" were "escapists." Furthermore, domestic consensus served freedom while differences of opinion aided the enemy. The "fomenters of disunity" who advocated negotiation with the Soviets, Acheson explained, contributed to American weakness. Other observers, noting how often "freedom" was invoked to support dictators abroad and to suppress dissent at home, suggested that language, and therefore communication, became a serious casualty of the cold war.

Korea

Koreans, long dominated by Japanese power, had looked forward to liberation and independence after Japan's defeat in World War II. By 1946, however, zones of occupation, as in Germany, had hardened into political jurisdictions. The communist North under Kim Il Sung allied with the Soviet Union and carried out land and labor reforms on a communist model. The South under the elite-based rule of Syngman Rhee allied with the United States and resisted reformist challenges. Korea remained the playground of expansionist foreign powers and soon would become their battleground as well.

In June 1950, communist North Korea attacked South Korea across the Thirty-eight Parallel dividing line in an attempt to unify the country. Committed to a policy of containment, possibly even a rollback of communism in Asia, the Truman administration invoked the assumptions and fears articulated in NSC 68. There was no evidence that Stalin had ordered the attack or that he knew of it in advance, yet Americans still viewed the Korean conflict as a showdown with the Soviets. Using the logic outlined in his Truman Doctrine for Greece and Turkey, the president announced that "if aggression is successful in Korea, we can expect it to spread through Asia and Europe to this hemisphere." One weak spot in the "free world" defense would start the "dominoes" falling.

In line with this worldwide containment policy, Truman responded globally. He gained United Nations support for an American-controlled defense of Syngman Rhee's South Korean regime (the Soviet delegation was boycotting the United Nations and could not exercise its veto); he also announced protection for Jiang Jie-shi's exiled regime in Formosa and ordered support for the French in their efforts to hold off communist-led nationalists in Vietnam. Assistance was extended to the Philippine government's attempts to suppress leftist Huk rebels, and the administration accelerated its efforts to encourage Japan's emergence as a strong economic and anticommunist bastion in the Far East. In Europe, more troops were added to the NATO military force and a program for rearming West Germany was announced. The front line against communism lay everywhere, and America committed its power, prestige, and treasure as though there were no limits.

American policymakers were torn between two goals during the Korean War: simple containment (which would leave Korea divided) and rollback (which would unite it under American influence). As long as South Korean and American troops were retreating southward early in the war, restoration of a boundary at the Thirty-eighth Parallel seemed victory enough. But when a regrouped force under General Douglas MacArthur landed at Inchon behind enemy lines and drove the North Koreans back from the Thirty-eighth Parallel, decisions became more complicated. Could MacArthur "liberate" North Korea, and would the Soviet Union and China intervene if he did? The president gave MacArthur authority to pursue the war in the north as long as it did not bring a wider war with China, but the general underestimated Chinese reaction. After crossing the Thirty-eighth Parallel, American soldiers began to encounter Chinese "volunteers." Then, as American forces penetrated farther into North Korea and approached the border of China, the provocation became too great for China to ignore. Chinese troops streamed into Korea and sent MacArthur's armies reeling backward across the Thirty-eighth Parallel once again. When MacArthur regrouped and once more pushed northward, Truman ordered him to seek a negotiated settlement.

Truman's order provoked a dramatic clash between civilian and military authority. The general publicly opposed Truman's "limited war" and balked at his instructions. He pressed for a full-scale commitment to victory over North Korea, even over China, and claimed that this was America's chance to roll back communism in Asia. Truman, however, held to his position that a lengthy conflict in Korea would weaken America's defense posture in other, more vital areas. He viewed the Soviet Union as the real enemy and believed a costly Asian land war would only play into Stalin's hands. Responding to MacArthur's challenge to presidential authority, Truman had only one choice: He removed the general from command.

Those "Asia-firsters" who had denounced Truman following Jiang Jie-shi's fall in China now had new ammunition and a popular martyr. They condemned the "no-win policy" against communism, and MacArthur returned home a hero. Telegrams demanding Truman's impeachment flooded the Capitol. Huge crowds greeted the general in San Francisco, Washington, and New York. A parade in New York on his behalf attracted 7.5 million people (compared with 4 million for Eisenhower at the end of World War II) and produced over three thousand tons of litter. George Gallup reported that only 29 percent of those polled supported President Truman's action against MacArthur.

The outpouring of support, including a MacArthur-for-president boomlet, subsided quickly. Senate hearings on the general's dismissal convinced the public that most military strategists opposed a wider conflict in Asia, and few Americans wanted full-scale war. Admiration for MacArthur's military achievements remained, but most Americans welcomed negotiation. When the 1952 Republican nominee for president, General Dwight D. Eisenhower, promised to go to Korea and end the struggle, he received applause and votes. By the end of Truman's presidency the war in Korea had grown less intense and both sides had gathered around a conference table. Hammering out the details of a negotiated settlement (which eventually reestablished the Thirty-eighth Parallel as a dividing line) would fall to the new Republican administration.

New Policies in New Areas of Concern

The rise of America's global power and the decline of European power in the Middle East, India, Africa, and Southeast Asia necessitated developing policies toward new areas hardly considered by American policymakers of the past. Significantly, decisions were forged less out of experience, which was scant, than out of the bipolar, cold war thinking of NSC 68. Whereas during World War II American policymakers had frequently formed ties to anticolonial movements and encouraged allies to plan for decolonization, the growing conservatism and preoccupation with anticommunism that characterized the late 1940s and early 1950s tilted American policies into misunderstanding, even hostility, toward popular nationalist movements.

In Southeast Asia, Americans severed their wartime contacts with the popular Vietnamese communist-nationalist Ho Chi Minh and supported French efforts to maintain the old colonialist order.

In India, United States policymakers persistently confused Jawaharlal Nehru's nationalist policy of nonalignment with Soviet-sympathizing. American policymakers and media pictured Nehru, a widely respected leader of Third World nationalism and an influential interpreter of nationalist aspirations, as a slightly befuddled mystic who lacked the clarity of vision to recognize the Soviet threat and ally with the United States. Dean Acheson, after meeting Nehru during his goodwill trip to the United States in 1949, wrote, "I was convinced that Nehru and I were not destined to have a pleasant personal relationship. . . . He was one of the most difficult men with whom I have ever had to deal." Such condescending attitudes and the policies that emerged from them hardly provided a promising basis for future United States relations with the Third World.

Issues of race and international politics emerged with special clarity in the late 1940s in South Africa. The white, Afrikaner-based Nationalist party came to power in 1948 and began erecting apartheid—an elaborate system of racial separation and systematic, legally sanctioned discrimination against the nonwhites who comprised more than 80 percent of the South African population. Although some American policymakers, fresh from fighting Nazi ideas of a "master race," questioned the wisdom and morality of such a racially based governmental system, the desire to open South Africa to growing American trade and investment and to maintain friendly access to South Africa's copious store of strategic raw materials took precedence. The South African government also garnered United States support by portraying black aspirations as communist-inspired and casting its own minority rulers as stalwart defenders of capitalism in Africa. In addition, strong criticism of South Africa seemed difficult in light of America's own racially segregated society.

America's burgeoning economic presence in South Africa after 1948, attracted by the cheap labor supply that apartheid ensured, provided the basis for a growing alliance between the United States and the white South African government. Within the next two decades nearly fifty African nations became independent, and American policy toward these states— nearly all black-ruled and determinedly hostile to South Africa's racially repressive regime—took shape within the context of the close South African–U.S. alliance.

The Middle East also presented the need for new policies. Only in Saudi Arabia, particularly through oil investments, had the United States maintained a substantial presence before the war. After 1940, strategic and economic bonds with that desert kingdom increased dramatically, and United States interests expanded into other areas as well. When, in 1946, the Soviet Union attempted to extend its own economic and political influence into northern Iran, for example, the United States made it clear that Britain's postwar weakness in this traditional zone of British influence should not mean gains for the Soviets. The Soviets retreated, leaving Iran and its rich oil fields within the perimeter of Anglo-American power and interest. Policies in this area would continue to be shaped through the prisms of anticommunism and the maintenance of access to oil.

Elsewhere in the Middle East, American support for the creation of Israel proved to be the new policy with the most far-reaching implications. In Western Europe the problem of homeless Jewish refugees, displaced by Nazi atrocities, pressed urgently upon policymakers, and Truman supported large-scale resettlement of Jews as part of his concern over the social stability of Europe. At the same time, powerful Jewish groups in the United States and abroad stressed the world's moral obligation and recalled certain assurances given Jews during World War I to provide a Jewish homeland in Palestine.

The Truman administration backed the idea of a new Jewish state. Over the objections of Middle Eastern experts in the State Department, who urged that the interests of Palestinian Arabs and other nations in the Middle East needed to be factored into some comprehensive, internationally formulated solution, the Truman administration recognized the state of Israel in May of 1948, just minutes after it was officially proclaimed by the Israeli forces who had wrested the land in a bloody fight with Arab inhabitants. The tangle of hatreds, of demographic and boundary problems, and of new refugee issues remained to fester and provide the seeds of future conflicts and foreign-policy dilemmas.

LONG-TERM TRENDS IN FOREIGN POLICY

World War II vastly changed the United States government bureaucracy. Before the war the federal government employed about 800,000 civilians,

10 percent of whom were involved with national security; by the end of the war the figure had risen to nearly 4 million, with 75 percent working for national security agencies. Although the new government bureaus were designed to increase the efficiency of wartime operations, their sheer size and complexity often complicated decision making. New photocopying techniques brought additional problems. The "paper revolution," designed to assist interdepartmental communication, often beleaguered policymakers, burying both the important and the trivial under a mountain of duplicate copies.

The State Department, the agency traditionally responsible for creating and executing foreign policy, was transformed during the war. The department and its related agencies outgrew old quarters and, during the 1950s, expanded into twenty-nine buildings throughout Washington, D.C. When all of these offices were finally brought together in 1961, it took eight stories covering a four-block area to house them. Before the war a few people would meet in the secretary of state's office, discuss world problems, and set policy. By the end of the war cozy familiarity and easy communication had given way to faceless bureaucratic routine. Truman's secretary of state, Dean Acheson, once asked Cordell Hull, Franklin Roosevelt's secretary of state, to come by the department and meet the assistant secretaries. Hull declined, wryly commenting that he had never done well in crowds.

The cold war also helped swell the State Department's support staff. In its new role as global superpower, the United States seemed to need a resident expert on every conceivable topic so that it could react quickly to a wide variety of situations. In this era of confrontation, the most casual decision could suddenly mushroom into a matter of major importance.

After 1949 the crisis atmosphere of the cold war delivered strong blows to the State Department's effectiveness. Mao's victory in China in 1949 outraged those Americans who believed that communism could never triumph on its own merits. The "China lobby," with its close ties to the popular media, drummed the refrain that the State Department officials "sold out" China, and pressure mounted to purge the "old China hands" who had advised against an open-ended commitment to Jiang Jie-shi. Throughout the 1950s many seasoned diplomats lost influence to newer people who took a harder anticommunist line. The immediate suspicion of anyone who questioned cold war verities quashed healthy differences of opinion. The State Department became less involved in forming policies according to world realities and more caught up in interpreting the world acording to a preestablished cold war viewpoint. The cold war consensus of the early and mid-1950s, combined with the attacks upon experienced diplomats, damaged the effectiveness, and ultimately the prestige and power, of the State Department.

Other agencies challenged the State Department's preeminence in international concerns. Before the war, nearly all foreign-policy functions were centralized at State; after the war, other departments—especially Agriculture, Treasury, and Commerce, as well as independent agencies such as the Central Intelligence Agency—assumed responsibilities in foreign nations. Policymaking became a complex process involving many different bureaucracies, each with its experts and points of view.

Overlapping jurisdictions sometimes even produced conflicting policies, particularly between the Central Intelligence Agency (CIA) and the State Department. The CIA grew out of the Office of Strategic Services (OSS), a wartime intelligence-gathering agency. After the war the State Department, the armed services, and the FBI all sought to assume the functions of the OSS. As a compromise in 1947, the CIA was created as an independent agency under the new National Security Act. Under the influence of its activist director, Walter Bedell Smith, the CIA began to narrow into a preoccupation with anticommunism. (Smith reportedly once confided that he even believed Eisenhower was a communist.) Although the CIA's finances and operations were kept secret, scholars have estimated that the agency rapidly surpassed the State Department both in number of employees and in budget. Personnel of the two departments sometimes worked at cross-purposes; American ambassadors in foreign lands often complained that their ignorance of the CIA's clandestine activities undermined their prestige.

The Pentagon also became a powerful rival in handling foreign affairs. During the war Roosevelt increasingly turned to the military for advice, and the Joint Chiefs of Staff, created in 1941, eroded the secretary of state's position as preeminent foreign-policy expert. The National Security Act of 1947 reorganized the military establishment, abolishing the Department of War and creating the Department of Defense and a new National Security Council to advise the president. These reorganizations further boosted the military's input into foreign policymaking.

Some elements of foreign policy were altogether external to the government. Although private businesspeople in foreign lands had always influenced international affairs, the giant United States-based multinational corporations that mushroomed in the postwar era exerted an unparalleled impact upon foreign relations. For example, the great oil giants—the so-called seven sisters—profoundly affected the world's economy through their agreements that set the world price of oil and divided up spheres of production and distribution. Many companies with far-flung investments began to view themselves as wholly new forces in international relations, developing company interests that could surpass national loyalties.

SUGGESTIONS FOR FURTHER READING

There are a number of fine studies of the United States and the world scene during the postwar era and beyond. A recent overview is Thomas J. McCormick, *America's Half-Century: United States Foreign Policy in the Cold War* (1989). Other broad treatments, from a variety of perspectives, include Walter LaFeber, *America, Russia, and the Cold War, 1945–84* (rev. ed., 1985); Stephen Ambrose, *Rise to Globalism: American Foreign Policy Since 1938* (rev. ed., 1988); John Gaddis's collection of essays entitled *The Long Peace* (1987);

Gabriel Kolko, *Confronting the Third World: United States Foreign Policy, 1945–1980* (1988); Thomas Paterson, *On Every Front* (1979) and *Meeting the Communist Threat: Truman to Reagan* (1988), a series of essays.

On "national security" policy during the late 1940s and early 1950s, consult Daniel Yergin, *Shattered Peace: The Origins of the Cold War and the National Security State* (1977); Gar Alperowitz, *Atomic Diplomacy* (rev. ed., 1985); Martin Sherwin, *A World Destroyed* (1985); Gregg Herkin, *The Winning Weapon: The Atomic Bomb in the Cold War* (1981); and John Gaddis, *Strategies of Containment* (1982).

On specific areas, see Terry H. Anderson, *The United States, Great Britain and the Cold War, 1944–1947* (1981); Bruce Kuklick, *American Policy and the Division of Germany* (1972); Akira Iriye, *The Cold War in Asia* (1974); Robert J. McMahon, *Colonialism and Cold War: The United States and the Struggle for Indonesian Independence* (1981); Nancy B. Tucker, *Patterns in the Dust: Chinese-American Relations and the Recognition Controversy, 1949–1950* (1983); Thomas M. Leonard, *The United States and Central America, 1944–1949* (1984); Thomas Noer, *Cold War and Black Liberation: The United States and White Rule in Africa, 1948–1968* (1985); Michael Schaller, *The American Occupation of Japan* (1985); Gary Hess, *The U.S. Emergence as a Southeast Asia Power* (1986); David Painter, *Oil and the American Century* (1986); William Roger Louis and Hedley Bull, eds., *The Special Relationship: Anglo-American Relations Since 1945* (1986); June M. Grasso, *Harry Truman's Two-China Policy* (1987); Nathan Godfried, *Bridging the Gap between Rich and Poor* (1987), on the Middle East; Howard Schonberger, *Aftermath of War: America and the Remaking of Japan, 1945–1952* (1989); and Gordon Chang, *Friends and Enemies: The United States, China, and the Soviet Union, 1948–1972* (1989).

For particular topics, see Richard Freeland, *The Truman Doctrine and the Origins of McCarthyism* (1971); Michael Sherry, *Preparing for the Next War* (1977); Fred J. Block, *The Origins of International Economic Disorder* (1977); Lawrence Kaplan, *The United States and Nato* (1984); Robert A. Divine, *Since 1945: Politics and Diplomacy in Recent American History* (3d ed., 1985); Robert A. Pollard, *Economic Security and the Origins of the Cold War* (1986); Michael Hogan, *The Marshall Plan* (1987); James Edward Miller, *The United States and Italy, 1940–50* (1987); Louis Liebovich, *The Press and the Origins of the Cold War, 1944–1947* (1988); Howard Jones, *A New Kind of War: America's Global Strategy and the Truman Doctrine in Greece* (1989); Erik Beukel, *American Perceptions of the Soviet Union as a Nuclear Adversary* (1989); and Ronald L. Filippelli, *American Labor and Postwar Italy, 1943–1953: A Study of Cold War Politics* (1989).

There are excellent studies of the Korean War. Burton I. Kaufman, *The Korean War* (1986) is a brief synopsis. A more detailed analysis may be found in several volumes by Bruce Cuming: *The Origins of the Korean War* (1981); *Child of Conflict* (1983), a series of essays that he edited; and *Korea: The Unknown War* (co-authored with Jon Halliday) (1988). See also William S. Stueck, Jr., *The Road to Confrontation* (1981), and Joseph Goulden, *Korea: The Untold Story* (1982).

Biographical studies include Ronald Steele, *Walter Lippman and the American Century* (1980); Robert Ferrell, *Harry Truman and the Modern American Presidency* (1983); Walter Issacson and Evan Thomas, *The Wise Men* (1986), which looks at six leading architects of cold-war policy; Mark A. Stoler, *George C. Marshall* (1989); Walter Hixson, *George F. Kennan* (1989); and Anders Stephanson, *Kennan and the Art of Foreign Relations* (1989).

Chapter Two

Postwar Readjustments, 1946–1953

The years from 1945 to 1952 seemed peculiarly marked by a popular mood that oscillated between visions of great peril and almost unlimited promise. The American film industry, only beginning to be challenged by television, brilliantly captured the deep ambivalence in postwar society. On the one hand, Hollywood turned out films celebrating happiness, innovation, and prosperity. The 1952 classic *Singing in the Rain* epitomized this mood. This brightly colored musical traced Hollywood's own transition from the silent era to sound, driving home the theme that upbeat, flexible people could adapt to changing times. The film became a great popular and critical success. Yet Hollywood also found millions of filmgoers drawn to motion pictures that emphasized the dark side of postwar life. A whole cycle called *film noir* tore away at the easy optimism of pictures like *Singing in the Rain* and portrayed deeply troubled people fighting among themselves, confronting sinister forces, almost never succeeding, and oftentimes even failing to survive. In many of these films, the pursuit of the American Dream seemed a blind, foolish, fatally flawed obsession. Only a fool would want to sing about rain-soaked city streets, suggested films like *The Asphalt Jungle* (1950).

The tension between promise and peril appeared in almost every area of postwar life. From the programs of the Truman administration that simultaneously trumpeted both the dangers of a vast communist menace and the dream of a harmonious welfare state, to the problems of American workers, who faced both the perils of technological innovations and the promise of higher living standards, the postwar era seemed shot through with contradictory hopes and fears.

RECONVERSION, 1946–1948

Postwar Tensions

Throughout World War II, most Americans sacrificed to preserve the "American way of life." But as the global conflict dragged into 1945, it became evident that the United States had changed in fundamental ways. The war's end would terminate one struggle but would also usher in new problems, both at home and overseas.

President Harry S Truman and his close advisers had awaited the end of the war with both hope and fear. The return of peace, they hoped, would allow the Democratic party to retrieve the fallen standard of domestic reform, to revive the New Deal spirit. But the end of war also brought fears of economic stagnation. Economists recognized that it was not New Deal programs but World War II, with its huge government expenditures, that had finally ended the Great Depression of the 1930s. Remembering the sharp economic downturn that had followed the first Great War—and the bitter social conflicts that the depression of 1919 had brought—many national leaders dreaded the transition from war to peace. What would happen when wartime production slowed? Only a few weeks after the final victory, almost 100,000 defense workers in Detroit alone lost their jobs. Could production for civilian consumption take up the slack and put people back to work?

Wartime mobilization had touched most areas of American life. During World War II more and more women had entered the wartime labor force where they sometimes received traditionally male jobs and equal pay with men. "Latchkey children," kids who returned from school while parents were still at work, became a familiar sight during the war, and the national government, under the Lantham Act, even provided federal financing for a limited number of child-care centers. Although wartime publicists tried to portray such changes as temporary, many women held a different view. The Women's Bureau of the United Auto Workers Union reported in April 1945 that, "In one shipyard, 98 percent of the women want to continue working in shipyards." Other surveys confirmed that women overwhelmingly hoped to retain their wartime positions and wages.

Greater independence for women and children, however, provoked great controversies. Some social observers blamed working women for new strains on the family, including discontented husbands and an allegedly rising tide of juvenile delinquency. Traditionalists argued that, in the postwar period, women must abandon the workplace in order to restabilize family relations and to alleviate the prospect of male unemployment and potential labor strife over job seniority. Returning male war veterans, they argued, "needed" jobs to bring home a "family wage." Despite attempts by the Women's Bureau in the Department of Labor and a variety of women's groups within labor unions to support women's employment concerns, men who were hostile or indifferent to the needs and desires of female workers dominated the numerous committees charged with planning postwar reconversion. Very quickly after the war, psychologists, economists, politicians, and the media all endorsed closing doors of economic opportunity for women in the workplace. For many women, the decision to center their work around home involved no meaningful choice at all; for many who continued to work outside the home, opportunities for wage-work were again narrowed to low-paying jobs in domestic service or clerical positions.

Issues of war and reconversion also intertwined with racial tensions. Large numbers of African-Americans, American Indians, and Mexican-Americans responded to new wartime job opportunities by relocating, particularly to urban industrial areas. These rapid demographic and occupational shifts stirred racial hostility between newcomers and established residents or jobholders. Racism became an explosive problem that touched every section of the country. So-called zoot-suit riots in Los Angeles and throughout the Southwest highlighted cultural tensions between Mexican-American and Anglo communities. Battles in Northern cities and industrial workplaces, particularly between blacks and whites, dramatized fears of job scarcity during the expected postwar retrenchment. Japanese-Americans, deprived of their property holdings in the West and relocated to barbed-wired internment camps in the interior of the nation, struggled to recover from wartime economic deprivation and to rebuild their communities in the face of continued postwar suspicion.

Although social issues such as the future of women workers and the new demographic and racial trends failed to capture the kind of consistent media coverage reserved for economic and foreign-policy questions, they deeply affected the lives of millions of Americans in the postwar era. Questions of gender and race thus symbolized a broader point: Social changes of the war years affected postwar society in all kinds of ways that had never been expected during the early 1940s. And the disorders and tensions of the immediate postwar period forcefully raised the question of the government's future role in postwar social policy. Liberal economists and many Democratic politicians argued that the national government should continue the social and economic programs—and also solidify the political gains—of the Roosevelt era. Government welfare measures could not be limited to times of acute economic depression, liberal economists contended, but must become a permanent part of the postwar economic system. Increased spending for social welfare programs would pump money into the economy, easing the problem of reconversion and providing a cushion against social conflict. Unless the national administration took decisive action, some forecasters claimed, postwar unemployment might reach 11 million workers.

Only three weeks after the Japanese surrender, President Truman proposed twenty-one domestic spending programs. These included an increased minimum wage, money for hospital construction, funds for small businesses, permanent government price supports for farmers, and legislation to ensure full employment. The Truman administration faced congressional opposition from a coalition of anti-New Deal Republicans and southern Democrats, but the Seventy-ninth Congress did pass a number of Truman's proposals, including the Hospital Construction Act, the Veterans Emergency Housing Act, funds for power and soil conservation projects, and a modified version of the highly controversial Full Employment Bill of 1945.

The Full Employment Bill produced bitter political and economic debates. The bill's drafters hoped to "establish a national policy and program for assuring continuing full employment," largely through continual planning, direction, and spending by the national government. Washington would take responsibility for ensuring that the "free enterprise" system would produce full employment. But the specter of government planning and massive spending in peacetime alarmed many conservatives; to them the Full Employment Bill seemed another giant leap toward a centrally planned economy, or even toward socialism.

The employment bill and similar economic proposals drew their inspiration not from socialism but from the theories of British economist John Maynard Keynes. A complex capitalist economy, Keynesians argued, required active governmental intervention. Whenever consumer spending declined, for example, increased spending by government could take up the slack, maintain full employment, and prevent recession. Funds for public housing, hospitals, schools, and social welfare would provide assistance for the poor while maintaining a high level of economic growth. In addition, government officials could use controls over taxation as an economic tool: In times of slow growth they could lower personal and business taxes to stimulate buying power and output; when inflationary pressures developed, they could raise taxes as one means of reducing the amount of spending. Keynes's American disciples did not follow all of his ideas—political pressures, for example, made it difficult to raise taxes or reduce government expenditures—but the Keynesians' "new economics" became orthodoxy to most Democratic liberals after World War II.

By the late 1940s most Americans accepted some type of continuing economic role for the federal government, and a modified version of the Full Employment Bill did become law in 1946. Economic oversight and heavy government spending became prominent features of the postwar welfare state. The modern "free enterprise" system seemed too fragile to be left entirely to the mechanisms of the marketplace.

Although it did not satisfy advocates of centralized planning, the Employment Act of 1946 established an important precedent and provided the institutional framework for more extensive governmental action. Congress created a new executive body, the Council of Economic Advisers, and charged it with advising the president and establishing policies to "promote free competitive enterprise, to avoid economic fluctuations . . . and to maintain employment, production, and purchasing power." Citizens soon came to expect that the national government, especially the presidency, would confront economic problems. Any administration that failed to develop effective programs, to maintain high levels of employment, or to curb inflation invited political disaster. In retrospect, the Employment Act of 1946, with its authorization of positive action by the national government, assumed almost the status of a constitutional amendment, signaling a new political-constitutional order that one legal analyst has called "the positive state."

Inflation, Black Markets, and Strikes

Despite this greater governmental involvement, a variety of problems still beset the nation's economy following the war. Most liberal economists had feared that peacetime consumer spending would not maintain wartime levels of production and employment, but the gloomy forecasters were proved wrong. Consumers took the money in their savings accounts—funds that they had been unable to spend because of wartime rationing and production controls—and went on a buying spree. They wanted all the items that had been scarce or out of production during the war: refrigerators, new-model cars, nylon stockings, cameras and film, rubber-centered golf balls, wire coat-hangers, and toy electric trains. Taking advantage of greater supplies of gasoline, Americans began to travel again, and hotel and motel owners complained that they could not handle the crowds of tourists.

In most areas of the economy, supply could not equal demand, and a steep inflationary spiral began. As prices soared, supplies dwindled. Producers could not provide enough meat, cars, and new homes. In June 1946 a deliveryman in Denver lost his entire truckload of bread to a crowd that overpowered him outside a grocery store; rumors of a shipment of meat produced an angry, shoving crowd of over two thousand in front of a Brooklyn store; and outside a Detroit supermarket, employees served coffee and doughnuts to placate angry shoppers who were waiting in line. A thriving black market soon developed. If people wanted a new car or a juicy steak, they often had to tip the automobile salesperson or the butcher. Some butchers tried a barter system: a meat cutter in Atlanta offered steaks and roasts in exchange for nails, flooring, and plumbing fixtures for his new home.

Harry Truman received much of the blame for postwar economic problems. While Republicans berated him for rising prices and black-market conditions, he also faced opposition from labor unions, which had been firm supporters of the Democratic party and Roosevelt's New Deal.

The year 1946 saw bitter labor disputes in most major industries. During the year following V-J day, more than 5 million workers were involved in nearly five thousand work stoppages. One of these, the United Auto Workers (UAW) strike against General Motors (GM), lasted almost four months. Here, the UAW's leader, Walter Reuther, advanced an idea abhorrent to management: He tried to include a provision in the new GM-UAW contract pledging GM not to raise the price of cars. Reuther argued that such a clause would prevent GM from using wage gains by the UAW as an excuse for price hikes that would affect the entire economy. GM stoutly resisted, claiming that this provision impinged upon one of the company's "managerial prerogatives." GM expressed special displeasure at the UAW's insistence that the company open its books so that the union could verify its contention that the auto giant could easily absorb any of the union's gains out of corporate profits.

The UAW's stand enraged the business community and drew little support from the Democrat in the White House. The editors of *Business Week*, the widely read "bible" of American industry, expressed a common theme. The "time had come," argued *Business Week*, to beat back decisively "further encroachment into the province of management." A GM attorney used even stronger terms: To accept the UAW's position "would mean the end of free enterprise and efficient management." And Reuther's claim that his position actually bolstered Truman's own drive for price stability and social justice failed to move the president against GM. In the end, the UAW won a wage increase, but Reuther's dream of gaining organized labor a broader role in determining basic political-economic decisions collapsed.

As November of 1946 neared, Truman seemed to be losing support among organized labor and among liberals who had supported Franklin Roosevelt's New Deal of the 1930s. A number of pro-Democratic labor leaders questioned Truman's capabilities; many liberal Democrats also became disenchanted, dismissing Truman as an inept politician with a weak social conscience.

Throughout his first year in office Truman did appear confused and inept. Seeking political popularity by promising rapid discharges for service personnel, his administration mishandled demobilization of the armed forces. At one point the navy found it lacked the ships to transport the large number of soldiers scheduled to return to the States. By Truman's own admission the process soon "was no longer demobilization . . . it was disintegration." Although he did face extremely difficult economic decisions, Truman made things even worse by failing to develop clear and consistent policies. He hesitated, for example, to support the Office of Price Administration (OPA), an executive agency that regulated wages and prices, and listened instead to people who favored a quick end to economic controls after the war. In June 1945 Truman vetoed a bill that would have renewed the OPA's authority while limiting its powers. But after a short period with no controls at all, he signed a second bill that differed very little from the first. Finally, in November 1946, Truman proclaimed an end to virtually all controls. In all of these matters Truman seemed an indecisive president, a person who leaned too heavily upon old political cronies and representatives of special-interest groups. Even Truman's supporters could find few examples of effective leadership during his first year in the White House.

Truman Takes Command

Republicans hardly lacked campaign issues in 1946; soaring prices, black-market conditions, labor strikes, an unpopular president. By October the Gallup polling organization reported that only 32 percent of their sample approved of Truman's performance, compared with a figure of 87 percent a little over a year earlier. One pro-Republican columnist suggested that the Democrats nominate W. C. Fields for president: "If we're going to have a comedian in the White House, let's have a good one." Other Democrats were the targets of similar jibes, and after nearly fifteen years as the minority party, Republicans found themselves almost back in control. Summing up all the Democratic sins, Republican posters asked, "Had enough?" In the November 1946 elections Republicans gained control of the new Eightieth Congress and captured twenty-five governorships. Jersey City's political boss, Frank Hague, was expecting the defeats. "The Republicans would have won even had they put up a German," an aide quoted Hague. And 1948 promised to be an even better election year for Republicans.

Truman, however, rebounded from his problems. In foreign affairs, of course, his administration embarked on a vigorous anticommunist crusade, one that eventually carried over to the domestic front as well. And Truman warmed up for the domestic battles of 1947–1948 by thrashing John L. Lewis, the colorful leader of the United Mineworkers Union and by attacking the Republican dominated Congress.

Lewis's union was trying to go beyond traditional wage issues and raise basic questions about safety and health conditions in the mines. The supposedly prolabor Democrats, Lewis argued, should be prepared to join the battle on the side of the mineworkers. With his unruly lion's mane of white hair in constant disarray, Lewis stalked both the mineowners and the Truman administration. Responding to Lewis's decision to call the mineworkers out on strike, however, Truman obtained a federal court injunction in late November of 1946 against both the union and its officers. Lewis initially defied the injunction as illegal but ultimately backed down from a test in the Supreme Court.

The Truman-Lewis confrontation carried considerable significance. First, Truman's action provided yet another sign that labor unions lacked support, even from Democrats, for pushing labor-management negotiations into new areas. In the final analysis, political leaders would line up for protecting management's traditional bargaining prerogatives. To the president's close advisers, the defeat of John L. Lewis also signaled the man from Missouri's arrival as a political force. "There was a big difference in the old man from then on," one aide remembered. "He was his own man at last."

The president proved particularly feisty with the new Republican-controlled Eightieth Congress (1947–1949) on domestic issues. He challenged Republicans to pass legislation he knew they opposed and refused to seek common ground on measures such as a higher minimum wage and labor legislation. At the same time, the president consulted congressional Democrats infrequently, failing to give them any clear indication of the White House's domestic priorities. At one point Democratic Senator Alben Barkley grumbled that working with Truman was like playing a night baseball game without lights: "I'm supposed to be the catcher and I should get the signals. I not only am not getting the signals, but someone actually turns out the light when the ball is thrown." Thus, while Truman proposed expensive social-welfare programs, he also urged reduction in federal expenditures. Such double-talk passed little social legislation, but it helped Truman build a record upon which to run in 1948.

In reality, Truman could point to few domestic innovations of his own and could cite few instances of Republicans trying to tear down popular programs of Roosevelt's New Deal. By the late 1940s many Republican politicians saw that outright opposition to liberal Democratic measures such as Social Security offered little hope for increasing the GOP's vote totals. This pragmatic attitude gained most of its support from younger Republicans, particularly those who came from larger northern cities or held state offices. Increasingly, they battled older, more tradition-bound Republicans in Congress for influence within the party.

Ridiculed by Truman as a do-nothing body, the Eightieth Congress actually passed several significant pieces of legislation. The National Security Act of 1947 reorganized the armed forces and the entire military establishment. In recognition of the new importance of air power, the air force became a separate branch of the military; a new Department of Defense, under a civilian head, replaced the old departments of War and Navy; top-ranking uniformed officers from the air force, navy, army, and marines sat on a new coordinating body called the Joint Chiefs of Staff; and the new National Security Council and Central Intelligence Agency assumed important tasks in planning and executing foreign policy. In a highly popular move, the Eightieth Congress also approved and sent to the states the Twenty-second Amendment, which prohibited presidents from serving more than two terms. In addition, Congress accepted Truman's suggestion that it create a special commission to study reorganization of the federal bureaucracy. Under the leadership of former President Herbert Hoover, the commission submitted a plan that became the basis of the Reorganization Act of 1949. By clarifying lines of authority and reducing the number of executive agencies, the Hoover Commission hoped to make government administration more efficient.

Robert Taft, Republican majority leader in the Senate, emerged as the dominant figure in the Eightieth Congress. Son of President William Howard Taft, the middle-aged Ohioan was a shy, thoughtful man who often seemed uncomfortable in the glare of national politics. Certainly he lacked the charm of Roosevelt or the fire of Truman. But Taft's close attention to detail won him respect from Senate colleagues, and a reputation for honesty and integrity gained him the admiration of older, more conservative Republicans. "Mr. Republican" argued that liberal Democrats were abandoning the New Deal measures of Roosevelt and moving toward socialism. Their programs, he charged, threatened to bankrupt the country and to place individual liberties at the mercy of an overbearing federal bureaucracy. But by 1946 Taft was also moderating some of his more extreme anti-New Deal views: To the consternation of reactionary Republicans, he even supported some federal aid to education, a limited program of public housing, and some social-welfare measures. In view of Truman's increasing problems, Taft hoped that his vision of "modern Republicanism" would make him the GOP's nominee in 1948.

Passage of the Taft-Hartley Labor Act of 1947 demonstrated the Ohio senator's economic ideas and legislative skills. The law, clearly aimed at reducing the political and economic power of organized labor, outlawed the closed shop (the practice of hiring only union workers), prohibited use of union dues for political activities, and authorized presidential back-to-work orders whenever labor strikes threatened national security. The law, Taft claimed, would not destroy labor unions; it would actually help workers by curbing the abuses of corrupt labor bosses. Taft skillfully managed the bill through the Senate and worked out a compromise with House Republicans who wanted a stronger antiunion statute. Truman vetoed the measure, but Taft collected the votes to override. Labor leaders denounced the bill as "a slave-labor act" and the "Tuff-Heartless Act"; pickets even appeared at the wedding of Taft's son.

Enactment of Taft-Hartley epitomized the ambiguous place of organized labor in the postwar political economy. On the one hand, the act struck at certain gains that labor had made during the 1930s and early 1940s; on the other, Taft-Hartley acknowledged that labor unions would retain more power than conservatives considered acceptable. In time, with the law courts and political leaders supporting the overall structure, the postwar labor-management settlement emerged. Management expected labor unions to press aggressively on wage issues, including cost-of-living increases, and other compensation questions such as pension plans and fringe benefits. In exchange, labor would become more productive, turning out more products in the same units of time, and concede management's prerogatives over a wide range of basic issues including the organization of the work process and investment decisions about where to locate and move plant facilities. This arrangement offered union members the promise of higher wages, more benefits, and greater job security; at the same time, however, it removed a whole range of fundamental issues from the process of collective labor-management bargaining and assigned them solely to the prerogatives of industry. Negotiations between the UAW and the Detroit automakers in 1948 followed this general compromise and set the pattern for labor-management relations during the first three decades of the postwar era.

The Election of 1948

The congressional and presidential elections of 1948 revealed more conflict than the UAW-auto industry negotiations of that same year. Despite his impressive leadership in Congress, Robert Taft lost the 1948 presidential nomination to Governor Thomas E. Dewey of New York, the GOP's standard-bearer in 1944. Taft's old reputation as a poor vote-getter and a conservative worked against him. Republicans, who had not nominated a winning candidate in twenty years, desperately wanted a winner, and Dewey and his running mate, Governor Earl Warren of California, appeared to be shoo-ins. Dewey had run well against FDR in the last presidential contest, had won a smashing victory in the 1946 New York gubernatorial race, and belonged to the more progressive, Eastern wing of the GOP.

But the victor in 1948 was not Tom Dewey: Harry Truman surprised almost all the political "experts," his Democratic critics, and the entire Republican party. "You've got to give the little man credit," admitted Republican Senator Arthur Vandenburg. "Everyone had counted him out, but he came up fighting and won the battle. That's the kind of courage the American people admire." To the extent that the presidential sweepstakes was a "beauty contest" between competing images, Truman emerged the clear winner. Dewey displayed little of Truman's warmth and personality. "I don't know which is the chillier experience—to have Tom ignore you or shake your hand," claimed one of his detractors. "You have to get to know Dewey to dislike him," another complained. Overconfident and overly cautious, "Thomas Elusive Dewey" made far fewer personal appearances than Truman. When Dewey did speak, he fell back upon platitudes and bland appeals to national unity.

In contrast, Harry Truman slashed away at the Republicans' Eightieth Congress. With his arms in perpetual motion, Truman denounced Republican representatives as "errand boys of big business" and bragged that he had vetoed more legislation than any other president of the twentieth century. During the brief interval between the Democratic convention and the November election Truman even called the Eightieth Congress into special session and presented it with a list of "must" legislation. When the Republican-controlled body predictably adjourned after passing only a few minor bills, Truman escalated his attacks upon Dewey and the Eightieth Congress. The president's seventeen-car, armor-plated campaign train whistle-stopped across the country to shouts of "Give 'em hell, Harry."

When he was not roasting the "no-account, do-nothing" Republican Congress, Truman emphasized his own version of the positive state. His chief strategists, especially Washington lawyer Clark Clifford, urged an aggressively liberal stance. Truman called for a higher minimum wage,

The man from Independence. Harry Truman projected an image as an ordinary citizen, one who never lost the common touch after he gained office. Source: *National Archives.*

repeal of Taft-Hartley, more public housing, and higher farm prices. During the final week of the campaign he became the first president to appear in Harlem. There he told a crowd of 35,000 African-Americans that he supported the "goal of equal rights and equal opportunities" for all Americans.

The civil rights question, which would become a more pressing political issue after 1948, did cost Truman some southern votes. His advisers wanted the party convention to adopt a mild statement in support of civil rights, but liberals and big-city bosses, who relied upon black voters, pushed through a stronger proposal. Following the heated floor fight, delegates from Alabama and Mississippi stalked out of the convention, and segregationists eventually formed the States Rights, or "Dixiecrat," party. The Dixiecrat platform denounced "totalitarian government" and advocated "segregation of the races." With Strom Thurmond of South Carolina as their presidential nominee, the Dixiecrats hoped to gain one hundred electoral votes in the South—enough ballots, they thought, to throw the presidential election into the House of Representatives. Thurmond, however, lacked enough financial support for an effective campaign, and the strategy failed. Most southern Democrats stayed with Truman, and Thurmond gained only 39 electoral votes.

Truman survived another revolt within his party: the Progressive party candidacy of Henry Wallace. Truman had fired Wallace as secretary of commerce because Wallace had publicly criticized the administration's hard-line anti-Soviet foreign policy. With support from a wide range of left-wing groups, inluding the Communist party, Wallace launched a new party that advocated greater cooperation with the Soviet Union, an end to the military draft, more federal money for social and economic programs at home, and American support for a United Nations Reconstruction Fund to promote worldwide economic recovery. If the United States could avoid conflict with the USSR, Wallace believed, American liberals could not only revive the New Deal at home but also extend its spirit of social reform overseas. Wallace's rallies resembled old-time revival meetings, as folk singers such as Pete Seeger and Woody Guthrie campaigned for Wallace and his running mate (another guitar player), Senator Glen Taylor of Idaho. One of Guthrie's songs, sung to the tune of "The Wabash Cannonball," expressed the class-based appeal of Wallace's left-wing supporters.

> *There's lumberjacks and teamsters and sailors from the sea,*
> *And there's farming boys from Texas and the hills of Tennessee,*
> *There's miners from Kentucky and there's fishermen from Maine,*
> *Every worker in the country rides that Wallace-Taylor train.**

But the Wallace-Taylor special never reached the White House. Following Clark Clifford's advice, Truman highlighted his own role as the nation's commander-in-chief while allowing subordinates to tie Wallace to the enemy in Moscow. "A vote for Wallace," the Democratic National Committee claimed, "is a vote for the things for which Stalin, Molotov, and Vishinsky stand." Wallace's acceptance of support from the Communist party of the United States, bitter opposition from large labor unions, the defection of anticommunist liberals, his forthright stand on civil rights, and the insurmountable problems of any newly formed party all caught up with Wallace. In December 1947 a poll showed that 13 percent of the electorate favored Wallace's candidacy; by election day his campaign had collapsed, and he received less than 3 percent of the popular ballots and not a single electoral vote.

Truman's victory demonstrated the staying power of the old Roosevelt coalition. Midwestern farmers, urban ethnic voters, organized labor, African-Americans, and most southerners continued to support the Democratic party. Many voted Democratic because of family tradition and because of the social and economic programs begun during the New Deal. Truman's energetic campaign, like most political efforts, did not suddenly convince great numbers of voters to support the Democratic party; it revived many Democrats' party loyalty and raised fears that GOP reactionaries would mount a general assault on New Deal measures. The four-way contest also

*The Farmer-Labor Train by Woody Guthrie © Copyright 1947 by Woody Guthrie Publications, Inc. All rights reserved. Used by permission.

apparently confused some voters. The 1948 election was what political scientists would call a "decline election," and only 54 percent of the electorate turned out. The election maintained the basic political configuration of the late 1930s and provided a mandate for following the basic outlines of the New Deal's positive welfare state.

THE FAIR DEAL

Truman's Domestic Program

After the victory of 1948, Truman and his advisers planned a new set of domestic proposals that they hoped would move beyond the New Deal. FDR's programs had been designed to stop the Great Depression and to restore the prosperity of the 1920s; Truman's Fair Deal offered measures aimed at sustaining an ever-expanding economy.

Truman's liberal economists believed that they had solved the mysteries of economic management. One aide, Charles F. Brannan, championed an ambitious proposal that he claimed would give farmers higher prices while providing consumers with cheaper food. Under Brannan's program the government would lift New Deal restrictions on the number of acres planted and would maintain farm income through direct price supports.

Another of Truman's economic advisers, Leon Keyserling, predicted that the national government could guarantee full employment, higher wages, and greater profits through well-planned and well-executed spending programs. Americans had no need to take from the rich to care for the poor. Properly managed, America's capitalist economy could outproduce any socialist system in the world. In 1948 nearly two-thirds of all American families lived on incomes of less than $4000 a year; by 1958 it would be possible, Keyserling predicted, to generate enough economic growth to make $4000 the minimum income for *every* family. "The people of America need to be electrified by our limitless possibilities," he proclaimed.

In addition to government measures designed to stimulate economic growth, Truman's Fair Deal promised a variety of programs to promote social and economic justice. Truman proposed expansion of Social Security, generous federal funding for public housing projects, a national plan for medical insurance, federal aid to education, and civil rights legislation. Truman and his liberal advisers believed that the Fair Deal represented the middle way between socialism and fascism. "Between the reactionaries of the extreme left with their talk about revolution and class warfare, and the reactionaries of the extreme right with their hysterical cries of bankruptcy and despair, lies the way of progress," Truman declared. The Democratic historian Arthur Schlesinger, Jr., provided an appropriate title for this postwar liberalism—"the vital center."

The Truman administration achieved some of its social programs, and economic conditions improved. Congress passed measures that extended

Social Security benefits; raised the minimum wage (to seventy-five cents an hour); and appropriated federal funds for soil conservation, flood control, and public power. Despite some fluctuations, the economy performed fairly well during the late 1940s and early 1950s. The United States came nowhere near Leon Keyserling's optimistic predictions, but real income did rise. People who had survived the Great Depression of the 1930s with help from the New Deal continued to do well in the era of the Fair Deal.

The Fair Deal: An Assessment

Sandwiched between FDR's New Deal of the 1930s and LBJ's Great Society of the 1960s, the Fair Deal of Harry Truman has too often been ignored. Many historians have viewed it as an addendum to the New Deal, as a grab bag of social-economic programs left over from the 1930s; others have seen it primarily as a prelude to the burst of legislation enacted during Lyndon Johnson's Great Society. But the Fair Deal deserves its own assessment. The Fair Dealers' optimistic assumptions about economic and social policies helped to shape the dominant view about the nation's future and about the role of government.

The Fair Deal rested upon an abiding faith that the United States economic system, so severely criticized during the 1930s, had proved itself far superior to any type of planned economic order. Capitalism, not democratic socialism or Soviet communism, represented the wave of the future. Classical defenders of the "free enterprise" system, of course, had always argued that a marketplace economy maximized individual freedoms and efficiently allocated resources and finished products. But during the cold war era, capitalism's liberal defenders also claimed that it could advance the cause of social justice, the banner under which the political left marched. One of the main virtues of America's economic system, postwar liberals argued, was its apparently unlimited ability to generate economic growth, a side of American life that economists proudly measured by a relatively new statistical gauge, the gross national product (GNP). A steadily rising GNP— the total dollar value of all goods produced and services rendered—attested to the fact that the economic collapse of the 1930s would not recur. Indeed, given the new economic wisdom now available, it could not!

Visions of economic growth bedazzled postwar social planners. An ever-expanding economy, Truman's advisers promised, ensured security for those people and for those organized interests that had already benefited from legislation of the New Deal era. More important, the promise of an ever-expanding economic pie offered hope to those Americans, estimated in 1937 by Franklin Roosevelt himself to be one-third of the population, who had been largely untouched by New Deal programs. In seeking to aid the poor and advance social justice, the United States could deftly sidestep difficult issues involving redistribution of wealth, income, and political power. As long as there was a growing GNP, new economic growth could provide the material basis for aiding those who had somehow fallen behind in the race for success. As Walter Heller, an economist who began his distinguished career during the Truman era, later explained, economic growth was both "the pot of gold and the rainbow."

But, as the dwindling band who still embraced classical laissez faire complained, proponents of this new economic wisdom did not place their faith in capitalism alone. The economic collapse of the 1930s, Keynesian economists warned, showed that a complex market economy was not always self-regulating. The Great Depression prompted governmental policies that would assist, and guarantee, economic growth. As passage of the Employment Act of 1946 suggested, even a majority of Congress, hardly a body known for its radical economic ideas, agreed that government officials had some responsibility to intervene in the "free enterprise" economy. Liberal economists welcomed this responsibility. Brandishing their new tools for monitoring the economy and for diagnosing its health, postwar economic doctors were generally confident that they could administer the kind of remedies—including measures to adjust interest rates, levels of taxation, and amounts of government spending—that could cure an ailing economy or merely pep up a sluggish one.

Confidence in the essential soundness of American capitalism and in their own expertise allowed the Fair Dealers to think beyond the old goals of the New Deal—economic recovery and reform. Instead, they could frame programs and establish bureaucratic institutions that could ensure steady economic growth; they could then use the results of this growth to attack ancient social problems, such as the grossly unequal access to medical care. Truman's proposals for domestic reform, more than anything envisioned by FDR, remained the basic aims of the Democratic party for almost two decades. A whole generation of Democratic liberals—individuals like Hubert Humphrey and John Kennedy—began their careers during the Fair Deal. Most never moved beyond it or questioned its basic assumptions.

The Fair Deal, and the larger postwar liberal vision, contained significant limitations. Despite the general affluence, especially in contrast with the economic situation in other parts of the postwar world, the American welfare state expanded its boundaries relatively little in the two decades after 1945. In 1962, Michael Harrington's *The Other America* reminded affluent liberals that nearly one-fourth of the population of their country still lived in deep poverty, largely unaided by federal programs. Defenders of the Fair Deal's approach could, of course, argue that the more ambitious portions of Truman's program never got through Congress. Determined lobbying by the American Medical Association, which raised the cry of "socialized medicine," helped kill the plan for national health insurance. Opposition from other powerful pressure groups encouraged a coalition of Republicans and conservative southern Democrats to block a program for general federal aid to state school systems and the Brannan plan for agricultural subsidies. In addition, many of the Fair Deal's programs lacked effective political support. Most middle-class Americans, the people who made up the bulk of the active electorate, wanted to enjoy the benefits of expanding economic production themselves—in the form of a new home, a second car, new consumer goods, and greater recreational opportunities.

But the limits of the Fair Deal cannot be blamed solely on the conservative coalition in Congress, on special-interest groups, or on voter apathy. The Truman administration itself placed greater weight on foreign than on domestic issues. America's national security and its economic well-being, Truman and his internationalist advisers believed, depended primarily upon the successful conduct of a global foreign policy. Preoccupied with foreign affairs and often inept in his dealings with Congress, Truman failed to provide vigorous leadership on domestic social issues. America's liberal crusaders focused most of their attention, and most of their energies, on problems overseas.

Civil Rights

The limited enthusiasm, among liberal elites, for new domestic crusades was most evident in the fate of civil rights legislation. Revulsion against Nazi racism helped encourage greater rhetorical denunciations of discrimination at home; wartime economic gains produced a desire among African-Americans for broader attacks on discrimination; and the outbreak of racial violence immediately after the war intensified liberal efforts to calm racial hatreds. Even the climate of the cold war seemed to call for measures to improve race relations at home. As the United States proclaimed that it, not the Soviet Union, offered the proper model for other nations to follow, continued legal discrimination against nonwhites in the United States itself proved difficult to explain. Desite these forces for change, however, the Fair Deal meant only small gains for the anti-discrimination effort.

As part of his broader domestic program President Truman pushed for a variety of civil rights measures, including a ban on poll taxes, an anti-lynching law, and legislation to guarantee equal employment opportunities. During the 1948 presidential campaign he issued executive orders that ended (at least on paper) discrimination in federal employment. Truman took great pride in his civil rights record; he once went so far as to claim that desegregation of the armed forces, which began during his second term, was "the greatest thing that ever happened to America."

The Truman administration also played a role in several important Supreme Court decisions that affirmed the legal rights of African-Americans and other minority groups. In *Shelly* v. *Kraemer* (1946) the justices unanimously held that no court could enforce restrictive covenants, agreements that prevented minority groups from acquiring real estate in certain areas. In two other cases—*Sweatt* v. *Painter* (1950) and *McLaurin* v. *Oklahoma Board of Regents* (1950)—the Court ruled that a separate law school established for blacks violated the Fourteenth Amendment's requirement for equality in education and that graduate schools could not segregate students according to race. Although these cases did not declare all segregated educational facilities inherently unequal, they did point the way toward the broader school-desegregation decision in *Brown* v. *Board of Education* (1954). In all these cases Truman's Justice Department supported the claims of African-American plaintiffs.

Despite these positive marks on Truman's record, civil rights provided another example of the gap between promise and performance in the Fair Deal. Some civil rights activists blamed Truman himself for the lack of new legislative initiatives: They claimed that the president gave their cause a low priority and too often deferred to the feelings of southern Democrats. Truman did try to avoid a direct stand on civil rights; the threat of African-American voters defecting to Henry Wallace in 1948, for example, prompted his executive orders barring racial discrimination in federal hiring. But Truman was not entirely to blame for his administration's failure to achieve more. The conservative coalition in Congress effectively bottled up legislation that would have aided African-Americans, and some military officials did their best to delay desegregation of the armed forces. Similarly, the president's initiatives in ending job discrimination ultimately depended upon the attitude of other officials in the federal bureaucracy. No executive order could be self-enforcing.

There was also a good deal of popular opposition to even limited moves toward racial equality. In the southern states the Confederate flag became the symbol of resistance: One flag company boasted that Virginians

A store for "colored only." The rural South in 1945. Source: *National Archives.*

owned more Confederate banners in 1951 than during the Civil War, and a New York City firm reported that the demand for rebel flags exceeded orders for the Stars and Stripes. Throughout the nation, racists violently opposed the drive for integration. When an African-American couple attempted to move into an apartment in Cicero, Illinois, a mob of about five thousand angry whites broke through National Guard lines and set the building ablaze. In the same year, 1951, a black school principal and civil rights leader died when explosives destroyed his Miami home on Christmas Day. Decrying the increased use of explosives in racial attacks, Walter White of the National Association for the Advancement of Colored People (NAACP) observed that "the bomb has replaced the lynchers' rope" as the main weapon of racist resistance.

The upsurge in white violence was one more impediment to the pace of national action against racial discrimination. Advances in the commitment to legal equality came slowly during the Truman years. Still, Truman's record looked better than that of any previous twentieth-century president. He was the first chief executive to make civil rights a national political issue, and his administration at least proposed a comprehensive legislative program. After 1948, the issue of race would inexorably move to the center of the national political stage and dramatically alter politics in the United States.

ANTICOMMUNISM AT HOME

The Communist Issue

Although the Truman administration moved cautiously on civil rights and social welfare issues, it acted decisively against the alleged threat of communist subversion in the United States. In 1947 Truman established a comprehensive "internal security" program designed to uncover "subversives" in the federal bureaucracy. Employing broad definitions of disloyalty, agencies purged a number of supposed security risks. The president did oppose suggestions for more Draconian measures—such as abolition of the Fifth Amendment in national-security cases—but the White House often failed to restrain the Department of Justice. J. Edgar Hoover's FBI, with the administration's consent, pried into the private lives and political beliefs of alleged subversives. Extending a practice begun during the Roosevelt years, the FBI also used wiretaps in violation of the Federal Communications Act of 1934. In 1949 Truman rejected suggestions that a special commission investigate the FBI. "Hoover has done a good job," the president told a press conference. The Attorney General's List of Subversive Organizations, first issued in 1947, demonstrated the Justice Department's propensity for establishing guilt by association. Noncommunists who happened to belong to one of these groups sometimes found themselves branded as reds, "pinkos," or "fellow travelers." Civil libertarians charged that the government too often equated legitimate political dissent with communist subversion.

Fears of subversive elements within the United States helped to justify creation of a massive surveillance–national security state. Citing the dangers the nation faced in the postwar era, members of the new CIA, the FBI, military intelligence, and other surveillance agencies began to broaden their oversight of domestic dissenters. Those on the political left, who could be most easily linked to a vague "communist conspiracy," came under intense scrutiny. Phones were tapped, dossiers collected, innuendos spread. Summing up the activities begun after World War II, the civil liberties lawyer Frank J. Donner called the postwar period "the age of surveillance."

How real was the domestic threat of communism? Did the White House and the Justice Department exaggerate the dangers? Although no researcher has uncovered any evidence that procommunists shaped United States policies, the government did possess intelligence about the activities of communist agents and the passing of military information to the Soviet Union. The FBI captured several authentic spies, and J. Edgar Hoover firmly believed that "the ignorant and the apologists and the appeasers of Communism in our country" consistently minimized the "danger of these subversives in our midst."

Still, the amount of spy activity and its actual danger to national security remain open questions. Historians, for example, continue to debate whether or not the Justice Department possessed sufficient evidence against Ethel and Julius Rosenberg, who were executed in 1953 for giving atomic secrets to the Soviets, and whether or not the couple fell victim to anticommunist hysteria. Similarly, controversy continued into the 1990s over the guilt or innocence of Alger Hiss, a prominent Democratic leader accused of passing secret documents to the USSR. Defenders of the Rosenbergs and Hiss claimed that governmental officials and witch-hunters largely manufactured the cases against these alleged spies, assertions that increasingly seemed impossible to prove, or to disprove. Greater access by scholars to previously classified materials, released through new government regulations or through suits under the Freedom of Information Act of 1974, only provided new ammunition with which to refight the old cold war battles. New books and articles have helped to intensify, not to settle, disputes over the nature of the communist threat during the 1940s and the 1950s. Although classified material about nuclear weaponry was passed to the Soviet Union, recent historical studies argue that the information received by the Soviets in the late 1940s contained badly flawed data. Ironically, suggests one study, these atomic "secrets" may have hindered, rather than assisted, Soviet efforts to acquire an atomic arsenal.

Whatever the impact of Soviet spying, the Truman administration had other reasons to mount a vigorous anti-red crusade. Since the late 1930s, anti-New Deal Democrats and conservative Republicans—particularly members of the House Committee on Un-American Activities (HUAC)—had claimed that communists and fellow travelers infested the Roosevelt administration. Charges of communist influence in the federal government often accompanied general attacks upon the "socialistic" New Deal welfare programs. Responding to Republican taunts of being "soft on communism," the Truman administration tried to improve its anticommunist credentials. Truman hoped that his own hard-line stance would prevent Republicans from seizing the anticommunist issue for themselves.

Fears of an active communist conspiracy within the United States also dovetailed with the administration's strong anti-Soviet foreign policy. During the period immediately following the war, public opinion polls revealed that few Americans considered communism a major problem. Truman's advisers feared that such attitudes—along with the strong popular sentiment against expensive overseas commitments—might hamstring the president's foreign policy. A tough stand against communism at home and a constant barrage of anticommunist rhetoric, administration strategists hoped, would counteract domestic resistance to Truman's sweeping foreign policy proposals.

Consequently, the Truman administration dramatically publicized its plan for dealing with internal subversion; officials continually stressed the need for greater vigilance; and the government orchestrated a vigorous pro-American campaign. In 1947, for example, Attorney General Tom Clark developed the "Freedom Train" program. This historical society on rails carried important documents, including a copy of the Truman Doctrine, to more than two hundred major cities. When the train returned to Washington in the fall of 1947, the government staged a "week of rededication." At a series of patriotic demonstrations, government employees took a "freedom pledge" and everyone sang "God Bless America." In a similar vein, the Office of Education promoted its "Zeal for Democracy" program: Washington encouraged local schools "to vitalize and improve education in the ideals and benefits of democracy and to reveal the character and tactics of totalitarianism."

Government leaders did not manufacture this crusade by themselves; but the broad anticommunist effort in Washington did help to shift attention from a specific problem, namely the extent of Soviet espionage, to the less tangible fear of an "alien" communist "invasion" of the nation's institutional and cultural life by subversives. Partly encouraged by government leaders, then, many Americans became less concerned about foreign agents than about communist sympathizers spreading dangerous ideas through an unsuspecting, overly tolerant society.

During the 1940s, a variety of official anticommunist activities began. The Post Office Department banned communist materials from the mails; many states adopted laws banning subversives from state-government jobs; bar associations and school boards required prospective attorneys and teachers to sign loyalty oaths. Congressional committees looked into red webs that supposedly stretched from Hollywood to Washington, D.C. Members of HUAC, including young Richard Nixon, claimed that their committee had discovered extensive procommunist networks in the United States; even if it stopped short of espionage, this pro-communist activity allegedly hindered execution of the nation's anticommunist containment policy. Critics of HUAC and of Truman's Justice Department countered with claims that, not only had very few dangerous people been fingered, but far too many innocent reputations had been smeared. Moreover, overzealous witch-hunters seemed less focused on rooting out subversives than on stigmatizing political dissidents, especially those who considered containment of the Soviet Union unnecessary and unwise.

Hollywood and the entire entertainment industry became an important focus of debates over the legitimacy and efficacy of postwar anticommunism. In 1947, HUAC began its effort to find communist infiltration of the movie colony. The committee's widely publicized hearings, which featured both "friendly" witnesses (who testified about an allegedly extensive communist involvement in film making) and "unfriendly" ones (who refused to say anything about political affiliations), badly divided the motion picture community. The Hollywood Ten, a group of witnesses that included past and present members of the Communist party, went to prison, after being found guilty of contempt of Congress, for defying HUAC by refusing to "name names" of suspected communists.

After some early resistance, studio heads cooperated with the red-hunters. Ultimately, several hundred people suspected of dangerous ideas or affiliations found themselves on an entertainment "blacklist"; blacklisted writers and performers found it difficult, if not impossible, to find work. (Typing away in anonymity, writers could be luckier than well-known performers; under an assumed name, one of the Hollywood Ten even won an Oscar for screen-writing while still on the blacklist!) The easiest way to escape the blacklist was to appear before an investigative committee, admit political errors, ritually condemn communism, and name at least one alleged subversive. In time, many prominent people in Hollywood, and throughout the entertainment industry, cooperated with anticommunist groups.

This search for subversives became—and remains to this day—a highly controversial subject. Despite overwhelming evidence to the contrary, some participants have tried to deny even the existence of blacklisting. Ronald Reagan and John Wayne, for example, denied knowing anything about a blacklist; yet both actors proudly talked about their helping to rid Hollywood of people they considered subversives. Reagan not only served as the anticommunist head of the Screen Actors Guild during the cold-war years but also as a secret informant for the FBI, known to the Bureau as Agent T-10. Such activities, observers and historians sympathetic to the anticommunist effort insist, represented a legitimate effort to root out pro-Soviet Stalinists and others who dishonestly tried to conceal their true political loyalties. The vast majority of "victims," they insist, actually had been associated with the Communist party or with other procommunist organizations; they were political hacks who betrayed their own artistic independence for a dubious political cause.

But the anticommunist probe of the entertainment industry also has its critics. Not surprisingly, writers and artists on the left, such as the writer Lillian Hellman (whose companion, the writer Dashiell Hammett, went to jail for refusing to cooperate with HUAC), condemned the "immoral" behavior of the "scroundrels" who testified about the affiliations and ideas of one-time friends and political allies. The anticommunist crusade in Hollywood, critical historians have further noted, coincided with a conservative assault on labor unions and the progressive political coalitions that had developed in the movie capital during the 1930s and early 1940s. In this view, industry leaders not only wanted to eliminate political opponents but also to recast Hollywood as a symbol of the postwar possibilities of anticommunism, corporate production, and mass consumption—the same set of values that Ronald Reagan subsequently carried from Hollywood into national politics. The search for subversives, then, fed upon itself. Fueled by powerful social and political pressures, investigations of the entertainment industry became "degradation ceremonies," ritualistic exorcisms in which dissident ideas and the people who held them could formally be labeled as deviant. The whole process of overseeing people's political ideas thus created powerful pressures for conformity: Rather than risk the ordeal of being accused, many individuals simply decided to censor themselves.

A series of disturbing events appeared to give credence to wild tales of communist machinations. Mao Zedong's success in China in 1949 and Russia's first atomic test frightened those who wrongly believed that the United States had "lost" China to the communists and that the "backward" Russians had stolen vital atomic secrets from the United States. Stories about communists in the State Department and atomic spies offered attractive explanations. The year 1950 brought new shocks: The government uncovered a Soviet spy ring in the United States, and American troops entered the Korean conflict. If these developments were not troubling enough, there were a series of scandals within the Truman administration, corruption in the Internal Revenue Service, a televised investigation of organized crime, and even an assassination plot against the president by Puerto Rican nationalists.

McCarthyism

Militant anticommunism reached its apogee in—and eventually took its name from—Senator Joseph McCarthy. Red-baiting existed before McCarthy ever discovered the anticommunist issue, and other witch-hunters made even wilder charges than the Wisconsin senator. But McCarthy dominated the headlines. His tactics were disarmingly simple: He flung accusations as fast as newspapers could print them but avoided specific proposals for fighting the communist "menace." When an acquaintance asked McCarthy how he would change the Voice of America's allegedly ineffective programs, "the Senator looked blank; obviously he had never thought about it." Nor did McCarthy spend much time documenting his sensational charges. His famous Wheeling, West Virginia, speech of 1950—in which he charged that the State Department employed more than two hundred communist sympathizers—rested upon a hodgepodge of questionable evidence from old congressional files. Even though the Senate later gave him broad investigatory powers, McCarthy never bothered to pursue his allegations against the State Department. Instead, he went after new demons, who he claimed were hiding in other government bureaus.

Because of widespread publicity, McCarthy soon gained an undeserved reputation as a powerful political force. The Wisconsin senator, his opponents feared, led a massive right-wing movement that seemed to appeal to the great numbers of lower-middle-class people with little formal education. Looking more like a heavy in a B movie than a tribune of the people, McCarthy pressed his image as a tough guy and a rebel. He railed against "establishment Democrats" such as Alger Hiss and Dean Acheson. All these "bright young men who were born with silver spoons in their mouths" and all those "striped-pants diplomats," McCarthy charged, were "selling the nation out." As he escalated his attacks, anticommunist liberals and moderates worried about a new threat from the "radical right."

McCarthy's power, however, did not come from a mass movement of fanatics. Instead, he gained attention because important people, such as members of the United States Senate, either supported his attacks or failed to oppose him. Influential middle western Republicans, who formed the traditional base for anti–New Deal conservatism, gave McCarthy vital political assistance. Republicans who would not personally stoop to McCarthy's smear tactics—Robert Taft of Ohio, for example—tacitly encouraged the Wisconsin senator. Anything that hurt the Democrats, Taft reasoned, would help the Republican party regain power. In addition to aid from conservative Republicans, McCarthy received help from other important sources. Most newspapers, regardless of their political allegiances, splashed McCarthy's charges over their pages. Sensational scoops about communist influence provided good copy—and greater sales. And many prominent liberal politicians avoided direct confrontation with McCarthy and his supporters for fear of being labeled "soft" on communism.

The passage of the McCarran Internal Security Act of 1950 demonstrated the widespread fear of opposing anticommunist measures. Rather than openly fighting Senator Pat McCarran's harsh proposals, the White House and congressional Democrats offered their own internal-security bills. In so doing, they accepted the McCarthyites' basic position: Communists should not expect the same civil liberties as other Americans. In its final form, the McCarran Act required communist and "communist-front" organizations to register with the attorney general, barred foreign communists from entering the United States, and authorized secret prison camps for detention of domestic subversives during wartime. Only seven senators and a handful of representatives voted against the McCarran Act. Truman vetoed the bill, but Congress quickly overrode the president's action. McCarthyism and McCarthy continued to influence national policy.

Eventually, however, McCarthy ran out of obvious targets and overstepped even his fertile imagination. By 1953 he was charging the Voice of America, the new Republican administration of Dwight Eisenhower, and the

United States Army with playing into the hands of the communists. In one celebrated incident, two of McCarthy's aides traveled around Europe to search for procommunist literature in libraries run by the United States Information Service. His agents and other witnesses charged that these libraries contained shelves of communist books and only a handful of pro-U.S. works; one investigator even suggested that libraries manipulated card catalogs so that readers would not find books critical of communism.

McCarthy's charges of communist influence in the army resulted in a special Senate investigation. The Army-McCarthy hearings, an ongoing television spectacular, contributed to McCarthy's demise. With McCarthy exposed to the harsh glare of TV, many viewers came to dislike his brash manner and bullying tactics. Many others simply became bored with the whole communist issue. Emboldened by McCarthy's problems, his critics escalated their attacks. Some of his Republican allies began to temper their support, and a few anticommunists even claimed that McCarthy's extremist position discredited the fight against Moscow and unwittingly aided the Kremlin. Finally, the United States Senate, the source of his prestige, turned against him. In 1954 a majority of senators voted to "condemn" McCathy for conduct unbecoming a member of the Senate. Stripped of his prestige and influence, McCarthy disappeared from the headlines, began drinking heavily, and died in 1957 at the age of forty-eight.

McCarthyism represented one of the more extreme examples of a general culture of anticommunism that dominated the 1940s and early 1950s. Fears about subversion and invasion by "alien" elements flourished, to one degree or another, in most parts of postwar life. Put simply, a wide spectrum of opinion considered communism—which different groups defined in very different ways—a domestic as well as a foreign danger and supported various efforts to contain it.

Anticommunism produced its own literary genre. Exposés of alleged communist infiltrators became a staple of postwar literature. The exploits of Mike Hammer, Mickey Spillane's brawny crime fighter, attracted paperback readers; by 1950, consumers had bought more than 6 million of Spillane's detective novels. The Hammer stories, though set on the domestic front, represented an exaggerated fear of communist-led subversion. With a single-minded devotion to 100 percent patriotism, Spillane's fictional hero loathed sexual "perverts," bleeding-heart liberals, civil libertarians, and communists. The stereotyped "lady-killer" around women—no female could withstand Hammer's charms—this vigilante hero mowed down communists and their corrupted followers with equal, though usually more violent, ease. To their many literary and political critics, Spillane's Hammer series expressed the same ends-justify-any-means approach as McCarthyism itself.

In time, even committed anticommunists saw their faith veering out of control. A growing conviction that McCarthy, after his foray against the U.S. Army, had stepped over the line, of course, speeded his downfall. Similarly, even many anticommunists dismissed groups on the "radical right," such as the John Birch Society, as purveyors of hysteria. With their wild claims about communist subversion—Dwight Eisenhower became a target of the Birch Society in the mid-1950s—the extreme anticommunists possessed the power to injure the reputations of individual liberals and moderates, but not the political support to influence the day-to-day shape of anticommunist measures. At best, they gave anticommunist policymakers a reserve army of committed loyalists; at worst, they projected a fanaticism that embarrassed larger anticommunist efforts.

The New Conservatism

McCarthy did receive cautious praise from a new source of conservative, anticommunist activism, William F. Buckley, Jr., who established the magazine *National Review* in 1955. The precocious product of a wealthy Catholic family, whose dread of communism traced back to the 1920s, Buckley saw promotion of anticommunism, at home and abroad, as his religious and patriotic duty. Moreover, Buckley detested the liberal-Democratic welfare state; its programs, he insisted, threatened the liberty of individuals while underestimating the communist threat. In this sense, Buckley considered Joe McCarthy—and even most of his tactics—as a justifiable response to a dangerous political world, one that liberals, even Republicans, failed to acknowledge. Buckley provided a powerful conservative magnet and eventually attracted a number of talented right-wing writers to his magazine.

Even before Buckley entered the scene, however, a number of other writers were setting the stage for a "new conservatism." Frederick von Hayek's *The Road to Serfdom* (1944) condemned the New-Deal welfare state, with its programs for using governmental power to supplement the "natural" workings of the economic marketplace, as a major step toward totalitarianism. Offering academic support for an argument that conservative Republicans had been making since the 1930s, Hayek's scholarly publication gained a broad audience when *Reader's Digest* issued a condensed version. Much to his surprise, the Austrian-born scholar became a popular source of postwar conservative ideas, especially on economic issues. Other conservative writers championed ideas such as strict construction of the Constitution, respect for the concept of states' rights, and concern about a possible "tyranny of the majority." Conservatives thus insisted that the activist New Deal dishonored the nation's intellectual heritage and endangered traditional liberties.

During the 1950s several conservative think tanks tried to enter public-policy debates. The Foreign Policy Research Institute, headed by Robert Strausz-Hupe, wanted a stronger anticommunist foreign policy, one that would go beyond simply containing to rolling back communism. Strausz-Hupe urged the United States aggressively to "carry the battle to the vital centers of communist defense." William F. Buckley took up another important conservative theme in his 1951 jeremiad, *God and Man at Yale*. His alma mater, Buckley charged, typified institutions of higher education in the ways that its faculty championed liberal, collectivist ideas and derided conservative, Christian ones. Thus, Buckley and other postwar conservatives launched an effort that would continue into the 1990s: a concerted campaign to interject conservativism into academic life.

This new conservatism, from the very outset, covered a wide range of ideas and personalities. Russell Kirk, one of the most cerebral and pessimistic of the postwar conservatives, criticized democratic government and wanted a greater sense of deference, among the unruly masses, to the nation's "natural leaders." In contrast, other prominent conservatives such as Peter Viereck and Clinton Rossiter praised democratization and even much of the New Deal. Viereck, for example, saw welfare-state programs, such as Social Security, providing the stabilizing influences that conservatives should favor. And whereas Russell Kirk urged censorship of "dangerous" ideas, libertarian conservatives often joined liberals in seeking broad interpretations of constitutionally protected civil liberties.

Despite all of the activity by the new conservatives, their movement remained largely one of ideas during the 1940s and 1950s. If social liberals could not rally the country behind a new crusade for moving beyond the New Deal, conservatives found even less enthusiasm for rolling back the Democratic party's welfare state or moving beyond a foreign policy based on containment. The center of postwar conservatism remained literary and cultural, bolstering the larger culture of anticommunism.

Anticommunism and Intellectual Life

Most prominent writers and social commentators of the late 1940s and 1950s agreed that communism threatened the "American way of life" and that Marxism was a pernicious doctrine without any intellectual respectability. As the liberal journalist Tom Braden put it, the cold war was being "fought with ideas instead of bombs," and a number of prominent postwar intellectuals consequently joined the Congress for Cultural Freedom (CCF), an international organization pledged to promote ideas of liberty and oppose "state-sponsored ideologies" such as Soviet communism. Behind the scenes, however, the CCF received secret CIA funding. Although the CIA never told members of the CCF what to believe, or what to print in their influential publication *Encounter*, the organization rarely, if ever, endorsed intellectuals who opposed the anticommunist foreign policies of the United States. Did this dominant anticommunism significantly narrow social criticism in the United States?

Consider, for example, the postwar media. Certainly the press remained free from direct government censorship, and many journalists, especially those on the political right, vigorously criticized official execution of specific cold-war programs. Yet, after the collapse of Henry Wallace's Progressive party movement in late 1948, it became difficult to find media people who criticized the basic assumption that the greatest threat to the nation came from international communism. Attending Washington cocktail parties, listening to officials' "off-the-record" justifications, and accepting governmental handouts at face value, influential journalists might be seen, in effect, as part of the ideological apparatus by which the state encouraged a culture focused on anticommunism. Truly independent writers such as I.F. Stone, who subjected government explanations to critical scrutiny, seem to have been the exception. In contrast to Stone's one-person operation. *I.F. Stone's Weekly* (which assumed every official statement to be suspect until independently confirmed), the mainstream media rarely scrutinized cold-war orthodoxies.

A similar pattern emerged in academic life. During the 1930s, for example, scholarship stressing social conflict, the limits of capitalist institutions, and skepticism of received wisdom had figured prominently in academic debates. By the late 1940s, in contrast, the horrors of Stalinism, fears about radicals from both the right and left, and the hopeful performance of postwar capitalism all helped to produce an academic culture that ignored perspectives that might be labeled "radical."

Like prominent journalists, academic leaders proudly proclaimed their cold-war, anticommunist credentials. University-based research labs, after some early postwar debates about the role of scientists in nuclear weapon-making, enthusiastically enlisted in the anticommunist fight. Similarly, academics in the humanities and social sciences often lent their talents to the containment crusade. American historians, for example, embraced containment as a continuation of the internationalist, anti-totalitarian thrust of enlightened, post-1937 foreign-policy making. And in the social sciences, with the dominant emphasis upon objective, disinterested, and value-free analysis, any passionate work of social criticism risked being labeled as old-fashioned and out-of-step with currently scholarly standards.

Leading intellectuals still proclaimed themselves skeptics, but, in retrospect, this postwar skepticism had clear limits. Most prominent academics, in the words of one later scholar, were "believing skeptics," people whose distrust of left-wing pieties did not produce an equally rigorous scrutiny of the pragmatic, political system they believed operated in the United States. Once deeply committed to Marxism and left-wing politics, the sociologist Daniel Bell spoke for most postwar intellectuals when he proclaimed an "end of ideology." Welfare-state programs of both the New Deal and the Fair Deal offered everything needed to fix the nation's problems. Through economic and social fine-tuning, done in accordance with the best scientific and social-science expertise, political managers could advance social and economic justice without any fundamental restructuring of capitalist institutions or rethinking of consumer values. Within the nation's fast-growing system of higher education, a celebratory mood dominated: The United States should be praised for its broad virtues rather than criticized for its narrow vices.

This general mood of celebration, according to mainstream intellectuals, did not mean that academic freedom had been compromised. While admitting a few cases in which left-wing academics lost their jobs, the postwar liberal academy emphasized that prominent dissenters, such as the sociologist C. Wright Mills, were not silenced as they would have been in a communist state.

In recent years, however, histories of academic culture have suggested considerable surveillance of campus life by the FBI and CIA. In one case, for example, J. Edgar Hoover's agents pilfered a draft copy of a law-review article that criticized the FBI as a threat to civil liberties, a move that enabled the bureau's director to begin planning a campaign to discredit the article's author. In other cases, prominent academics covertly worked with anticommunist agencies much more closely than they admitted at the time, or subsequently. As in the entertainment industry, the history of higher education seems to have involved more dismissals, a longer blacklist and a wider history of cooperating with surveillance institutions than once thought.

THE PERILS OF PROGRESS

Publicists for the giant electronics firm of General Electric coined a phrase that captured the essence of postwar optimism: "Progress is our most important product." (During the 1950s, GE's primary spokesperson became a fading Hollywood star named Ronald Reagan.) According to the widely shared vision, the future, largely defined in terms of the increased consumption of goods and services, seemed preordained: It would be a bigger, better, streamlined version of the present. Public-spirited business corporations, employing the latest scientific and technological advances, would produce an ever-expanding array of improved products for wealthy, middle-class and even poor families.

In time, thanks to the miracles of mass production and the mechanics of mass consumption (including expanded use of installment buying), the lifestyles of the nation's diverse population would ultimately converge. New "communities" would emerge, based upon the mutual consumption of similar products. The richest Americans, to be sure, would always have the most, but even those at the bottom of the socioeconomic scale could live increasingly comfortable lives. Skilled technocrats, the kind of people who had proved so adept at harnessing science and technology for production during World War II, would ensure that this vision became reality. And if technocrats and the "private sector" failed to accomplish all this by themselves, postwar futurists observed, the national government stood ready to act as the ultimate cheerleader and banker for the new future.

Science and Technology

Postwar discussions of science and technology raised both fears and hopes about new developments. The atomic explosions that ravaged Japan, for example, initially produced terrifying images of worldwide destruction alongside optimistic pictures of how America's growing nuclear prowess might open an entirely new age in human history. After several years of fierce debate, in which vastly different images of a nuclear future competed against one another, opposition to full-scale nuclear development by the United States faded away. Critical scientists gradually found themselves marginalized and, in the more extreme cases, ostracized by colleagues and the increasingly powerful nuclear-research lobby. For years, the government conducted experimental tests of nuclear weapons on islands in the South Pacific and in the western United States. But it kept secret the devastating effects of radioactive fallout on humans—islanders, service personnel, nuclear-industry workers, and westerners—who were downwind of the explosions or who came in contact with radioactive materials.

By 1950, arguments urging bigger bombs for national security and a domestic nuclear power industry effectively dominated public discussion. Correctly developed and properly harnessed, atomic energy, it was claimed, could power the nation's growing cities, propel its naval vessels, and carry explorers into outer space. In a similar way, radioactive technology in medicine promised exciting new advances, including victory in the fight against cancer.

By the early 1950s, a comprehensive legal network helped to legitimize the nuclear industry. The Atomic Energy Act of 1946 gave the president sole authority to order use of nuclear weapons but vested day-to-day control over nuclear materials to a new executive agency, the Atomic Energy Commission (AEC). Run by civilians, the AEC initially conducted research and made basic policy decisions about the use of nuclear technology. Under the Atomic Energy Act of 1954, however, this system of tight federal control was modified in favor of an arrangement by which the AEC would grant licenses to private users of nonmilitary atomic energy. The goal of this new system, according to its supporters, was rapid growth of privately owned, but governmentally regulated, nuclear generating plants. Few people questioned the wisdom of this important step toward creation of a private nuclear power industry in the United States.

The national government became more involved in a wide range of other, nonnuclear scientific activities after World War II. The wartime experience suggested the need for peacetime support of military research, and advocates of federal aid also urged the government to appropriate more money for nonmilitary experimentation. In a report to the president entitled *Science—The Endless Frontier* (1945), Vannevar Bush, who had managed scientific projects for the government during World War II, called for a single national agency to administer grants for scientific research. Scientists, he argued, were about to make important new discoveries that could protect the nation from foreign enemies and dramatically improve the quality of citizens' daily lives. In 1950 Congress established the National Science Foundation, and NSF grants soon allowed scientists to explore subjects unknown a generation earlier. Within two decades federal funds underwrote most scientific research in the United States.

Encouraged by government funds (and by grants from tax-exempt private foundations), scientific activity accelerated in the postwar era. Ever since the late nineteenth century the number of scientists and technicians had been growing faster than the general population, and this trend continued after 1945. The United States had once been a nation of basement tinkerers. But the corps of highly trained specialists who dominated science and technology after World War II could not build their own laboratories, as Thomas Edison had once done. The new discoveries—in fields such as chemistry, biology, electronics, and nuclear energy—rested upon highly sophisticated equipment and complex scientific theories about the physical universe.

The postwar enthusiasm for scientific and technological innovation overwhelmed doubts about the social impact of new developments. The postwar era seemed to promise almost unbelievable, and overwhelmingly positive, changes. Instead of merely adapting human institutions to the natural environment, scientists celebrated their ability to go beyond the natural to create an artificial world. Knowledge of scientific theories permitted them to rearrange molecular structures and to produce synthetic fibers, high-strength adhesives, man-made construction materials, and many other new products. In 1944 scientists at Rockefeller Institute isolated a compound called DNA, which opened the secrets of genetic reproduction. Throughout the 1940s biochemists tried to unravel the molecular structure of DNA, and finally in 1953 an American and a Briton constructed a model of a DNA molecule. Scientists were on the threshold of creating life itself. Abstract theoretical knowledge and sophisticated technology were becoming important national resources, like iron and coal; indeed, scientific know-how and up-to-date technology now seemed the most vital resources of all.

Developments in the computer-electronics industry, however, suggested ambiguities in the dominant, postwar vision of "progress." From management's perspective, for example, the ideal factory seemed one almost totally devoid of workers. In 1946, *Fortune* magazine featured a section on the "Automatic Factory," including an article entitled "Machines Without Men." By the use of new, computer-assisted technology, this article predicted, the factory could be emptied of dirty, troublesome laborers and run by a handful of skilled technocrats who looked after the "accurate," "untiring," and highly efficient "electronic gadgets." The following year an executive at Ford Motor Co. offered a term that has remained, depending upon one's point of view, either a threat or a promise—"automation."

What, for example, would be the fate of workers who faced computer-assisted technologies? Viewed from the vantage point of corporate managers and other apostles of progress, the answer seemed obvious. A more efficient production process could only be eminently democratic: More consumers would obtain more goods and services at lower prices. But if one reversed the perspective, and looked at this kind of "progress" from the position of workers, substantial difficulties appeared. New technologies, developed by management (often with hefty governmental subsidies), controlled by management, and explained to the public by management, promised to strip workers of a good deal of power and control over both the work process and ultimately their job security.

In 1952, a youthful GE publicist-turned-author, Kurt Vonnegut, Jr., criticized the "progress as our product" vision in his novel *Player Piano*. Based on many of Vonnegut's own experiences at GE's complex in Schenectady, New York, *Player Piano* fantasized a dystopic future in which automation obliterated the skills, self-confidence, and human spirit of workers; Vonnegut imagined a world in which one-dimensional technocrats presided over a moral and spiritual wasteland. The future, he warned, might not be characterized by evolutionary progress, as the publicists for the cold war consensus confidently predicted; instead, postwar America could be headed down a dark, dangerous, and disorderly path of "devolution." Although *Player Piano* became a cult classic, Vonnegut himself later recalled that the GE technocrats he so bitterly lampooned remained wedded to the mainstream, postwar vision: New technologies were automatically good, and automation would bring the benefits of consumerism to a wider audience, while relieving workers of the burdens of repetitive labor.

Changes in postwar medicine also showed the ambiguous nature of scientific "progress." Undeniably, there were positive breakthroughs. After World War II, for example, the United States experienced severe, unprecedented epidemics of poliomyelitis. Between 1947 and 1951 this disease, which generally crippled those it did not kill, struck an annual average of 39,000 Americans, mostly children. (Between 1938 and 1942 the annual average had been only 6,400, a figure that rose to 16,800 between 1942 and 1947.) In 1952 doctors reported some success using gamma globulin as a preventative, and three years later Jonas Salk pioneered the first truly successful vaccine. A nationwide program to inoculate people with this and the later Sabin vaccine resulted in the vital elimination of polio by the 1960s. After World War II, doctors also introduced a series of "wonder drugs." Penicillin, an antibiotic discovered in the 1920s and refined during the war, came into general use between 1945 and 1952; a powerful set of antibiotics—streptomycin, aureomycin, terramycin, and magnamycin—appeared after World War II; and antihistamines, which proved important in the treatment of allergies, became available in the late 1940s. These drugs and new surgical techniques allowed many Americans to lead longer and sometimes more comfortable lives. Also, they encouraged more determined research into cures for cancer and heart disease, two afflictions that became increasingly common as the United States became more urbanized and industrialized.

Changes in medicine, however, did not automatically bring better health care to everyone. Exotic new drugs, complicated treatment procedures, and lavish hospital facilities increased the costs of medical care. The very poor and many elderly people simply could not afford the new "wonder" cures; many rural areas and small towns, unable to compete with metropolitan areas for younger physicians, found themselves short of competent doctors as well as of up-to-date hospital facilities. Largely as a result of this maldistribution of medical services, the United States actually lost ground, compared with other industrial nations, in reducing its infant mortality rate.

In addition to the unequal distribution of medical treatment, postwar technology created other problems. New developments accelerated the disappearance of the family doctor—the general practitioner celebrated in Norman Rockwell's paintings—and the proliferation of specialists—doctors trained to diagnose and treat only a limited number of conditions. Indeed, after World War II new medical technologies meant that large hospital complexes, with their costly array of machines and their large staffs of specialists, did replace the home and the doctor's office as primary treatment centers. Fewer and fewer doctors made house calls; more and more people went to hospital emergency rooms or outpatient centers. At the same time, people who needed extensive medical care found that the new medicine often meant a costly stay in the hospital. In 1946 only 1 of every 10 Americans was admitted to a hospital for inpatient care; twenty years later the figure had risen to 1 of every 6.5 persons. Unfortunately, a hospital visit did not always result in either an instant cure or, in some cases, even the proper treatment. According to numerous studies, perhaps half of many common surgical operations, particularly those performed upon women and children, were unnecessary. Other critics of the postwar medical establishment cited the proliferation of iatrogenic illnesses, ailments brought on by the "treatment" for some other malady. Many iatrogenic illnesses, these critics argued, resulted from a naive faith in new medicines, from improper testing and regulation of supposedly effective drugs, and from the popular belief that doctors possessed a miracle cure for every ache and pain. Assessing the impact of exotic medical technologies would, by the 1990s, require a complex dialogue in which philosophers who specialized in "medical ethics," as well as the medical community and the general public, would take part.

Agriculture

Postwar science and technology affected all segments of American society, and few people saw more changes than farmers, supposedly the slowest to alter settled ways. Farming became more mechanized and scientific than ever before. Sophisticated biological research produced new types of seeds, such as hybrid corn. Introduced in some areas during the 1930s, hybrid corn had spread to all parts of the country by the 1950s. Equally important to grain producers, the chemical industry provided the knowledge to make cheaper fertilizers and pesticides. Farmers quickly turned to these chemicals to boost output: They used three times as much fertilizer in 1950 as they had ten years earlier. Farmers also began to adopt labor-saving machines on a massive scale. Between 1940 and 1960, for example, the number of tractors increased by more than 200 percent, and the number of grain combines rose nearly as much. Meanwhile, engineers were increasing the size of these machines, boosting their horsepower with higher-compression engines, and offering a variety of attachments. The new machinery and chemicals drastically reduced the number of farm laborers needed to bring in key crops (see Table 2–1).

TABLE 2–1   **Declining demand for farm labor accelerated the rush to urban areas and left pockets of rural poverty.**

MECHANIZATION OF AGRICULTURE:
WORKER-HOURS PER 100 BUSHELS OF SELECTED CROPS

CROP	1945–49	1955–59	1962–66
Corn for grain	53	20	9
Sorghum grain	49	20	9
Wheat	34	17	11
Hay	6.2	3.7	3.0
Potatoes	12	6	5
Sugar beets	6.3	2.9	2.1
Cotton	146	74	39
Tobacco	39	31	25
Soybeans	41	23	20

Source: *Agricultural statistics*

As a result, rural life in the United States changed significantly after World War II. For many years agricultural production had been increasing, but now—with hybrid seeds, better equipment, cheaper fertilizers, and new irrigation facilities—output rose at a much faster rate than before. Farmers could cultivate hitherto unproductive land and areas once set aside as pastures for horses and mules. (In 1920 farmers had used more than 90 million acres of potential croplands to graze draft animals; by 1960 they needed less than 10 million acres for pasturage.) In addition, the new agricultural methods permitted farmers to utilize their old land more effectively, and the yield per acre rose substantially after World War II. But irrigation required massive amounts of water, and fertilizers and pesticides raised serious health hazards for both farm workers and consumers.

Meanwhile, steadily increasing production kept farm prices low, thereby altering the bases of agricultural production. After 1947 agricultural prices leveled off until the sudden rise of the early 1970s. While most of the world's people spent almost half their incomes for food, Americans needed only about 20 percent of their paychecks to feed their families. The majority of farmers did not enjoy the rising incomes of most other Americans, and only the largest and most efficient operations could show substantial profits. Although Washington tried to support farm incomes by using the same basic programs devised during Roosevelt's New Deal—direct subsidies and various plans for restriction of acreage—nothing really raised farm incomes. Low prices and steadily rising costs continually plagued small operators. Taking advantage of their private economic power and their ability to secure federal assistance, larger corporate farmers gained larger shares of the agricultural market while the number of smaller "family farms" declined steadily.

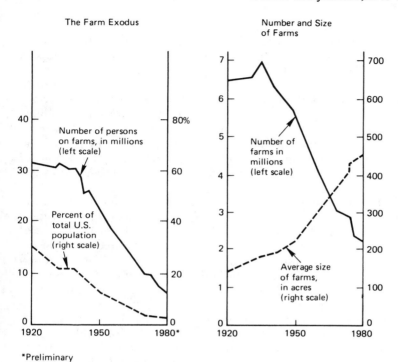

The Farm Exodus

Number and Size
of Farms

*Preliminary

In the post war period the trends toward fewer but larger farms and toward a much smaller rural population accelerated. By 1980 three of every four Americans lived in a metropolitan area.

The United States at Mid-Century: The Taint of Scandal and the End of Truman's Presidency

The ambiguities of developments in science and technology, along with more immediate political tensions, produced considerable unease about everyday life in mid-twentieth century America. The promise of the postwar era seemed particularly marred by signs of widespread corruption. In 1950 and 1951 an ambitious Democratic senator from Tennessee, Estes Kefauver, dramatically unveiled the shadowy world of organized crime. Skillfully using television, Kefauver brought underworld figures—from top mobster Frank Costello to petty gamblers and prostitutes—into millions of living rooms. Keufauver's Senate hearings held all the drama of a Hollywood production. "It was difficult at times to believe that it was real," said the *New York Times*.

Other stories of corruption appeared during the postwar period. In 1950 the United States Military Academy, the citadel of gentlemanly honor and patriotic values, expelled ninety West Pointers, including nine starting members of the football team, for cheating on examinations. That same year, prosecutors in New York uncovered a point-shaving scandal in college basketball. Star players on several top teams—including national champion City College of New York and the University of Kentucky—were found to have taken bribes in exchange for rigging game scores in favor of professional gamblers. Bernard Malamud's novel *The Natural* (1952) captured at least some of this mid-century disillusionment: A talented, but gullible, baseball star, Roy Hobbs, falls prey to corrupt owners and mysterious gamblers, eventually disgracing the national pastime. (In contrast to the film version of the 1980s, Malamud's novel of the 1950s ends on a note of despair: Hobbs fails to redeem himself and comes to symbolize an unreflective, naive national spirit.)

By the 1950s, big-time sports had become an important part of cultural life, and revelations about scandal at the highest levels produced widely different reactions. Some people, such as Senator J. William Fullbright of Arkansas, blamed the spirit of corruption on a general decline in moral principles. The National Collegiate Athletic Association (NCAA) banned the basketball players who had taken bribes from further competition, and the National Basketball Association blacklisted them forever. But others were not so quick to accept or to assign moral blame. The West Point cadets refused contrition, claiming they were being punished for a practice followed by most of their classmates. Army's football coach, Colonel Earl Blaik, whose son had been one of those dropped from the academy, refused to condemn his players and publicly reaffirmed his faith in football as a character-building sport.

In time, the search for corruption reached into the White House. Along with McCarthyite charges of being soft on communism, accusations about "the mess in Washington" drove Truman's popularity lower and lower. During his last years in office, scandals seemed to pop up everywhere. An old crony, Harry Vaughan, was accused of accepting illegal gifts; Senator Fulbright (an old Truman foe known as Senator Halfbright around the White House) uncovered examples of apparent political favoritism in the Reconstruction Finance Corporation; the wife of a former RFC official received a mink coat as part of a questionable transaction; the *New Republic* leveled charges of bribery or political favoritism at no less than six federal agencies; the head of the Democratic National Committee appeared guilty of influencing a government decision in exchange for legal fees; and Republicans constantly complained that the Truman administration was full of "five-percenters" who traded their political influence for kickbacks on public contracts. Cantankerous and stubborn as ever, Truman lashed out at his critics. Despite clear evidence to the contrary, he proclaimed that "my house is always clean." Although no one ever connected any of the scandals with Truman himself, he left Washington with his reputation as a presidential leader badly tarnished. Only with the passage of time and the uncovering of far greater scandals in subsequent presidential administrations would Harry Truman become a national folk hero, a president lionized by both Republicans and Democrats, liberals and conservatives.

Meanwhile, as the nation passed the midpoint of the twentieth century, the perils of the postwar years appeared to have passed; the promise of "the American Century" seemed in view. To be sure, even the most optimistic observer conceded lingering problems: the Soviet threat overseas; McCarthyism at home; economic problems at the fringe of a growing affluence; and the explosive issue of race relations. But even social critics generally accentuated the positive: though hardly tranquil, labor-management conflict now centered on clearly defined issues; the welfare state, assisted by newly developed social-science expertise, seemed firmly in place; supported by judicious governmental intervention, the capitalist economy appeared to have outgrown traditional cycles of boom and bust; a new scientific-technological elite promised to produce progress for all; the national security establishment seemed entirely capable of safeguarding the nation's global interests. And perhaps most important, the apparent "end of ideology" suggested a future in which rational planners and practical compromisers could solve remaining difficulties. During the mid-1950s, popular debates would generally focus on questions of how best to adjust to the self-evident promise of the United States, but beneath the surface the unresolved postwar tensions remained.

SUGGESTIONS FOR FURTHER READING

Lary May, ed., *Recasting America: Culture and Politics in the Age of the Cold War* (1989) is a collection of essays on different aspects of postwar life. Eric F. Goldman's *The Crucial Decade—and Afterward* (1960) remains a good introduction, but John Patrick Diggins, *The Proud Decades: America in War and Peace, 1941–1960* (1988), and Michael Barone, *Our Country* (1990), offer more recent syntheses. Two very useful accounts, especially for labor and mass culture, are Marty Jezer, *The Dark Ages* (1982) and George Lipsitz, *Class and Culture in Cold War America* (1982). Alan Wolfe, *America's Impasse* (1981); Margaret Weir, Ann S. Orloff and Theda Skocpol, eds., *The Politics of Social Policy in the United States* (1988); and Steve Fraser and Gary Gerstle, eds., *The Rise and Fall of the New Deal Order, 1930–1980* (1989), all take wider views of postwar themes.

Robert Ferrell, *Harry Truman and the Modern American Presidency* (1983), and William Pemberton, *Harry S Truman: Fair Dealer and Cold Warrior* (1989), offer good introductions; Robert J. Donovan's two-volume biography, *Conflict and Crisis* (1977) and *Tumultuous Years* (1982), provides more detail. Truman's own views can be found in his *Memoirs* (2 vols., 1955—56) and in Merle Miller's *Plain Speaking* (1974), a series of interviews that helped spark the rehabilitation of Truman's reputation. Michael J. Lacey, ed., *The Truman Presidency* (1989), offers a set of recent interpretive essays, while Alonso Hamby, *Beyond the New Deal* (1973), remains a useful look at Truman's Fair Deal.

Specialized studies include R. Alton Lee, *Truman and Taft-Hartley* (1966); Allen J. Matusow, *Farm Policies and Politics in the Truman Administration* (1966); William C. Berman, *The Politics of Civil Rights in the Truman*

Administration (1970); Maeva Marcus, *Truman and the Steel Seizure Case* (1977); Monte Poen, *Harry S Truman Versus the Medical Lobby* (1977); Andrew J. Dunar, *The Truman Scandals and the Politics of Morality* (1984); and Steven M. Gillon, *Politics and Vision: The ADA and American Liberalism, 1947–1985* (1986).

Economic and labor issues can be traced in Robert Leckachman, *The Age of Keynes* (1966); John Bernard, *Walter Reuther and the Rise of the Auto Workers* (1983); Gerald D. Nash, *The American West Transformed* (1985); Robert H. Zeiger, *American Workers, American Unions, 1920–1985* (1986); Milton Derber and others, *Labor in Illinois: The Affluent Years, 1945–1980* (1989); and Mark Friedberger, *Farm Families and Change in Twentieth-Century America* (1988).

There are many excellent studies of the postwar red scare. Richard M. Fried, *Nightmare in Red: The McCarthy Era in Perspective* (1989), is a recent synthesis, but David Caute's *The Great Fear* (1978) still offers the most comprehensive overview. Specialized studies include Michael Belknap, *Cold War Political Justice* (1971); Frank J. Donner, *The Age of Surveillance* (1980); Peter Steinberg, *The Great "Red Menace"* (1982); Stanley I. Kutler, *American Inquisition* (1982); Larry Ceplair and Steven Englund, *The Inquisition in Hollywood* (1983); Ronald Radosh and Joyce Milton, *The Rosenberg File* (1983); David Oshinsky, *A Conspiracy So Immense: The World of Joe McCarthy* (1983); Gerald Horne, *Black and Red: W.E.B. DuBois and the Afro-American Response to the Cold War* (1986); Ellen Schrecker, *No Ivory Tower: McCarthyism & the Universities* (1986); Herbert Mitgang, *Dangerous Dossiers: Exposing the Secret War against America's Greatest Authors* (1988); Bernard Dick, *Radical Innocence: A Critical Study of the Hollywood Ten* (1989); and Robert P. Newman, *The Cold War Romance of Lillian Hellman and John Nelby* (1989). Athan Theoharis has a number of outstanding studies on the culture of surveillance and anticommunism; see, for example, *The Truman Presidency: The Origins of the Imperial Presidency and the National Security State* (1979), and *Beyond the Hiss Case*, two volumes which he edited. See also the relevant chapters of Theoharis and John Stuart Cox, *The Boss: J. Edgar Hoover and the Great American Inquisition* (1988).

On cold-war cultural and intellectual trends, see Robert Booth Fowler, *Believing Skeptics* (1978); Mary Sperling McAuliffe, *Crisis on the Left: Cold War Politics and American Liberals* (1978); Serge Guilbaut, *How New York Stole the Idea of Modern Art: Abstract Expressionism, Freedom, and the Cold War* (1983); Richard Pells, *The Liberal Mind in a Conservative Age* (1984); Paul Boyer, *By the Bomb's Early Light; American Thought and Culture at the Dawn of the Atomic Age* (1985); Alexander Bloom, *Prodigal Sons: The New York Intellectuals & Their World* (1986); Alan Wald, *The New York Intellectuals* (1987); Lawrence H. Schwartz, *Creating Faulkner's Reputation: The Politics of Modern Literary Criticism* (1988); Robbie Lieberman, *"My Song Is My Weapon": People Songs, American Communism, and the Politics of Culture, 1930–1950* (1989); and the early chapters of Andrew J. Ross, *No Respect: Intellectuals and Popular Culture* (1989).

Science and technological issues are discussed in Daniel Ford, *The Cult of the Atom* (1982); George T. Mazuzan and J. Samuel Walker, *Controlling the Atom: The Beginnings of Nuclear Regulation* (1984); David Noble, *Forces of Production* (1984); Bryan Jennett, *High Technology Medicine: Benefits and Burdens* (New ed., 1986); Howard Ball, *Justice Downwind: America's Atomic Testing Program* (1986); James Patterson, *The Dread Disease: Cancer and Modern American Culture* (1987); Jonathan Liebenau, *Medical Science and Medical Industry: The Formation of the American Pharmaceutical Industry* (1987); Rosemary Stevens, *In Sickness and in Wealth: American Hospitals in the Twentieth Century* (1989); David A. Hounshell and John K. Smith, Jr., *Science and Corporate Strategy: Dupont R&D, 1902–1980* (1988).

Chapter Three

Politics and Culture
In the 1950s

MODERATE REPUBLICANISM

The broad smile of Dwight Eisenhower dominated politics during the mid-1950s. A successful general in World War II, Ike surely was shrewder than his simple popular image suggested. Army promotions and success as a commander required ambition and a politician's keen sense of timing, and Eisenhower put the political skills he had learned in the army to good use during his presidency. But to his admirers of the 1950s, he simply radiated good, down-home common sense rather than political guile. Even his nickname had a folksy ring, lacking the efficient staccato of JFK and LBJ or the distant formality of Richard M. Nixon. Though old doubts persisted and new problems emerged during the "Eisenhower years" from 1952 to 1960, the emphasis would be upon the bright facets of postwar life. Ike symbolized a faith that traditional values remained the key to tapping the full possibilities of postwar life.

The Elections of 1952 and 1956

In 1952, encouraged by the Truman administration's many problems, Republicans anticipated the victory that had slipped away four years earlier. Still, GOP leaders wanted to take no chances, and the desire to pick a winner worked in favor of Dwight Eisenhower.

Some people doubted that Eisenhower would ever run. In 1948 the popular general had firmly rejected a presidential race because of the "necessary policy" of subordinating the military to civilian rule. And despite a Republican background, his postwar political affiliation remained a mystery. As late as 1951 Truman suggested that Eisenhower become the Democrats' standard-bearer.

But while president of Columbia University from 1948 to 1951, Eisenhower formed close ties with influential members of the Republican party's eastern establishment. He came to share their belief that another GOP defeat would greatly strengthen the more conservative and the McCarthyite wings of the party. A moderate on almost every issue, Eisenhower did not want the GOP to swing so far to the right. He also believed that the United States must play an active role in Europe, and he feared that Senator Robert A. Taft, the leading contender for the Republican nomination, was not firmly committed to NATO. When eastern supporters convinced Eisenhower that Taft's reputation as a midwestern reactionary would prove a serious political liability, the old soldier decided that both the GOP and the nation needed him. After twenty years of Democrats in the White House, the GOP could not pass up a seemingly sure winner: Eisenhower won a first-ballot victory at the 1952 Republican convention. To soothe ruffled feelings, he selected Richard Nixon, a Republican regular and anticommunist crusader, as his vice-presidential candidate. The thirty-four-year-old Nixon was also expected to attract younger voters.

During the 1952 presidential campaign, Eisenhower encountered some difficulty transforming himself from General of the Army to good old Ike. Gradually, though, he developed his own style and learned the rituals of American politics. To the displeasure of some, he made symbolic concessions to right-wing Republicans, holding a highly publicized session with Senator Taft and campaigning alongside several outspoken McCarthyites. In a Wisconsin speech Eisenhower deleted a favorable reference to General George Marshall, his close personal friend but one of McCarthy's favorite targets. And though Ike piously announced, "I shall not and will not engage in character assassination, vilification and personalities," Nixon and other McCarthyites sought votes by extravagant attacks on communist influence in Washington, corruption in government, and the "no-win" war in Korea. Nixon even reverted to the communist-conspiracy theme when stories about an improper political slush fund threatened his place on the ticket. His televised reply to the charges featured insinuations that the "reds" wanted to deny him the vice-presidency and contained self-pitying comments about his wife's "Republican cloth coat," his worn-out Oldsmobile, and his one political payoff—his daughters' little dog Checkers. The "Checkers Speech" saved Nixon's career and made him an even greater asset to the Republican ticket. It also gave Nixon a reputation as a skilled television performer.

By contrast, Democrats found few bright spots in 1952. Their presidential nominee, Governor Adlai Stevenson of Illinois, won the plaudits of liberal columnists for his cleverly phrased speeches. But critics complained that the erudite Stevenson aimed his addresses well over the average voter's head. His image as an egghead and a recent divorce became frequently noted handicaps. In addition, Stevenson had to outrun the unpopular shadow of Harry Truman, who insisted upon taking part in the campaign. Political pollsters, who had substantially revised their techniques after the miscalculations of 1948, discovered that many voters simply felt that the Democrats had been in power too long. Election results corroborated their predictions. Eisenhower carried all but nine states, and the Republicans also gained control, though by very narrow margins, of both houses of Congress.

Eisenhower appeared to be a person who could restore old-time virtues to government, and most voters seemed satisfied with his leadership. Four years later, when the Eisenhower-Stevenson presidential contest was replayed, Eisenhower's popularity remained undiminished. Retaining Richard Nixon as a running mate (after several unheeded hints that Nixon might prefer a cabinet post), Eisenhower received almost 10 million more popular votes than Stevenson. Ike's popularity, however, did not carry over to his own party. The Democrats had regained control of both houses of Congress in 1954, and they solidified their position in 1956.

The Eisenhower Presidency

Eisenhower promised a "constitutional presidency." Extolling the traditions of local government and state autonomy, he felt that Democratic administrations had extended national power too far and had spent the public's tax dollars too freely. Eisenhower also believed that Harry Truman, whom he held in very low esteem, had provoked Congress, needlessly embittering relations between the White House and Capitol Hill. Ike came to Washington determined to get along with Congress; such cooperation became a necessity after the Democrats gained control of both houses in 1954. Eisenhower instructed cabinet members to avoid antagonizing members of Congress. The art of leadership, he told one associate, did not require "hitting people over the head. Any damn fool can do that. . . . It's persuasion—and conciliation—and education—and patience. That's the only kind of leadership I know—or believe in—or will practice." During his two terms he received much help from congressional Democrats led by two cagey Texans, Sam Rayburn and Lyndon Johnson. Political centrists themselves, Rayburn and Johnson approved of many of Eisenhower's policies; one historian described their version of "loyal opposition" as three parts loyal and one part opposition. Although the executive branch and Congress often clashed, there was little of the bitterness that characterized relations between them during the late 1960s and early 1970s.

Eisenhower also sought harmony within his administration. Believing that Democratic administrations had ignored sound managerial practices, Eisenhower filled his first cabinet with Republican business leaders. "Engine Charley" Wilson, secretary of defense, came from General Motors; Treasury Secretary George Humphrey had headed the giant Mark Hanna Company; Postmaster General Arthur Summerfield owned a huge car agency in

Michigan. A liberal magazine dismissed Eisenhower's appointees as "eight millionaires and a plumber." The plumber was Democrat Martin Durkin, president of the United Association of Plumbers and Steamfitters. Eisenhower hoped that a union man might smooth relations between his administration and organized labor, but appointment of a Democrat as secretary of labor only angered conservative Republicans. Within eight months Durkin was gone. Eisenhower also drew heavily from business and the military to fill White House staff positions.

The president shrewdly managed his new team. He picked Sherman Adams as his chief aide (some people called Adams the assistant president) and granted him broad authority. Adams acted as gatekeeper, allowing Ike to see people who had important business but blocking those who might waste his time. He also handled many sensitive duties that Eisenhower wished to avoid. Adams soon became notorious for his brusque phone calls—he made more than two hundred every day—in which he barked orders and then hung up without waiting for a reply. This style gained Adams many enemies in Washington, but it also allowed Eisenhower himself to avoid some ticklish situations. In foreign affairs and in economic policy, Eisenhower adopted a similar strategy, letting Secretary of State John Foster Dulles and Treasury Secretary George Humphrey take the heat while he remained above the battle.

Eisenhower's skillful use of subordinates as political lightning rods reflected his deep conviction that, after all of Harry Truman's troubles, he must restore the image of the presidency. Although he had formed no church ties during his army career, Eisenhower quickly joined Washington's National Presbyterian Church (seven previous presidents had been members) and became a Sunday regular. He opened cabinet meetings with a silent prayer and began the tradition of "prayer breakfasts" at the White House. His inaugural parade contained a hastily constructed entry called "God's Float." Flanked by slogans proclaiming "In God We Trust" and "Freedom of Worship" and topped by a curious structure that was supposed to resemble a nondenominational church, the creation struck one minister as "an oversized model of a deformed molar left over from some dental exhibit." But Eisenhower rarely stumbled in his public relations efforts. Unlike Lyndon Johnson and Richard Nixon, who unsuccessfully used many of the same symbols during their stormy presidencies, Eisenhower apparently convinced most people of his sincerity. Although liberal critics questioned the wisdom of Eisenhower's policies, few doubted his integrity or decency. And through his much-publicized addiction to golf and bridge, pastimes that millions of ordinary citizens also enjoyed, he projected the image of the common person.

In recent years, many historians have revised earlier estimates of Eisenhower's abilities. For a long time people believed that strong figures such as Dulles, Humphrey, and Adams dominated Eisenhower and really ran the government. Early in Eisenhower's first term a familiar joke asked, "What if Ike died and we got Nixon as president?" "Yes," went the punch

President Dwight David Eisenhower's emphasis upon his leisure-time activities was part of the "hidden-hand presidency." Often pictured on the golf course, he also fished and dabbled in painting. Source: *National Archives*

line, "but what if Adams died, and we got stuck with Ike?" But Eisenhower now gains higher marks. According to his associates, he skillfully presided over cabinet sessions and meetings of the National Security Council, and he apparently retained a firm, though often unseen, rein over those areas he considered critical. During his second term all three of his key advisers resigned (scandal forced Adams's resignation, Humphrey returned to business, and Dulles fell victim to cancer), yet Eisenhower carried on without any noticeable disruption in the presidential routine.

Still, many questions about Eisenhower's presidency remain unanswered. Did Eisenhower, who left office with an extremely high rating in the opinion polls, simply ignore controversial domestic problems such as environmental pollution and urban decay? Did Eisenhower's obvious lack of sympathy toward the civil rights movement help inflame racial tensions? (See Chapter 5.) And was he as shrewd a president as his close associates claimed, or did he simply have extraordinarily good luck in handling the affairs of state? All these questions and many others await further research and contemplation. But one thing is clear: At a time when many people wanted a respite from the perils of the immediate postwar period, the former general from the Great Plains provided a symbol of old values, traditional virtues, and hopes for a bright future.

Economic Policies

Two weeks after taking office Eisenhower announced, "The first order of business is the elimination of the annual deficit" in the federal budget. Guided by Secretary of the Treasury George Humphrey, Eisenhower curtailed federal spending whenever possible. To this Republican administration—the first since Herbert Hoover's—mounting unemployment and possible recession were always less frightening than inflation or the "creeping socialism" of big government.

Eisenhower pledged to reduce government's role in the economy. During his first year in office he turned over some nationally owned offshore oil deposits to the states of California, Louisiana, and Texas for subsequent lease to private oil companies. He also attempted to undercut the federal government's Tennessee Valley Authority by giving the privately owned Dixon-Yates utility a contract to supply power for the Atomic Energy Commission. (Public furor over the questionable circumstances surrounding this deal, however, forced the government to repudiate the Dixon-Yates agreement.) Ike frequently used his veto power against housing, public works, and antipollution bills; after the end of the Korean War he quickly lifted economic controls (too quickly many economists believed); and his secretary of agriculture attempted to lower farm subsidies. Following his vision of moderate Republicanism, Eisenhower did not dismantle New Deal programs—during his eight years as president Congress raised Social Security payments, minimum wage rates, and unemployment benefits—but the president clearly opposed any new, large government expenditures.

One new spending program that Eisenhower did support had a profound effect: the interstate highway program. Begun in 1956, it committed the federal government to a thirteen-year, $26 billion program to help states construct interstate highways according to a national plan. As costs steadily mounted, Congress appropriated additional revenues. The program represented a major national commitment to the internal combustion engine; in effect, it subsidized the trucking industry and those individuals who could afford cross-country travel in private automobiles.

Interstate highway construction had a host of spinoffs: Construction companies boomed; new gas stations sprang up; lines of motels stretched out along the highways. Around big cities the maze of interstate exchanges stood as monuments to human ingenuity, and engineers lent their latest techniques to the planning and control of traffic flows. But the positive effects of the interstate highway program often obscured its drawbacks. Railroads, a less expensive and less polluting means of transportation, could not compete with truckers who used free interstate highways, and rail lines fell into deep financial trouble. In New York City mass-transit facilities decayed; in Los Angeles and many other cities light-rail transit was ended, and miles of concrete and asphalt crisscrossed the landscape. Americans became more car-crazy than ever, and the more they drove, the more there seemed to be no alternative to driving. Those without cars—the old, the handicapped, the poor—were the losers. The "highway lobby," an informal alliance of auto manufacturers, oil producers, and construction companies, were the winners. The graft sometimes associated with the purchase of right-of-ways and the award of contracts tainted local politics and recalled the railroad corruption of the late nineteenth century.

In general, the Eisenhower administration kept federal spending down, and the economy grew at a slow but steady pace. The refusal to increase governmental spending, as a means of pumping up the economy, disturbed devotees of the new economics who insisted that Washington could stimulate greater economic growth. After the end of the Korean War, in 1953, the country slid into a small recession, but Eisenhower's advisers still refused to pump in additional federal money in hopes of stimulating recovery. The economy picked up, but by 1957 leading indicators showed an even more alarming downturn. By the spring of 1958, the signs of recession were everywhere; the official unemployment rate reached 7.5 percent. Even leading business people, who had been among Ike's strongest supporters, began to consider at least the possibility of more active governmental intervention. Still fearing that greater expenditures could trigger an inflationary spiral, Eisenhower opposed tax cuts or increased spending, the prescriptions ritualistically offered by advocates of the new economics for curing economic slowdowns.

Eisenhower's partisans credited the Republican administration's cautious approach with helping to promote the general prosperity of the 1950s. During that decade, according to most estimates, large segments of the blue-collar, working-class population saw their incomes and life styles raised to levels that could be called "middle-class." If the Pentagon became the center of a "military-industrial complex," the suburbs became the focus of what might be called the "auto-house-electrical-appliance complex." Both home ownership, especially in the new postwar suburbs, and a host of new consumer products, made available by credit buying, became real possibilities for millions more people.

Liberal advocates of the new economics still considered the rate of economic growth too slow to keep up with population growth. America's economic-growth rate, they pointed out, lagged behind that of the Soviet Union, and the large baby-boom generation would soon demand a greatly enlarged job market. Moreover, Germany and Japan were beginning to rebuild the infrastructures of their war-shattered economies, while economic planners in the United States were resting on their laurels, apparently blind to their increasingly outdated industrial plants and deteriorating infrastructure. Finally, social liberals charged that the lack of new federal spending programs stemmed not from the lack of pressing problems—such as urban and rural poverty, air pollution, central-city blight, and an inequitable system of health care—but from a determination to ignore them.

By the mid-1950s, liberal social observers became more critical of the direction of postwar society. Breaking with the celebratory tone of the immediate postwar period, they increasingly pointed to tears within the social fabric. Much of this attention first focused upon the alleged discontents of the middle class: their lack of purpose, sense of aimlessness, and desire for greater peace of mind. The sociologist Daniel Bell, who had earlier proclaimed the "end of ideology," gradually became less sanguine about technological expertise as the solution to all social problems, especially those related to work. In 1956, he catalogued the discontents of the work process, criticizing preoccupation with issues of efficiency and managerial control. Beneath the semiofficial public tranquility, social critics observed a seething strata of private tensions.

A few liberal social critics shifted the focus from private discontents to public social problems. In *The Affluent Society* (1958) John Kenneth Galbraith denounced the parsimony of public welfare programs. He contrasted the personal affluence of most Americans with the lack of decent public services, writing of the travelers who steer their "mauve and cerise air-conditioned, power-steered and power-braked car" through badly paved and littered streets; who "picnic on exquisitely packaged food from a portable icebox by a polluted stream and go on to spend the night at a park which is a menace to public health and morals." Galbraith scathingly attacked the American tax system, which permitted such a disparity between public services and private comfort. He called for higher levels of taxation and greater government spending.

Ignoring such criticism, Eisenhower and his advisers held fast to their economic policies. They pointed out that real wages for an average family had risen 20 percent during Ike's years in office, a gain that meant a great deal to blue-collar workers. In addition, policies of modest growth kept the inflation rate low, and this price stability moderated labor disputes and helped maintain a relatively healthy dollar abroad. If Ike's administration deferred problems until later, many people probably wanted it that way. Eisenhower, after all, had not promised to reform and crusade but to soothe and assure. Many years later, Ike proudly remembered his principal accomplishment as having created "an atmosphere of greater serenity and mutual confidence."

But, as social critics increasingly noted, all was not serene and calm during the 1950s. The population was expanding at a tremendous rate; people were flocking to the suburbs in unprecedented numbers; a booming popular-culture industry rapidly altered older patterns of leisure and socialization; and people at the lower end of the economic spectrum, many of them nonwhite, found it difficult to believe that the United States really was a land of affluence.

SOCIAL TRENDS

The Baby Boom

During the ten years after World War II the number of children born each year in the United States rose by nearly 50 percent, the biggest increase in births ever recorded anywhere. Throughout the 1950s, towns and cities

Coney Island, 1950. Though the old-style amusement park would not last, prosperity and the baby boom ensured that other youth-oriented forms of leisure, such as massive theme parks like Disneyland, would flourish. Source: *National Archives.*

busily constructed brick-and-glass schools to hold youngsters until they were about seventeen, socializing them into the dominant value system and economic structure. Everywhere baby boomers turned, they spilled out of conventional facilities. They needed unprecedented quantities of diapers, toys, books, and teachers. Their very numbers gave them a generational identity and tagged them as somehow extraordinary. During the 1950s the pressure of this generation was contained in homes and schools; in the 1960s it would find its way into overcrowded subways, unemployment lines, student revolts, and a "counterculture"; in the 1970s and 1980s it would swell the market for consumer goods and services and provide a key target for politicians with programs to sell.

Demographers seeking explanations for the postwar baby boom have arrived at a few tentative conclusions. From 1940 to the mid-1950s couples began marrying and having children at a much earlier age than their parents. There has always been a close correlation between average age of marriage and number of children—the two factors rise or fall inversely—so the extraordinarily high birth rate comes as no surprise. But why did couples marry early and have large families?

Economic security was one reason. The tremendous economic expansion that came with the war opened new jobs and created a general scarcity of labor. The shortage of younger workers throughout the late 1940s and the 1950s meant unusually rapid economic advancement, especially for white males. Not only did pay scales within each job category shoot up, but upward occupational mobility was far greater than in the 1930s or even in the 1920s. Throughout the 1950s business analysts noted a decline in the average age of corporate executives, and older people grumbled at how easily the younger generation could reach positions that had taken them years to attain. Favorable employment and high income levels gave young middle-class couples greater security than ever before.

Certain economic innovations also contributed to the affluence of young, particularly white, couples. Government-sponsored benefits for veterans provided extra sources of income; unemployment compensation made savings seem less necessary. The whole array of New Deal programs—Federal Housing Administration (FHA) home loans, the Agricultural Adjustment Administration soil bank, Rural Electrification Administration energy, Federal Deposit Insurance Corporation insurance, and Social Security payments—particularly assisted middle-income Americans. In addition to these welfare state measures, wider use of credit allowed families to spend beyond their income. Installment buying, finance agencies, charge accounts, and credit cards helped many consumers buy whatever they wanted, whenever they wanted it. The financial well-being that encouraged early marriage and large families was based upon certain employment, rising income, the new welfare role of government, and the availability of credit.

The baby boom probably also had psychological foundations. Its beginnings in the war years may have stemmed partially from the fears associated with separation as men entered the military. The bright economic picture after the war provided couples with the self-confidence and optimism that are important ingredients in decisions to marry and have children. Then too, Americans had deferred having children throughout the Depression. The meteoric rise of the birth rate during the 1950s must always be viewed against the backdrop of its decline during the 1930s.

"Women's Work" and Domesticity

Although the baby boom helped create a climate of opinion that emphasized the home as women's proper place, the number of women employed outside their home rose substantially after the late 1940s. By 1960 over one-third of the women of working age were employed, and nearly one-third of all wives worked. Historically, a large percentage of women from working-class families and women of color had always participated in the paid labor force; for women from these groups employment trends of the 1950s represented little change. But for a growing number of middle-class families, the extra income contributed by a wife often provided the essential key to the middle-class status. The rising consumption and apparent prosperity of the 1950s rested, in part, on the growing number of women in the paid labor force.

This 1958 display, in a department store window, presented a tableau of the ideal suburban family. It links the latest consumer goods—including home movie cameras and backyard barbecue equipment—with advice on "How to Keep a Man." Source: *Norton and Peel Collection, Minnesota Historical Society*

Women's work had important distinguishing characteristics during the 1950s. Jobs were often part time, held after the age of thirty-five or forty when children were no longer at home during the day, and not career oriented. Furthermore, employment for women was generally very low paying, on the theory that women's income was always a secondary one, providing niceties, but not necessities, for a family. The greatest job opportunities, associated with structural changes in the economy as a whole, were in occupations that came to be designated specifically as "women's work": clerical and secretarial jobs, teaching, and certain sectors of retail sales. Although women attended college in unprecedented numbers, few received graduate degrees, and employment of women in prestigious professions actually dropped. Women's employment, while becoming more widespread, retained the stigma of low pay and low status.

The dominant social imagery of the 1950s disregarded both the growing employment among women and the diversity of women's experiences. Instead, psychologists, educators, magazine writers, and advertisers emphasized a single "proper" life style for women: domesticity. Most social analysis simply assumed that home and childrearing provided the "natural" sphere and function for women while the public world and moneymaking comprised the "natural" male realm.

Although this idea of separate and complementary gender spheres was not new, it emerged in fresh garb. Most psychologists diagnosed any signs of women's discontent in the 1950s as a failure to adjust to "natural" passive and subordinate roles. Popular magazines featured articles that equated happiness with mediocrity: A *Good Housekeeping* column advised that a woman with a grade-point average of C was "more likely to succeed" than a woman of great intelligence, because she had a greater chance for a lasting marriage and a family. If a woman showed concern about issues related to equal rights or feminism, in this dominant view, such an interest very likely reflected some deep-seated neurosis or social maladjustment.

Women's educational institutions mirrored the emphasis on the importance of marriage and family. College presidents and campus speakers urged an education that prepared women to marry and serve the nation by raising virtuous, industrious sons and dutiful, domesticated daughters. A national poll in 1957 reported that 80 percent of the respondents believed that people who chose not to marry were sick and immoral.

Images of domesticity in the 1950s became inextricably linked to women's roles as consumers. Under the influence of the rapidly expanding advertising industry, the word *housewife* less frequently evoked sewing and baking and became closely associated with shopping. Advertisers geared their appeals to women, even for expensive, durable goods. *Better Homes and Gardens*, a women's magazine (edited by men) with a circulation of millions, exemplified the trend. Advertisements took up far more than half the space, and the remaining pages contained tips on how to consume efficiently and "scientifically"—how to plan quick meals, determine which washing machine to buy, keep a family budget, etc. Both the ads and the articles often emphasized saving money, but even these pieces were, in fact, designed to stimulate consumer tastes, and teach about new products. The popular women's magazines of the 1950s, always projecting a white middle-class life style as the universal norm, both reflected and reinforced the unity between domesticity and consumption.

Along with "scientific" housekeeping came an emphasis on "scientific" childbearing and childrearing. Before World War II the majority of births did not take place in hospitals; in the postwar era, childbearing became more impersonal and institutionalized. More and more women had their children in hospitals, attended by male physicians using a variety of painkilling methods. Accompanying this trend toward more births taking place in hospitals, sales of commercial baby food also soared, and women shifted in massive numbers from breast feeding to bottle feeding. In childrearing practices, outside expertise was also exalted. Dr. Benjamin Spock's *Baby and Child Care* rivaled the Bible in sales and stood next to it as a guide to appropriate conduct in most middle-class homes. Although Spock cautioned mothers against becoming too tied to their children, he nonetheless implied that full-time motherhood was the most desirable role for women and was essential to a child's physical and emotional health.

Although the dominant media portrayed any kind of feminist activism as outmoded and deviant, some women associated with the strong prewar women's rights movements continued to speak out. Members of the National Woman's Party consistently lobbied Congress on behalf of an Equal Rights Amendment throughout the 1950s. Groundbreaking studies in women's history appeared with the publication of Mary Beard's *Woman as Force in History* (1946) and Eleanor Flexner's *Century of Struggle* (1959). Zora Neale Hurston continued her studies on African-American women. And the sociologist Mirra Komarovsky published her classic work on behalf of gender equality, *Women in the Modern World* (1953). These and similar efforts laid a basis for a revitalized "women's liberation movement" in the late 1960s.

Suburbia

Rising incomes, the baby boom, and the emphasis on domesticity became closely associated with life in the suburbs. Throughout the country the more affluent white, middle-class families built new residences farther from the center of cities in order to accommodate their larger families, to flee urban problems, and to achieve new levels of comfort and status. Outside of major cities and even smaller towns, neat rows of homes intruded upon the surrounding countryside. Real estate builders and developers such as Levitt & Company pioneered tract homes, which were rapidly constructed according to standardized, preestablished plans. Building innovations, in addition to the FHA and VA loan programs, brought the suburban "paradise" within the reach of millions. One-fourth of all the housing that existed in 1960 had been built in the 1950s.

Giant suburban shopping malls followed the suburbanization of the 1950s and continued to spur even greater urban sprawl in subsequent decades. Source: *Tacoma Public Library Neg. TPL 400.*

Suburban living promised contentment. The predominantly white, middle-class residents aspired to economic success, and although preoccupation with status often bred rivalries, a shared value system also brought a sense of comfort and community. Conformity seemed a balm for rootlessness and a cushion against the anxiety of change. But every glimpse of suburban happiness had its darker side of unforeseen problems. Burgeoning residential sections often overcrowded existing facilities, creating the congestion that residents had hoped to escape. Payments for mortgages, autos, and consumer goods sometimes brought new financial worries, and the mounting personal indebtedness among Americans alarmed many economists. Distances to work grew longer and longer; those who commuted in comfortable private cars contributed to clogged freeways and polluted air.

Suburban life easily lent itself to caricature and derision. The folk singer Malvina Reynolds labeled suburban homes "little boxes made of ticky-tacky" and jabbed at the conformity of men who all "drink their martinis dry" and of children who all "go to summer camp and then to the university." In the 1960s Andy Warhol made the slickly packaged consumer culture associated with suburbia a subject of pop art, creating still-life portraits of monotonous rows of Campbell's soup cans. Upper-class critics of suburbia snorted at its bad taste—the lack of greenery (except for the spindly tree per lot that FHA mortgages required); the cheap construction; the clutter of too many autos, tricycles, lawn mowers, and children. Poor people and nonwhites, trapped in decaying inner cities, also attacked the suburbs, envying the comparative space and quiet while resenting the drain of tax revenue to outlying areas. Suburbia, however, with its popularization of "California-style" houses and informal, family-oriented life styles, exemplified the 1950s for most white families.

Organization Men and Women

The large business organization dominated the lives of many suburban men during the 1950s. The person whom William H. Whyte described in *The Organization Man* (1956) established his primary roots not in a particular town or region but within a corporate structure. The business corporation provided the society in which he defined himself and gauged his status. He did, of course, withdraw from the corporate world to his home and family each day, but this retreat occupied only a few evening hours. Sociological studies revealed that success as a husband and father and occupational advancement often varied inversely. Home and office were separate and competing spheres, and the organization often won out as the primary frame of reference.

The economic growth and occupational mobility of the 1950s reinforced corporate loyalty. A young executive with dedication was almost sure to rise. But advancement often meant moving around the country at the company's behest. "We never make a man move," one company president explained. "Of course, he kills his career if he doesn't. But we never make

Hat n' Boots Gas. Such examples of oversized and commercialized art disgusted some critics, but others found them an appropriate reflection of a society that loved large-scale, ambitious undertakings. Source: *Robert Peterson.*

him do it." Geographic mobility only strengthened the bond between employee and company, for it hindered development of strong ties to a local community and brought the organization right into the family circle as a most important decision maker. Popular culture of the 1950s was replete with the theme of organizational loyalty.

The relationship of women to the large business organization was quite different. Especially to young women, corporate life seemed to promise excitement and independence. But during the 1950s most corporations generally hired women for positions in the secretarial ghetto, where pay was low and a woman remained a "girl" no matter what her age. The illusion of glamour and independence darkened into the reality of boredom and bare subsistence. Research showed that illicit relationships between boss and secretary, one of the principal subjects of humor of the 1950s, were largely male fantasies seldom duplicated in reality or in the thoughts of secretaries. For most organization women love for boss or for business did not transcend dollars and cents, and many women rapidly deserted secretarial jobs for domestic life. The rapid turnover of women in corporations bolstered the myth that they were poor risks at any level in the business hierarchy. Organization "girls" were entrapped in a vicious circle of low pay, rapid turnover, and discrimination.

The wives of most corporate employees were also organization women, deriving income and even status from their husbands' jobs. A wife's identity often came through her husband—upon meeting a middle-class woman many people did not ask "What do you do?" but rather "What does your husband do?" Restricted to the sphere of home and children, the model corporate wife was nonetheless supposed to feel devotion to the business world that she seldom saw. But this obligation of loyalty, together with the husband's unfamiliarity with his spouse's domestic routine, drove subtle wedges between married couples. At home, as in the office, the great corporations contributed to deep social tensions.

Sexual Politics

The 1940s and 1950s represented, in some ways, a period of liberation for homosexuals and lesbians. The familiarity of military life during World War II provided new opportunities for single-sex relationships, and postwar urbanization allowed homosexuals to gather, away from glare of small-town scrutiny, in a growing urban subculture. While most large cities had a number of bars catering to gay men, lesbians generally prefered to seek companionship through more private "friendship networks." Nevertheless, the results were the same: a growing sense of individual and group identity among homosexuals.

The issue of homosexuality gained considerable visibility when Dr. Alfred Kinsey first published his studies, in 1948 and 1953, on sexual behavior in the United States. Kinsey's research, conducted at the University of Indiana, suggested that people with "homosexual histories" could be found "in every age group, in every social level, in every conceivable occupation," and in virtually every part of the country. Kinsey's findings, in one sense, helped to empower homosexuals; they suggested that homosexuality was not limited to the fringes of society. On the other hand, the idea that homosexuality could be anywhere increased the fears among people who were already opposed to homosexual life styles.

Homosexuality became, as did communism and juvenile delinquency, another of those infectious "diseases" that could rally the forces of containment. Anticommunists even worried that homosexuals and lesbians, if not already inclined toward communism because of their own "alien" life styles, could prove particularly susceptible to blackmail by Soviet agents. In 1953, the Eisenhower administration endorsed this theory with an executive order that prohibited homosexuals from holding government jobs. And in another parallel with anticommunism, such blacklisting at the national level energized local "purity crusaders." Police departments and district attorneys could claim greater legitimacy when unleashing their own antihomosexual campaigns.

The wider issue of "sexual revolution"—sexual relations outside a heterosexual marriage—became increasingly visible during the 1950s in a number of ways. The *Kinsey Reports*, based on thousands of interviews with white informants, suggested that people were engaging in a wider range of sexual practices, more often, and with more partners than anyone had ever thought. Despite almost antiseptic prose, Kinsey's studies on the sexual behavior of men and women became best-sellers and their data widely popularized. The dominant emphasis on monogamous relationships, within the idealized nuclear family that was featured on network television, clearly existed alongside powerful centrifugal forces.

The greatest popularizer of the sexual revolution was not the scholarly Dr. Kinsey, however, but the flamboyant (or pathetically juvenile, according to his critics) Hugh Hefner. During the late 1940s and early 1950s, laws aimed at sexually explicit publications had been facing greater scrutiny from the courts; the First Amendment to the Constitution, civil libertarians argued, prevented government censors from writing their own sexual standards into law. Although legal definitions of what was obscene or pornographic remained uncertain, there was still too much liberalization for traditionalists but just enough for magazine entrepreneurs like Hefner. In December 1953, Hefner published the first edition of *Playboy*, heralded as "entertainment for men," expanding the boundaries of First Amendment protection for sexually oriented literature.

Playboy offered more than pictures of unclothed young women and articles by respected popular writers; Hefner used the publication to expound his philosophy of a "liberated" life style based upon mass consumption and sexual experimentation. The "Playboy Philosophy," as Hefner expounded it throughout the 1950s, also stressed liberation, for men, from all of the restraints associated with marriage; the nuclear family was a trap that ensnared males and robbed them of money that could be spent on hi-fi equipment, sports cars, and attractive young women. *Playboy*'s philosophy, according to the social historian Barbara Ehrenreich, was part of a larger "male revolt" of the 1950s, against the prevalent image of a husband-dominated home in which the man earned most of the family's income and the woman presided over its consumption and childrearing.

MASS COMMERCIAL CULTURE

After World War II, people could choose from an ever-expanding array of cultural and entertainment products aimed at a mass consumer audience. With blue-collar workers enjoying larger take-home paychecks, while suffering from increasing regimentation in their workplaces, leisure and cultural markets expanded significantly. Meanwhile, the general postwar affluence, in which the majority of people did share, made the entertainment business more profitable than ever before. By 1950, consumers were spending twice as much money on entertainment as on rent; total expenditures equaled one-seventh of the GNP.

Travel and Sports

The travel industry grew tremendously after World War II. To those who could afford the price, travel agencies marketed package tours to Europe. In only two weeks travelers could absorb the culture of the Old World—from Paris, to Brussels, to Geneva, to Rome, to Vienna, to Hamburg, and finally to London. For those who lacked the money to visit Europe (or who had already toured the Continent), the United States provided its own vacation spots. New motels, their quality certified by motor clubs or franchise owners, began to replace the old, independent tourist cabins. When affluent travelers reached Southern California, Las Vegas, or Miami Beach, they found luxury-resort complexes that offered expensive night-clubs for adults, professional recreation directors for children, and deluxe kennels for family pets.

After the reduced schedules of the war years, sports promotions regained, and then surpassed, their earlier pace. Promoters welcomed back the young people who had served in the armed forces, abandoning the lesser talents and fading veterans who had performed during World War II. (The supply of quality baseball players had become so low that during the war the St. Louis Browns employed a one-armed outfielder.) Although all levels of professional baseball revived, the late 1940s and early 1950s proved to be the last hurrah for baseball's minor leagues. Before the full impact of competition from network television, many cities and smaller towns eagerly supported their own professional baseball teams. And with only sixteen major-league clubs, there was a surplus of good players to stock the minor leagues. Until the late 1960s African-Americans complained, with much justification, that only outstanding athletes such as Jackie Robinson could play in the newly integrated majors; white ballplayers generally received preference for jobs such as second-string catcher or reserve infielder. Even talented white players found themselves tied to a monopolistic business system in which major-league teams owned vast numbers of players whom they could freely transfer from team to team, from league to league.

Yet in the patriotic spirit of the cold war, baseball served as a symbol of the openness and equality of American society. Sportswriters, following in the star-struck tradition of their calling, still lavished praise on the game, celebrating it as an integral part of the American way. One prominent writer-broadcaster, Bill Stern, constantly invented uplifting stores about the national pastime. A dying Abraham Lincoln, Stern once solemnly claimed, had told an aide to "keep baseball going; the country needs it."

Professional boxing, plagued by hints of fixed fights and underworld domination, lacked baseball's hallowed reputation but attracted large audiences in the postwar period. Massive promotions for world championships and small neighborhood fight clubs all made money during the late 1940s and early 1950s. Joe Louis, the symbol of sports as an avenue of opportunity for African-American men, finally concluded his long reign as heavyweight champion; between 1943 and 1951 the flamboyant Sugar Ray Robinson lost only one of nearly a hundred bouts and won general acclaim as the greatest fighter, "pound for pound," of all-time; and a stocky Italian-American from Massachusetts, Rocky Marciano, battered forty-nine opponents before retiring, in 1955, as the undefeated heavyweight champion. Professional boxing quickly became a staple of network television: During the early 1950s, the networks carried four nationally televised prime-time main events every week.

Professional wrestling and Roller Derby, pseudosports that dated back to the 1930s, also reached prime-time TV. Carefully contrived and pre-scripted, professional wrestling (as distinguished from the amateur sport) offered familiar morality plays: Stereotyped villains, often posing as Germans or "Japs," abused long-suffering heroes until some dramatic reversal sealed the bullies' fates. Justice—and "the American way"—ultimately triumphed. But a variety of different gambits and a flexible catalogue of "rules" allowed promoters to vary scenarios and lure fans to the next big card. Only Roller Derby, with two teams of skaters careening around a banked, wooden track, offered a comparable blend of mayhem and ritualistic symbolism. According to Roller Derby's publicity, "two [recent] impacts have hit the American public—the atom bomb and the Roller Derby—and it appears the latter will have the most permanent effect."

Alas, Roller Derby soon faded from prime time into a minor oddity, but most other sports, at all levels, continued to thrive in the postwar era. Bowling, golf, and tennis attracted growing crowds to professional tournaments and matches, while millions of amateurs took to the lanes, links, and courts. Hockey and basketball, established as professional sports primarily in the Northeast, slowly gained national audiences, and professional basketball achieved needed continuity with formation of the National Basketball Association in the years between 1946 and 1949. Football remained the premier sport on college campuses, but the professional version also made great strides in the postwar years; the Cleveland Browns, Detroit Lions, and Los Angeles Rams became the dominant powers during the early 1950s in a revamped National Football League.

Motion Pictures

While the sports industry attracted new fans, the motion picture industry was struggling to retain its mass audience. In 1946, Hollywood enjoyed the most profitable year in its history, with nearly nine-tenths of all the money spent on entertainment in the United States going to the movie industry. By 1950, though, TV offered a serious challenge, and the giant movie factories could no longer churn out a steady supply of traditional films and expect a mass audience to buy tickets. In response, film moguls tried to lure people back to the half-empty theaters with two new types of films: Expensive "blockbusters," often based upon a successful book (including the Bible) or stage play, aimed at attracting a mass clientele, and "specialized" offerings, such as the *film noirs*, targeted specific audiences.

Director Billy Wilder's *film noir, Sunset Boulevard* (1950), bade a cynical goodbye to the old Hollywood. It begins with a corpse floating in a Beverly Hills swimming pool, and this dead man, formally a second-rate screenwriter, narrates the remainder of the story. A middle-aged silent film star, played by Gloria Swanson, lives under the illusion that she will triumphantly return to the silver screen in a biblical epic. But a call from her old studio turns out to be merely a request to use her antique automobile, and she drifts even deeper into her fantasy world. The final scenes reveal that the actress has killed the screenwriter and gone completely mad. *Sunset Boulevard* suggests that mid-century Hollywood, like the middle-aged actress, was living on illusions while madly searching for successful artistic formulas that might revive its former glories.

During the 1950s, Hollywood's products often became entangled in the kinds of political issues affecting the nation at large. A number of filmmakers, for example, used the silver screen to stump for postwar, anticommunist culture. Some of the efforts were one-dimensional jeremiads on the evils of communism, but other films delivered their messages more subtly. In *On the Waterfront* (1954), screenwriter Budd Schulberg and director Elia Kazan, Hollywood liberals who had cooperated with anticommunist investigative committees, glorified the brave individual who informed upon those who threatened the democratic process. Filled with Christian imagery, *On the Waterfront* featured Marlon Brando, the punk hero of *The Wild One*, as a former prizefighter who testified against corrupt labor union bosses. Critics of "red-baiting" denounced the film for simplifying complex moral and political issues, while cold war liberals and moderates praised its portrayal of the democratic promise. Gaining no less than eight Academy Awards, *On the Waterfront* became a controversial symbol of Hollywood's uneasy relationship with larger political forces.

Hollywood also offered movies that broke away from mainstream political and artistic formulas. A few offbeat films featuring no great stars and eschewing glamor appeared during the 1950s. Adapted from a successful television production, *Marty* told the simple story of a Bronx butcher, played by Ernest Borgnine, who fell in love with a woman who considered herself plain and unexciting. After the decline of McCarthyism several films treated controversial social issues. *Paths of Glory* indicted military leaders for their values and portrayed war as anything but a glorious enterprise. Shot in black and white, *Paths of Glory* did poorly at the box office but gained much critical acclaim for its youthful director, Stanley Kubrick. Kubrick would become recognized as one of America's most innovative directors during the 1960s. Racial tension provided the backdrop for several films, the most popular being *The Defiant Ones*, a chain-gang story in which brotherhood triumphed over bigotry. Although the film would seem trite and overly cautious to many later viewers, Stanley Kramer's production appeared at a time when racial prejudice was still considered a dangerous subject in Hollywood.

During the 1950s a prominent school of film criticism, popular in both the United States and France, praised those Hollywood directors who could surmount the restraints of the industry and use their films to make personal statements. These *auteur* critics generally concentrated on so-called lesser films, finding much to admire in the work of directors like Budd Boettcher, Orson Welles, Anthony Mann, and Samuel Fuller. Always controversial, the *auteur* approach gained considerable power among critics when the giant Hollywood film factories began to break down in the 1960s and individual directors tried to wield greater control over their cinematic products.

Television

While the motion picture industry was struggling, television was thriving. In 1945, only a few people had ever seen a television set; by 1957, the United States claimed 40 million sets, and most cities boasted several local stations, including one for each of the major national networks. Research suggested that the larger the household size, the more likely it was to have at least one TV set.

Industry executives aggressively pushed family images. Many popular shows featured those now legendary TV "families"—the Andersons, the Cleavers, the Ricardos—and their never-ending familial conflicts, such as the now classic tussles between Wally and Theodore (Beaver) Cleaver. So that everyone could better watch Ward and June Cleaver save the day, television executives urged viewers to convert their living rooms into centers of family—and TV—culture. One TV advertisement from the 1950s advised parents that their children needed the tube "for their morale as much as they need fresh air and sunshine for their health."

Advertising, of course, was the fuel that carried "free" TV into millions of homes. As had been the case in network radio, some early TV shows even bore the names of their "sponsors"—the *Colgate Comedy Hour*, the *General Electric Theater*, or *Hallmark Hall of Fame*. More commonly, in contrast to the later practice by which networks would sell brief commercial spots to different advertisers, a single sponsor would often underwrite an entire series of shows, as Texaco did with TV's first smash hit, *The Milton Berle Show*. This arrangement obviously gave sponsors considerable leverage over program content. Sponsors consistently urged story lines and imagery that showed people working their way up the ladder of "success" by buying more and better products.

Consequently, many TV programs, as well as the commercials that sustained them, stressed the glories of mass consumption. A familiar theme in early TV situation comedies, for example, found working-class families trying to move from older, Depression-era values of thrift and careful saving to postwar consumerism. Story lines on shows such as *The Life of Riley*, which focused on a working-class family in Los Angeles, or *The Goldbergs*, which featured a Jewish family in New York City, suggested that the road to happiness could be paved by the purchase of consumer goods and leisure-time activities, rather than by faithfulness to ethnic rituals and traditions. Nonwhite ethnics were almost invisible except for *Amos 'n Andy*, a show that angered many African-Americans and eventually frightened away corporate sponsors.

By the mid-1950s, network programmers were eliminating working-class, ethnic sitcoms altogether, in favor of shows that featured upper-middle-class families who were clearly part of the culture of mass consumption. *The Adventures of Ozzie and Harriet*, for instance, came to television with *The Goldbergs* but lasted well into the 1960s; still a cable-TV staple in the 1990s, Ozzie and Harriet's "adventures" included frequent shopping forays, extensive leisure time, and even a live-in rock star, their son Rick Nelson.

Television touched politics as well as cultural values. During the 1952 presidential campaign, Richard Nixon used TV to defend his beleagured reputation and to salvage his political career. Two years later, the televised Army-McCarthy hearings helped bring down Wisconsin Senator Joe McCarthy. And toward the end of the 1950s, John Kennedy's media image aided his drive for the 1960 Democratic presidential nomination.

At a time of important social and cultural change in the United States, then, television was coming to replace movies and radio as the primary media for representing everyday life and transmitting cultural and political values across generations. Moreover, the small tube not only carried its pictures into people's homes, but it seemed to have the capacity, much more than the motion picture screen or radio set ever could, of providing representations that sometimes looked more "real" than the actual events themselves.

The rigged quiz shows of the 1950s came to symbolize most of what seemed so disturbing about TV culture. Once staples of prime-time programming, quiz shows offered tests of knowledge that paralleled pro wrestling's simulated tests of strength and power. Fearing the uncertainties of unrigged contests, quiz-show producers found they could transform unknown contestants into instant (and cheaply paid) celebrities simply by giving them answers in advance. In the most celebrated case, a Columbia University professor, who had thrilled more than 50 million TV viewers week after week by answering questions on virtually every subject, admitted that his entire performance had been rehearsed. Producers provided the answers and hints for making his replies as dramatic—and, therefore, as "real"—as possible. Critics who were already deriding the daily fare offered on the "boob tube" gained new ammunition from the quiz show scandals.

Rock Around the Clock: The Popular Culture of Youth

Accompanying the rise of TV, the 1940s and 1950s also saw the emergence of a distinctive youth culture. As with other aspects of postwar life, this phenomenon was closely linked to consumerism. Young people, as advertisers and business people recognized, provided exciting new possibilities for mass marketing. In 1944, a new magazine appeared and aimed (in its own words) at giving teenagers "a sense of identity, of purpose, of belonging." Not coincidently, this perennial drug-store favorite, *Seventeen*, also gave teenagers a sparkling, constantly up-dated array of consumer products and mass-consumption life styles. Within a few years, as postwar economic growth and the baby boom took hold, a new set of specialists played it both ways: Monitoring the burgeoning teenage consumer market, they consulted with companies about what to produce and, at the same time, advised teens about what they might consume.

Another group of specialists looked after the nonconsumer behavior of young people. During the early postwar years, explaining the problem of juvenile delinquency became a growth industry. After surveying juvenile unrest, the award-winning journalist Harrison Salisbury concluded that delinquency stretched from the nation's worst slums to its most affluent suburbs. In an age of increasing world tensions, this "shook-up generation"—a song written for Elvis Presley, "I'm All Shook Up," parodied Salisbury's title—even constituted "a matter of national security," Salisbury (with apparent seriousness) concluded.

After the juvenile delinquency scare of the late 1940s and 1950s had passed, criminologists generally agreed that there had been no startling upsurge in youthful deviance, a finding that makes the postwar concerns about the issue all that more puzzling. Why were so many people convinced that postwar youth were getting out of control?

A common theory focused upon changes in the nation's culture: Worries about juvenile deliquency, in many different analyses, went hand-in-hand with concern about the impact of postwar mass culture. Images of juvenile deliquents filled mass culture. Movies such as *The Wild One*, featuring Marlon Brando, and *Rebel Without a Cause*, which rocketed James Dean to an ill-fated stardom, indicated that Hollywood might attract a new youthful audience; but the sympathetic portrayal of rebellious youth in these films also threatened to cause studios problems with already-angry critics of youth and "experts" on juvenile delinquency. Officially marketed by Hollywood as explorations of juvenile deliquency, the films seemed, to their detractors, more likely to serve as guidebooks for future rebels.

Comic books were another cultural product that allegedly provided lessons in juvenile delinquency. Between the end of World War II and 1953, according to one study, the comic book industry marketed a billion books every year. This flood tide did include familiar characters from other media, including Bugs Bunny, Donald Duck, and various detective and western heroes; but it also contained new comic-book genres that featured stories of crime, horror, and exaggerated violence. In addition to offending genteel standards, such comics became linked to violence among troubled and rebellious youth. In one of the widely cited examples of gruesome comic art, ghouls played baseball with various parts of a dissected human body.

Arriving at about the time that concern over comics was waning, rock-and-roll music raised deeper and longer-lasting concerns. To those who considered Frank Sinatra as animated as pop music stars should ever get—and even to those who were embracing avant garde trends in postwar jazz—rock appeared to be merely gratuitous noise, wild "jungle" sounds that set young people into frenzied new dance crazes. Moreover, the sexual innuendos in many songs seemed yet another dangerous incitement to misbehavior. And the fact that rock grew out of rhythm-and-blues, a musical style popularized by urban African-Americans, alerted racists to the possibility of some plot, perhaps by subversive "communists," to sway young people toward integration.

Rock-and-roll thus had to grow up, as ragtime had done at the turn of the century, outside the major channels for producing and distributing popular music. Many rock artists, such as Chuck Berry and Carl Perkins, wrote their own material, and young producers, such as Sam Phillips of Sun Records in Memphis and the Chess brothers in Chicago, began to market what the major labels hesitated even to record. During the mid-1950s, Phillips unveiled the now legendary figures of early rockabilly—Perkins; Johnny Cash; Jerry Lee Lewis; and, of course, Elvis Presley. The Chess brothers, who had been featuring rhythm-and-blues artists such as Muddy Waters, introduced rock-and-roll pioneers like Berry and Bo Diddley in the mid-1950s. In other parts of the country, other small producers were also experimenting, releasing songs by both black and white artists that smashed old categories of popular music. Musical purists might break all this down into new pigeonholes—such as "Chicago rhythm-and-blues" and "West Texas country rock"—but millions of young people knew it simply as rock. While established radio stations and prominent radio personalities steered clear of the new sound, smaller stations and younger DJs hitched their fortunes to rock. The most prominent early rock-and-roll DJ, Alan Freed, soon found himself atop a burgeoning musical empire, a kingdom that collapsed when the federal government prosecuted him for payola—accepting bribes to promote certain records.

Freed's place was soon taken by Dick Clark, host of a popular television show, *American Bandstand*. Clark's program gave the emerging rock and dance culture a national audience, but many purists also accused Clark of "selling out." Believing that the unruliness of the new music had to be tamed, Clark pushed for "cleaner" lyrics and mass-produced a new generation of singers, such as Frankie Avalon and Fabian, who offered something of a compromise between the wildness of a Jerry Lee Lewis and the blandness of a Perry Como. Rock soon lost its roughness, its regional identity, and its spontaneity. (Clark, for example, insisted that all artists appearing on *American Bandstand* "lip-synch" their songs, a requirement that masked the ineptitude of a Fabian and squelched the artistry of a Chuck Berry.) By the late 1950s the major record companies were absorbing rock, merging it into the mainstream of popular music.

Like rock-and-roll, automobiles became a special passion of the middle-class, youth culture. Automobiles—especially the increasingly common second car—made young people mobile and provided status symbols, entertainment, and makeshift bedrooms. They provided transportation to teenage gatherings out of parents' sight and gave the freedom of privacy. In the rapidly growing South, stock-car racing became a preeminent sport. Detroit's auto manufacturers vied to contribute innovations that, by giving daredevil drivers an edge on the track, would win loyalties within the vast youth market. In both North and South, in city and small town, this was an age of souped-up hot rods, of dual exhaust systems, of raked bodies, of rolled and pleated interiors. For many youths, the transformation of one of Detroit's stereotyped products into a special personal creation may have represented a subtle, though tangible, revolt against the mass-produced world of their parents. Although only a small proportion of young people actually owned such a creation, the "Kandy-Kolored Tangerine-Flake Streamline Baby," to use writer Tom Wolfe's phrase, was the envy of the teenage "scene."

The youth culture thrived, especially in the suburbs, where the general affluence trickled down from parents to children. The youth market became a multimillion-dollar business. Sales of the new 45-rpm records and long-play albums exploded, and a collection of the latest hits became an important teen status symbol. Other items also tempted teenagers to spend money: record players, the latest in penny loafers or saddle shoes, the charm bracelets displaying pictures of rock idols. The youth generation of the 1950s was a peculiar amalgam: In its crass commercialism and unabashed materialism it mirrored, even caricatured, the rest of society; in its hedonism and stylistic iconoclasm it set itself decisively apart from the 1950s and anticipated the 1960s.

The Postwar Debate over Mass Culture

The association of comics, rock music, and hot-rod cars with rebellious young people gave a special urgency to discussions about mass culture. Invoking the disease metaphors, which were prominent in so many other postwar discussions, critics portrayed mass culture as a cancerous invader that threatened to overwhelm the nation's cultural immune system. The violence in comic books was said to eat into young minds and produce juvenile delinquents. Some social psychologists hypothesized that the simplicity of any comic book (or TV) story, violent or not, hindered young people's emotional development by teaching them to ignore complexities and conditioning them to expect quick, simple solutions to all of their problems. Pressure groups urged Congress to ban comic books or, at a minimum, impose censorship over their contents. Quickly responding, the comic book industry established its own regulatory code, a step that eliminated the more controversial offerings from the store racks and drove publishers like EC Comics into retirement. (The people behind EC's offbeat brand of culture quickly regrouped and produced the long-running satirical classic, *MAD* magazine.)

The passing of the great comic book scare and the taming of rock music hardly ended the larger debate over postwar mass culture. Elite critics found most of what millions of people liked to read, hear, and see as beneath contempt.

One line of criticism focused on the issue of "taste." Mass culture seemed just another sorry example of how a mass production and mass-consumption economy ignored issues of quality. In contrast to works of "high culture," mass-marketed books and TV programs made no effort to deepen understanding about the nature of life and beauty. Cultural products aimed at the millions seemed more like chewing gum than "real" art: They were to be consumed as rapidly as possible and then discarded. And unlike true "folk culture"—what critics identified as authentic art produced by ordinary people from their communal traditions—popular culture was stamped out by hack writers and mediocre image-makers, people only concerned with meeting their quota of marketable "stuff." By its very existence, mass culture represented an affront to everything noble and uplifting in the realm of culture.

Mass-marketed culture, to these critics, acted like an intellectual cancer. Even talented writers and artists succumbed to the allure of easy money, abandoning difficult projects in favor of producing easily marketable junk; consequently, consumer tastes became too vulgarized even to recognize good art. Mass culture thus carried the seeds of intellectual decay: High and folk cultures could eventually be totally destroyed or, at best, reduced to some grotesque mutation such as a mindless "middlebrow culture." Worse still, as mass culture proliferated, the ability of consumers to discriminate good from bad could become so eroded that they could fail to recognize the ways in which mass culture manipulated their desires and opinions. Especially in the view of writers who had fled Nazi Germany in the 1930s, mass culture provided the basis by which a native totalitarian movement could brainwash the innocent masses.

Not every student of mass culture sounded such bleak notes. Gilbert Seldes, a long-time partisan of the popular arts, insisted that most of what was now being offered to the public was only getting better, and he chided mainstream critics for their elitism. Although lacking Seldes' enthusiasm for the cultural products themselves, others shared his skepticism of theories that mechanically traced all manner of cultural and social problems to mass culture. Robert Warshow, for example, decided that his own son's taste for EC Comics was hardly a "serious problem." His boy was a "fan," not an "addict." Some sociologists even argued that the new popular culture could help people, especially children and adolescents, adjust to the demands of a complex society. The popular children's book *Tootle the Train*, for example, showed young people the need to "stay on the tracks" and adjust to community expectations of proper behavior.

Perhaps the most buoyant theorist of mass culture, especially television, was Marshall McLuhan. He predicted that TV would eventually homogenize and standardize global culture, just as it was already doing with

North American culture. McLuhan foresaw a "global village" in which peoples of previously distinct cultures could expeience a common bond of sensory awareness simply by abandoning themselves to the "cool medium" of television. Initially hailed as one of the twentieth century's foremost visionaries, McLuhan saw his reputation plummet as later media theorists recognized that TV could not, as McLuhan implied, become an independent technological force or be analyzed apart from social-economic-political contexts.

Reinterpreting the Mass-Culture Debate

McLuhan's successors, drawn from a generation actually raised on postwar consumer culture, tried to anchor their own analyses in more specific contexts. By the 1970s, younger academics and journalists saw postwar intellectuals' contempt for mass culture as a historical phenomenon to be explained, rather than a cultural judgment to be endorsed. Consequently, some recent studies argue that prominent postwar intellectuals feared that mass culture, with its new sources of inspiration and its eclectic creativity, threatened their own cultural authority, which was rooted in the mastery of traditional works of high culture. And the fact that the new mass culture drew upon sources outside the educated, white, middle-class—such as the music of urban African-Americans, Mexican-Americans, and southern whites—only underscores the elitism and cultural blinders of cold war intellectuals. The music of Elvis Presley and Chuck Berry, which blended white and black sounds, represented a daring crossing of racial boundaries, a kind of cultural civil-rights movement. And though 1950s rock-and-roll invariably reinforced subordinate images of women's roles, in both the lyrics of the songs and the performances of its male stars, it also displayed a healthy skepticism about many other social "truths" and traditional sources of cultural authority.

Other examples of postwar commercial culture also now find more favorable reception. Television, its recent defenders point out, contributed to a virbrant, quickly changing postwar culture. It extended the careers of popular vaudeville stars—including George Burns and Gracie Allen, Groucho Marx, and Milton Berle—and developed or refined newer forms of mass culture, including the sitcom (*I Love Lucy*), the police drama (*Dragnet*), and the psychological western (*Gunsmoke*). Even professional wrestling and Roller Derby have recently found their own sympathetic analysts; both spectacles provided working-class heroes for blue-collar audiences and offered more opportunities for participation by women than most of the "real" sports. In a similar way, other works of mass culture, even quickly written romance novels, one cultural anthropologist argues, could provide women with sources of information and lead them to question, at least in tentative ways, the hierarchical, male-dominated structures that shaped daily lives in the 1950s. The mere act of sitting down to read a novel for pleasure, for example, represented a small revolt against the home-front ethic that a woman-and-mother's work was "never done." The automatic contempt for commercial culture, the position championed by the literary elite of the 1940s and 1950s, now dominates neither contemporary cultural criticism nor the writing of cultural history.

THE OTHER SIDE OF AFFLUENCE

As middle-class city dwellers moved to the suburbs, many people from rural areas arrived to replace them. These new migrants were usually not white and not middle class. For them, the 1950s did not bring ebullient affluence; their small economic gains came only against a background of oppressive discrimination and entrapment in decaying central cities.

African-Americans

Black people from the rural South flooded into northern cities during World War II to take jobs in war-related industries. But even though employment possibilities increased, the overall quality of life remained low. With the nation's resources being poured into national defense, little money remained for housing programs. In Detroit's new black ghetto, for example, one investigator reported that an old converted one-family dwelling might hold over a hundred black people, one family to a room.

But overcrowding, discrimination, and harrassment by whites did not curb the postwar flow of black people into urban areas. With the new emphasis on corporate farming and mechanized agriculture, many southern blacks who had traditionally hired out as farm laborers found themselves with little hope of employment. Others who had scratched out livings on small farms felt their always marginal existence slip below self-sufficiency. In 1940, 77 percent of the black population had lived in the South, mostly in rural areas; by 1960 nearly half lived in the North, and three of every four blacks resided in a city.

Although the gap between the living standards of white and black Americans remained large, northern migration did advance the economic position of black people as a group. Between 1947 and 1952 the median income of nonwhite families rose from $1614 to $2338, and the gap between black and white narrowed slightly. In 1940, 80 percent of all black workers were employed in unskilled jobs; by 1950 the figure had dropped to 63 percent. Similarly, life expectancy of blacks advanced from 53.1 years in 1940 to 61.7 in 1953 (compared with 64.2 to 69.6 for whites). Throughout the 1950s, the expanding economy and favorable job market helped maintain the economic gains that the war had initially stimulated.

During the Eisenhower years almost every area of southern society still had segregated facilities for blacks and whites. "Jim Crow" extended to public transportation, rest rooms, drinking fountains, even parking lots and cemeteries. Often required by law and always demanded by custom, these separate, but rarely equal, facilities reminded black people of the inferior status assigned them by white society. The National Association for the Advancement of Colored People (NAACP) financed a series of successful legal challenges during the Truman years, and their success in *Brown* v. *Board of Education* (1954) marked the most important victory.

In *Brown*, all nine Supreme Court justices agreed that legally sanctioned segregation of public schools violated the equal-protection clause of the Fourteenth Amendment. In a simple, straightforward opinion, Chief Justice Earl Warren argued that separate schools were "inherently unequal" and deprived black children of equal educational opportunities. But one court decision, by itself, could not produce a revolution in race relations. Bowing to political pressures and the practical problems of education, the Supreme Court later ruled that school desegregation need not be immediate; it should proceed "with all deliberate speed." Ten years after the *Brown* decision only about 1 percent of black children in the South attended desegregated schools.

Resistance to desegregation hardened after the *Brown* case. Most white southerners protested this "invasion of states' rights"; some denounced the ruling as part of a communist plot to destroy "the white race"; many pledged massive resistance to school integration. The Ku Klux Klan revived, and a new organization, the White Citizens Council, became a powerful force in many areas. Not all members of the KKK and Citizens Council endorsed violent resistance, but some did use force against blacks who "didn't know their place." In 1954 a crowd of whites lynched a young black man, Emmet Till, for allegedly whistling at a white woman.

Southerners also used legal and political strategems to delay changes in race relations. In 1957, 101 members of Congress signed the Southern Manifesto, a protest against "federal usurpation" of states' rights, and southern senators employed the filibuster to block civil rights legislation. A segregationist image was essential to political survival in many southern states; after a moderate young lawyer, George C. Wallace, lost badly to a segregationist, he announced that he would never be "outnigraed again." The most spectacular example of official resistance came in 1957 when Arkansas governor Orval Faubus defied a federal court order to desegregate Little Rock High School and used his national guard to keep black children out of the building. With national authority openly challenged, the Eisenhower administration could not avoid the issue. Although never a firm supporter of school desegregation, Eisenhower placed the Arkansas National Guard under federal control, augmented it with regular Army troops, and enforced the court order. The following year Arkansas officials tried to block desegregation through the courts. Meeting in emergency session, the Supreme Court rejected Arkansas' claim that the state need not obey national court orders and buried once again the states' rights argument. After the Little Rock incident the Supreme Court declared unconstitutional the evasive tactics of closing down public schools and gerrymandering school districts, and it pressed southern school districts for realistic desegregation plans.

Desegregation of public facilities in the South gained the support of influential people. Fighting a war against Nazi racism and crusading against "atheistic communism" had made American liberals more sensitive to injustices at home. The success of American institutions, they argued, required a greater commitment to racial justice. Policymakers, competing with the Soviets for the goodwill of Third World nations, found it difficult to explain away discrimination against nonwhites in the United States. When diplomats from the new African states experienced segregation firsthand, the whole system of Jim Crow became highly embarrassing to influential whites. Many religious leaders and scientists also lent their prestige to the civil rights cause.

At the same time, the migration of northern-based corporations and industries to the southern states was producing important socioeconomic, and ultimately cultural, changes: In many ways the South was becoming more like the North. To a new generation of white southern leaders, this process of "northernization" made old patterns of racial domination, such as Jim Crow and political exclusion, seem both embarrassing and anachronistic. This new group of "white southern liberals" lacked a deep-seated commitment to segregation and possessed some genuine impulses to change settled ways.

The introduction of new industries and new technologies also affected black southerners. With the rise of white-owned agribusinesses patterned on northern models, and the use of new agricultural techniques, the largely rural southern black population came under severe pressure. Old living patterns were disrupted: Slowly at first, and then at a much more rapid rate, black people found themselves pushed off the land. Many moved to cities within the South or to urban areas in the northern states. During the 1940s and 1950s, it should be recalled, more than 3 million black people left the South. This disruption helped to break old deferential patterns and to encourage a new spirit of militancy among younger blacks. By the mid 1950s white leaders found it impossible to ignore black demands, for within the black community new leaders and new organizations were spearheading the fight for equality.

The Montgomery bus boycott of 1956–1957 provided an impetus for community action against Jim Crow. Massive resistance against segregation on municipal buses began when Rosa Parks, a seamstress who had been involved in the local NAACP chapter, sparked defiance when she was arrested for refusing to surrender her bus seat to a white man. Very quickly, African-American leaders rallied behind Rosa Parks and organized a boycott of all municipal transit, refusing to ride until facilities were desegregated. Lasting for more than a year, the Montgomery boycott ended in a victory for antidiscrimination forces and brought to prominence a young Baptist minister, Martin Luther King, Jr.

Raised and educated in Atlanta, and earning a doctorate at Boston

University before moving back to the South, Dr. King quickly gained recognition as a charismatic presence and a skilled strategist. Casting himself as a moderate, he nevertheless went beyond the courtroom tactics of the NAACP and the calm lobbying of the Urban League. While still in his twenties he led the successful boycott against segregated public transportation facilities in Montgomery, Alabama. King's tactics of nonviolent civil disobedience and economic pressure soon became the civil rights movement's primary weapons. Citing the success of Mahatma Gandhi's passive resistance in India, King preached the importance of laying one's body on the line and of loving one's enemy. "If we are arrested every day . . . if we are trampled over every day, don't ever let anyone pull you so low as to hate them. We must use the weapon of love." In 1957 King and other black ministers formed the Southern Christian Leadership Conference (SCLC), which quickly became the most active civil rights organization in the South.

King and the SCLC worked primarily through churches and drew their heaviest support from middle-class black people. The son of a prominent Atlanta minister, King had enjoyed a sheltered childhood and a good education at Morehouse College before going north to get his doctorate. He spoke in the measured cadence of the black preacher, the person who traditionally led the black community, but he also had the oratorical power to move white audiences and touch their consciences with his message of Christian love. Whether he sought the role or not, King became the symbolic leader of the nation's entire black population. Such a position gained him the enmity of angry whites and, eventually, of more militant black activists.

Puerto Ricans

Thousands of Puerto Ricans moved to New York City in the decade after World War II, transforming that city's ethnic makeup. New York's Puerto Rican community grew by over half a million in twenty years, from 70,000 in 1940 to 613,000 in 1960. A variety of circumstances contributed to this massive migration. Throughout the 1940s Puerto Ricans had experienced increased contact with the United States mainland through mass media, advertisements, and military life (65,000 Puerto Ricans served in the armed forces during World War II). Especially to young Puerto Ricans, life in the United States seemed alluring. New York's unemployment rate was lower than Puerto Rico's, and its social services seemed superior. The administration of Luis Muñoz Marín in Puerto Rico encouraged the trend, hoping to raise Puerto Rico's per-capita income by reducing the island's population. Comparatively inexpensive air service between San Juan and New York, begun in 1945, facilitated movement. In addition, United States businesses encouraged migration; Puerto Ricans provided cheap labor for agriculture and the garment trades. Once a sizable Puerto Rican community existed in New York, it generated its own growth through a high birth rate and the additional migration of friends and relatives.

The Puerto Rican community crowded into East Harlem and then into other ethnic neighborhoods throughout the five boroughs of New York City. Studies showed that the newcomers generally had a higher level of education and skill than the average Puerto Rican, but their Spanish language, skin color, and close ties with the island left them outside the mainstream of city life. During the 1950s most Puerto Ricans could obtain only the lowest-paying jobs, and few entered New York City politics. Puerto Ricans suffered the fate of many groups that lacked economic power and political muscle: discrimination, deteriorating schools, overcrowded housing, and indifference to their problems. Every year around 30,000 people returned to the island, but Spanish Harlem still continued to grow rapidly throughout the 1950s and 1960s.

Mexican-Americans

New immigration from Mexico and the attraction of urban jobs swelled southwestern cities with another Spanish-speaking population: Mexican-Americans (Chicanos). Before World War II Chicanos, like blacks, lived largely in rural areas, but by 1960, 80 percent resided in cities. According to the 1960 census, over half a million Mexican-Americans lived in the Los Angeles–Long Beach area. Large Spanish-speaking neighborhoods *(barrios)* also existed in El Paso, Phoenix, and other southwestern cities; and northern industrial centers such as Chicago, Detroit, Kansas City, and Denver attracted growing numbers of Chicano workers.

City life and the favorable job market of the 1950s raised the overall living standards of Mexican-Americans, but racial prejudice still kept a lid on opportunity and advancement. Discrimination, coupled with the ethnic awareness that grew in city *barrios*, produced racial tensions between Chicanos and white "Anglos."

During World War II, for example, young Chicano men in Los Angeles defied conventional styles of dress by donning "zoot suits" (or "drapes")—pleated, high-waisted pants with tight cuffs and long, wide-shouldered, loose coats. The ducktail haircut (which would become standard for fans of Elvis Presley in the 1950s) topped off the costume. Many whites, feeling threatened by the display of ethnic separateness, tended to see zoot suiters as hoodlums. In 1943, after zoot-suited youth reportedly beat up eleven sailors who were strolling through a Chicano neighborhood, large-scale violence erupted. About two hundred sailors, joined by scores of soldiers and marines, cruised through the city attacking anyone who wore a zoot suit. The Los Angeles police followed, arresting only the injured Chicanos. The one-sided rioting went on for several days, and similar disturbances quickly flared up in other cities throughout the country.

Despite widespread racial prejudice against Chicanos, the United States government welcomed additional Mexican migrants under the bracero (farm-worker) program. The executive agreement between the United States and Mexico that started the bracero program in 1942 was part of an effort to increase manpower during World War II. But under pressure from large agricultural enterprises Congress continued to authorize migration of farm laborers long after the war. Throughout the 1950s the number of incoming Mexican workers climbed each year, reaching a peak of almost a million in 1959 alone. Mexican migrants provided cheap, unorganized labor to harvest seasonal crops from Texas to Montana, and growers profited enormously. By the early 1960s, however, the rising unemployment rate among Americans, combined with anti-Mexican prejudice, convinced Congress to discontinue the bracero program. Over the protests of large growers, but to the satisfaction of labor unions that feared competition from cheap labor, the bracero program ended in 1965, although illegal immigration continued.

American Indians

American Indians also flocked to urban areas during and after World War II. Army life and lucrative industrial jobs initially attracted Indian people away from reservations, and the federal government's policies during the 1950s substantially increased flight to the cities. The policy of the Eisenhower administration, as passed by Congress in 1953, called for the government to end Indians' "status as wards of the United States, and grant them all of the rights and privileges pertaining to American citizenship." The plan sought to "terminate" dependence upon the national government, to liquidate the reservation system, and to permit states to assume legal jurisdiction over Indians. Six bills of termination, applying to tribes who supposedly no longer needed a special relationship with the federal government, passed Congress in 1954.

While pursuing termination, the government also set up a Voluntary Relocation Program (later called the Employment Assistance Program) to coax more Indians into urban areas. Begun in 1952, this program helped Indians move to one of ten cities with "field relocation offices" and paid living expenses until first wages were received. Within about a decade, more than sixty thousand (approximately one of every eight) Indians had migrated from reservations to urban centers.

Termination and relocation greatly disrupted Indian life. Some terminated tribes, now subject to state tax requirements, fell upon hard times. Others sold tribal lands to private developers. Indians who moved to the cities found themselves ill equipped for the transition from a semicommunal rural existence to the isolation of urban life. Federal officials had hoped that termination and relocation would assimilate Indians into the American mainstream and end federal outlays to support them, but assimilation proved more complicated than a geographical move. The Bureau of Indian Affairs estimated that 35 percent of all relocated Indians eventually returned to the reservations, but other studies suggested that about 75 percent would probably have returned had the reservations offered more job opportunities.

Few Indians favored the federal policy of termination and relocation, and protests mounted against the breakup of reservations and the destruction of Indian culture. Although the Eisenhower administration never abandoned the goal of termination, officials finally promised not to force it upon unwilling tribes. By the 1960 presidential campaign, termination was so discredited that both the Democratic and Republican parties repudiated it. During the 1960s the government revised the policy and attempted to provide opportunity on reservations rather than to force Indians to leave.

Urban Problems

Although the term *urban crisis* did not become a cliché until the 1960s, people who understood urban life recognized severe tensions and strains during the 1950s. Construction of new office buildings and highways, reduction of the number of substandard housing units, and a decrease in population density gave some evidence of urban growth. In addition, the diversity of life in the United States allowed people to cite vastly different information about "the American city." Obviously, problems such as pollution, racial conflict, and crime did vary from city to city, but local discomforts increasingly appeared to be variations on a general trend. By 1960 almost every city confronted serious problems that seemed beyond the capacity of established urban institutions.

Most cities were paying the price for more than a century of largely uncontrolled development. Even after the advent of planning and zoning commissions during the early twentieth century, the private decisions of business leaders exerted the greatest influence on the direction and pace of urban change. The needs of business enterprises largely determined what land would be used, how it would be developed, and what groups would pay the highest social costs. All cities faced another problem with a long history. Unlike Europeans, with their long tradition of city living, many Americans continued to view urban life as less virtuous than rural or small-town living. This antiurban bias created a curious situation: People moved toward cities to exploit the economic opportunities located there, while feeling that urban life was not really what they wanted for themselves or their children. This feeling was not limited to affluent whites: Many black and Spanish-speaking parents also feared, with more reason than most whites, that urban life might harm their children.

Whatever their apprehensions, people still flocked toward urban areas after World War II in search of greater economic rewards. As a result, the urban population grew tremendously during the late 1940s and throughout the 1950s. Sprawling across the landscape, urban areas became more fragmented than ever before. After studying cities along the eastern seaboard during the 1950s, a French geographer called this new social organization the "megalopolis." "We must abandon the idea of the city as a tightly settled and organized unit in which people, activities, and riches are crowded into a very small area clearly separate from its nonurban surroundings," wrote

Jean Gottman. A city would spread out "far and wide around its original nucleus" until it melted into the suburban neighborhoods of other cities.

Many people blamed this geographical expansion for many of the failures of the modern American city. Larger urban areas made coherent centralized administration difficult, and any decentralized arrangement left less affluent areas saddled with poor schools, inadequate services, and too little money to solve social problems. Many sociologists also argued that urban sprawl exacerbated people's sense of isolation and contributed to their sense of being transients rather than parts of a community. As long as more affluent urbanites could hope to escape to suburbia, they would hesitate to commit themselves or their tax dollars to projects that aimed at long-range solutions to urban problems.

Ironically, many attempts to meet urban needs seemed only to accelerate fragmentation. Significant federal aid for construction of low-cost housing rarely reached central cities during the 1950s. Even the modest goal of 810,000 public-housing units by 1955, the target of the Housing Act of 1949, was not achieved until the end of the 1960s. In fact, the Housing Act began another program—urban renewal—that actually reduced the number of dwellings available to poor people. In theory, urban renewal allowed local governments to obtain federal funds to clear out old and dilapidated buildings and to replace them with new public-housing units or with other projects, including almost anything from new cultural complexes to concrete parking garages. In practice, the Eisenhower administration began to permit urban planners and private developers to evade the responsibility of replacing or increasing the supply of living units.

New York's Robert Moses, a person who held no elective office but who came to dominate building and urban planning in the nation's largest city, epitomized the postwar approach to urban issues. Moses ridiculed critics of his grandiose schemes. "When you operate in an overbuilt metropolis, you have to hack your way with a meat ax," he once explained. Flaunting his power as City Parks Commissioner and City Construction Coordinator, Moses taunted opponents that he was "just going to keep on building. You do the best you can to stop it." Moving poor people as if they were disposable commodities, Moses held fast to his vision of urban progress. For those who "like things as they are," Moses offered this advice: "Keep moving further away. [New York] is a big state, and there are other states. . . . go to the Rockies." And even though most of New York City's postwar residents owned no automobiles, Moses cut through, around, and even above the city with expensive freeway projects.

The vast networks of multilane expressways, in New York and elsewhere, brought paradoxical changes to urban life. The new freeways allowed people to travel to work in the privacy of their automobiles rather than on public transportation and enabled affluent commuters to live even farther from decaying urban centers. In addition to accelerating uncontrolled urban sprawl, the freeways created other problems. The new concrete conveyors accelerated decay of existing mass transit facilities and worked against construction of any new ones. The stream of cars creeping to and from the central cities every day also increased air pollution without noticeably speeding the pace of urban commuting. Finally, the new express-ways destroyed even more old buildings and further contributed to the fragmentation of urban life.

By the 1960s urban problems seemed of growing concern. During the presidential campaign of 1960 both Richard Nixon and John Kennedy pledged their support for creation of a new cabinet-level office to coordinate federal assistance to urban areas.

The "Invisible" Poor

Despite urban deterioration, the people who congregated in central-city neighborhoods were often better off than those who remained in rural areas. During the 1950s great agribusiness combinations mechanized opera-tions and engulfed more land. By 1954, 12 percent of the farm operators made nearly 60 percent of total agricultural sales, and this imbalance grew. Unemployment accompanied this agricultural revolution; severe rural poverty became a major, if often unnoticed, problem. Throughout the rural Midwest in the 1950s, many young people left their family farms rather than try to compete with large agricultural enterprises. A million and a half people abandoned unproductive patches of land in Appalachia. The many old people who remained were those least able to cope with mechanization and changing markets. Whether a person was a black tenant farmer in Georgia, an Indian on an isolated reservation, a white farmer in the hills of Appalachia, or a Mexican-American migrant worker, poverty often domin-ated their life.

While growing affluence and comfort characterized the postwar years for some Americans, what Michael Harrington called *The Other America* (1962) of persisting and systemic poverty remained. The medium of televi-sion made middle-class comforts highly visible to the poor, yet poverty and degradation grew more invisible to the affluent. Suburbanites in fast-moving automobiles skirted the slums and rarely penetrated the pockets of rural poverty. A gap grew between the aspirations of the lower sectors and the social consciousness of the affluent. Bitterness mounted in the central city as complacency spread through the suburbs.

In 1960, John F. Kennedy promised to "get this country moving again" and help revive the old liberal-Democratic approach to social problems. But for the decade of the 1950s, Dwight Eisenhower's desire to limit social welfare programs and the size of government prevailed. By the 1970s, when the nation had "moved" in directions that liberals could neither foresee nor control, more than a few people would look back to Ike with a touch of nostalgia. What often becomes forgotten, however, is that the "real fifties," though perhaps more placid than the immediate postwar period, still exhib-ited tensions and strains that could not always be papered over by the official gospel of affluence and affability. This was especially true in foreign affairs, where the United States struggled to preside as the "Protector of the Free World."

SUGGESTIONS FOR FURTHER READING

Charles Alexander, *Holding the Line* (1975), offers a useful introduction to the Eisenhower years, and the early sections of Martin P. Wattenberg, *The Decline of American Political Parties, 1952–1980* (1984), set the political background. Stephen Ambrose's two-volume study *Eisenhower* (1983, 1984) will likely remain the standard source for years, but Fred Greenstein's *The Hidden-Hand Presidency* (1982), Herbert J. Parmet's *Eisenhower and the American Crusades* (1972), and Robert F. Burk's *Dwight David Eisenhower* (1986) should also be consulted. Ike's own memoirs, *Mandate for Change* and *Waging Peace* (1963, 1965), are worthwhile. Specialized studies include Gary Reichard, *The Reaffirmation of Republicanism* (1975); Burton J. Kaufman, *The Oil Cartel Case* (1978); Mark Rose, *Interstate: Express Highway Politics* (1979); and Robert F. Burk, *The Eisenhower Administration and Civil Rights* (1984); Duane Tanabaum, *The Bricker Amendment: A Test of Eisenhower's Political Leadership* (1989); and R. Alton Lee, *Eisenhower and Landrum-Griffin: A Study in Labor Management Politics* (1990).

The baby boom is the focus of Richard A. Easterlin, *Birth and Fortune* (1980), and Landon Y. Jones, *Great Expectations* (1980). See also the relevant chapters of John Modell, *Into One's Own: From Youth to Adulthood in the United States, 1920–1975* (1989). On women's issues, see the final chapters of Susan Strasser, *Never Done* (1982); Ruth Schwartz Cowen, *More Work for Mother: The Ironies of Household Technology from the Open Hearth to the Microwave* (1985); Alice Kessler-Harris, *Out to Work: A History of Wage-Earning Women in the United States* (1982); Jacqueline Jones, *Labor of Love, Labor of Sorrow: Black Women, Work and the Family, From Slavery to the Present* (1985); Paula Giddings, *When and Where I Enter* (1984); and Sara Evans, *Born for Liberty* (1989). General surveys that focus more directly on this specific period include Eugenia Kaledin, *Mothers and More* (1984); Leila Rupp and Vera Taylor, *Survival in the Doldrums* (1987); Cynthia Harrison, *On Account of Sex: The Politics of Women's Issues, 1945–68* (1988). Family and gender issues are nicely tied to cold war culture in Elaine May's *Homeward Bound* (1989). Barbara Ehrenreich, *The Hearts of Men* (1983), relates women's issues to her theory of a "male revolt" during the 1950s. On issues related to sexuality, see the relevant chapters of John D'Emilio, *Sexual Politics, Sexual Communities: The Making of a Homosexual Minority in the United States, 1940–1970* (1983); Paul Robinson, *The Modernization of Sex* (1976); and John D'Emilio and Estelle B. Freedman, *Intimate Matters* (1988).

On suburbia and urban issues, see Robert J. Caro, *The Power Broker* (1974), a fascinating study of the machinations of New York City's Robert Moses; Mark Gelfand, *A Nation of Cities* (1975); Kenneth Fox, *Metropolitan America: Urban Life and Urban Policy in the United States* (1986); Herbert Gans, *The Levittowners* (2nd ed., 1982); Robert B. Fairbanks and Kathleen Underwood, *Essays on Sunbelt Cities and Recent Urban America* (1989). See also the relevant chapters of Kenneth T. Jackson, *The Crabgrass Frontier* (1985).

The mass-culture debate can be sampled in Bernard Rosenberg and

David Manning White, *Mass Culture* (1957) and *Mass Culture Revisited* (1971). James Gilbert, *A Cycle of Outrage* (1986), offers a fine analysis of the mass-culture debate and how it related to an emerging youth culture. On sports, see Randy Roberts and James S. Olson, *Winning Is the Only Thing: Sports in America Since 1945* (1989). Different views of Hollywood's role emerge from Peter Biskind, *Seeing Is Believing* (1984); Andrea Walsh, *Women's Film and Female Experience, 1940–1950* (1984); Robert Ray, *A Certain Tendency in the Hollywood Cinema* (1985); Dana Polan, *Power and Paranoia: History, Narrative, and the American Cinema, 1940–1950* (1986); and Mary Doane, *The Desire to Desire: The Woman's Film of the 1940s* (1987); and J.P. Tellotte, *Voices in the Dark: The Narrative Patterns of Film Noir* (1989).

On TV, see David Marc's two books—*Demographic Vistas* (1984) and *Comic Visions* (1989)—which offer an appreciative view of television. More critical are Erik Barnouw's various works such as *Tube of Plenty* (rev. ed., 1982). For an overview of recent, critical approaches see the various essays in Robert C. Allen, ed., *Channels of Discourse* (1987). On music, see Greil Marcus, *Mystery Train* (rev. ed., 1990); Charley Gillet's *Sound of the City* (rev. ed., 1984); Ed Ward, Geoffrey Stokes, and Ken Tucker, *Rock of Ages: The Rolling Stone History of Rock & Roll* (1986); and Nelson George, *The Death of Rhythm and Blues* (1988).

On social issues, see Michael Harrington's classic study, *The Other America* (1962) and his later work, *The New American Poverty* (1984); James T. Patterson, *America's Struggle Against Poverty, 1900–1980* (1981); Doug Mc-Adam, *Political Process and the Development of Black Insurgency, 1930–1970* (1982); Harvard Sitkoff, *The Struggle for Black Equality* (1983); Larry Burt, *Tribalism in Crisis* (1982); Tony Freyer, *The Little Rock Crisis* (1984); Manuel Alers-Montalvo, *The Puerto Rican Migrants of New York* (1985); David Garrow, *Bearing the Cross; Martin Luther King, Jr., and the Southern Christian Leadership Conference* (1986); the relevant chapters of Earl Black and Merle Black, *Politics and Society in the South* (1987); Jack Bloom, *Class, Race, and the Civil Rights Movement: The Political Economy of Southern Racism* (1987); David Garrow, ed., *The Montgomery Bus Boycott and the Women Who Started It: The Memoir of Jo Ann Gibson Robinson* (1987); Joseph P. Fitzpatrick, *Puerto Rican Americans: The Meaning of Migration to the Mainland* (2d ed., 1987); Taylor Branch, *Parting the Waters: America in the King Years, 1954–1963* (1988); Steven J. Whitfield, *A Death in the Delta: The Story of Emmett Till* (1988); Herbert Haines, *Black Radicals and the Civil Rights Mainstream, 1954–1970* (1989); Mario Garcia, *Mexican-Americans: Leadership, Ideology, and Identity, 1930–1960* (1989); Ricardo Romo, *East Los Angeles: History of a Barrio* (1983); Nancy J. Weiss, *Whitney M. Young, Jr., and Struggle for Civil Rights* (1989); the relevant chapters of Ronald Takaki, *Strangers from a Different Shore: A History of Asian-Americans* (1989); Henry Hampton, ed., *Voices of Freedom: An Oral History of the Civil Right Movement* (1990); and Robert Weisbrot, *American Crusade: A History of the Civil Rights Movement* (1990).

Chapter Four

Protector of the Free World

REPUBLICAN FOREIGN POLICIES

President Dwight Eisenhower's personal style contrasted with that of his flamboyant predecessors. For years Eisenhower had reconciled diverse opinions into consensus, first as commander of the world's greatest amphibious invasion, the D-Day attack against occupied France, then as president of Columbia University, and from 1950 to 1952 as leader of NATO's vast military apparatus in Europe. Distrustful of expansive government and its potential for public waste, Ike championed conservative economic principles and scrutinized defense expenditures carefully. This general enjoyed quiet games of golf and, unlike "give 'em hell, Harry Truman," vowed to "wage peace."

John Foster Dulles, an austere corporation lawyer who became secretary of state, helped chart Eisenhower's foreign policy. A fervent anticommunist, he extended the position of the 1952 Republican platform that condemned Truman's containment policy as "negative, futile, and immoral" by stridently calling for a psychological and political offensive to roll back communism. Dulles saw himself, one biographer wrote, "as the chess master of the free world, daily engaged in a mortal contest against a monolithic adversary."

100

The New Look

How could the Eisenhower administration reconcile a suspicion of large government with its rhetorical commitment to an open-ended struggle against anything perceived as socialist or communist? The cost-conscious president, his secretary of state, and Pentagon generals recast America's strategic doctrines into a "New Look" stressing the deterrent of massive retaliation. Modern technology could increase American military power while reducing its cost: Secretary of Defense Charles Wilson quipped that nuclear weaponry provided "more bang for the buck." Doomsday bombs, together with sophisticated delivery systems, could protect the United States from attack, since no nation would risk "second-strike" reprisal.

Determined to stake out the boundaries of the "free world" as broadly as possible, Dulles also dramatically expanded the nation's collective-security arrangements. He spent months traveling around the world, signing up allies. A succession of bilateral defense pacts with Taiwan, Korea, and Japan extended America's nuclear umbrella to the shores of China. Even more grandiose schemes shored up Britain's weakness "east of Suez." The Southeast Asia Treaty Organization (SEATO) of 1954 linked Australia, the Philippines, Thailand, and Pakistan with the United States, Britain, and France. The next year Washington sponsored England's Central Treaty Organization (CENTO) with Turkey, Iraq, Iran, and Pakistan. Turkey tied CENTO with NATO; Pakistan connected SEATO with CENTO. Each of these multilateral covenants pledged that an attack against one member, either by overt aggression or, as Dulles put it, "by internal subversion," would bring all into consultation to decide common action. Eisenhower, already skeptical about the military value of large American army reserves, thought that local forces, financed partly from Washington and linked to a network of alliances controlled by the United States, could contain regional threats and prevent them from escalating into nuclear cataclysm. Although designed to decrease America's obligations, regional pacts could also increase them by involving the United States in local disputes.

The New Look stressed atomic weaponry, but it also brought other tools into what Republicans viewed as a global struggle between good and evil: an increase in overseas bases; a larger commitment to foreign military aid; employment of economic assistance programs to accomplish political goals; more aggressive use of techniques of psychological warfare (such as Radio Free Europe); and a stepped-up program of covert action, run by the CIA, to subvert unfriendly governments. The Eisenhower administration talked about limited government, but historians now recognize how thoroughly it expanded and employed new techniques, controlled by executive branch discretion, of conducting foreign policy. Use of economic, psychological, and covert diplomacy—all fairly hidden from public view or scrutiny—sharply distinguished Eisenhower's foreign policy from prewar patterns and significantly shaped future capabilities. More and more, the United States' "defense" posture against communism looked like a global offensive; Ike's "limited" government like a budding leviathan.

Korea

Armistice negotiations with the North Koreans and the Chinese had broken down in October 1952, largely because of a complicated impasse over the issue of prisoners of war. The communists demanded that the usual international practice of returning all POWs to their homeland be observed. The United States, however, insisted upon voluntary repatriation. Since many enemy soldiers wanted to stay in South Korea, this formula meant that the South could gain, and the North lose, as many as 50,000 trained soldiers. Stalemate also continued on the battlefield.

True to his campaign promise, Eisenhower toured the front in November 1952 and then, with Dulles, orchestrated an exercise in New Look diplomacy. Nuclear weapons might be used to terminate the conflict if negotiations failed. The president wired General Mark Clark, the United Nations commander, that the United States might "carry on the war in new ways never yet tried" if the communists remained intransigent. Dulles dispatched more specific warnings through third parties: America might drop atomic bombs.

Before the United States took such a fateful step, however, negotiations resumed, and both sides quickly initiated armistice terms. Korea would stay divided, as before the war; neutral powers were to tackle POW repatriation (an issue eventually settled according to the voluntary formula). On July 27, 1953, a truce—not a peace treaty—ended a war that had killed over 2 million Asians, mostly civilians, and 33,000 Americans.

The Korean War sharply focused the nature of United States policy during the 1950s. To American policymakers of the time—and many subsequent historians—it represented a clear case of communist expansionism: aggression across international boundaries to take over a "free" state. In this view, expansionism was successfully "contained" by a strong military response topped off by use of an atomic threat. The Korean War seemed to exemplify the cold war premises of NSC 68 and to require a rapid buildup of American military strength and nonmilitary leverage.

Yet this version of the war speaks more about the mentality of the 1950s than about Korean realities. Korea was a deeply divided society—factionalized between right and left and divided, since 1946, by an arbitrary border that cut across lines of ethnicity, religion, and political allegiance. The governments of both North and South were deeply committed to reunification of the country and both were, simultaneously, attempting to consolidate their control. Within this fragmented society, the cast of characters simply did not match the cold war morality play. Kim Il Sung was a communist dictator but undoubtedly acted on his own, not as an agent of Soviet expansionism. And Syngman Rhee was poorly cast as a defender of democracy. The South seethed with discontent against his autocratic rule;

indeed, the civil turmoil in the South may have convinced Kim Il Sung that the time had come to make a bid for unification. After gaining United States support for his own ambitions, of course, Rhee had little reason to reorient his regime in a more popular direction. Portrayed by the United States as a defender of freedom—because he was anticommunist—Rhee could continue to block needed reforms, imprison dissenters, and expand his tyranny.

Korea was consistent with a predominant trend in Eisenhower's overall foreign policy toward the Third World: the support for conservative, often autocratic dictators as the only presumed alternative to a supposedly monolithic communist menace.

"Summitry"

Although New Look calculations about the Soviet Union assumed an international communist conspiracy led by a Stalinist police state, Soviet communism, in fact, began to mellow after the mid-1950s. On March 5, 1953, the Soviet dictator, Joseph Stalin, died, and his tyranny partially withered. Stalin's theories had proved wrong: World war had revived liberal capitalism, not doomed it. The troika that replaced Stalin—Foreign Minister Vyacheslav Molotov, Defense Minister Nikolai Bulganin, and Nikita Khrushchev, first secretary of the Communist party—went along with Premier George Malenkov's plan to ease tensions with the United States. Within three years Khrushchev had triumphed over the others, and the Soviet people, tired of fear and poverty, enthusiastically responded to his promises of "peaceful coexistence" and more consumer goods. After Khrushchev denounced Stalin's "Gestapo tactics" in 1956, Russians dreamed of less regimentation, less sacrifice.

This new direction in Soviet policy not only substituted competition for confrontation but also reduced the dangers of massive retaliation. The Soviet Union reduced its armed forces from 4 million to less than 3 million by the mid-1950s. Though primarily an effort to shift economic priorities toward consumer industries, the unilateral gesture did seem to contradict Dulles' hard-line premises. It also calmed European fears of Soviet power. Increasingly, Eisenhower became interested in refashioning America's relationship with the Soviet Union, perhaps by easing the nuclear arms race. During the halcyon months of the Russian thaw, English leaders had urged a conference of heads of state to settle European problems, particularly German reunification. The idea of a summit meeting intrigued Eisenhower, despite Dulles' pessimistic admonitions. Summitry offered not only an alternative to grim crusades but also a new forum for long-stalled disarmament negotiations.

In July 1955 the president traveled to Geneva, where he met with his counterparts from the Big Four: Premier Bulganin and First Secretary Khrushchev, Prime Minister Anthony Eden of Britain, and Premier Edgar Faure of France. The drama of face-to-face sessions obscured otherwise desultory talks about Germany's future and East-West cultural exchanges.

Then Eisenhower submitted a plan for disarmament. The United States and
the Soviet Union would exchange blueprints of all military installations and
permit reconnaissance flights over each other's territory. The proposal had
little chance for practical success because the Soviets were deeply and historically suspicious of opening their territory to Western scrutiny, but "open
skies" did represent a propaganda victory for the United States. More
important, it inaugurated "the spirit of Geneva": Leaders in the two blocs had
moderated their intractable rhetoric, and cultural exchanges accelerated.

The dangers of radioactive fallout from atomic tests spurred further
efforts toward accommodation. In mid-1958 the Russians unilaterally suspended nuclear testing, presumably to probe American intentions while
converting more of their economy to consumer production. Britain and the
United States followed later that year, finally responding to growing evidence that atmospheric tests represented a severe health hazard. The movement toward a "test-ban" showed that in the mutual danger of the atomic age
there could lie mutual interests in constructive solutions.

In the same spirit of summitry, leaders of both nations embarked upon
personal diplomacy. In the fall of 1959 Khrushchev visited the United States
for twelve days. He addressed the United Nations, talked to Iowa farmers,
and watched Hollywood stars. Then premier and president conferred privately at Camp David, a mountain retreat in Maryland. Though achieving
nothing concrete, the "spirit of Camp David" further moderated rancor in
both countries. The leaders also launched much-publicized goodwill trips
elsewhere. Eisenhower went to Europe, the Middle East, Latin America, and
the Far East, though anti-American riots protesting a bilateral defense treaty
forced him to cancel a trip to Japan. Khrushchev appeared in Western
Europe, Afghanistan, and India.

In early 1960 Khrushchev called for another summit meeting, this time
in Paris to deal with issues of German reunification and nuclear armament.
On May 1, 1960, however, the Soviets shot down an American U-2 spy plane
over their territory. Khrushchev trumpeted Russia's injury, demanding
both an apology and an end to such spy flights. Eisenhower knew that
Khrushchev would use the Paris meeting to embarrass the West. The summit collapsed.

The summitry of the Eisenhower years did not narrow fundamental
disagreements nor provide diplomatic breakthroughs. Its essence lay less in
substance than in media-attracting pageantry and in the display of cold war
rituals for home consumption on both sides. Still, the cold war was created by
people in power, and it had to be ameliorated by people in power. The gains
from face-to-face conversations, though small, seemed worthwhile.

Challenges to Superpower Dominance

Even as Soviet-American tensions eased, discontent spread within the
alliance systems of both superpowers. The New Look, based upon America's
strategic superiority, inspired resentment against American dominance.

Russia's thaw spread throughout its Eastern European empire, creating unrest—even outright rebellion. Aligned nations in both blocs rejected crucial parts of their overlords' prescriptions for the future.

Of all its crisscrossed security pacts, America's alliance with Western Europe was the oldest and strongest, but tensions nonetheless mounted. Washington had strongly urged an integrated NATO force armed with conventional weapons. A joint effort would force Europe to finance a larger portion of its defense, increase pressure against the Soviet Union, and rope German power into a regional enterprise. Dulles advocated creation of a European Defense Community (EDC), but many Europeans, particularly the French, opposed its transnational approach and its lack of nuclear weapons. In response, Dulles ruminated at a press conference about "an agonizing reappraisal" of America's relations with Europe if EDC was not supported.

Dulles' tactics only angered politicians in France and England, who asserted national defense to be the province of their own parliaments, not of foreign leaders. Specialization—an American nuclear force paired with conventional European armies—would continue Europe's second-class status in the NATO alliance. Would the United States risk nuclear war, and thus its own destruction, to save Western Europe? Conversely, might not Washington and Moscow pull back from direct superpower confrontation after mushroom clouds rose over Paris and, say, Warsaw? When the French National Assembly finally refused to ratify the EDC treaty on August 30, 1954, most Europeans happily approved. Britain and France accelerated their own plans for nuclear armament.

Nowhere were superpower hopes for mastery wrecked more consistently than in the Middle East. There nationalism and charismatic leaders defined the contours of change. In Egypt, for example, military leaders destroyed King Farouk's corrupt monarchy in a 1952 coup, intending to modernize the country and escape Britain's economic domination. Two years later a "colonels' revolt" gave Gamal Abdel Nasser near dictatorial power. The new president dreamed of making Egypt the chief military power in the Middle East so that he could lead Arab nationalism. Popular resentment at Israeli statehood and English control over much of the Middle East's political life encouraged rearmament programs; "positive neutralism" garnered money and technological aid from both East and West. Nasser's successes soon enraptured Arabs but alienated Britain and frightened Israel. Then, after an Israeli raid into Egypt's Gaza Strip, Nasser signed an agreement to buy advanced weapons from Czechoslovakia. Angry with this threat to the Western-dominated status quo, Dulles withdrew American support for loans for the construction of Egypt's Aswan Dam, a huge project that would improve harvests along the Nile River and provide hydroelectric power for Egypt's developing industries. Nasser then seized the Suez Canal on July 25, assuming that its duties could finance the dam's construction.

Britain, France, and Israel resolved to act. Israelis saw the Suez crisis as a pretext for preventive war; Europeans hoped to destroy Arab nationalism in the Middle East. French premier Guy Mollet also reckoned that a militant response would shore up his foundering coalition government. Then too, a blow at Nasser would discourage Arab rebels in Algeria, where France was attempting to suppress an anticolonial guerrilla movement. Meanwhile, the British had created their own domino theory: Nasser was a Hitlerian figure who, if unopposed, would unite the Arab world and confiscate Britain's most valuable investments. When Eisenhower cleverly ducked the Suez crisis during his 1956 presidential campaign, the British Foreign Office chose to interpret his obscure statements as a negative endorsement of their intervention in the Middle East. The United States, they thought, could not abandon its closest ally once military operations began. On October 29, 1956 Israel attacked Egypt, and several days later Anglo-French forces retook the Suez Canal.

The war ended quickly, partly because Egypt's armies proved surprisingly inept, but largely because of superpower reactions. The United States angrily reasserted its leadership of the Atlantic community. Opposed to "any aggression by any nation," Eisenhower threatened to support cutting oil shipments to the invaders and to destroy the English pound by opposing renewal of British loans from the International Monetary Fund. Unencumbered by alliances with former colonial powers, the Russians condemned Britain and France more forcefully and even hinted at a nuclear strike. Mollet and British prime minister Eden could only acquiesce in a Canadian-American plan for the United Nations troops to police the Sinai Peninsula.

The affair severely damaged America's prestige in most parts of the world. Egyptians did not forget that the "American peace" had stationed foreign soldiers in their country but not in Israel, the aggressor. The Suez crisis of 1956 interjected Russia into Egyptian affairs, especially after the Soviets took over financing the Aswan Dam, and insured Nasser's leadership of the Arab world. Neither prospect pleased Dulles. Washington's criticism had also alienated the Europeans. Franco-American relations never quite recovered. Suez convinced most French people that Washington had sacrificed their national interest; France, indeed all of Europe, would have to chart a new course. The British were stunned but unwilling to give up their "special relationship" with the United States.

Strains within the Western alliance over nuclear policy and the Suez crisis coincided with a similar restiveness within the Soviet bloc. After World War II, Stalin had backed pro-Soviet regimes throughout Eastern Europe. These "satellites" embarked upon industrial programs designed to complement Soviet reconstruction. Never content with Stalinist tactics and the distortion of national economic needs, some Eastern Europeans challenged these local regimes once the Russian thaw began. Yet how much liberalization would Moscow's new rulers allow? In June 1956 over 15,000 factory workers rioted at Poznan in Poland. Their three-day rebellion set off a popular upsurge of support for Wladyslaw Gomulka, a former minister removed by Stalin when he publicly opposed collectivization and advocated

national development regardless of Russian orders. After complicated maneuvers with Poland's old guard and Moscow's politburo, revisionists forced
Moscow to accept the unorthodox Gomulka. Events had caught Soviet
leaders off guard, but their recognition of Gomulka seemed to indicate the
feasibility of economic reform that did not threaten the integrity of the
Soviet bloc.

Misunderstanding this subtlety, Hungarians reached for true political
independence a few months later. Emboldened by Poland's success and by
its own suffering from the same Stalinist exploitation, a huge crowd demonstrated on October 23. Students and workers, intellectuals and housewives
paraded for hours, demanding the return of Imre Nagy, like Gomulka a
former minister disgraced for his liberal views. Nagy formed a new government, but strikes and unrest continued. Protests against subservience to the
Soviet Union turned into armed rebellion in the countryside and within days
paralyzed the capital as well. Misled by broadcasts from America's CIA-
financed Radio Free Europe, the revolutionaries hoped for United States
assistance. Nagy pledged free elections and a multiparty system. "No nation," he declared, "can intervene in our internal affairs." Although Moscow
tried to negotiate, the lure of independence and Dulles' talk of "liberating
captive peoples" betrayed the Hungarians into tragic illusions. As violence
continued, the Russians sent a huge army into Hungary and crushed the
Hungarian revolt. Moscow would not tolerate neutrality on its strategic
borders and benefited from the simultaneous British and French action
against Egypt. At the same time, however, the Kremlin learned that it could
not assume passive subservience in Eastern Europe.

THE THIRD WORLD AND THE COLD WAR

During the 1950s the focus of international affairs shifted toward Asia,
Africa, and Latin America, where charismatic leaders often pursued economic self-determination and control over national resources no less than
political independence. Nationalism was the dominant reality in the Third
World, and most leaders sought to steer between Russian and Yankee,
avoiding an exclusive, neocolonialist reliance on either. The Soviets
argued—often persuasively—that the Russian revolution, directed by centralized planning, was more relevant than the American to the twentieth-
century problems of industrialization. Through such an appeal, the Soviets
tried to build ties to anticolonial movements and to support nationalist
endeavors. United States policymakers under Eisenhower, by contrast,
looked suspiciously on centralized planning and often equated economic
nationalism, even liberal social reform, with communism. Under Eisenhower, the battle against communism became broad and vague and often did not
take into account the appeal of nationalist rhetoric and programs.

Vietnam

America's most perplexing involvement in Third World politics came in Southeast Asia, particularly Vietnam. French colonialism had dominated Indochina for eighty years, but Japan's initial victories over the area in 1940 unseated French rule and galvanized a coterie of nationalist intellectuals into a movement for postwar independence. Ho Chi Minh, a Marxist scholar dedicated to spreading the class struggle to his country of peasants, assumed leadership of the Viet Minh, a popular front of all revolutionary parties. As Japanese power collapsed at the end of World War II, Ho declared Vietnam's independence (on September 2, 1945) and hoped that he could attract support from the United States, whose leaders were then urging decolonization. Although his provisional government wanted to negotiate, France almost immediately launched a war of reconquest. Ho and an exceptionally skillful general, Vo Nguyen Giap, countered with guerrilla tactics, seeking to avoid defeat in the field while winning the people over to their nationalist-communist cause. Financed heavily by Washington, French armies struggled against the communist-nationalist forces led by Ho for control of Vietnam for nine years.

In 1954 the French met final defeat. Giap surrounded 25,000 French troops at a frontier outpost, Dien Bien Phu, while a constant artillery barrage cut off French reinforcements. The Viet Minh slowly advanced, using a complicated system of tunnels and munitions backpacked into the mountains by thousands of peasants. As the French public watched the sure strangulation of its army, the government under Pierre Mendes-France pledged to end the war, even if that meant leaving Vietnam to nationalist-communists under Ho Chi Minh. The French prepared for a peace conference in Geneva.

American policymakers were divided in their response. Shocked that yet another area might "go communist," John Foster Dulles and some Pentagon figures—notably Admiral Arthur W. Radford, chairman of the Joint Chiefs of Staff—proposed an air strike against Giap's army. Some even speculated that American troops could revitalize the French war effort. Eisenhower did not want to "lose" Indochina so soon after the Chinese debacle, but he was aware of America's limited power in so remote a place and worried about the federal budget. Congressional leaders refused to authorize intervention unless the United States first secured foreign support, and Britain quickly refused. After the army outlined cost and manpower estimates, Eisenhower concluded that intervention was impossible. Chief of Staff General Matthew Ridgway predicted that a million men, huge draft quotas, and enormous destruction might win this political-guerrilla war, but he thought that even then most Vietnamese would still likely support the Viet Minh.

Meanwhile, peace negotiations at the Geneva Conference reached a conclusion. France wished only to get out of the war. The Russians, afraid of aggravating Washington, and the Chinese, searching for international legitimacy, urged Ho Chi Minh to accept a compromise. Paris granted Vietnam, Laos, and Cambodia full independence, though none of the new states could join foreign alliances or permit foreign soldiers on its soil. French troops were to regroup in Vietnam south of the seventeenth parallel, communist forces north of it. A nationwide election to be held in 1956 would provide a single government for the reunified country. This solution—a graceful exit for the defeated French and a neutralized Indochina in exchange for a probably communist cabinet for Vietnam—satisfied almost everyone concerned.

Everyone, that is, except American policymakers. They saw a way to "save" at least some of Indochina, though it required unilateral action. The secretary of state refused to sign the Geneva accords and announced instead that the United States considered North and South Vietnam two separate entities. The State Department hurriedly completed plans for SEATO and gratuitously extended its coverage to South Vietnam, Cambodia, and Laos. After Bao Dai, the Vietnamese emperor who had served the French, stepped down in 1955, the Eisenhower administration pledged vast amounts of economic aid to his pro-Western successor, Ngo Dinh Diem. Diem, with American backing, called off the scheduled national elections in which a communist victory appeared certain. The Republican administration updated an old doctrine, long applied to Europe, to justify these expedient maneuvers: the domino theory. If South Vietnam "fell," Thailand would be next; then the rest of Indochina, and perhaps even India or Australia. If the West stood firm now, as Britain and France should have stood up to Hitler in 1939, communist advance would falter. A democracy in Southeast Asia could serve conveniently as an example for the Third World. But the connection between Washington and Saigon was so one-sided that Vietnam became more colony than sovereign state. Dependency reinforced the necessity for ever-increasing United States intervention.

Throughout the rest of the 1950s, Republicans richly supplied South Vietnam's pro-West Premier Diem with economic aid, military know-how, and diplomatic protection. The results at first seemed to vindicate their gamble that a limited commitment might not only stave off another communist victory but also build a capitalist model for the Third World. Between 1954 and 1957 South Vietnam ended wartime economic controls, initiated reconstruction, and began industrial development. Diem redistributed land confiscated from French landlords to peasants in the Mekong River delta. His steadily improving army brought order in Sagon and forced allegiance from the semifeudal religious sects in the countryside. But Diem could never really cement the nation together, and his Catholicism alienated the predominately Buddhist population. To ensure at least the appearance of popular support, Diem replaced local officials with his loyalists. A much touted "population relocation" program degenerated into political purges. Land reform ultimately benefited a new kind of absentee owner, the Saigonese bureaucrat. Corruption diluted American aid, so that little of it helped villagers trapped in the war-ravaged countryside or refugees hound-

ed into inflation-ridden cities. Diem retreated more and more into a contracting circle of family members and army generals. The regime's growing
isolation and dependence upon the United States frightened nationalists.

To protest such abuses, a coalition of anti-Diem intellectuals, nationalists, harassed politicians, and Viet Minh communists organized the National
Liberation Front (NLF) in 1960. Its platform promised return to village rule,
immediate land ownership for the peasants, and a coalition cabinet in
Saigon. Discontent in the countryside propelled many recruits into the NLFs
makeshift army which communist cadres soon dominated, partly because of
their experience during the earlier guerrilla struggle against France. The
NLF championed the communal traditions of the village rather than the
alien dictatorship in Saigon, which relied on Americans.

A communist-led war for national liberation set in motion a dangerous
spiral of escalation. The renewal of serious fighting panicked Washington
into supplying Diem with billions of dollars and a growing corps of American advisers—nine hundred by 1960. In response, Hanoi aided the insurgents, training recruits in the North. Then, after a five-year plan had made
their country the most heavily industrialized state in Southeast Asia by 1959,
the North Vietnamese shipped large amounts of war material south along
the Ho Chi Minh Trail. Although this primitive line of communications
depended as much on human backs as on gasoline engines, it permitted the
NLF to make great progress despite America's reinforcements. Shielded
behind popular resentments, raiders could strike almost anywhere. Their
opponents could only counter by garrisoning the entire country. Thus the
cycle of Saigon corruption and communist rebellion led to American rein-
forcement and then to more aid from Hanoi.

Washington tried to break this chain by asking Diem to reform his
regime. But the premier cared little about generating local popularity as
long as he could rely upon Americans to support him. Despite American
dissatisfaction with Diem, he seemed the only practical alternative to the
NLF. The more isolated Diem became, the more American support he
needed; yet the more aid he received, the more corrupt and unpopular he
became. Americans began to experience, if only dimly to perceive, the
frustration and the long-run dangers of building foreign alliances upon
client relationships.

Partly because of larger problems elsewhere, the Republicans avoided
final answers in their Vietnamese policy. The secretary of state blurted out
during a press conference that "the free world would intervene in Indochina
rather than let the situation deteriorate." Once involved, Dulles thought,
American's prestige required victory. But the president demurred. A charter member of the Never-Again Club—a group of generals who, after their
experiences in Korea, resolutely opposed another land war in Asia—
Eisenhower flatly contradicted his chief adviser on foreign affairs. "I can
conceive of no greater tragedy," he said "than for the United States to
become engaged in all-out war in Indochina."

Intervention: Iran, Guatemala, Lebanon, Cuba

Vietnam was only one area of concern in America's global anticommunist crusade. In the Middle East and Latin America, as in Southeast Asia, the decline of European dominance and the rise of local nationalism forced the United States into new policy decisions. In these areas, Eisenhower's extensive new foreign policy apparatus—encompassing a mix of economic pressure and covert action as well as conventional military strength—was tested and refined.

In Iran, American economic interests had always been small; Britain held tightly to its petroleum monopoly in that oil-rich land. But in 1951 Iranian Prime Minister Mohammed Mossadegh nationalized Britain's Anglo-Iranian Oil Company. The State Department feared that the precedent of nationalization might ultimately affect America's own holdings in Saudi Arabia or elsewhere and thereby damage the "free world" economy. The CIA, which had previously received explicit orders to make the protection of American-owned supplies of raw materials one of its prime duties, went to work organizing and financing opposition to Mossadegh. Kermit Roosevelt, the grand-nephew of Theodore, orchestrated one of the CIA's most stunning "successes." In a swift operation in 1953, CIA agents brought crowds into the streets, forced Mossadegh out of office, and reinstalled their friend, Shah Reza Pahlevi. Under the terms of a renegotiated oil contract American companies came out holding 40 percent of the Iranian oil concession previously held by British Petroleum, and the Shah launched a "modernization" program closely wedded to American corporate interests.

Events in Iran enabled the major oil companies to convince the Eisenhower administration to drop a large antitrust suit against them. In 1953 Eisenhower told his attorney general that because the giant oil companies supplied an essential commodity to the "free world," the enforcement of antitrust laws "may be deemed secondary to the national security interest." Iran's attempted nationalization thus proved timely and doubly beneficial to the American-dominated international oil cartel, a cartel that—at that time—controlled the world price of oil.

Success in Iran encouraged the Eisenhower administration to expand its use of the CIA. Headed by John Foster Dulles' brother Allen, the CIA escalated the use of subversion as a tactic against foreign enemies. It became clear that Ike's New Look extended toward the Soviet Union but that in the Third World covert action seemed the best substitute for outright military involvement.

Guatemala loomed as the next test of what the CIA could accomplish with covert operations. Guatemalan President Jacobo Arbenz, who had been legally elected on a reform platform, challenged United Fruit Company's longstanding dominance in his country by threatening to nationalize lands that the company had allowed to remain idle and unproductive. And as in Iran, American business interests and government policymakers easily confused nationalistic reform with communism. Dulles, himself closely connected with the fruit company, saw Guatemala as one more battle in the global struggle to contain communism, and Eisenhower, who knew little about Latin America, accepted Dulles' oversimplification and incorrectly perceived Arbenz as controlled by communists. Ike authorized and the CIA carried out a covert 1954 operation that included economic strangulation, psychological warfare, and the funding of a pro-U.S., conservative armed force to carry out a coup. Under these pressures the Arbenz government collapsed and an oppressive dictatorship friendly to the United States government and to United Fruit was saddled on the country.

United States-backed repression, however, only aggravated social hatreds in Guatemala and elsewhere. During Richard Nixon's goodwill tour of Latin America in 1958, for example, thousands of Venezuelans mobbed the vice-president's car in Caracas, upsetting not only Cadillac limousines but also American illusions. In response, Eisenhower supported creation of the Inter-American Development Bank, and the State Department stopped awarding medals to dictator allies and shifted its praises to such liberal reformers as Venezuela's Rómulo Betancourt. But only the image changed. American economic policies and military aid continued, in the name of anticommunism, to strengthen oligarchs and their military allies against rising popular demands for economic and political reforms.

As another part of its effort to contain communist influence, the Eisenhower administration tried to frame a general doctrine that would extend American protection into the Middle East, a region still reeling from the aftershocks of the Suez crisis and the Iranian coup. After weeks of dickering during the spring of 1957, Congress authorized the president to defend countries in the Middle East "against overt armed aggression from any nation controlled by international communism." This new "Eisenhower Doctrine" hardly fit with the political realities of this area, in which older imperial tensions, regional and religious distrust, and the rise of fervent nationalism shaped events more than did superpower contests. But the Eisenhower Doctrine, like the Truman Doctrine before it, forced complex events into simple molds and made it easy to label any local challenge to American interests as communist aggression.

During the summer of 1958, when rioting broke out in the small Middle Eastern country of Lebanon, the doctrine had its first test. Lebanon's government blamed the riots on saboteurs from the newly organized United Arab Republic (Egypt and Syria), but animosity between Christian and Moslem, city and countryside, Nasserites and moderates had long ago turned the tiny land into a tinderbox. Then nationalists in Iraq murdered King Faisal and his premier, Nuri el-Said. Iraq's new anti-Western leaders renounced ties with Washington and made overtures to the UAR. As violence in the Middle East accelerated, the established elements in Lebanon and Jordan asked the United States and Britain to "stabilize" the situation. Both powers quickly complied, anxious to check Nasserism and protect their dangerously exposed oil pipelines. Over 14,000 marines eventually waded ashore on Lebanese beaches in an intervention notable for its bloodlessness and short-range success. American troops set up a new, strongly anti-Nasser government in Beirut, and in Jordan the British restored King Hussein's control over Jordan's army.

Despite its superficial success, the Anglo-American intrusion provoked new fears of Western imperialism. The Eisenhower Doctrine may ultimately have pushed some Arab nationalists toward Moscow. Other Arabs began to turn away from the United States, not because they were procommunist, but because they suspected American motives.

American policy did not contain revolution everywhere. In fact, a leftist revolt succeeded in a place long considered a secure outpost of America's informal empire—Cuba. In 1959 a guerrilla leader, Fidel Castro, converted his mountaintop rebellion into a social revolution that not only deposed Cuba's dictator, Fulgencio Batista, but also ended the island's dependence upon the United States. The Cuban revolution at first attracted sympathy from many Americans. The rich sugar crop had benefited foreigners and Cuba's upper class, while the working population had suffered low wages and miserable living conditions. Batista's regime had grown notoriously corrupt. The prospect of honest government, social justice, and land redistribution provided support for the bearded, thirty-two-year-old Castro, like Nasser a charismatic leader. Initially welcomed by many Americans as an alternative to the repressive Batista, Castro soon encountered hostility as he tried to reduce his country's economic dependence on the United States. After a disagreement with some American companies, Castro nationalized their holdings; Eisenhower retaliated by curtailing the amount of Cuban sugar the United States would import; Castro stepped up nationalization and turned toward the Soviet Union for aid. By the time the spiral of deteriorating relations ended, Castro had nationalized over a billion dollars worth of Yankee assets, taken deadly reprisals against thousands as "enemies of the people," and frightened most of the Cuban upper-middle class into exile in Florida. During a visit to the United States, Castro appealed to America's racial minorities to follow his example. Later he joined hands with Khrushchev at the United Nations.

While some Ameicans wondered whether Castro was a true communist or had been driven to Moscow by United States intransigence, the Republicans moved methodically to drive him from power. Eisenhower ended American imports of Cuban sugar, which had maintained the island's prices above world market levels. Under great pressure from Washington, the Organization of American States expelled Cuba, thus cutting off all aid to Castro's regime from the OAS. These heavy-handed measures only reaffirmed the Cuban people's belief in Castro and forced him to rely upon the Soviets. Anxious to take advantage of American blunders and, no doubt, to check domestic critics, Khrushchev bought up Cuba's sugar crop in 1960 at an inflated price. CIA operatives began training a Cuban invasion force in Guatemala and plotting various kinds of sabotage against Castro's regime, but threats of American intervention only justified a further swing to the left by Castro. Shortsighted containment in the Caribbean, no less than in the Middle East, produced nationalist reactions often hostile to American goals.

REEVALUATION

On October 4, 1957, the Soviet Union orbited the first space satellite, Sputnik I; a month later Sputnik II, which weighed over 1300 pounds and carried a live dog, spent several days in space. The accuracy and large payload of the Russian rockets caused alarm throughout America because of the potential military implications. Most high officials recognized that America's manned bombers far outclassed Soviet defense systems. Though spectacular, Sputnik in no concrete way threatened the safety of the United States. Still, Sputnik proved a powerful symbol: Coming amidst a recession, it ended America's easy confidence in its technological ascendance and created new, oftentimes exaggerated fears of Soviet strength.

A sense of vulnerability pervaded American life. The Sputnik satellites frightened the Pentagon into deploying intermediate-range rockets in Britain, Turkey, and Italy. The Defense Department also channeled more and more money into research-and-development programs. Long restive about New Look economies, some military people publicly worried about the emphasis on bombers and carrier-based fighters. General Maxwell Taylor, army chief of staff, argued for "armament in depth" so that the United States could fight "low-level, conventional battles" if nuclear stalemate produced "brush-fire wars on the periphery of the free world." Sensing political advantage, many liberal Democrats saw more military spending as a means to stimulate the postwar economy. Defense intellectuals, gathered into research institutes by governments and universities, explained that atomic armaments required constant technological innovation to keep pace with scientific discoveries. The Korean War had spawned an industry dependent upon arms contracts. Research-and-development money produced ever more complicated weapons. Powerful interests in such politically important areas as Long Island, Texas, and Southern California pressed to increase lucrative defense production.

This combination of American generals, Democratic politicians, defense intellectuals, and enterprising business leaders coalesced into a powerful group that lobbied for more and more armaments. Eisenhower's immense prestige, and his skepticism about Pentagon claims, temporarily quieted the clamor. But opponents of the New Look wondered whether Eisenhower's economies had not misled the country. Gradually, the idea spread that the United States suffered a "missile gap" vis-à-vis the Soviet Union, a false analysis that John F. Kennedy nonetheless used as an election slogan against the Republicans in the election of 1960.

Eisenhower left the presidency a discouraged man. He confided to John F. Kennedy that "foreign affairs are in a mess" and warned the American people of "a burgeoning military-industrial complex." Eisenhower tried to be cost-conscious and to pursue peace, but he also launched an open-ended ideological crusade to refashion the world into a mold compatible with United States interests and greatly elaborated the government's foreign policy capabilities and techniques.

The more the Republicans tried to control world events during the 1950s, the more events seemed out of control. Massive retaliation did not guarantee security but instead required more and more doomsday weapons. A chain of anticommunist military alliances, the proliferation of bases abroad, and the growing role of the CIA entangled the United States in local complexities around the globe. Prosperity and a mellowing Russia diverted Western Europeans from the cold war and slowly ended their dependence upon Washington. The expansive rhetoric and international complexities of the 1950s heightened Americans' insecurities and set the stage for burgeoning defense spending and even more ambitious cold war crusading in the early 1960s.

SUGGESTIONS FOR FURTHER READING

Robert Divine, *Eisenhower and the Cold War* (1981), and Blanche Wiessen Cook, *The Declassified Eisenhower* (1981), offer two differing interpretations of the Republican president. See, also, Joanc P. Kreig, ed., *Dwight D. Eisenhower: Soldier, President and Statesman* (1987); H.W. Brands, *Cold Warriors: Eisenhower's Generation and American Foreign Policy* (1988).

The emphasis on covert operations may be seen in several general studies of the CIA: John Ranelagh, *The Agency* (1986); John Prados, *Presidents' Secret Wars* (1986); William Blum, *The CIA: A Forgotten History* (1986); Robin Winks, *Cloak and Gown: Scholars in the American Secret War, 1939–1961* (1987); Rhodi Jeffreys-Jones, *The CIA and American Democracy* (1989); and Loch K. Johnson, *America's Secret Power: The CIA in a Democratic Society* (1989).

More specialized works on the Eisenhower era include Douglas Kinnard, *President Eisenhower and Strategy Management: A Study in Defense Politics* (1977); Robert Divine, *Blowing in the Wind: The Nuclear Test-Ban Debate* (1978); Stephen Ambrose, *Ike's Spies* (1981); Stephen Schlesinger and Steve Kinzer, *Bitter Fruit* (1981); Richard H. Immerman, *The CIA in Guatemala* (1982); Burton F. Kaufman, *Trade and Aid: Eisenhower's Foreign Economic Policy* (1982); Richard E. Welch, Jr., *Response to Revolution: The United States and the Cuban Revolution, 1959–1961* (1985); Michael R. Beschloss, *Mayday: Eisenhower, Khrushchev, and the U-2 Affair* (1986); Richard A. Melanson and David Mayers, eds., *Reevaluating Eisenhower: American Foreign Policy in the Fifties* (1987); Stephen G. Rabe, *Eisenhower and Latin America: The Foreign Policy of Anticommunism* (1988); Richard G. Hewlett and Jack M. Holl, *Atoms for Peace and War, 1953–1961: Eisenhower and the Atomic Energy Commission* (1989); and William Rogers Louis and Roger Owen, eds., *Suez, 1956: The Crisis and Its Consequences* (1989).

On Eisenhower's controversial secretary of state, see Townshend Hoopes, *The Devil and John Foster Dulles* (1973); Ronald Pruessen, *John Foster Dulles* (1982); Mark Toulouse, *The Transformation of John Foster Dulles* (1985); and Richard Immerman, ed., *John Foster Dulles and the Diplomacy of the Cold War* (1990).

On the deepening U.S. involvement in Vietnam during the 1950s, see the opening chapters of George Herring, *America's Longest War* (1986); Andrew J. Rotter, *The Path to Vietnam* (1987); Lloyd C. Gardner, *Approaching Vietnam: From World War II Through Dien Bien Phu* (1988); Melanie Billings-Yun, *Decision Against War: Eisenhower and Dien Bien Phu* (1988). For works on the Korean War, see the suggested readings at the end of Chapter One.

The 1950s were a period of intense debate over the direction of U.S. foreign policy. Some of the various viewpoints may be found in Henry Kissinger, *Nuclear Weapons and Foreign Policy* (1957); Walt W. Rostow, *The United States in the World Arena* (1960); Maxwell Taylor, *An Uncertain Trumpet* (1960); and Robert Strausz-Hupe and others, *Protracted Conflict* (1961).

Memories include George B. Kistiakowsky, *A Scientist at the White House* (1976); Henry Cabot Lodge, Jr., *As It Was* (1976); and George F. Kennan, *Sketches from a Life* (1989).

Chapter Five

The Liberal Promise: JFK and LBJ

THE PRESIDENT WE HARDLY KNEW

A 1973 best-seller by one of John F. Kennedy's former aides expressed a common sentiment: *Johnny We Hardly Knew Ye.* The title was revealing. The Kennedy administration was always shrouded in legend, and books by his associates helped the myths grow larger. Only recently have historians begun to peek through the clouds of adulation that surrounded the thirty-fifth president.

Few fathers groom their children to be president, but wealthy Joseph P. Kennedy wanted one of his sons to gain the nation's highest office. When his oldest boy died during World War II, his other war-hero son picked up the family colors. John Kennedy attended an elite prep school and then graduated from Harvard, all while refining his social graces and developing a tough-minded view of public affairs. He also displayed an intolerance for those who did not share his pragmatic approach. People who could not say what they had to say quickly, who moralized or digressed, irritated John Kennedy. How could people who took so long to make up their mind do great things? Kennedy always surrounded himself with bright, ambitious young people who shared his distaste for sentimentality. The "public" Kennedy—idealistic, inspirational, and sometimes emotional—was very different from the calculating, "private" politician from Boston.

Kennedy's narrow victory over Richard Nixon in 1960 capped a rather unimpressive political career. In 1946 JFK won election to the House of Representatives and six years later ousted a distinguished scion of the Boston aristocracy, Henry Cabot Lodge, Jr., from the United States Senate. Kennedy considered the slow-moving, tradition-bound Senate undemanding and often boring. Kennedy usually supported generous expenditures for social welfare programs and championed a strong anticommunist foreign policy, but he sponsored no important legislative measures. During these years Kennedy did marry an attractive wife, who proved to be an important political asset, and he wrote a prize-winning book—*Profiles in Courage.* Between 1956 and 1960 Kennedy took full advantage of the new age of jet travel, personally visiting people in the Democratic party hierarchy and accumulating political debts that he could cash in during the 1960 presidential campaign. He and his close associates (the Irish mafia, some called them) put together a smooth-running organization that included pollster Louis Harris, speech writer Theodore Sorensen, the two younger Kennedy brothers, and a coterie of Harvard intellectuals.

The Election of 1960

The energetic Kennedy dominated the presidential campaign of 1960. As a politician Kennedy did few new things; he simply did the old ones better than other candidates. His speeches covered the standard postwar themes— the cold war with the Soviet Union, prosperity at home, and sacrifice for country—but they were cleverly phrased and, after some speaking lessons, effectively delivered. Kennedy's operatives employed old-fashioned arm twisting, and they generally knew just how much leverage to use and exactly where to apply it. Unlike Adlai Stevenson, who had let the Democratic convention choose his running mate in 1956, JFK made a highly political choice: Senate Majority Leader Lyndon Johnson of Texas. Even Kennedy's much-discussed "charisma" was not a new phenomenon; throughout the 1950s political observers had analyzed the charisma of President Eisenhower. But Kennedy's most distinctive qualities—his youth, good looks, and energy—did contrast his political image with that of the much older, more deliberate Eisenhower.

The Republican candidate, Eisenhower's vice-president Richard Nixon, tried to match his supposed maturity and experience against Kennedy's rather insubstantial political record. The tactic backfired in the widely heralded television debates: TV made the sharp-featured Nixon appear old and tired while it accentuated Kennedy's best qualities. The harsh lights highlighted Nixon's famous five o'clock shadow, leading some viewers to see him as "Tricky Dick," "the man you wouldn't buy a used car from." Most important, Kennedy's confident manner during the first debate undercut Nixon's claim about his opponent's immaturity. And though Nixon scrupulously avoided any hint of anti-Catholicism during the campaign, some of his supporters did not. Catholic voters tended to be Democrats anyway, and JFK piled up large Catholic majorities in several key states. The election of 1960 was still very close: Kennedy won by only 120,000 popular votes, and small shifts in several large states would have made Nixon president. The unexpectedly narrow victory probably increased Kennedy's political caution.

Camelot: The New Frontier

Although Kennedy could hardly claim a popular mandate, his publicists quickly built an imposing image for his administration—the "New Frontier," the energetic successor to the New Deal and the Fair Deal. First, JFK assembled his version of Roosevelt's brain trust. He appointed his brother and campaign manager, Robert Kennedy, attorney general; Robert McNamara, president of Ford Motor Company, became secretary of defense; Harvard's McGeorge Bundy assumed the important role of national security adviser to the president; and Dean Rusk, head of the Ford Foundation, got the coveted position of secretary of state. Even the secondary jobs claimed top individuals. (Henry Kissinger found himself outgunned in such fierce competition and took over Bundy's courses at Harvard, awaiting an administration that would better appreciate his talents.) Vice-President Johnson left the first cabinet meeting dazzled by the intellect that Kennedy had assembled. "You should have seen all those men," he told his old political mentor, House Speaker Sam Rayburn. "Well, Lyndon, you may be right and they may be every bit as intelligent as you say," replied Rayburn, "but I'd feel a whole lot better about them if just one of them had run for sheriff once."

The Kennedy White House became celebrated as a center of art and culture. Jacqueline Kennedy, a well-educated woman who spoke several languages, became the special guardian of culture: She invited artists such as cellist Pablo Casals to perform at the White House, redecorated the old mansion, and then conducted a tour of it for millions of television viewers. The Kennedy parties were lavish productions in the grand style; I.F. Stone, the dissenting journalist, complained that the atmosphere resembled that of "a reigning monarch's court." Such a comparison probably did not disturb Kennedyphiles. Many of the president's followers reveled in the reputation of the Kennedy White House as a modern-day Camelot.

In addition to intellect and style, the New Frontier emphasized toughness. John Kennedy boasted in his inaugural address that he and his advisers were all young men "born in this century, tempered by war, disciplined by a hard and bitter peace." Facing the challenges of a dangerous world, they believed that they could not afford to appear soft. In defending his space program, for example, JFK bragged that Americans would accept the challenges of space "not because they are easy but because they are hard." The Kennedy team displayed its toughness during impromptu touch football games; here the president's brother Robert gained the reputation as a hard-nosed scrapper who had no room for losers. After Floyd Patterson lost his heavyweight boxing title, the attorney general quickly removed the ex-champ's picture from his office.

All the Kennedy people boasted of their ability to handle any foreign or domestic crisis, and they seemed almost anxious to find them. In 1962 Kennedy massed the full power of the national government to combat a price increase by United States Steel and several other large firms. JFK denounced the companies as unpatriotic, contrasting their actions with the sacrifices of military officers who were already dying in Vietnam and reservists who had been called up to meet a feared confrontation with the Soviet Union in Berlin. The president coupled his verbal assaults with a massive legal offensive: The Justice Department sought evidence of price fixing; FBI agents started to investigate possible illegal activities by steel corporations; the Federal Trade Commission threatened to look into the same questions; and administration sources even hinted at antitrust actions to break up the steel giants. At the same time, the Defense Department refused to buy from companies that raised prices, and Kennedy aides pressured corporate friends to resist the lead of U.S. Steel. Confronted by this counterattack, Big Steel retreated and rolled back prices. Throughout the short skirmish the president viewed the controversy as an extension of foreign affairs, claiming that price increases threatened national security. It was the type of problem, he believed, that required crisis management.

The president's critics viewed the situation differently. Business representatives predictably denounced Kennedy for using "police state" tactics, but even some foes of large corporations expressed concern. A young law professor, Charles Reich (who would later gain fame as author of *The Greening of America*), argued that it was "dangerously wrong for an angry president to loose his terrible arsenal of power for the purposes of intimidation and coercing private companies and citizens." Other observers contended that Kennedy's actions reflected a dangerous crisis mentality and indicated a lack of consistent domestic policies. Within a year the steel firms raised prices twice, and the Kennedy administration did nothing.

Although JFK was more interested in foreign policy than in domestic affairs, he announced general goals for his New Frontier at home. The new Democratic administration revived many of Harry Truman's old Fair Deal proposals; federal aid to education, a national health program, and expansion of other welfare-state spending programs. Kennedy never saw educational or health programs or Medicare pass Congress, but he could take some credit for several less spectacular measures. Congress extended Social Security coverage to more American workers, covered more people by federal wage standards, raised the minimum wage to $1.25 an hour, appropriated nearly $5 billion for public housing, established the manpower training program, and passed an area-redevelopment act for West Virginia and other impoverished areas in Appalachia. These measures reflected JFK's preference for moderate, gradual reforms and his political caution.

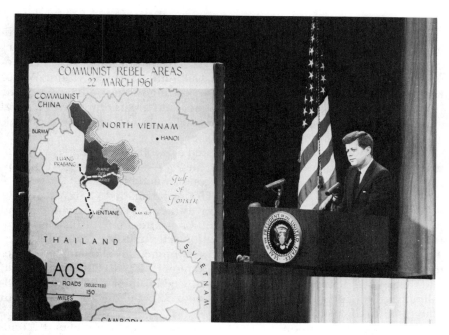

John F. Kennedy's Press Conference, 1961. Breaking with the practice of his predecessors, JFK held frequent press conferences. But he never completely revealed his administration's policies in Indo-China. Source: *National Archives.*

Kennedy also helped revive activism related to women's rights by appointing a Presidential Commission on the Status of Women, headed by Eleanor Roosevelt. The commission's report, issued in 1963, documented the discrimination in employment, the legal inequality, and the paucity of social services such as child care that kept women in subordinate status. The resultant Equal Pay Act of 1963 made it illegal for employers to compensate men and women at different rates of pay for the same job. Although equal pay legislation did not significantly raise the economic status of working women—most of whom were employed in job categories that included no men—the issue of economic inequality had at least been made a public issue. The commission's work spurred state governments to undertake similar studies and helped galvanize a new generation of activists on behalf of women's rights.

In addition to updating the Fair Deal's gradualist social welfare programs, the Kennedy administration tried to redefine the techniques of Truman's liberal economists. In his first state-of-the-union address, JFK promised that the sluggish economy would soon show both "a prompt recovery" and "long-range growth." Kennedy, of course, blamed the country's economic problems on the Eisenhower administration: The GNP had risen too slowly during the late 1950s, while the unemployment rate had climbed to around 6 percent. Although Kennedy shared Eisenhower's limited background in economics—JFK had received a C in his introductory economics course at Harvard—he gathered a distinguished group of economic advisers, including John Kenneth Galbraith of Harvard and Walter Heller of the University of Minnesota. According to these advocates of the "new economics," the national government could use its power over federal expenditures and its controls over monetary policy to promote economic growth and to "fine-tune" the economy.

The Kennedy administration adopted a number of strategies for stimulating economic growth and creating new jobs. Increased government spending pumped vital funds into the economy and brightened the general economic picture. In 1962 the White House persuaded Congress to give businesses a 7 percent tax credit for investments in new machinery and plants. At the same time, the administration granted one of business's top requests—the readjustment of depreciation schedules for corporate taxes. This action encouraged purchases of new equipment by allowing businesses to write off assets more quickly. Taken together, the investment tax credit and the revised depreciation schedules reduced business taxes and theoretically increased corporate spending by about $2.5 billion; the total tax cut amounted to almost 12 percent.

Although the economy picked up considerably, many liberal economists called for further steps to boost production and employment. John Kenneth Galbraith, who had become ambassador to India, continued to urge massive government expenditures for social welfare programs. Kennedy rejected this approach but did consider further tax cuts. A cut in tax revenues would increase the federal deficit; it would also, however, expand purchasing power for both consumers and businesses. Heller, who became head of the Council of Economic Advisers, and Paul Samuelson, an influential economist at MIT, were among those who urged an immediate tax reduction to ward off a possible recession. But advocates of a balanced federal budget, particularly Treasury Secretary C. Douglas Dillon and Federal Reserve Chairman William McChesney Martin, rejected this example of the new economics, and Kennedy finally shelved the proposal for 1962. The following year, however, the administration unveiled a comprehensive revenue bill that did include a $10 billion tax cut and tax reforms.

Kennedy's carefully calculated approach to social and economic problems reflected his basic assumptions about the new role of liberal government. The "old sweeping issues have largely disappeared," he told Yale's graduating class in 1962. Basic domestic problems were now "more subtle and less simple": how to manage a complex economy; how to ensure increasing productivity and rising prosperity for all citizens. The "sophisticated and technical questions involved in keeping a great economic machinery moving ahead" required "technical answers—not political answers." Rational bureaucrats, the cool technicians who could manage complex institutions, held the keys to effective government. Although his tenure in office tempered some of his early optimism, John Kennedy died confident that his view of government remained correct and that Camelot's bright young people could solve most problems.

Assassination

On November 22, 1963, the presidential motorcade was winding its way past unexpectedly friendly crowds in Dallas when a volley of shots—some claimed three, others four or five—raked Kennedy's open-topped limousine. Texas Governor John Connally was seriously wounded, and one shot ripped away the top of Kennedy's head. Within an hour doctors at Parkland Hospital pronounced the president dead; the thousand days of Camelot were over. Aboard Air Force One, Vice-President Lyndon Baines Johnson took the oath of office as the new chief executive.

News of the president's death stunned the nation. For two days people watched an elaborate televised memorial, and most people's respect for their fallen leader grew. Pictures of Kennedy's coffin, his riderless horse, and his grieving family clashed with scenes from Kennedy's past. Images of a vibrant JFK—sailing off Cape Cod, laughing with his children, or facing down the Russians—made his death seem all the more tragic. The Kennedy mystique grew.

The television spectacle also began to raise doubts about the cause of JFK's death. Within hours after the assassination, Dallas police officials announced the capture of Lee Harvey Oswald. A former marine who had lived in the Soviet Union for a short time, Oswald steadfastly proclaimed his innocence. On Sunday, November 24, while Dallas police were transferring Oswald to a new jail, millions of television viewers witnessed the assassination of a Kennedy's alleged assassin. A local nightclub operator with ties to organized crime, Jack Ruby, fatally shot Oswald at close range in the Dallas police station.

Oswald's bizarre death raised further doubts about his guilt. Was he part of a larger conspiracy? Was Kennedy's death somehow tied to pro- or anti-Castro forces? Was Ruby a hit man sent to silence Oswald? Were the Dallas police, or the CIA, or the FBI, part of some "plot"? Wanting to squelch such rumors quickly, President Johnson persuaded Chief Justice Earl Warren to head an official inquiry. After a ten-month investigation, the Warren Commission named Oswald the lone assassin and rejected evidence of any broader plot. Conspiracy buffs, however, were already offering an amazing variety of scenarios, and the Warren Commission Report merely gave them twenty-six volumes of evidence to piece through. More sober critics of the commission pointed out serious flaws in the hastily researched and sloppily documented report. Despite an intensive "sell" campaign conducted by the Johnson administration and the mass media, many Americans dismissed the Warren Commission's version of what had happened in

Dallas. Proponents of a conspiracy theory received some vindication when in 1979, a special committee of the House of Representatives concluded, on the basis of new evidence, that JFK had "probably" fallen victim to some kind of plot possibly involving organized crime figures. But the committee could offer little evidence about the details of the alleged conspiracy and Kennedy's killing remains a mystery.

THE GREAT SOCIETY

LBJ

When Teddy Roosevelt succeeded an earlier slain president, William McKinley, a conservative Republican expressed fears about "that damn cowboy"; sixty-two years later, many liberal Democrats felt much the same way about Lyndon Baines Johnson. Except for being a rich Democrat, LBJ had little in common with the cool, urbane Kennedy. Unlike JFK, Johnson loved the Senate, and during the 1950s he had dominated that body as its majority leader. John Kennedy always remembered how, as a senator, he had to beg Lyndon Johnson for favors. But despite years in Washington, Johnson never lost the earthy exuberance of "a good old boy from the ranch." (In his early White House days, Johnson showed a homemade film of deer mating and contributed his own ribald sound track.) A self-made entrepreneur, Johnson often was haunted by the hint of scandal. Critics snickered about "landslide Lyndon's" suspicious eighty-six-vote triumph in the 1948 senatorial primary, about his close association with convicted influence peddler Bobby Baker, and about his mysterious financial dealings throughout the Southwest. Lyndon Johnson came to Washington as an ambitious young politician attracted to Roosevelt's New Deal; he left as a former president and a multimillionaire. To some people LBJ looked too much like Jay Gatsby in a Stetson hat.

Johnson constantly worried about his public image. People would not give him "a fair shake as president," he often complained, "because I am a southerner." But Johnson realized that his problems lay deeper. "Why don't people like me?" he asked visitors to the White House. One elderly caller, who felt that his advanced years protected him, replied honestly: "Because, Mr. President, you are not a very likeable man." Defensive about his provincial roots in southwest Texas and perhaps still burdened by the conflicting childhood demands of his tough, hard-drinking father and his refined, intellectual mother, Johnson seemed to require constant reassurance. He also demanded unswerving loyalty from his subordinates. Among those around Johnson, no one wanted to be the bearer of bad news. He often flew into sudden rages, publicly berating staff members or arbitrarily summoning them at all hours of the night. He appeared to need the LBJ brand on everything. (His wife inherited the name Lady Bird, but LBJ christened his daughters Lynda Bird and Lucy Baines and called his dog Little Beagle.)

White House employees whom he suspected of antiwar sentiments dropped from favor, and only a few loyalists, such as Walt Rostow and Dean Rusk, stayed until the end. A critical reporter might receive the "Johnson treatment"—a private audience during which Johnson conducted a nonstop monologue on the glories of his presidency. A big man, the president liked to get close to his listeners, overwhelming them by sheer size.

Johnson smoothly handled the transition from the Kennedy administration, but after 1964 he watched his popularity decline steadily. Johnson often blamed the media for what became known as his "credibility gap." Stories about Johnson's pettiness, vanity, and duplicity colored people's perception of the president. Most reporters had genuinely liked Kennedy and had sometimes pigeonholed unfavorable stories about his policies and personal life. But Johnson, like Richard Nixon after him, considered himself the target of unfair reporting by journalists who compared Johnson unfavorably with the still untarnished image of JFK as well as with the vigorous reality of the Kennedy family. John Kennedy's youngest brother, Edward, represented Massachusetts in the Senate, and in 1964 Robert Kennedy overcame charges of being a carpetbagger to win election to the Senate from New York. The Kennedys only thinly veiled their distaste for Johnson, and many reporters expressed more sympathy for "Camelot-in-exile"—the intellectuals and politicians who swarmed around Bobby's home at Hickory Hill and Kennedy family compound on Cape Cod—than for Lyndon Johnson's entourage.

Toward the end of his presidency, as controversy over Vietnam obsessed both the president and the press, many people forgot Lyndon Johnson's domestic accomplishments and positive qualities. He could take much credit for the Great Society legislation passed between 1964 and 1968, and even most critics conceded his sincere commitment to social and racial justice. For all his faults, Johnson was an intelligent, complex, sensitive man. The American people, particularly the opinion-making elites, probably misunderstood Lyndon Johnson as much as he misunderstood them. He was, according to one observer of his last years, a tortured man who was torn between his fervent, populist hopes and his meaner, less noble impulses.

The Johnson Program

Lyndon Johnson moved to fulfill JFK's promise of promoting rapid economic growth. Aided by a reduction in taxes (the Tax Act of 1964, of course, was originally a Kennedy proposal) and by increased federal spending (particularly for the expanding war in Southeast Asia), the economy built upon gains begun under Kennedy. Between 1960 and 1964 the gross national product increased by 24 percent while corporate profits went up by 57 percent; the next year the GNP climbed by almost 7 percent and corporate profits by 20 percent; and by 1965 the nation reached what most economists considered "full" employment, an unemployment rate less than 4 percent. The boom lasted throughout Johnson's second term: Unemployment never exceeded 4 percent, and the GNP expanded at a rate of almost 5 percent a year. The median family income, measured in constant dollars, increased from $8,543 in 1963 to $10,768 in 1969.

Not everyone was impressed by the Kennedy-Johnson boom. Some economists warned that the expansion was too rapid and that the Johnson administration was ignoring the threat of inflation. Others argued that LBJ's economic wizardry was largely a fraud. Truman's old economic adviser Leon Keyserling contended that the Tax Act of 1964, which came out of Congress without most of its original reforms, primarily assisted the wealthy. According to Keyserling's calculations, the average taxpayer in the $10,000 income bracket received only a 3.5 percent increase in disposable income; in contrast, the taxpayer who earned $100,000 enjoyed a boost of 16.5 percent and the very wealthy, those in the $200,000 category, got a 31.1 percent windfall. Keyserling charged that the nation's basic economic problem remained an inequitable distribution of income. Radical economists concurred. Citing the tremendous rise in corporate profits during the Kennedy-Johnson years, they noted that large corporations were the primary beneficiaries of the high-growth policies of the "new economics."

Lyndon Johnson, the man who sincerely wanted to be "president of all the people," saw the situation differently. Of course, large businesses would benefit from economic expansion, but so would middle-income workers and budding entrepreneurs. And galloping prosperity enabled the country to advance beyond the limited goals of Truman and Kennedy and extend greater assistance to the very poor in the best LBJ style—with great breast-beating and with promises of much government money. Buoyed by his early successes and the economic boom, LBJ claimed "a broad, deep and genuine consensus among most groups within our diverse society" on behalf of his programs.

If only everyone would "sit down and reason together," they could realize the Great Society. Speaking in the spring of 1964 before an outdoor crowd of almost 100,000 people, LBJ heralded the coming of a society "where the meaning of our lives matches the marvelous products of our labor . . . a place where men are more concerned with the quality of their goals than the quantity of their goods." Even John Kennedy's speechwriters might have blushed at this rhetoric, but JFK had never approached the carload of legislative measures that LBJ rolled through Congress in 1964 and 1965.

In the wake of Kennedy's death and LBJ's own landslide triumph over Republican Barry Goldwater in 1964, Johnson broke a congressional stalemate that dated back many years. Never in recent memory had Congress done so much so quickly. When Johnson left Washington in 1969 his cabinet gave him a plaque commemorating the more than two hundred "landmark laws" passed during his administration. In LBJ's first full year alone, Congress approved the Tax Act of 1964, a new civil rights law, federally sponsored recreation programs, funds for urban mass transit, and the Economic Opportunity Act (the measure that signaled the beginning of Johnson's War on Poverty). And this was merely the prelude to the Great Society programs that Johnson took to the nation in the 1964 presidential race.

The Johnson Landslide

The Republicans graciously handed Johnson the 1964 election. Militant conservatives, most of whom lived in the "rim states" from southern California to Florida or in isolated enclaves in the Middle West, gained control of the GOP. Bragging that they would offer the nation "a choice, not an echo," they nominated Senator Barry Goldwater of Arizona. The hero of most conservatives, Goldwater soon acquired a reputation as an injudicious extremist. During a series of bitter primary campaigns, some of his over-zealous supporters reinforced this image by vehemently attacking more liberal Republicans, particularly New York's Nelson Rockefeller. When Rockefeller rose to address the GOP's 1964 convention, Goldwaterites in the galleries shouted him down. Goldwater's acceptance speech only increased doubts about his candidacy. "Extremism in the defense of liberty," he challenged his critics, "is no vice. . . . Moderation in the pursuit of justice is no virtue."

Goldwater ran squarely against Johnson's brand of liberalism. Ever since the New Deal, Republican candidates had ritualistically denounced the central government in Washington, but Goldwater really seemed to mean it. His strategists—highly disciplined professionals who emulated JFK's campaign techniques—hoped that a militantly conservative campaign would bring millions of alienated people to the polls and attract a blacklash vote from whites who were frightened by the anti-discrimination movement. A Goldwater administration, the senator from Arizona appeared to say, would sweep away all the baneful welfare programs established since the New Deal: agricultural subsidies, prolabor union legislation, civil rights laws, and all the other "socialistic" laws. "I will give you back your freedom," he promised. On several occasions he even hinted at making Social Security voluntary, a position that Democrats falsely translated into the charge that Goldwater planned to abolish the entire system. At the same time, missile-rattling statements about taking care of the USSR and gaining a quick victory in Vietnam enabled Democrats to paint Goldwater as a trigger-happy Neanderthal.

With the moderate center of the electorate deserting the Republican party, Johnson and his running mate, Senator Hubert Humphrey of Minnesota, recorded a landslide victory. The Democratic presidential ticket gathered 61.3 percent of the popular ballots and the electoral votes of all but six states. At the same time, Democrats gained thirty-nine seats in the House of Representatives and gained more than five hundred new seats in state legislatures across the country. Johnson celebrated his "politics of consensus," and some nervous Republicans even feared that the "Goldwater caper" might destroy the GOP.

The Great Society and the War on Poverty

After his smashing victory, LBJ pushed more Great Society measures through the new Eighty-ninth Congress. Medicare and Medicaid programs fulfilled Harry Truman's goal of some type of government-sponsored health care for people over sixty-five and for the very poor. Two other long-debated measures, the Elementary and Secondary Education Act and the Higher Education Act, extended federal funds to schools at all levels of the educational hierarchy. The Voting Rights Act of 1965 eliminated barriers against black voters in the South: It suspended literacy tests and authorized use of federal inspectors in areas where the attorney general suspected chicanery in voting procedures. To deal with urban decay, Congress passed the Housing Act of 1965, which created the new Department of Housing and Urban Development (HUD), and the Demonstration Cities and Metropolitan Development Act of 1966, which provided federal money for local "model city" projects. Prodded by advocates of automobile safety, Congress passed several bills dealing with highway and traffic safety. One measure, the Motor Vehicle Safety Act (1966), inaugurated federal safety standards for the auto industry and established a uniform grading system for tire manufacturers. As in the case of urban problems, Congress also created a new cabinet department—that of transportation—and gave its secretary the tasks of coordination and enforcement. Finally, Congress passed a number of "minor" pieces of legislation such as a new immigration act, which admitted newcomers primarily on the basis of their economic skills rather than their national origin, and the Truth in Packaging Act, which provided consumers with some protection against deceptive advertising practices.

Most people readily accepted these programs, measures once labeled "socialistic," as integral parts of an expanded welfare state. Controversies still erupted over details—how much Medicare patients should pay from their own pockets, or how quickly automakers should comply with safety standards—but few people suggested repeal of these Great Society laws. Much to LBJ's displeasure the loudest complaints came from social activists who charged that the programs required only minimal sacrifices from wealthy, corporate groups and provided too little assistance for needy citizens. Ralph Nader, for example, claimed that auto manufacturers blocked truly effective safety laws while using the cost of minimal improvements as an excuse to raise their prices. And despite all Lyndon Johnson's promises, basic needs such as better mass transportation systems and effective urban housing programs remained only dreams.

In addition to expanding the welfare state, Johnson launched a crusade of his own—elimination and prevention of poverty. Because of their material abundance, middle-class Americans had largely forgotten that one-fourth to one-fifth of the population, mostly white people, still lived in substandard housing and subsisted on inadequate diets. Michael Harrington's *The Other America* helped spark concern for the poor, and Johnson declared his own War on Poverty. At first glance, the array of programs seemed impressive: federal funds for public-works projects, particularly new highways in Appalachia; a Job Corps to train young people who lacked marketable skills; Work-Study, a program to supplement the incomes of college students; Volunteers in Service to America (VISTA), which would send young volunteers into impoverished areas; and Head Start, a program designed to provide compensatory education for preschoolers from "disadvantaged" families. Although these measures went far beyond any previous national efforts, even the programs' supporters conceded their traditionalist approach to social problems. In providing federal money and another federal agency (the Office of Economic Opportunity, or OEO), the Great Society borrowed the techniques of the New and Fair Deals.

One part of the War on Poverty, the Community Action Program (CAP), did represent a significant change in federal policy. Under Title II of the Economic Opportunity Act, Congress authorized funds for local groups—either private nonprofit or public organizations—that developed innovative programs to cure the symptoms of poverty. Sounding a theme that Richard Nixon and Ronald Reagan would later adapt to their own purposes, President Johnson argued that CAP rested upon "the fact that local citizens best understand their own problems and know best how to deal with these problems." At first, many people praised CAP as an attempt to check the extension of federal power into local affairs. Many poor people looked forward to being able to plan their own improvements.

The War on Poverty brought Lyndon Johnson—or the poor—few clear-cut victories. Many Republicans and blue-collar Democrats denounced the poverty program for giving money to people allegedly too lazy to help themselves. ("Yeah, I helped the War on Poverty," went one lame joke of the mid-1960s. "I threw a hand grenade at a bum.") Actually much of the available money went to white-collar bureaucrats or into expensive equipment. After their stints in public service, some antipoverty workers established consulting firms that received government contracts for "expert" advice on the problems of poverty. Early in the fight, some social critics declared that the "poverty-industrial" complex was a far bigger winner than the poor.

The widely heralded CAP also produced mixed results. Established welfare agencies and local political leaders opposed grants of funds to new community groups. When some of the CAP organizations espoused militant demands such as redistribution of wealth and political power, OEO's bureaucrats quickly sided with the vested interests and against poor people themselves. Even radicals, after all, could hardly expect the "establishment" to finance its own overthrow. In time, OEO placed more emphasis on "prepackaged programs" from Washington, such as Head Start, community-beautification projects, and legal aid, and employed local CAP groups as administrators rather than innovators.

Though Lyndon Johnson would not admit it, the nation simply could not wage both a war in Vietnam and one against domestic poverty without increased taxes. As a result of Johnson's determination not to hike taxes, the entire nation soon faced a rising rate of inflation, and the poor saw funding for social programs slowly level off. Federal expenditures for social programs, measured in proportion to the country's GNP, did increase between 1965 and 1975, but the sums appropriated never matched those LBJ had once projected, or those apparently needed to conquer poverty.

More than twenty-five years after Lyndon Johnson sounded his battle cry, historians and students of public policy continue to disagree about the exact results—and the larger meaning—of the conflict. Defenders of the basic premises behind the Great Society heralded its successes. They insisted that the goals were realistic, that the programs were managed with reasonable efficiency, that they provided tangible benefits to recipients, and that the Great Society demonstrated the untapped potential of welfare-liberalism. For example, by the middle of the 1980s, voting rights laws guaranteed that blacks, 90 percent of whom were effectively disenfranchised in 1965, could cast ballots, including ones for the more than 6000 black officeholders. Medicaid provided minimal health care for the poor, and Medicare offered coverage, albeit incomplete, for the elderly. Twenty years after the Great Society began, studies by the Census Bureau found more than 15 percent of all households in the country receiving benefits from Johnson-era programs.

But positive evaluations of the Great Society's accomplishments met stiff opposition, from analysts both to the left and the right of welfare-liberalism. To the conservative social scientist Edward Banfield, author of the highly controversial *Unheavenly City*, continuation of the programs begun under the Great Society could do little to deal with hard-core poverty, with the people Banfield called "the underclass." Social reforms by "guilt-ridden" liberals, Banfield claimed, only raised the expectations of the poor to "unreasonable and unrealizable" levels. Although critics from the left rejected this critique as a classic example of blaming the victims for their plight, many did come to distrust those liberal reformers who were committed to "doing good," even after it became clear that benevolence from above would not really liberate the poor. Liberal reformers, the radical critics of the Great Society argued, wrongly assumed that with a helping hand from the national government most poor people could work their way out of poverty. But bureaucratic programs, VISTA volunteers, and other "service strategies" were of minimal help, radicals claimed. The only sure cure for inequality, contended the sociologist Christopher Jencks, was a program for redistributing income.

But despite their rhetoric about curing poverty and achieving equality, the Great Society's liberals opposed any serious talk of redistribution of wealth, income, or political power. Their solution to what they themselves conceded was economic injustice remained essentially the same as Harry Truman's: Use the preexisting political machinery to promote economic expansion and try to target a portion of the new growth for social projects. The promise of an ever-growing economic pie could postpone, as it had in the 1940s, discussions about how large a slice should go to each citizen.

With the national government fighting a lengthy war overseas and a battle against inflation at home, an antipoverty program predicated upon an ever-expanding economy and upon steadily increasing expenditures for social welfare could not run its charted course. Some gains were made; even the program's severest critics allowed this. Yet even the Great Society's most enthusiastic supporters had to confront the cold realities: The government's own figures on income distribution and various independent studies on the distribution of individual and family wealth suggested that the gap between the rich and the poor narrowed very little during the 1960s. Johnson's program did not change the basic socioeconomic structure, nor was it intended to do so. But neither did the Great Society reach its stated goal—to deal seriously with the problems of poverty and social injustice.

The Warren Court and Liberal Reform

The Supreme Court also discovered the difficulties of effecting social change from above. Chief Justice Earl Warren, appointed by Dwight Eisenhower in 1953, and his "activist" colleagues believed that they could forecast the path of social progress and hasten the coming of justice and equality. The result was a flood of landmark decisions during the years of the Warren Court.

Even before Lyndon Johnson became president, controversy surrounded the Supreme Court and Chief Justice Warren. The famous desegregation decision, *Brown* v. *Board of Education* (1954), angered segregationists throughout the country. In a series of decisions handed down in 1956 and 1957, a divided Court also affirmed the rights of alleged communists. Anticommunist crusaders denounced the Court, and the ultrareactionary John Birch Society erected billboards that demanded, "IMPEACH EARL WARREN." And when the Court appeared to reverse itself on the communist issue in the later 1950s, civil libertarians criticized the justices, particularly Felix Frankfurter, for caving in to popular pressures. Because of internal divisions and external pressures, the Warren Court established no clear pattern during the chief justice's first years on the bench.

During the 1960s, however, the liberal activists gained ascendancy. Led by Chief Justice Warren and two veteran justices, William O. Douglas and Hugo Black, the Court began to require state and local governments to conform to the guarantees of the national Bill of Rights. The activists recognized, for example, that effective legal protection remained largely a matter of one's income and social standing. Rich people could afford good lawyers and thereby gain valuable legal protection. Poor people rarely employed attorneys, and they faced powerful government institutions with inadequate knowledge of their rights. In *Gideon* v. *Wainwright* (1963) the Court held that states must furnish indigents with lawyers in felony cases. Such decisions expressed the activists' commitment to a single standard of due process and to the principle of equality before the law.

In addition, the Warren Court attempted to align constitutional law with the larger political assumptions of New Deal–Fair Deal liberalism. Beginning with *Baker* v. *Carr* (1962), a majority of justices held that malapportioned electoral districts deprived some voters of equal protection. *Baker* v. *Carr's* "one man, one vote" rule aimed at correcting situations in which rural districts with comparatively few people had the same legislative representation as populous urban districts. Hoping to encourage more vigorous scrutiny of public officials, the Court made it more difficult for politicians to sue their critics for libel (*New York Times* v. *Sullivan*, 1964). In a series of highly controversial decisions, the majority declared that Bible reading and prayer in public schools violated the First Amendment's prohibition against establishment of religion. Earl Warren was declaring God himself unconstitutional, grumbled conservatives. Their mood remained sour when the same Court struck down laws against obscenity. Despite all the criticism, however, the Court seemed to have consolidated its new position by the mid-1960s. The Kennedy-Johnson appointees—particularly Arthur Goldberg, Abe Fortas, and the court's first black justice, Thurgood Marshall—offset the increasing conservatism of Justice Black and appeared to ensure an activist, liberal majority for years to come.

Then, after 1966, the liberal majority collapsed. One of the Court's own decisions did much of the damage. In *Miranda* v. *Arizona* (1966) the Court held that once a police investigation focused upon a particular suspect, the authorities had to inform the defendant that he or she could remain silent, have a lawyer present during questioning, and request a free attorney provided by the state. More than any other decision, *Miranda* angered the Court's critics and united them around one emotional issue. The decision coincided with rising fear of "crime in the streets," and people blamed the Warren Court for handcuffing the police. Although criminologists easily demonstrated that such charges were without foundation, popular criticism and pressure from within the legal establishment increased. Congress considered legislation to overturn the *Miranda* decision, and politicians such as George Wallace and Richard Nixon promised to appoint new justices who would "interpret the Constitution strictly." (This meant, of course, judges who favored *less* strict protection of individual liberties and who opposed the political assumptions of the Warren majority.)

Amid all this controversy, Chief Justice Warren announced his impending retirement. President Johnson wanted to replace Warren with his old friend Abe Fortas and then appoint another crony, Homer Thornberry, to the Court. Anticipating a Nixon victory in the 1968 election, Republicans and many conservative southern Democrats tried to block Johnson's reshuffling. Their job became easy when *Life* magazine uncovered what appeared to be evidence of official misconduct by Justice Fortas. Johnson had to withdraw his nomination, and Fortas eventually resigned in disgrace. Newly elected President Nixon thus gained two vacancies on the Court—the chief justice's post (which went to Warren Burger) and Fortas's old seat (which was ultimately filled by another Minnesotan, Harry Blackmun).

Even before the demise of the activist majority, however, legal scholars were beginning to question the impact of the Warren Court's decisions.

Obviously the Justices had eliminated some gross inequities in the American legal system and had established stricter standards for law enforcement officials. But the Court lacked the means—as it always had and always will—to enforce its ruling to the letter. Police departments could effectively evade the *Miranda* decision; publicly appointed lawyers often acted more as agents of the prosecutor's office than as representatives of their clients; and local pressures often made broad First Amendment principles superfluous. In an even more fundamental sense, decisions by five well-meaning activists were not always effective tools for social engineering. New interpretations of the law of libel, for example, could not make every journalist into a vigorous crusader for the public interest, and reapportionment of state legislatures would not automatically produce more effective bodies. On the most explosive public issue of the late 1960s the Court took no position at all: It avoided ruling directly on cases that challenged the legality of the undeclared war in Vietnam. And though the Warren Court played a vital role in the early movement for legal and political equality, the justices had no independent power to effect the sweeping social and economic changes that militants came to demand. When the black revolution turned away from narrow legal issues, during the Johnson presidency, the judiciary could play only a limited role.

CIVIL RIGHTS TO BLACK POWER

Civil Rights: The Kennedy Years

Several other groups joined forces with Martin Luther King's SCLC in the early 1960s. The Congress of Racial Equality (CORE) had employed nonviolent civil disobedience as early as the 1940s; led by James Farmer and later by Floyd McKissick, it became more active during the early 1960s. Another group, the Student Nonviolent Coordinating Committee (SNCC), evolved from demonstrations in North Carolina during the winter of 1960. Black college students, polite and neatly dressed, unsuccessfully tried to eat at a dime store lunch counter. Braving hostile whites—who tossed lighted cigarettes, dumped ketchup, and threw punches—the young blacks remained seated, patiently waiting for service. The sit-in movement quickly spread to other kinds of public facilities as thousands of young activists, both white and black, joined the protests. In April 1960 a group of these students formed SNCC and accepted King's approach—nonviolent protest. Some of the early "freedom songs" expressed their optimism:

Freedom's Comin' and It Won't Be Long
We took a trip on a Greyhound bus,
Freedom's comin' and it won't be long
To fight segregation, this we must
Freedom's comin' and it won't be long.

> Violence in 'bama didn't stop our cause. . . .
> Federal marshals come enforce the laws. . . .
> On to Mississippi with speed we go. . . .
> Blue-shirted policemen meet us at the door. . . .
> Judge say local custom shall prevail. . . .
> We say 'no' and we land in jail. . . .

The election of John Kennedy in 1960 seemed to offer hope of greater support of the civil rights movement from Washington. During his campaign JFK criticized the Eisenhower administration's reluctant support of integration and promised a new frontier for African-Americans. Once in office, he appointed a number of prominent blacks to federal positions, filed more desegregation suits than his predecessor, and supported a new civil rights act. (The previous civil rights laws of 1957 and 1960 had dealt primarily with voting rights; Kennedy supported a measure that would ban discrimination in public accommodations and give the attorney general authority to file desegregation suits.)

Kennedy's political caution, however, influenced his racial policies. During the campaign he had denounced Eisenhower's refusal to issue an executive order ending discrimination in housing—Ike could do it with "a stroke of the pen," claimed Kennedy—but he delayed his own order for two years. Desiring good relations with southern members of Congress, Kennedy often deferred to them on patronage questions, appointing several outright racists to the federal bench. (One Mississippi judge referred to black civil rights workers as "monkeys" and consistently demeaned African-American defendants.)

Kennedy also refused to cross J. Edgar Hoover, permitting the FBI leader considerable leeway to set his own rules in civil rights cases. In effect, this meant that Hoover, no friend of civil rights groups, would do as little as possible to help African-Americans and to jeopardize his close relationship with segregationist law officers in the South. Without thorough background investigations by the FBI, the Justice Department often lacked evidence to prosecute cases of alleged disrimination. Meanwhile, Hoover steadily stepped up his bureau's surveillance on African-American groups and leaders, with Martin Luther King, Jr., becoming the increasing focus of the director's attention. Hoover pondered how he might neutralize the civil rights movement, and the FBI slowly mounted a campaign of wiretaps, surveillance, and harassment that eventually touched every aspect of the movement, especially the personal and political life of Dr. King.

Dramatic events in the Deep South, more than symbolic and bureaucratic moves in Washington, however, determined the pace of change. In 1961, young activists from CORE and SNCC defied the Jim Crow laws on interstate buses and in southern terminals. Angered by these "freedom riders," segregationists used iron bars, clubs, and finally explosives against the nonviolent protestors. Increasing racist violence finally forced the government to respond: Attorney General Robert Kennedy dispatched his Justice Department troubleshooters and a corps of federal marshals to protect the demonstrators. He also asked the Interstate Commerce Commission to end segregation in interstate facilities, a request that the ICC honored in the fall of 1961. The use of federal personnel to protect the freedom riders established a pattern, and the following year President Kennedy reinforced the marshals with United States Army troops in order to quell violence that followed the enrollment of a black student at the University of Mississippi. Kennedy's actions probably prevented bloodshed on other campuses—two people died during disorders at Ole Miss—and a confrontation at the University of Alabama in 1963 ended differently. After symbolically "standing in the schoolhouse door," Governor George Wallace—who had championed "segregation now and forever"—stepped aside and watched Justice Department officials integrate the university without serious incident.

In the spring of 1963 the focus of integration efforts shifted from southern college campuses to the streets of Birmingham, Alabama. The drive to desegregate public facilities in this Alabama industrial center marked an important turning point in the struggle for racial equality. Police violence escalated into savagery. Police Commissioner Eugene "Bull" Connor, who fit perfectly the northern stereotype of a redneck southern law officer, turned fire hoses and dogs upon black demonstrators, including small children. Club-swinging police rounded up thousands of protestors and threw them into makeshift lockups. White vigilantes unleashed a terror campaign that culminated in the bombing of a black church; four children at Sunday school died in the blast.

Covered extensively in the media, the events in Birmingham had a significant impact on racial politics. Appalled by the violence, liberal opinion in the North and in Congress swung behind new civil rights legislation. Ultimately, then, the police and segregationist violence in Birmingham rebounded against Bull Connor and his allies. Equally as important, the militancy of Birmingham's young blacks gave a new urgency to liberal efforts, in both Alabama and Washington, to calm racial conflict. Seeking to avoid further violence and bloodshed, leaders of Birmingham's white business community compromised: Three thousand imprisoned demonstrators were released, and the city's white power structure agreed to begin desegregation efforts. In Washington, John Kennedy told the nation that the "rising tide of discontent that threatens the public safety" could not be calmed by "repressive police action"; it was time, JFK urged, for Congress to act. He would press them, he pledged, to enact a strong civil rights program.

Calm returned to Birmingham, but the events there presaged important changes in racial politics. Some people in crowded urban slums had never really accepted the rhetoric of nonviolence, and many young blacks voiced displeasure with Dr. King's stated philosophy. In retrospect, Birmingham began the long period of urban violence that transformed both the black movement and its white supporters. On the other hand, Birmingham also brought a subtle change in the strategies of Dr. King and the SCLC. He and his associates recognized that any violent white response ultimately rebounded to their benefit. Although members of the SCLC never admitted it, their organization turned increasingly toward "nonviolent provocation," a strategy designed to exploit coverage by the media and to use racist violence in the cause of civil rights. The SCLC relied upon this approach during their 1965 crusade in Selma, Alabama, a voter registration drive that helped push Congress to enact the Voting Rights Act of that year.

But in August 1963, the violence that lay ahead remained hidden beneath a glow of optimism and a temporary spirit of cooperation that climaxed in a March on Washington. Most northern newspapers and magazines praised the neat appearance, politeness, and commitment of the estimated 200,000 marchers. The unity within the movement also seemed exemplary: Young activists from SNCC shared the platform with the NAACP and the Urban League as well as with white church and labor leaders. And just when the August sun threatened to wilt the marchers, Martin Luther King revived their spirits with his immortal "I Have a Dream" speech. A carefully structured series of images, the address confirmed King's reputation as the movement's greatest spellbinder. With the formalities completed, civil rights leaders adjourned to the White House for a coffee hour with the Kennedys.

The Civil Rights Act of 1964: End of an Era

Even though civil rights leaders had recognized JFK's limitations, his death seemed a great blow to their movement; it brought a southerner with an even more ambivalent record into the White House. But Lyndon Johnson quickly dispelled doubts about his commitment when he helped push a stronger version of Kennedy's civil rights bill through Congress in 1964.

The Civil Rights Act of 1964 outlawed racial, religious, and sexual discrimination in private businesses that served the general public—such as restaurants and filling stations—and in public facilities such as swimming pools. It also authorized the executive branch to withhold federal grants or contracts from institutions that discriminated against nonwhites and empowered the attorney general to file school-desegregation suits at his initiative. To safeguard voting rights, the law contained a section that established a sixth-grade education as the basic requirement for literacy. This provision, it was hoped, would end "literacy" tests. (A white voting inspector in Alabama once rejected a black applicant because his literacy test contained "an error in spilling.") When properly enforced, the Civil Rights Act of 1964 changed the pattern of race relations. The law demanded no less than destruction of a settled way of life in the South, a system of racial discrimination that had evolved after the formal end of slavery. According to the act, blacks could now sleep in any motel, eat in any restaurant, or sit anywhere on any bus. Important as they were, however, such changes required no basic alteration in the socioeconomic structure or in the distribution of political power.

March on Washington, 1963. The peaceful mood and optimistic spirit of August 1963 would not survive the turbulent 1960s. Source: *National Archives.*

By 1964 many blacks were seeking more than equal access to public accommodations and government facilities; the victories of the early 1960s had raised the stakes. Black militants demanded monetary compensation for the years of discrimination, immediate economic assistance, and greater political power. Such things, white politicians argued, were clearly impossible; it had taken much bloodshed and political skill even to obtain the act of 1964. But young activists rejected arguments based upon what older black leaders and white politicians considered possible. Some charged that their own leaders were selling out. After the troubles in Birmingham, white philanthropists, perhaps worried about violence moving northward or perhaps sincerely moved by the rightness of the cause, pledged almost a million dollars to the leading civil rights organizations. Militants denounced this as a payoff and Kennedy's civil rights program as tokenism. During the March on Washington, leaders had forced John Lewis, the youthful head of SNCC, to rewrite his fiery address. Lewis had intended to criticize the Kennedy civil rights bill—"What is there in this bill to ensure the equality of a maid who earns $5 a week in the home of a family whose income is $100,000 a year?"—and to condemn "the cheap political leaders who build their careers on immoral compromises and ally themselves with open forms of political, economic, and social exploitation." To preserve the harmony of the day, Lewis softened his speech, but others did not attend the march or temper their words. One person who had not even been invited asked, "Who ever heard of angry revolutionists all harmonizing 'We Shall Overcome Some Day' while tripping and swaying along arm-in-arm with the very people they were supposed to be revolting against?" The angry young man was Malcom X, an eloquent advocate for political militancy and black pride.

A series of disturbing events in 1964 and 1965 made nonviolence and peaceful political appeals less attractive to some activists. In Mississippi three civil rights workers—Andrew Goodman, James Cheney, and Michael Schwerner—were brutally murdered; Cheney, the only black among the three, was apparently beaten to death with chains. That same year an inter-racial group risked their lives to organize the Mississippi Freedom Democratic Party (FDP), only to watch white liberals join with southern segregationists to deny the FDP formal recognition at the Democratic National Convention. And during the Freedom Summer of 1964—a SNCC-sponsored campaign to register voters and establish "freedom schools"—racial tensions within the movement itself increased. Blacks frequently ridiculed "paternalistic" whites and "fly-by-night freedom fighters who were bossing everybody around." Sexual relationships among the young civil rights workers, especially those between African-American men and Caucasian women, quickly added gender and racial conflicts to the list of problems with which those committed to the Freedom Summer had to deal. As SNCC and other inter-racial organizations tried to limp along, testing the viability of nonviolence in the South, African-Americans in some northern cities expressed their grievances and frustrations in very different ways.

The Ghettos Explode

Less than three weeks after Lyndon Johnson signed the Civil Rights Act of 1964, violence broke out in several northern cities. Immediately recognizing that some politicians would use violence by African-Americans in the North to cripple his civil rights and Great Society programs, Johnson enlisted the aid of J. Edgar Hoover in orchestrating a report that blamed poverty and racial discrimination, rather than some subversive plots, for the violent outbreaks.

Although Johnson's theory implied that further Great Society spending would calm northern cities, a second violence-filled summer followed the first. In August 1965, a clash between a white highway patrol officer and an African-American motorist touched off four days of violence in the Los Angeles neighborhood of Watts. Thirty-four people lost their lives; property losses, from fires and looting, reached more than $20 million; and the National Guard patrolled the streets of Los Angeles. According to one administration official, the president "just wouldn't accept it. He refused to look at the cables from Los Angeles" that described the escalating violence in Watts.

Several more years of urban disorders followed the outbreak in Watts. The worst was 1967, with trouble in 128 cities, and major clashes in Newark and Detroit. In Detroit, regular Army units assisted police and the National Guard; at least forty-three people died, while fires and looting left permanent scars on Detroit's African-American neighborhoods. In all the confrontations, the vast majority of people killed were African-Americans, and property damage remained largely confined to their communities. Investigations revealed indiscriminate shooting by authorities and even a few incidents of outright murder by white police officers. In addition to burned-out buildings and escalating tensions in African-American neighborhoods, these long, hot summers produced growing unease among white liberals. Johnson himself was reported to have asked, "How is it possible after all that we've accomplished? . . . Is the world topsy-turvy?" Certainly, he had a point; the violence had come during a period of at least some progress in fighting racial discrimination. What could explain the urban violence?

Official explanations tried to steer between right-wing theories of a grand revolutionary conspiracy and left-wing claims of an incipient popular revolution against white exploitation. Investigating the Watts disorder, the McCone Commission (headed by former CIA director John McCone) propounded a "rotten apple" or "riff-raff" interpretation. A small group of troublemakers, the McCone Report concluded, had precipitated the trouble and fueled the violence. The "riots" were not legitimate protests against substantive grievances but "formless, quite senseless, all but hopeless" outbursts of looting and burning—"engaged in by a few but bringing great distress to all." The commission theorized that most of these "rotten apples" had recently migrated from the rural South and had not yet adjusted to urban life. Though it refused to call Watts a ghetto (because it contained mostly single-family dwellings and fairly wide streets) or to concede a serious issue of police brutality, the commission did see problems in Watts. It had inadequate mass transit to jobs, poor educational facilities, and a small number of poorly trained police. Suggesting that the situation required no fundamental social or economic changes, the report called for greater job opportunities near Watts, more money for education, and "better understanding" between police and citizens. Throughout the report, McCone and the other commissioners viewed greater respect for the law enforcement system as the major issue.

Other investigators quickly challenged the McCone Commission. These observers sympathized with the people of Watts and considered the disorders to be political protests rather than formless riots. The violence in Watts, they claimed, involved a sizable portion of the community, not a few misfits. The protesters, in fact, had lived in Watts for some time, usually held low-paying jobs, and possessed the best education ghetto schools could provide. Disputing the idea that the violence had been senseless, some researchers argued that protesters had tried to avoid black-owned businesses and had concentrated upon white firms that were considered dishonest. Much of the housing in Watts was dilapidated, many businesses exploited black customers and employees, and police brutality was an every-day occurrence. Many of these writers concluded that the violence grew out of deep-seated, legitimate grievances.

This dispute between "riot" and "protest" theorists involved more than a semantical difference. The riot view upheld the quick suppression of such disorders and pointed to the need for changes within the existing system; the protest position at least implied the legitimacy of the violence and supported the need for more sweeping social changes. Equally as important, the riot view tended to see the problem as one between good people and bad people. The protest theory pointed to a deep-seated socioeconomic and racial crisis.

As disorders continued, official explanations changed very little. The most extensive government investigation, done by President Johnson's National Advisory Commission on Civil Disorders (commonly called the Kerner Commission), rejected evidence that suggested fundamental prob-lems with the political system. In the end, the commissioners did identify "white racism" as part of the trouble, but not before they had fired 120 staff members who wanted stronger language and had suppressed the staff's radical report, "The Harvest of American Racism." The commissioners' own document recommended a moderate two-pronged approach: increased social-welfare expenditures and more effective use of force to suppress disturbances. The last solution proved more acceptable to most white politi-cians, and Congress voted additional funds to beef up local law enforcement agencies and to train the National Guard in more efficient riot control. Saddled with burgeoning expenditures for Vietnam, the president filed away the commission's other recommendations. Lyndon Johnson, like most other national leaders, ultimately preferred to ignore the broader implica-tions of the commission's report.

Black Power

Meanwhile, some African-American leaders were already citing white intransigence as justification for rejecting integration—the traditional goal of the civil rights movement. An established separatist group, the Black Muslims, suddenly gained prominence in the early 1960s. The Muslims preached the superiority of black people and black institutions, predicted eventual collapse for the decadent white society, planned the creation of separate black areas in the United States, and stressed the necessity for hard work and self-discipline. The sect gained converts during the 1950s, includ-ing Malcolm Little, a self-educated man with a keen intellect. Rejecting his "Christian slave name," Malcolm X became Muslim leader Elijah Muham-mad's top aide and his most eloquent spokesperson. Malcom's fiery oratory and the conversion of the heavyweight boxing champion Cassius Clay (who became Muhammad Ali) gained the Muslims national attention.

Malcolm X anticipated the African-American militancy of the late 1960s. Malcolm ridiculed Martin Luther King's philosophy of nonviolence: "If someone puts a hand on you," he preached, "send him to the cemetery." He advised black people to join together "to lift the level of our community, and to make our society beautiful so that we will be satisfied in our own social circles and won't be running around here trying to knock our way into a social circle where we're not wanted." A series of disputes with Elijah Muhammad led Malcolm to form in 1963 the Organization of Afro-American Unity. After leaving the Muslims, he began to temper his separatist rhetoric and to suggest a working alliance with a variety of black and white groups. Such ideas seemed heresy to the more isolationist followers of Elijah Muhammad. In 1965 Malcolm was assassinated, allegedly by his Muslim enemies. After his death, growing numbers of people read his *Autobiography*, and Malcolm became a hero to young radicals. "Black history began with Malcolm X," proclaimed Eldridge Cleaver of the Black Panthers.

By 1965, racial politics in the United States were in a state of flux; the forward march of the civil rights movement toward legal and constitutional change seemed at an end. Southern resistance to the Civil Rights Act of 1964 and the new Voting Rights Act of 1965 produced further bloodshed and death; to some blacks, the urban disorders in the North suggested the possibility that violence might bring more concessions than nonviolent civil disobedience. In May 1966, SNCC, officially committed to integration, urged blacks "to begin building independent political, economic, and cultural institutions that they will control and use as instruments of social change in this country." Later that summer SNCC joined other civil rights groups, including the SCLC and CORE, in a protest march through Mississippi, an effort that widened divisions within the civil rights movement. Stokely Carmichael, SNCC's new head, took the spotlight away from Martin Luther King, who was often absent. Carmichael vowed that he would never go to jail peacefully again and declared that "every courthouse in Mississippi ought to be burned down to get rid of the dirt." In the most publicized event of the march, he coined the movement's new slogan: Black Power!

The people in SNCC and CORE had tried nonviolence and cooperation with whites, and they believed that these tactics had failed. Integration, wrote Stokely Carmichael, "reinforces among both black and white, the idea that 'white' is automatically better and 'black' is by definition inferior." And to blacks like Carmichael, political and legal equality, the basis of the civil rights movement, now seemed less important than economic power. Black people, they argued, had to gain control of their communities and expel the "white power structure"—the "dishonest" businesspeople, the "rent-gouging" landlords, and the "crooked" politicians. Along with economic independence, young nationalists promoted black pride. Since many whites would always see blacks as inferior, they contended, black people must reject the values of white society and forge a cultural identity based upon their own heritage. As a means of stimulating black pride and cultural nationalism, militants demanded community control of neighborhood schools and, where this was not immediately possible, black studies courses taught and administered by African-Americans.

There were many variations on the themes of black power and black nationalism. Some people, identifying with dark-skinned peoples in the Third World, viewed African-Americans as colonized people subject to the domination of alien, white masters. Others adopted a Marxist framework, seeing blacks as the most exploited group in an exploitative capitalist society. Violent revolution, a few extremists suggested, offered the best means of redressing grievances. But most warned against open confrontations with the overwhelming firepower of white America and sought to build bases of local support before pressing the movement for significant social change.

The history of the Black Panthers, an organization that attracted the media spotlight in the late 1960s, revealed the tensions generated by debates over black power and black nationalism. Formed in Oakland, California, the Panthers gained attention primarily through a shootout with Oakland police and through the success of Eldridge Cleaver's book, *Soul on Ice*. Outfitted in paramilitary garb, the Panthers frightened many people, and law enforcement officials denounced the group as a grave threat to American society. Panther leaders Huey Newton (who was convicted of killing a police officer during the Oakland shootout) and Bobby Seale urged "self-defense groups that are dedicated to defending our black community against racist oppression and brutality." The Panthers also demanded a guaranteed income for all citizens, exemption of blacks from military service, government funds for cooperative housing facilities, reparation payments "as retribution for slave labor and mass murder of black people," release of all black prisoners "because they have not received a fair and impartial trial," and use of all-black juries to try black defendants. Such demands borrowed from black nationalist ideas, but they also owed much to a curious blend of Marxism and the rhetoric of American constitutional law. (Huey Newton always carried a stack of law books in his car.) The Panthers found it difficult to fix a transformational strategy: Should they ally with white radicals and prepare for revolutionary action, or should they avoid ties with nonblacks and go it alone? The Panthers finally did seek ties with both white and black radicals, a course that helped to divide the party's members.

By 1968 neither black power nor black nationalism had carried the day. Most black people—if opinion polls are to be believed—still supported the traditional aims of integration and equal rights, and they considered Martin Luther King the foremost leader. But the spirit of militancy had prompted African-American people to reexamine goals and aspirations. Most saw no real contradiction between greater racial pride and some type of integration with white society, no real conflict between greater political power and acceptance of the basic American system. Black politicians, gaining crucial white votes to add to their power base, won elective office in many large cities. Throughout the 1960s the income of black families did rise, and the gap between whites and blacks narrowed. New styles of dress—Afro haircuts and dashikis—appeared to be more than fashions; black studies seemed more than a passing fad. When he was killed in 1968, Martin Luther King had never used cries of "Black Power!" but he had begun to recognize the limits of the old SCLC approach, to stress racial pride, and to place his greatest emphasis on the need for significant socioeconomic change.

The Civil Rights Act of 1968, the last major civil rights measure, indicated the ambivalent attitude of white politicians toward militancy. Title VIII of the law prohibited discrimination in the advertising, financing, sale, or rental of most homes and charged the executive branch with acting "affirmatively" to achieve integrated housing. Together with a Supreme Court decision and state open-housing laws, the act pointed toward integration of the largely white suburbs. If coupled with generous funding for inner-city projects, it also promised better urban housing for minority families. The urban violence of the 1960s did, therefore, produce some positive responses, in the form of congressional legislation and bureaucratic attention, from the political system.

But in the Civil Rights Act of 1968 the majority of whites in Congress also indicated their fear of the radical implications of black militancy. At the insistence of Strom Thurmond of South Carolina, Congress also made it a crime to use the facilities of interstate commerce "to organize, promote, encourage, participate in, or carry on a riot; or to commit any act of violence in furtherance of a riot." In approving this vague provision, most members of Congress knew exactly what they wanted: a federal law that would stop the activities of black power advocates such as H. Rap Brown of SNCC. This "Rap Brown section" gave national authorities a catchall statute to halt the travels and organizing efforts of radicals.

The movement for political and economic power and the renaissance of black pride, then, affected white as well as black people. The sight of young persons shouting "Black Power!" and of black men and women with Afro haircuts represented a threat to settled ways. But many whites recognized the need for greater black pride and self-assertiveness. Potentially at least, the message that black is beautiful could also liberate white Americans from narrowness and old prejudices.

But, in many ways, the liberal promise of the early 1960s was beginning to fade; the failure of liberal politics to solve the riddles of race constituted only one of the legacies of the JFK-LBJ years. Problems in foreign affairs, largely the result of efforts to maintain earlier cold war policies in the face of new circumstances, also helped to wither the promise of the 1960s and demonstrate the perils of power.

SUGGESTIONS FOR FURTHER READING

The best study of the problems of liberalism in the 1960s is Allen J. Matusow, *The Unraveling of America* (1984); the relevant sections of Alan Wolfe's *America's Impasse* (1981) also offer critical perspectives, as does Garry Wills' *Nixon Agonistes* (rev. ed., 1980) and *The Kennedy Imprisonment* (1983). More favorable, though not uncritical, is David Burner, *John F. Kennedy and a New Generation* (1988); see also David Burner and Thomas West, *The Torch Is Passed* (1984). For more detail, Herbert J. Parmet's two volumes— *Jack* (1980) and *JFK* (1983)—are excellent. There are many sympathetic accounts of Kennedy's presidency by close associates; by far the best is Arthur Schlesinger, Jr., *A Thousand Days* (1965). See also, Richard N. Goodwin, *Remembering America: A Voice from the Sixties* (1988), and Thomas Brown, *JFK: History of an Image* (1989).

Events surrounding Kennedy's death have attracted almost as much attention as his life. Edward Jay Epstein's two studies, *Inquest* (1963) and *Legend* (1978), are the best of the older accounts that reject the Warren Commission's version of JFK's assassination. Michael J. Kurtz's *The Crime of the Century* (1982) tries to offer historical grounding, but there have been many subsequent conspiracy theories. See, for example, Henry Hurt, *Reasonable Doubt* (1988), and John H. Davis, *Mafia Kingfish: Carlos Marcello and the Assassination of John F. Kennedy* (1989). But also see the attempt to rehabilitate the Warren Commission's general conclusions in David Belin, *Final Disclosure* (1989).

Other aspects of the Kennedy administration can be explored in Grant McConnell, *Steel and the Presidency–1962* (1963); Jim F. Heath, *John Kennedy and the Business Community* (1969); Victor Navasky, *Kennedy Justice* (1971); Carl M. Brauer, *John F. Kennedy and the Second Reconstruction* (1977); James Tobin and Murray Weidenbaum, eds., *Two Revolutions in Economic Policy: The First Economic Reports of Presidents Kennedy and Reagan* (1988); and John Walton Cotman, *Birmingham, JFK, and the Civil Rights Act of 1963* (1989).

In addition to general studies on the civil rights movement cited at the end of Chapter 3, in this text, the following studies are also recommended: Howard Zinn, *SNCC* (1965); Elliot Rudwick and August Meier, *CORE* (1972); David Garrow, *Protest at Selma* (1980); William Chafe, *Civilities and Civil Rights* (1980); Clayborne Carson, *In Struggle* (1981); Steven Lawson, *In Pursuit of Power* (1985); the relevant chapters of Earl Black and Merle Black, *Politics and Society in the New South* (1987); Doug McAdam, *Freedom Summer* (1988); Emily Stoper, *The Student Non-Violent Coordinating Committee: The Growth of Radicalism in a Civil Rights Organization* (1989); David Garrow, ed., *Birmingham, Alabama, 1956–1963: The Black Struggle for Civil Rights* (1989); Ralph David Abernathy, *And the Walls Came Tumbling Down: An Autobiography* (1989); Kenneth O'Reilly, *Racial Matters: The FBI's Secret Files on Black America, 1960–72* (1989), and Hugh Davis Graham, *The Civil Rights Era* (1970). See also Stewart Burns, *Social Movements of the 1960s: Searching for Democracy* (1990).

Many of the works cited on gender and family issues at the end of Chapter 3 are also relevant here. In addition, see Susan M. Hartman, *From Margin to Mainstream: American Women in Politics Since 1960* (1989).

On Lyndon Johnson, begin with Paul K. Conkin, *Big Daddy from the Pedernales: Lyndon Baines Johnson* (1986); Robert Caro is writing a multivolume history, two of which have appeared: *The Path to Power* (1982) and

Means of Ascent (1990). Ronnie Dugger's *The Politician* (1982), like Caro's volumes, is highly critical. Vaughn Davis Bornet's *The Presidency of Lyndon Baines Johnson* is more sympathetic, while Doris Kearns' *Lyndon Johnson and the American Dream* (1976) remains insightful.

On the Great Society and the War on Poverty, start with the critical assessment in Matusow, cited earlier. A much more positive view is *The Promise of Greatness* by Sar Levitan and Robert Taggert. John E. Schwarz's *America's Hidden Success* (rev. ed., 1988) is equally upbeat. The most influential analysis from the right of Great Society liberalism has been Charles Murray's *Losing Ground* (1984); for views from the left of the Great Society, see, for example, William P. Ryan, *Equality* (1982), and Richard Cloward and Francis Fox Piven, *Poor People's Movements* (1978). *The Great Society Reader* (1965), edited by Marvin E. Gettleman and David Mermelstein, remains a useful documentary collection.

On the Warren Court and liberal reform, see the unabridged edition of Bernard Schwartz, *Super Chief* (1983); G. Edward White, *Earl Warren* (1982); and the relevant parts of Mark Tushnet, *Red, White and Blue: A Critical Analysis of Constitutional Law* (1988), and of Samuel Walker, *In Defense of American Liberties: A History of the ACLU* (1990). See also Neil McFeeley, *Appointment of Judges, The Johnson Presidency* (1987).

Chapter Six

The Perils of Power: Foreign Policy in the 1960s

KENNEDY'S FOREIGN POLICIES

New Programs

John F. Kennedy's New Frontier asserted a new activism into the cold war. In the presidential campaign of 1960, Kennedy charged that the Eisenhower-Nixon team had created a dangerous "missile gap" between the United States and the Soviet Union and had not worked vigorously to eliminate Castro. (Neither charge was true.) Once in the White House, Kennedy waged the cold war in a determined way and with a great variety of techniques. Kennedy promised that his foreign policy would provide a "flexible response": It would challenge communism on every level, from atomic weaponry to "counterinsurgency units" to economic pressure to enlarged covert capabilities.

General Maxwell Taylor, army chief of staff, told Kennedy, "We must show the Russians that wars of national liberation are not cheap, safe, and disavowable but costly, dangerous, and doomed to failure." Believing that ground combat was relevant, even in the era of atomic brinkmanship, Taylor and his staff sketched a heady new mission for the army: "nation building." Highly trained elite forces would teach local troops the techniques of counterinsurgency against guerrilla fighters and instruct them in twentieth-century technology and liberal democracy. Air cavalry and special units such as the Green Berets were to ensure that the Third World would be stable and friendly to the United States. For Kennedy even more than for Dulles, the front lines of the cold war were everywhere, and Capitol Hill enthusiastically funded Taylor's experiments.

Others in the new administration stressed using America's wealth to promote development. In a fervor of can-do activism, these individuals talked about short-circuiting the poverty and sense of helplessness that they felt fueled communist appeals to the underdeveloped world. Ironically, while Kennedy found it difficult to secure congressional approval for reform at home, Congress authorized new departures in foreign aid, such as the Alliance for Progress and the Peace Corps. The Alliance for Progress, the New Frontier advocates calculated, would thwart radicalism in Latin America and encourage moderate, reformist leaders while breaking oligarchic or anti-American regimes. This "ten-year plan for the Americas" was signed at Punta del Este, Uruguay, in August 1961 by all nations of the Western Hemisphere except Canada and Cuba. The United States promised new credits and private investment that, over the next decade, would finance social programs, such as health care, housing, and education; boost local rates of growth by 2.5 percent annually; and encourage industrial diversification and land reform. The Agency for International Development (AID), operating on a smaller scale in all Third World areas, also promoted anticommunist modernization.

An even more imaginative program, the Peace Corps, sent volunteers to willing nations throughout the world. Functioning primarily in rural areas, the Peace Corps worked to improve health, education, and economic efficiency. Director R. Sargent Shriver expected no dramatic results, only "cumulative years of goodwill among the common folk." By 1963 volunteers were working in over forty countries as teachers, corp specialists, and construction supervisors.

The Alliance for Progress became a disaster because reform stalled and expectations outran growth. Latin America grew more debt-ridden and even more dependent on United States-based multinationals. The Peace Corps also came under attack from some who suspected its motives; Bolivia, for example, expelled volunteers. But both programs reflected the New Frontier's confidence in the ability to shape the world in its own image.

Cuba

Events in Cuba made an activist foreign policy not only feasible but almost mandatory. The Eisenhower administration had given the green light to a CIA project to invade Cuba with a small force of anti-Castro expatriates, and Kennedy decided to follow through on his predecessor's plan. The disgruntled population of Cuba, America's spies predicted, would welcome these rebels as liberators. On April 17, 1961, two days after CIA mercenaries had attacked Cuba's air bases with B-26 bombers, approximate-

ly 1400 Cuban exiles waded ashore at the Bay of Pigs. Local peasants ignored
the unlikely army, most of them pro-Batista urbanites, and Castro's forces
soon surrounded them. Though some in the State Department urged full-
scale intervention, Kennedy reluctantly accepted the fact of disaster. "Victory has a hundred fathers," he said, "but defeat is an orphan." The Bay of Pigs
fiasco only tightened Castro's control in Cuba, reinforced his dependence
upon the Soviet Union, and loosed yet another round of Yankeephobia
throughout most of Latin America. The debacle also raised Kennedy's
anxiety about being perceived as weak-willed and thus increased his determination to "get tough" in future showdowns.

Before Washington officials could recover from this setback, another
confrontation loomed. Perhaps hoping to gain easy concessions from an
inexperienced president, at an informal summit meeting in Vienna in June
1961, Khrushchev hinted at war unless NATO abandoned West Berlin. If
the United States did not agree, the premier explained, he could secure the
same result by signing a separate peace with his East German ally Walter
Ulbricht. Determined to uphold America's credibility, Kennedy mobilized
the National Guard, accelerated arms production, and tripled draft calls.
Khrushchev blustered about "thermonuclear holocaust" but acted much
more cautiously. Barbed wire and then a wall of cement blocks sealed off
West Berlin from the rest of East Germany, ending an embarrassing flow of
defectors to the West (some 3 million since 1945) and cutting off a black
market in goods and currencies. Kennedy gracefully accepted this compromise, realizing the substance of victory.

Stung by rebukes from domestic critics for his poor showing, Khrushchev quickly looked for a major strategic victory. Frightened of America's
aggressiveness, Castro apparently asked the Soviet Union for military hardware, and Khrushchev replied with massive shipments of sophisticated
weapons, including missiles armed with atomic warheads. Kennedy responded with a week of crisis diplomacy. In a televised address on October
22, 1962, he vowed, "The United States will not compromise its safety," and
ordered the Strategic Air Command to full alert. Two days later the navy
quarantined the island, its destroyers ready to turn away any Soviet merchant ships carrying missiles. But Kennedy also began searching for compromise: If The Soviet Union removed its weapons, the United States would
not attack Cuba again. While public prodding continued—United Nations
Ambassador Adlai Stevenson urged the Soviets "to save the peace"—complicated secret messages between the Kremlin and the White House soon
confirmed Kennedy's offer. Amid headlines warning of imminent nuclear
war, Khrushchev ordered Soviet ships to return home, and the missiles
began to be dismantled. Castro's Cuba continued to be harassed by CIA plots
to destabilize the regime, but superpower confrontation there was over.

The Cuban missile crisis highlighted the perils of cold war diplomacy.
The swiftness of nuclear escalation frightened both sides; mutual blackmail,
if miscalculated, could easily get out of control. Then, too, both powers had
other concerns. In late 1962 China overran Tibet and ostentatiously began

atomic tests near the Soviet border. Mao Zedong openly challenged Moscow for leadership of the Communist bloc. The Americans looked toward Vietnam, experimenting with counterinsurgency, "nation building," and the other tactics of flexible response. Superpower rhetoric mellowed, Khrushchev admitting, "If the United States is now a paper tiger, it has atomic teeth," and Kennedy calling for "mutual tolerance." During the summer of 1963 the two countries set up a "hot line," a direct telephone link between their capitals. And on July 25, 1963, America, Britain, and the Soviet Union initialed a nuclear test-ban treaty that ended all except underground atomic explosions. (Soviet fears that on-site inspections might reveal too much about its industrial potential made a total ban impossible.) Such gestures did little to ease rivalry between the two superpowers, but they did indicate a mutual desire to find some areas of common agreement.

If Cuba daily reminded Washington officials of cold war dangers, peaceful coexistence allowed them to act elsewhere in the Third World. And most Americans, proud of their ingenuity, did not easily recognize limits to what was possible. Surely, with such riches, such power, such determination, the United States could build nations in the Third World like itself: prosperous, democratic, and anticommunist. Nurtured by this self-confident, activist atmosphere within the Kennedy administration, the American role in Vietnam fatefully expanded.

STRUGGLE IN VIETNAM

Hoping to sharpen the nation's credibility while pushing back a communist liberation movement, the Kennedy administration tested its new flexible approach in Southeast Asia. Diem still blocked reform, despite pressure from American ambassadors. Nonetheless, the Democrats undertook a military defeat of the National Liberation Front (NLF). Billions of dollars, tons of sophisticated weapons, and 16,000 American support and combat troops had inundated the Vietnamese countryside by 1963. At first, the communist effort wavered, seemingly justifying the Pentagon's tactics. But then Hanoi increased its aid to the insurgents, and Kennedy widened the American intervention to include a covert war against North Vietnam. More discouraging, Diem's regime came apart at the seams. Limitless treasure from Washington brought jolting corruption in Saigon. The scramble for loot hindered normal operations of state. Land reform collapsed.

In May 1963, the Catholic Archbishop forbade the carrying of Buddhist flags, and Diem's anti-Buddhist persecution grew strong throughout the provinces. Now, forced either to abandon some religious practices or to face charges of treason, Buddhists organized massive demonstrations, which culminated on June 16, 1963, when a priest martyred himself by setting fire to his gasoline-soaked robes. As if finally convinced of Diem's turpitude, city people paraded in the streets and prayed at pagodas for his downfall. For nearly two months the regime waited for animosities to abate, but more self-immolations and the growing violence of student strikes convinced Diem and his brother, Ngo Dinh Nhu, that only strong measures could restore order. On August 21, detachments from American-trained special-forces units attacked Buddhist sanctuaries in Saigon, Hue, and most provincial capitals. This repression, coupled with political arrests, prompted another, even more violent, cycle of protests and autocratic response. Intellectuals and the urban middle class abandoned the Diem regime, which was now consumed in self-destruction.

No one in Washington knew what to do. One obvious reaction was to excise the cancer: Diem must go. The internal chaos of his regime enervated the war effort against the communists and mocked hopes for a democratic example for the Third World. Religious persecution bothered Americans, including the president, himself a Catholic. During the fall of 1963 several Vietnamese generals suggested plans for a coup to the American ambassador, Henry Cabot Lodge. They received the encouraging reply that Washington would not intervene in "an internal matter." The CIA also began to work toward Diem's replacement. In October the Kennedy administration unexpectedly canceled the commercial-import program that financed Diem's government and publicly disavowed the rest of his family. Reassured that Washington would support Diem's ouster, the generals wheeled into action, and on November 1 Vietnamese battalions near Saigon captured administrative centers and surrounded Diem's palace. The man whom Americans had vainly tried to turn into the George Washington of Vietnam died that night, murdered while trying to escape his country.

American Goals and Vietnamese Realities

That same month an era also ended in the United States. On November 22, 1963, President Kennedy died in Dallas, Texas, victim of an assassination. Anxious to maintain continuity, Lyndon Johnson did not challenge the policy of growing involvement in Vietnam, and White House advisers put forth new variations on cold war themes. The United States must repel communist aggression now or face repeated nibbling elsewhere. If Washington faltered, many Third World leaders might question America's ability, even its willingness, to protect their countries against subversion. The Soviet Union must understand Yankee determination to contain communism. Walt Whitman Rostow, the president's special adviser on foreign affairs, speculated that American pressure in Vietnam would divert Chinese attention away from the Pacific and toward central Asia, thus aggravating the Sino-Soviet split. Vietnamese problems thus became absorbed into global strategy: A Pentagon expert explained in 1968 that repelling communist aggression in Asia was "only 10 percent" of America's purpose; the war was being fought primarily to reassure allies and frighten enemies elsewhere.

Seeking larger goals, bureaucrats lost sight of their tool, Vietnam, still a very traditional peasant society. For centuries, ritual emperors had symbolized universal order for thousands of economically self-sufficient villages.

Individuals molded themselves into a historical process that emphasized continuity with the past, not progress toward a different future. The Vietnamese valued harmony, unanimity, and adherence to legitimate authority as a means of insuring the day-to-day functioning of society and its primary institution, the village. French colonialism had ripped away the emperor's "mandate of Heaven"—popular confidence in his right to rule—and warped the agrarian economy. The new masters demanded surplus, not self-sufficiency, and herded Vietnamese together on rice or rubber plantations. Saigon and Hanoi became parasitic pleasure spas for these *colons* and their upper-class mandarin supporters. Although ethnocentric French teachers tried for decades to "civilize" the population, they educated only a class of intellectuals, who were thereby alienated from the rest of the people. Despite such changes, the villages' agrarianism remained the basis for both society and ethics.

The first Indochinese war, followed by Diem's ruthless centralism, aggravated the rural-urban split, the tension between old and new, familiar and foreign. Westerners preached development, while the National Liberation Front extolled the communal basis of life in Vietnamese villages. Red cadres talked of traditional ways and enacted land reforms immediately. Rulers in Saigon tried to impose forms of democracy, but peasants feared Saigon as a hostile place with novel, disruptive ideas.

Americans never realized how hard it would be for their revolution from above to compete with the NLF restoration from below. In one sense, however, Lyndon Johnson had few, if any, options. Only a strong American presence could stave off internal collapse in South Vietnam, now without a leader or even a government. The new president's advisers did not readily abandon old rationales. Johnson accepted their theories about credibility as much as he had earlier theories about dominoes: "The United States must take a strong stand," he said, "or else no one will believe our promises." After a month-long inspection tour, Secretary of Defense Robert S. McNamara and Chief of Staff Maxwell Taylor reported on October 2, 1963, that the United States could probably begin pulling out its troops by early 1964. The opposite occurred.

A Vigorous Beginning, 1964–1965

America began the second Indochinese war during the winter of 1964–1965, responding to growing chaos in South Vietnam. A revolving door of military juntas undermined the anticommunist effort on the battlefield and aggravated Diem's legacy of corruption and malaise. The NLF rapidly filled the political vacuum in the countryside, appealing to many Vietnamese frustrated by years of indecisive warfare. By the middle of 1964 the NLF, always supported by military aid from Hanoi, had begun preparations for a major assault on provincial capitals. Considerably frightened at this prospect, Pentagon officials drew up plans for an air war against North Vietnam. No other option seemed feasible, short of an embarrassing disengagement or total war. But escalation required legal, if not moral, justification. The White House drafted a congressional resolution authorizing air attacks and waited for an opportunity.

It came almost too quickly. In early August a confrontation developed in the Gulf of Tonkin. The United States spy ship *Maddox* violated Hanoi's self-proclaimed twelve-mile territorial sea limit. Assuming that the destroyer was part of a larger operation, North Vietnam ordered several PT boats into the area and several volleys were exchanged. Two days later the *Maddox* and another destroyer, the *C. Turner Joy*, returned to the Gulf of Tonkin. In the midst of a storm on the night of August 4, anxious naval captains and malfunctioning sonar equipment reported an attack. By afternoon the commander of the *Maddox* wired that there had been no visual sighting and that freak weather effects may have explained the sonar and radar signals. But the Johnson administration sought an excuse for retaliation and chose to believe the first reports of an attack.

Denouncing "unprovoked aggression" during a nationally televised speech, President Johnson ordered reprisal raids against North Vietnamese naval bases. The temporary feeling of crisis prompted Congress to pass the so-called Gulf of Tonkin resolution. Its open-ended phraseology authorized

Johnson "to take all necessary measures" to repulse communist advances. Unaware of the dubious nature of Hanoi's attacks and, like the chief executive himself, ill informed about Vietnamese complexities, the Senate adopted the de facto declaration of war, eighty-eight to two. Only Senators Wayne Morse and Ernest Gruening voted against this potentially unlimited commitment.

During his 1964 presidential campaign, Johnson presented himself as a peace candidate, firmly rejecting prescriptions from critics, such as former air force chief of staff Curtis Lemay, for "bombing Hanoi back into the Stone Age." After the 1964 presidential election, however, United States officials launched a sustained air assault. Pentagon bureaucrats argued that the Saigon clique could not reform itself as long as insurgency continued. Guerrilla attacks would go on as long as North Vietnam supplied them. Bombing strikes against the North and elite counterinsurgency operations in the South would defeat this war of national liberation, Washington's best and brightest told each other, and restore America's global credibility. But analysis could not alter reality. Anger and discontent with the Saigon regime, together with carefully cultivated affinities between Vietnamese communism and Vietnamese traditionalism, fueled the NLF's success.

More and more, the problem of Vietnam preoccupied Washington's planners. The treadmill of escalation continued. It seemed reasonable: just a little more aid, just a few more soldiers would break the rebellion. Victory seemed always so close. Johnson himself believed that a steady, predictable escalation would avoid intervention by China or Russia and at the same time convince the NLF and Hanoi that they would not win.

Determination Becomes Self-Delusion, 1965–1967

The war slowly intensified. Sustained bombing of North Vietnam began on February 15, 1965, ostensibly in reprisal for an NLF mortar attack against a Marine Corps base at Pleiku. That spring, American combat troops began to aid Vietnamese army units under fire. Johnson authorized the first "search-and-destroy" missions—independent sweeps involving large numbers of GIs—in June 1965, several miles northwest of Saigon. Most military experts guessed that victory required a ten-to-one numerical advantage over NLF-North Vietnamese troops. But the enemy, then recruiting the bulk of their troops within South Vietnam itself, more than matched, at this ratio, Pentagon escalations.

Against a backdrop of Johnsonian rhetoric about "winning the hearts and minds of the Vietnamese people," a plethora of bureaucrats crisscrossed the countryside with experiments. AID officials ostensibly brought health care and modern agricultural techniques. Combat units built hospitals, schools, orphanages. Government programs assured farmers of high prices for their crops but low prices for consumers. The junta in Saigon periodically deployed urban volunteers to counteract the work of communist cadres. Such "nation-building," however, barely touched communist strength in rural areas. By 1967 frustrated officials adopted still another device for rural pacification: the strategic-hamlet program. To protect villagers from NLF attack and ensure their loyalties to Saigon, American soldiers garrisoned many rural towns, often erecting makeshift forts. Herded into barbed-wire enclosures, living under American machine guns, the peasants were expected to continue their agrarian way of of life. Such concentration camps did achieve their military purpose, but they alienated farmers, now isolated from land and tradition.

Bewildered and angered by the failure of their good intentions, Americans came to rely upon more direct and even savage tactics. Computer printouts in Washington explained that improved "kill ratios" were needed. Bombs, artillery, and rifles could kill so many enemy soldiers that eventually the NLF and North Vietnamese could not replace them, given their relatively small population base. If such thinking skirted genocide, the nature of guerrilla war made it almost inevitable. The NLF did not wear uniforms. Taking Mao Zedong's advice, insurgents "swam like fishes in a sea of people" and fought a war of stealth: ambush, booby trap, sabotage, and quick mortar barrage.

To many American soldiers, both enthusiastic volunteers and scared draftees, the war became one against the Vietnamese themselves. Search-and-destroy missions created a misconception that "body count" alone mattered. Some officers, realizing that careers depended upon numbers, lied to superiors about enemy dead; GIs tortured NLF suspects, matching the tactics of their foe. The United States command in Saigon charted "free-fire zones," huge areas in which helicopter gunships strafed anything alive. Chemicals defoliated the earth, and bombers pulverized North Vietnam's industry and South Vietnam's farms. Some devices may have limited communist freedom of movement, but they also destroyed American prestige. In a traditional society whose members valued their ties to ancestral lands and to village communities, terror, free-fire zones, and wholesale murder steadily discredited the American cause.

The Americans miscalculated badly, but few admitted it. Middle-level civilians and field officers reported what higher officials in Saigon wanted to hear, not the actuality of stagnation. America's ambassadors and generals further refined the stylized ritual: We are winning the war, they wired Washington, but send us more money, more men. For many in the administration, tough-mindedness became not a style but an end. A militant stand ensured approval as a "realistic appraisal," and giving assurance of victory garnered points in bureaucratic infighting. Having shoehorned the conflict into America's global strategy, Johnson isolated himself completely from Vietnamese realities and vowed that "I will not be the first president to lose a war."

Neither Diplomacy nor Reform

Unrealistic calculations scuttled opportunities for compromise. Johnson and his advisers used diplomacy either to justify further escalation or to secure an American victory. When U Thant, secretary-general of the United

Nations, suggested in July 1964 that the Geneva Conference reconvene, Johnson righteously refused: "We do not believe in conferences called to ratify terror." But nine months later, the war firmly escalated, the president told an audience at Johns Hopkins University that the United States would discuss peace. He even offered American capital to rebuild "a peaceful Southeast Asia," almost a bribe for surcease. Yet his continued demand for a noncommunist regime in Saigon was unrealistic, tantamount to a Hanoi-NLF capitulation. The enemy routinely rejected such transparent efforts to achieve at the bargaining table what American soldiers had not won in the field. Every rebuff, the president chided his critics, proved communist perfidy.

Johnson used diplomacy more for warmaking than for peacemaking. During a thirty-seven-day period in December 1965 and January 1966, he halted the Rolling Thunder bombing raids against North Vietnam and ostentatiously sponsored a far-flung peace initiative. His closest friends applauded his cleverness. The air war had not materially impaired Hanoi's war production, and few military targets remained. Ho Chi Minh had simply decentralized, then camouflaged his industry in the countryside. Although Ho responded to Johnson's pause with hints about a coalition or neutralist government for South Vietnam, Johnson rejected further talks. Instead he pointed to enemy "truculence" and unleashed a new air war, this one directed against Hanoi's supply routes through Indochinese mountains and jungles. At the same time Johnson vigorously escalated the ground war. Troop levels jumped from 150,000 in February 1966 to 550,000 at their peak in 1968. For nearly twenty-four months, America saved South Vietnam from communism by destroying its land and its people.

Washington bureaucrats also tried to reform Saigon's government. Absorbed in its coups and intrigues but assured of American money, the military junta became not only dictatorial but also useless. Johnson summoned the two most recently installed generals, Nguyen Van Thieu and Nyguyen Cao Ky, to a meeting in Honolulu in February 1966. He extracted promises from the quiet Thieu and the more flamboyant Ky that they would redistribute land, end corruption, and rule more liberally. Like Kennedy before him, the president had few levers to enforce the glib assurances from Vietnamese leaders who could always cash in profits, leaving the country to the NLF. Thieu and Ky were elected president and vice-president by suspiciously lopsided victories in 1967 after a "constitutional convention," but they "postponed" reforms and ruled through fiat and secret police. This facade of democracy in Saigon only aggravated discontent in the countryside.

The ugliness of brutal, unending war in Vietnam began to repulse many American citizens. A growing protest movement questioned the country's purposes. Although he had guided the Gulf of Tonkin resolution through the Senate, J. William Fullbright lashed out against what he called "the arrogance of power." "Power," the head of the Foreign Relations Committee observed, "tends to confuse itself with virtue." Many thought dangerous the Pentagon's sense of omnipotence and the president's voluble self-righteousness. Perhaps America could not reshape other societies. More and more people expressed their moral distaste for the Vietnam adventure. Months of general peaceful protest marches culminated October 1967 in a giant three-day rally in Washington, D.C. The mushrooming antiwar movement deprived Johnson of part of his natural constituency among liberal Democrats. More ominous, the protests polarized American society into "hawks" or "doves"—those who favored pursuing victory or a compromise peace.

Tet and the President's Discontent, 1968

The year 1968 became a turning point. Many people already doubted whether the United States could ever win in Vietnam at any reasonable cost. But a majority of Americans still believed in the cause. Walt Rostow told reporters that the captured documents showed a communist collapse to be "imminent." Then in late January 1968, during Tet, Vietnam's lunar-new-year celebrations, NLF guerrillas and North Vietnamese armies coordinated a massive attack against Saigon and Hue, the imperial capital of Vietnam, and also against nine provincial capitals. The insurgents overran much of Cholon, the Chinese section of Saigon, and even penetrated the American embassy, killing several guards. In Hue the rebels executed a reign of terror against their political opponents. The attacks on regional cities had the greatest military repercussions. To restore control, General William Westmoreland had to shift troops from northern South Vietnam and from rural areas to take and then garrison places like Tay Ninh, Quang Tri, Pleiku, and other towns. Communist cadres quickly infiltrated the now unprotected countryside.

The United States command saw silver in the lining of the Tet offensive cloud. The NLF had overextended itself, exhausting months of supplies in an unsuccessful effort to end the war. "The enemy is on the ropes," Westmoreland said. "Tet was his last gasp." If only he had 200,000 more men, the American commander promised, he would crush the rural insurgency "once and for all." But several civilian advisers had for months counseled diplomatic compromise. McNamara recommended a coalition government for South Vietnam and then resigned. George Ball, the undersecretary of state, repeatedly pointed out the folly of shooting a people into allegiance and had already resigned; the CIA for years had counseled against the effort. But Johnson had, until now, listened more to his generals, demanding only good news and then relying on their promises. After the Tet offensive, the president asked an old friend and much-respected confidant of Democratic presidents, Clark Clifford, to chart a fresh course. As the new secretary of defense, Clifford soon discovered that the military numbers game was relatively straightforward. To send 200,000 men to Southeast Asia and still protect American commitments elsewhere, the president would have to call up the army reserves or triple already high draft quotas. Only new taxes and wide-ranging controls on an overheated economy could ensure war production at a reasonable cost and temper an accelerating

LBJ, 1964. In 1964 Lyndon Johnson was widely celebrated as a political genius; by 1968, largely as a result of the Vietnam War, and the growing protests against it, his popularity and his political reputation were in eclipse. Source: *National Archives*.

inflation. Senators privately told their former majority leader what many citizens knew instinctively: The country would reject such steps toward mobilization for war. Clifford urged Johnson to negotiate.

Events, not advice, finally shoved the president toward diplomacy. The Tet offensive had convinced many in Vietnam that the war could never end until the United States left. "Before the Americans came," an old man told a reporter in Saigon, "my home was on the land of my ancestors and my family was honorable. Now I live off my daughter's earnings as a hooch-girl." Morale cracked in the U.S. Army. Helicopter pilots refused to fly during their last four weeks "in country." Some units sought escape in drugs or "fragging"—surreptitious assaults upon their own officers. Others lost all restraint, as at My Lai, where American soldiers bayoneted children, women, and old men, apparently without thought or guilt. Both Vietnamese society and the army were coming apart under the strain of a stalemated war.

Amid the pressures for peace, Johnson gradually lost control of his party. Senator Eugene J. McCarthy, an outspoken Democratic critic of Pentagon policy, nearly won New Hampshire's presidential primary, and Robert F. Kennedy announced his candidacy and pledged to stop the conflict. And the president, a great campaigner, could not defend himself publicly on the hustings: The Secret Service considered the security risk too great. Trapped in the White House, losing both the presidential nomination and popular respect, Johnson brooded about his nemesis, Vietnam. Finally, on March 31, 1968, Johnson told a nationwide television audience that he had rejected Westmoreland's request for more troops. American escalation would stop. To signal his good intentions and lure Hanoi to the bargaining table, he halted bombing north of the nineteenth parallel. Then, almost as a postscript, Johnson announced that he would not run for reelection.

Yet the level of violence within South Vietnam actually increased. Thieu promised to conscript another 135,000 men, a figure that together with more Americans already in training camps, would almost fulfill Westmoreland's request. Proscribed from attacking the North, American pilots intensified the air war in the South. The president was still attempting to "negotiate from strength." Moreover, he intentionally omitted any reference to a coalition government. Johnson still sought an American peace, a noncommunist South Vietnam.

Ho Chi Minh, wanting to ensure the bombing halt, took up Johnson's offer for talks, and in private American and Vietnamese negotiators gradually worked out a practical arrangement that reflected battlefield realities. America would end all bombing if North Vietnam agreed "by its silence" not to escalate support for the NLF. Both sides might then consider possible coalition governments for South Vietnam. In this compromise, however, Johnson had not reckoned with his obstreperous ally in Saigon. Thieu thought that the Republican candidate could arrange better terms: "I will win the peace," Richard Nixon had vowed. So Saigon obstructed multilateral talks with the NLF, thus scuttling the compromise. Johnson stayed the bombing anyway, but he could not guarantee Saigon's good faith. If he cut off American aid, the communists would win by default. Thieu could always discipline Washington with threats that he would quit and thereby bring on chaos. Nixon's victory pleased Thieu immensely, but the new president required time to formulate specific policies. Diplomats marked time by haggling over the shape of the bargaining table. By the beginning of 1969, the Republicans faced an extraordinarily difficult situation: stalemated war, ungovernable allies, domestic impatience with half-measures.

VIETNAM FALLOUT

Washington's fixation with Southeast Asia distorted United States foreign policy. The war in Vietnam simultaneously pleased and worried the Soviets; America's burgeoning armies flanked their Chinese rival while it consumed capitalist treasure. Yankee search-and-destroy missions in the Mekong Delta freed the Soviets for attempts to expand their influence in the Middle East. Yet Johnson's very willingness to use force convinced Khrushchev's successors, Leonid Brezhnev and Aleksei Kosygin, that the Americans respected only military strength. Then, too, many Soviet scientists worried about the implications of the National Aeronautics and Space Administration's mammoth space rockets and plans for orbiting platforms. The Soviets stepped up production of their most sophisticated missile, the SS-9, and accelerated atomic stockpiling. Unable to match this buildup weapon for weapon, given Vietnam's huge drain on available resources, the United States intensified the technology of nuclear war, developing Multiple Independent Re-entry Vehicles (MIRVs), which vastly increased the payload of a single rocket, and "smart bombs," which guided themselves to their target through electronic devices.

But neither power wanted to let cold war rivalry escalate beyond its control. During June of 1967 Johnson and Kosygin conferred privately at Glassboro State College in New Jersey. Worried that the enormous success of Israel's just completed Six-Day War might somehow bring on a Soviet-American clash, each promised to respect his rival's vital interests in the crucial Middle East region. Rather than jeopardize the Nuclear Nonproliferation Treaty, finally signed in early 1969, Washington ignored Moscow's brutal repression of Czechoslovakian reform efforts in 1968. Such tradeoffs symbolized, once again, the high priority both nations placed upon avoiding atomic war.

Though consistently proclaimed as a crusade to reassure its allies, America's adventure in Southeast Asia further fragmented the Atlantic alliance. Western Europe's accelerating prosperity—itself a reflection of American spending overseas—eroded its sense of dependency. Arguments over strategy vitiated traditional comradeship. Determined to build a national nuclear force and, more grandiosely, to break out of "sterile bipolarity," Charles de Gaulle took France out of the NATO alliance, though he did not relinquish its protection. Many West Germans, hoping to build better relations with their neighbors, chafed at Washington's rigid anticommunism. Even the "special relationship" between Great Britain and the United States withered a bit. As economic obsolescence shoved the English toward the Common Market, they realized more and more their junior membership in the "atomic club." Prime ministers and many other Britons opposed America's policy in Vietnam. If Johnson felt somehow betrayed, England, no less than the rest of NATO, worried that its powerful protector had lost a sense of proportion. The United States seemed so drained by Vietnam that it could hardly attend to other pressing problems (its balance of international payments, for example). Vietnam became the most visible wedge that drove the Atlantic community apart, Europe's regional interests clashing with America's global visions.

Throughout the Third World the conflict in Southeast Asia resuscitated old devices in American diplomacy. Determined to create an Asian consensus for his policy, Johnson did not challenge oppressive regimes in the Philippines and South Korea, as long as they supported the American effort in Vietnam. Both countries sent troops to Vietnam. American money once again supported a military oligarchy in Indonesia after General Suharto ousted the increasingly pro-Chinese Sukarno in 1965. Only Japan resisted Johnson's embrace, but regardless of politics, the tendrils of a vast commerce clamped the two nations together. During the late 1960s, then, the United States forced everyone into roles as pro-United States or pro-communist, ignoring throughout Asia, as in Vietnam, both nationalism and indigenous cultures.

Such attitudes reverberated in policies toward Latin America. Once again Washington honored dictators. In 1964 in Brazil, for example, a cabal of generals supported by the United States toppled the populist Joao Goulart, who was showing growing interest in the nationalization of foreign businesses. Panicked by fears of "another Cuba," Johnson even resorted to military intervention in the Caribbean. In the Dominican Republic, a right-wing coup had ousted the constitutionally elected reformist government of Juan Bosch. But when Bosch's supporters attempted to regain control, American representatives on the island reported that communists had infiltrated Bosch's movement and requested Johnson to send the marines. Some 20,000 troops landed in mid-1965, and despite the quickly discovered inaccuracy of American reports, Johnson left the troops there until September 1966, when carefully supervised elections installed another pro-American leader, Joaquin Balaguer, as president. American gunboat diplomacy and alliances with dictators complemented a geyser of private investment by American corporations looking to Latin America for a quick profit but demanding political stability.

Preoccupied with Vietnam, Johnson either ignored change elsewhere or woodenly enforced the status quo. In this way the Southeast Asian war blinded America to the future, distorting its foreign policies and pushing others into a ready-made mold. The tensions could not be checked for long, but Johnson contained them for the moment.

Johnson's Legacy

If complex, the Democrats' legacy was not unmanageable. Peace talks in Paris provided a continuing structure for negotiation, but Johnson (and his successor) still hoped to win. South Vietnamese troops, presumably more motivated than America's dispirited soldiers, and sophisticated firepower, American leaders hoped, could "Vietnamize" the war while winning it. However plausible in the short run, such tactics could not remedy the flaw of American involvement. More years would pass before the nation's leaders abandoned this goal. By then, Johnson's war had become Nixon's war.

Most people did not immediately recognize another casualty of war—American socioeconomic stability. To pay for the most expensive war in the country's history, the White House loosed an inflation at home and a dollar crisis abroad that developed their own momentum. By the 1970s America's wealth and self-confidence had visibly atrophied. The adventure in Vietnam, far from protecting American institutions from foreign dangers, helped to bring them under increasing attack both from domestic reformers and external forces. Opposition to the Vietnam War served to unite the diverse protest movements of the 1960s.

SUGGESTIONS FOR FURTHER READING

Many of the general studies listed in the suggested readings for Chapter 1—such as McCormick, LaFeber, and Ambrose—remain relevant for the 1960s. In addition, see, generally, Richard J. Barnet, *Intervention and Revolution* (rev. ed., 1972); Thomas G. Paterson, ed., *Kennedy's Quest for Victory* (1989); and Bernard Firestone and Robert C. Vogt, eds. *Lyndon Baines Johnson and the Uses of Power* (1988).

On specific issues, consult Graham Allison, *Essence of Decision* (1971) on the missile crisis; Warren Cohen, *Dean Rusk* (1980); Henry Jackson, *From Congo to Soweto: United States Foreign Policy toward Africa Since 1960* (1982); Walter A. McDougall, *The Heavens and the Earth: A Political History of the Space Age* (1985); Richard D. Mahoney, *JFK: Ordeal in Africa* (1983); Glen Seaborg, *Stemming the Tide: Arms Control in the Johnson Years* (1987); Jane Stromseth, *The Origins of Flexible Response* (1988); Robert A. Divine, ed., *The Cuban Missile Crisis* (2nd ed., 1988); Trumbell Higgins, *The Perfect Failure: Kennedy, Eisenhower, and the CIA at the Bay of Pigs* (1989); and Bruce Palmer, Jr., *Intervention in the Caribbean: The Dominican Crisis of 1965* (1989).

Much of the scholarly debate, like most of the contemporary debate during the 1960s, has focused on Vietnam. In addition to volumes listed earlier—such as George Herring's *America's Longest War* (1986)—the following are good places to begin: William Appleman Williams and others, *America in Vietnam* (1985), provides a very valuable set of documents; Leslie Gelb and Richard K. Betts, *The Irony of Vietnam* (1978); Paul Joseph, *Cracks in the Empire* (1981); Larry Berman, *Planning a Tragedy* (1982); the relevant chapters of Lawrence Wittner, *Rebels Against War: The American Peace Movement, 1933–1983* (1984); Bruce Palmer, Jr., *The 25-Year War* (1985); William Conrad Gibbons, *The United States Government and the Vietnam War: Executive and Legislative Roles and Relationships* (1986); R. B. Smith, *An International History of the Vietnam War* (2 vols., 1985, 1987); Gabriel Kolko, *Anatomy of a War* (1986); Melvin Small, *Johnson, Nixon, and the Doves* (1988); Larry Berman, *Lyndon Johnson's War: The Road to Stalemate in Vietnam* (1989); John P. Burke and Fred Greenstein, *How Presidents Test Reality: Decisions on Vietnam, 1954 and 1965* (1989); Mark Clodfelter, *The Limits of Air Power: The American Bombing of North Vietnam* (1989); Marilyn Young and Jon Livingston, *The Vietnam War; How the United States Intervened in the History of Southeast Asia* (1990).

Also see Loren Baritz, *Backfire: A History of How American Culture Led us into Vietnam and Made Us Fight the Way We Did* (1985); Susan Jeffords, *The Remasculinization of America* (1989); Dean Rusk, *As I Saw It* (1990); and Patrick Lloyd Hatcher, *The Suicide of an Elite: American Internationalists and Vietnam* (1990). Michael Herr's *Dispatches* (1977) remains the most popular journalistic account of American involvement in Vietnam, while Peter Braestrup's *Big Story* (1978) is highly critical of the way that journalists such as Herr covered the war. Kathleen Turner's *Lyndon Johnson's Dual War* (1985) looks at LBJ's problems with the press. Finally, see Gilbert Adair, *Hollywood's Vietnam* (1989).

Chapter Seven

The Youth Movement and Search for a "New Politics," 1963–1968

For more than two decades now, people have been debating the meaning of the dissenting youth culture of the 1960s and early 1970s. Bitter divisions, personal as well as political, among people who once joined together in radical protest—against virtually every foreign and domestic policy of both major parties—suggest how heated debates about the 1960s can become. In recent years, for example, many former activists have turned public conferences and symposia into confessionals about their "sins" committed during the 1960s. They now dismiss their antiestablishment ideas and activities as the dangerous fantasies of youth, not a historical legacy that anyone, certainly not another generation of young people, would want to reclaim. In stark contrast, many others rejected the need for confessions or apologies. Still committed to the dissenting spirit of the 1960s, they insist that the old insurgency remains alive and relevant to the problems of the 1990s. But even people espousing these polar positions, as well as those whose interpretations of the decade fall somewhere in-between, agree on one point: The outpouring of dissent represented one of the central events in postwar history.

The "youth movement" is an imprecise term that was applied to a loose collection of very diverse groups with different styles of political and cultural dissent. Members of the New Left concentrated on political solutions for what they considered the failures of postwar liberalism; they believed that radical action by youthful community activists could bring significant social change and "power to the people." In contrast, cultural radicals displayed much less interest than members of the New Left in traditional political concerns; devotees of "the counterculture" advocated altered forms of social consciousness and a revolution in values as the best antidotes for what they saw as the sterility and repressiveness of postwar society.

Radicals never discovered how to change, at least as quickly as they desired, the direction of postwar society. The New Left did gain allies and make headway on specific issues—especially opposition to America's involvement in Vietnam—but radical politics also sometimes tailed off into ineffectual gestures and, on a few occasions, random acts of violence. Cultural radicals also left an ambiguous legacy. Many young people did adopt the outward symbols of cultural revolt, such as drugs and faded blue jeans, but most retained a desire to settle down, one day, within the existing social and economic structure. Some of the impulses toward cultural liberation, such as self-gratification, proved perfectly compatible with the ethos of a mass-consumption society. Moreover, as the sociologist Todd Gitlin, himself a veteran of the youth movement has argued, both political and cultural protests became captives of the mass media; film, television, and the popular press helped to contain and even trivialize protester's messages.

Still, the youth movements touched nearly every area of life. By challenging the dominant political and cultural values of the 1950s, they exerted a significant impact on the nation and widened opportunities for diversity and dissent. Especially for women of all races and for members of minority groups, the cultural and political insurgency helped to emphasize that the political was personal and the personal was political. This understanding contributed to a diverse and activist political culture during the late 1960s and 1970s, one that heightened social justice concerns and environmentalism.

THE REVOLT OF YOUTH

Young people's enthusiasm for John Kennedy led supporters of the New Frontier to expect that the 1960s would be a decade of steady liberal reform. But even before JFK's death, some young people were becoming disillusioned with his gradualism and with liberalism itself. The potpourri of sources from which disaffected young people sought insight and inspiration underscored the diversity of this new radicalism. Unlike the "old left" of the 1920s and 1930s, which looked primarily to Marxism, radicals of the 1960s sampled a variety of social theories. "Beat" writers, Eastern mystics, academic mavericks, and the civil rights movement helped provide the youth movement's eclectic intellectual base.

Radicals of the 1950s

While the middle-class protesters of the 1960s were still opening their school day by saluting the flag, the Beat poets and novelists of the 1950s had already dismissed society as an "air-conditioned nightmare." Jack Kerouac's novel *On the Road* (1957) glorified the drifter, the rebel who resisted the temptation to conform. The poems of Allen Ginsberg denounced materialism and middle-class morality and celebrated the satisfaction of marijuana, Eastern mystical religions, and homosexual love. In their best works, Beat poets such as Ginsberg and Gary Snyder displayed a free-flowing style that challenged restrictive cultural forms. Part hipster and part huckster, Ginsberg kept alive the spirit of the Beat movement, becoming a revered elder-in-residence to the radicals of the 1960s.

While the Beats condemned postwar cultural values, the sociologist C. Wright Mills concentrated on the postwar political system. In response to efforts by colleagues to marginalize his work, Mills effectively cultivated his image as an marverick outsider. (Although he taught at Columbia University, Mills mocked Ivy League style in favor of a motorcycle jacket and a Harley Davidson.) He also consciously rejected the dispassionate, carefully nuanced stance of cold war academics in favor of politically committed, rhetoric-filled analysis. Mills's writings helped popularize theories that became the New Left's central tenets: that an undemocratic "power elite" dominated American society; that liberalism had lost its social consciousness and become an ideology of the status quo; and that most liberal intellectuals merely offered rationalizations for an unjust society. Mills also condemned American foreign policy as an extension of the same corrupt values: He warned that a small group of politicians, military officials, and business leaders enjoyed virtually unchecked power. An activist as well as a scholar, Mills visited Cuba and wrote a short book praising Fidel Castro's social experiments. After his death in 1962, Mills became one of the youth movement's most revered saints.

The critique of American liberalism received greater philosophical development in the works of Herbert Marcuse. A German-born Marxist, Marcuse attacked the sophisticated technology and economic prosperity that liberals praised so highly. The United States, according to Marcuse, was a quasi-totalitarian "technocracy." Real power lay with the "technocrats"—the experts in government, business, science, and other dominant institutions, who defined social policies and national priorities. In such a one-dimensional society, people became slaves to a technological imperative. The political process offered no real choice: Voters could choose only among candidates who endorsed the same social and economic policies and who ultimately relied on the same group of technocrats. The mass-production, mass-consumption economic system satisfied only "false" needs—new automobiles, electronic gadgets, and thousand of other products that provided no real sense of happiness or personal fulfillment.

Disaffected young people borrowed from Marcuse and his many popularizers. Terms such as *false consciousness and technocracy* became parts of the radical vocabulary. Marcuse, like Mills, endorsed the thesis that the liberal "good guys"—including the people who ran the big universities and the big government in Washington—were really the villains. Some young people came to see liberalism as a new form of conservatism; others saw it as a kind of suave totalitarianism, one that dominated people with mass-mediated images and popular illusions rather than with guns and concentration camps.

Paul Goodman, another radical social critic, also helped to popularize the theory that liberal institutions actually repressed young Americans, especially males. In his book *Growing Up Absurd* (1960), Goodman argued that educational institutions stifled naturally healthy instincts and subtly indoctrinated young people with the values of a badly flawed society. Order and regularity, he claimed, took precedence over spontaneity and creativity; memorization of meaningless data became more important than critical thought; the interests of teachers and administrators outweighed the needs of students. Goodman applied his anarchist critique to all of postwar society, contending that large bureaucracies run by technocratic experts rarely performed their appointed tasks. Goodman did not see technology as an uncontrollable demon, as did some of his younger disciples; the problem, he argued, lay in the way that centralized institutions misapplied technology to social situations.

Books were not the only source of radical inspiration. Experiences in the civil rights movement also propelled many young radicals, white as well as African-American, toward an open break with liberalism. Lacking financial resources, civil rights leaders relied upon youthful volunteers for time-consuming, labor-intensive jobs: preparing leaflets, running copying machines, and canvassing neighborhoods. In time, the ways in which tasks divided along gender lines would encourage many women to embrace a new feminism; but, initially, these activities brought young people together in a common cause. Often travelling long distances and "crashing" together in makeshift accommodations, civil rights workers discovered a vision of community that seemed missing elsewhere in the United States. As one woman later wrote, the civil rights movement to her "was everything: home and family, food and work, love and a reason to live." In such a community atmosphere, many young people found personal fulfillment in a crusade that they expected would also change the entire society.

Seeking immediate solutions, civil rights workers inevitably confronted hostile or cautious political leaders. Segregationists in Alabama and Georgia would make no concessions, and liberal politicians stressed the need to move slowly and to avoid sudden changes in race relations. On many occasions southern crowds beat up civil rights workers while FBI agents simply looked on and took notes. After confronting the racial hatred of Oxford, Mississippi, or Cicero, Illinois, many young activists charged that liberals offered Band-Aid solutions for deep national wounds. Segregation and racism, young civil rights workers charged, were evils that no decent society would tolerate.

Beyond Liberalism and toward a New Left

Not all young people protested, and the new radicals constituted only a minority of those between eighteen and twenty-five. Others remained true to the liberal spirit of John Kennedy, voting for Lyndon Johnson and going off to fight a war for "democracy and freedom" in Vietnam. Many young people bitterly resented long-haired "hippie" protestors, and they embraced the consumer products and the nine-to-five jobs scorned by the radicals. Talk of a "generation gap" obscured equally large fissures within the youth generation itself and ignored the small, yet significant, group of older radicals who joined the Movement. But the young people who protested seemed to overshadow their peers; certainly they dominated the media and the political debates in the 1960s. Deeply disturbed by the direction of society and convinced that they could find alternatives, the youthful rebels become the symbols of their entire generation.

What distinguished the young radicals from others of their age? Drawing upon several studies of college students, the psychologist Kenneth Keniston argued that the rebels were "psychological adults" but "sociological adolescents." Contrary to conventional wisdom, Keniston found that protesters tended to be excellent students, usually in the humanities, who suffered no great psychological difficulties. But as the products of affluent or solidly middle-class homes, they possessed the freedom, as well as the desire, to postpone settling into permanent social roles. Instead of leaping into an established career pattern, the young radicals wanted to adopt a less conventional role—that of social activist and agitator for political change. The fact that many believed their parents shared many of their ideals, but were forced to compromise them in their day-to-day lives, only intensified the desire to remain free from settled, adult routines.

To the young dissenters, liberalism's failures seemed more important than its admitted successes. Postwar America did enjoy greater material affluence, but at a price: Most jobs seemed boring; life lacked adventure and excitement; racial discrimination oppressed millions of people; and personal relationships seemed artificial. The cool, rational world of John Kennedy appeared to lack genuine feeling and to substitute rhetoric for meaningful social change. In contrast, a stance of opposition seemed to offer hope for immediate personal fulfillment as well as the chance for basic social change. Through a commitment to radicalism young people could instantly complete Paul Simon's "dangling conversations" or explore Bob Dylan's "smoke rings of the mind."

During the late 1950s and early 1960s small groups of college students helped to spark a revival of radical politics in the United States. At various universities—especially the University of Wisconsin at Madison, the University of California at Berkeley, and the University of Michigan—students tried to link "radical scholarship" and social activism. How could university professors avoid the kind of "scholarly dispassion" that radicals considered a means of justifying a repressive status quo? In time, a number of graduate students came to see themselves as prototypes for a new breed of college teacher: In the style of C. Wright Mills they would awaken campus life and revitalize radical thought. Other university students took more direct action. In the San Francisco Bay area, activists from Berkeley joined older activists to demonstrate on behalf of such causes as dissolution of HUAC, abolition of capital punishment, and elimination of racial discrimination. Young people were also active in the South, helping miners fight the large coal companies in Hazard County, Kentucky, in addition to working for civil rights organizations.

The predominately white Students for a Democratic Society (SDS), which began as an arm of the old left's League for Industrial Democracy, epitomized the New Left. SDS's Port Huron Statement of 1962 pleaded for a dramatically new social and political system in which people "shared in those social decisions determining the quality and direction" of their lives. As an alternative to the liberal political order—one that "frustrates democracy by confusing the individual citizen, paralyzing policy discussion, and consolidating the irresponsible power of military and business interests"—SDS espoused "participatory democracy." The search for a true participatory democracy, the Port Huron Statement argued, was "governed by two central aims: that the individual share in those social decisions determining the quality and direction of his life; that society be organized to encourage independence in men and provide the means for their common participation." Though the rhetoric of the Port Huron Statement hinted at the radicalism that SDS would soon embrace, the manifesto of 1962 remained essentially a leftist-liberal document. It sounded no call for revolution and endorsed specific political programs only slightly to the left of the Fair Deal–New Frontier agenda.

SDS's leaders initially viewed community organizing as the first step toward participatory democracy. Poor people fell victim to better-organized elites, SDS argued, because they could not exert political pressure commensurate with their numbers. SDS branched out from the college campuses and launched grass-roots programs among the urban poor. By moving into urban neighborhoods SDS hoped to form new organizations and to channel poor people's discontent into local politics. In cities such as Newark, New Jersey, SDS mounted drives against urban renewal and in support of better housing, more jobs, and school lunch programs. The first SDSers displayed a missionary zeal. While cultural radicals were smoking dope, the SDSers bragged that they were turned on to political organizing. But despite their commitment, they quickly discovered the difficulties of organizing poor people, especially by a group committed to participatory democracy. Inexperience in organizing, impatience with endless rounds of face-to-face meetings, and doubts about their initial visions of participatory democracy all led most SDS members to abandon the community projects. Seeking a more congenial environment and switching to the issue that seemed most pressing—the Vietnam War—SDS moved back to the college campus, the center of the youth revolt of the 1960s.

Campus Protests

The most-publicized campus protest occurred at the University of California at Berkeley in the fall of 1964. When university officials tried to limit political activity by radical students, protesters charged the university's administration with bowing to pressures from right-wing business leaders in the Bay Area and destroying free speech on campus. As protests against restrictions on speech escalated and a temporary truce collapsed, mass rallies, takeovers of university buildings, and raids by local police highlighted the Berkeley Student Revolt. A number of campus groups, not all of whom represented New Left factions, joined under the banner of the Free Speech Movement (FSM). Thus, the earliest protests represented more of an attack upon the paternalistic, bureaucratic routine of Berkeley than a revolt against the entire university structure. In early December 1964 student protesters began wearing computer cards as name tags; militants soon called a campus-wide strike. Student leaders claimed that almost three-quarters of the student body—and a sizable portion of the faculty—supported their three-day walkout.

The FSM also expressed cultural and political impulses that transcended campus life. Some of these seemed trivial. A young New Yorker who had drifted West, just to "check out the scene," arrived with a simple protest sign—FUCK. (Some people claimed that this really stood for "Freedom Under Clark Kerr," the president of the university). His example inspired a group of imitators, the "word mongers," and FSM to be identified by its opponents as simply the "Filthy Speech Movement." But the FSM also represented much deeper concerns and personal commitments. As one of the movement's leaders put it, there were times when the social-political machinery "makes you so sick at heart . . . [that] you can't even tacitly take part. And you've got to put your bodies upon the gears and upon the wheels, upon the levers, upon the apparatus, and you've got to make it stop." By the spring of 1965, many of the campus issues that had precipitated the first student protests had faded, replaced by larger concerns, especially the war in Vietnam.

The unrest at Berkeley provided a scenario that repeated itself on many large college campuses. Increasingly, the tone and the aims of the protesters grew more militant. In banding together to fight college administrators and their outside supporters—a student observer of the 1968 disturbances at Columbia, called them "the biggies"—young people often discovered a sense of community. As the civil rights workers in Mississippi had done earlier, though, they also developed a kind of garrison mentality, viewing themselves as victims of a faceless power structure.

The modern "multiversity" provided a perfect target. Big universities displayed what radicals considered the major sins of modern liberalism: emphasis on competitiveness, reliance on bureaucratic structures, restrictions on personal life styles, and feeling that bigger inevitably meant better. Many nonradicals shared some of these concerns. Sensitive young students, many of whom had been reared in families that stressed openness and concern for individual feelings, felt especially frustrated by the impersonality and routine of universities such as Berkeley and Columbia. They complained that large, impersonal lectures and haphazard discussion sections exemplified the multiversity's assembly-line approach to education. Many students felt reduced to faceless numbers, subject to the whims of giant computers, and dependent on faceless bureaucrats. Even the University of California's liberal president Clark Kerr saw himself as the administrator of a large "benevolent bureaucracy," a huge enterprise that produced knowledge instead of consumer goods. "The university and segments of industry are becoming more alike," Kerr observed in 1960.

Finally, most students resented what they considered invasions of their personal freedoms by university officials. Women, even those who were legally of age, had to observe dress codes and dorm hours on most college campuses during the early 1960s; men at many state universities were required to take two years of ROTC; and faculty-dominated committees censored student publications. Dissidents began to demand that universities abandon or relax these restrictions, reduce the number of required courses, and offer programs "relevant" to mid-twentieth-century society.

When student muckrakers examined the multiversity's role in American society they found additional grievances. Professors conducted classified research for the Defense Department; Harvard chemists, not Dow Chemical, had developed napalm. Seeking additional space for new buildings, athletic stadiums, and parking lots, many universities expanded into neighboring areas and pushed out the residents. Some private universities, radicals also discovered, owned inner-city properties and qualified as genuine slum landlords. To make the indictment complete, big universities rarely admitted minority students; when they did, recruitment efforts centered on talented athletes and a few academic superstars. Viewed from within, the multiversity seemed to offer mind-numbing courses and senseless regimentation. Seen as part of liberal society, it appeared implicated in war and racism.

Student and faculty pressures brought significant changes and a few strategic retreats by the old guard. Most colleges relaxed life style restrictions, abolished compulsory ROTC, adjusted curriculum requirements, made special efforts to recruit minority students, and established minority-studies programs. Some professors encouraged social activism by permitting students to substitute "relevant" outside projects for more traditional assignments. Although a number of spectacular "busts" temporarily halted protests, many campuses continued to serve as staging areas for forays against the outside world. At many urban universities large groups of street people provided additional troops for campus demonstrations and swelled the ranks of the "student" opposition. A radicalized university, activists began to hope, would be an important tool for changing the larger society.

The protests against growing U.S. involvement in the war in Vietnam demonstrated the value as well as the limitations of the university in radical politics. The crusade against the Vietnam War did not begin on the campuses, but dissent there gave the antiwar movement influential forums. Early in 1965, after President Johnson mounted an all-out bombing campaign against North Vietnam, antiwar activists organized a nationwide series of teach-ins, meetings at which supporters and opponents of LBJ's policies debated before largely student audiences. Initially, some protestors hoped that the teach-ins would spark vigorous exchanges with government officials and that the confrontations might eventually change policies. But by 1966 most militant opponents of the war were charging that teach-ins only wasted precious time. Obviously, the meetings were having little effect on President Johnson's actions, and the novelty of the gatherings was wearing thin. Although teach-ins continued sporadically throughout the 1960s—and even into the 1970s on some campuses—the antiwar movement began to desert the lecture platforms for the streets.

Antiwar demonstrations borrowed from both the tactics of the civil rights movement and the techniques of the teach-in. Beginning with a mass march, demonstrations invariably concluded with a series of speeches and musical entertainment. Organizers hoped large numbers of people in the streets would dramatize the strength of the youth movement, increase "radical consciousness," and pressure the national government to change its policies. Thus, each new march had to outdo the last; organizers struggled to attract more people or to devise new strategems for lampooning the liberal establishment. During the October 1967 March on Washington, a group of what the *East Village Other* called "witches, warlocks, holymen, seers, prophets, mystics, saints, sorcerers, shamans, troubadours, minstrels, bards, roadmen and madmen" tried to exorcise the Pentagon, hurling "mighty words of white light against the demon-controlled structure." Alas, the five-sided bastion of the military-industrial complex hardly budged, but such productions raised the spirits of the protesters.

The politics of simply organizing such demonstrations helped cover up deeper differences over goals and tactics. Negotiations with political leaders, police chiefs, rock entrepreneurs, and portable-toilet vendors sometimes seemed as complex as the conduct of the war itself. For many people, marches and demonstrations served much the same function as religious revival meetings: The faithful assembled, felt their faith renewed, and then went back home to prepare for the next assembly. And by gathering tens and then hundreds of thousands of people at a single demonstration, antiwar leaders could reassure themselves that all was going well. Even a fraction of a percent of the baby-boom generation, when assembled in one spot, made a good-sized crowd, and a sprinkling of older people raised hopes that the movement was edging outside its core youth market.

What was the political role of the mass demonstrations and marches? Critics have claimed that they actually rebounded against the antiwar forces by daring the combative LBJ to "hang tough" and to conduct more of the war in secret. Others argue that the techniques did help end the war. Although policymakers publicly denied that they took any notice of the mass protests, the gatherings undoubtedly helped to convert some former hawks and embolden doves. Moreover, they made it more difficult for Johnson to claim any consensus for his war policies and, once the "secret" portions of his policies became public knowledge, to mount any bold escalations. Even so, mass demonstrations became increasingly ritualistic. Protesters sprawled on the grass, half-listening to familiar rhetoric, and reminisced about previous gatherings.

The vast majority of youthful protesters strongly opposed the war and felt estranged from liberal society, but many also came to lose interest in sustained political activity. In time, antipathy toward the liberal establishment extended to "peace bureaucrats" in the New Left. Cultural radicals, whom the mass media eventually labeled "hippies," emphasized "doing your own thing" rather than joining political organizations. San Francisco, the old haunt of many of the Beats of the 1950s, once again became a mecca for cultural dissidents.

Radical Youth Culture

In the mid-1960s the San Francisco Bay area, especially the Haight-Ashbury neighborhood of San Francisco, became famous, or notorious, as the focus of cultural revolution. "Hip" people from all over the country flocked to northern California, hoping to enjoy the "laid-back" life styles of the "age of Aquarius." Soon, the media highlighted the comings and goings of the hippies. Many young people were intrigued by communal living arrangements, "liberated" views on sex, experimentation with drugs, and the electrified sound of folk-rock music. Hippies celebrated their emancipation from "hang-ups" such as work and clothing fashions. Attired in America's castoffs, including old military uniforms, the new rebels espoused philosophies that stressed mystical experiences and universal love.

Unlike members of the New Left, most devotees of the counterculture showed little interest in political questions or new political organizations. Following the Beat writers of the 1950s some began to study Eastern faiths such as Zen and Taoism; a few joined Timothy Leary's League for Spiritual Discovery or eclectically sampled psychedelic drugs; many simply relied upon slogans. "Make Love, Not War" and "Flower Power" became familiar parts of the hippie litany. Sociologists eagerly studied hippie culture; pop journalists such as Tom Wolfe breathlessly covered it; and middle-class vacationers made a quick bus tour of Haight-Ashbury an essential part of their visit to San Francisco.

But Haight-Ashbury soon became something other than a quaint haven for "flower children." San Francisco's political establishment declared war on "this hippie thing," and the city's police chief condemned the young rebels as people without "the courage to face the reality of life." Quickly taking their cue, many patrol officers ruthlessly searched for drugs and often harassed any unkept young person. At the same time, the Haight faced an invasion of petty criminals, drifters who saw hippies as easy prey. The community also developed internal divisions; "hip entrepreneurs" took control of Haight-Ashbury's economic life, and phony "weekend hippies" invaded the area. Dope became big business, and pushers began to peddle stronger and stronger chemicals. The wiser "heads" warned about the dangers—"Speed Kills," proclaimed posters—but the naive became hooked on hard drugs or experienced bad "trips" on powerful hallucinogens. A few died from overdoses. A handbill printed in August 1967 expressed the growing disillusionment with Haight-Ashbury.

> The trouble is that the hip shopkeepers probably believe their own bullshit lies. They believe that dope is the answer and neither know nor care what the question is.
>
> Have you been raped? Take acid and everything will be groovy. Are you cold, sleeping in doorways at night? Take acid and discover your inner warmth. Are you hungry? Take acid and transcend these mundane needs.
>
> You can't afford acid? Pardon me, I think I hear somebody calling me.

Despite the rapid rise and fall of Haight-Ashbury, the counterculture grew, especially as it became closely linked to new trends in rock music. By 1966 the Beatles and the Rolling Stones were dominating rock, and Bob Dylan was augmenting his acoustic guitar with the amplified sound of folk-rock. Groups from San Francisco took the lead in exploring the possibilities of electronic rock. Jerry Garcia and the Grateful Dead attracted a particularly devoted following. The Dead gradually added various kinds of light shows, and the Merry Pranksters (a group of young people attracted to the novelist Ken Kesey) laced the audience with LSD. ("Can you pass the acid test?" the Pranksters slyly asked concertgoers.) The result was "acid rock" and a whole new genre of drug-related, "mindblowing" sounds. Soon, something called "progressive rock" became a smashing success, financially as well as artistically. Although cautious programmers and disc jockeys generally excluded the new sounds from AM radio's Top-40 play lists, progressive rock spawned its own medium—"free-form" FM radio. The popularity of San Francisco groups—particularly the Dead, Jefferson Airplane, and Big Brother and the Holding Company (featuring Janis Joplin)—rapidly spread across the country.

The union of disaffected youth, drugs, and rock music—the combination that made the Woodstock Rock Festival of 1969 briefly appear to represent the flowering of a true cultural revolution—was consummated. By the later 1960s the counterculture appeared everywhere. Aided by modern technology—mass-produced books and magazines, stereo record albums, automobiles, airplanes, and psychedelic chemicals—the radical youth culture became a nationwide phenomenon. The counterculture was difficult to classify; it was variously a state of mind, a way of life, or sometimes merely a style of dress. It developed its own mass media. The success of the *Berkeley Barb* and the *Los Angeles Free Press* encouraged other "underground newspapers," and radical journalists soon formed their own Liberation News Service. Although few of these enterprises survived for any length of time, the proliferation of underground papers did suggest the counterculture's broad aspirations. The growing populations of countercultural students and street people created little Haight-Ashburys around major college campuses and in most large cities.

New York's East Village, a run-down area near fashionably radical Greenwich Village, quickly became the East Coast's version of Haight-Ashbury. Here Abbie Hoffman and Jerry Rubin conceived the spurious Youth International party—the Yippies. A free-wheeling attempt to blend political and cultural radicalism and to gain attention from the media, the short-lived Yippie movement made Rubin and Hoffman national celebrities.

Yippie philosophy owed more to Groucho, Harpo, and Chico than to Karl Marx. The Yippie program was theater in the streets, an updated, drug-inspired vaudeville of the radical left. With the Yippies, revolution and symbolic defiance became one and the same. In one of their most famous escapades, Yippies invaded the New York Stock Exchange, hurling currency at brokers who were wildly trading their paper securities. Hoffman facetiously suggested that such theatrics would eventually produce upheaval through a mystical process he called "cultural jujitsu": Confronted by the taunts of the Yippies in the streets and by its own innate contradictions, corporate America would hack itself to pieces. The Yippies' penchant for playing radicalism for laughs—Hoffman entitled his treatise *Revolution for the Hell of It*—and their adolescent bravado—which oftentimes took the form of media-oriented theatrics—only underscored their lack of any serious program for social change, let alone for political transformation. Rubin and Hoffman drew more support from the managers of the mass media than from members of the youth movement; but, certified as hippie celebrities, they came to enjoy the visibility that more thoughtful dissidents could never obtain.

The Meaning of the Counterculture

From the very beginning, critics denounced radical youth culture as a dangerous and foolish attack on the realities of modern life. The prominent psychologist Bruno Bettelheim dismissed the outcries against technology as the babbling of "obsolete youth" in a technological age that required discipline and order. Zbigniew Brzezinski, who would later be President Carter's National Security Adviser, condemned the youthful protesters as "twentieth-century Luddites." Noting that most college dissidents came from the humanities rather than from the sciences or engineering, Brzezinski claimed that the rebels were blindly attacking the new learning because it threatened their power and prestige. He dismissed both the cultural rebellion and the politics of the New Left as "a reaction to the more basic fear that the times are against them, that a new world is emerging without either their assistance or leadership." The counterculture, Brzezinski concluded, was "the death rattle" of the historically obsolete.

Even people critical of the dominant emphasis within postwar liberalism criticized the spirit of the counterculture. Writing in the 1970s, Peter Clecak saw leaders of the cultural insurgency vying with one another for the chance to be packaged and sold as media celebrities. Having been raised on the juvenile television fare of the 1950s, he complained, the eternal adolescents of the 1960s "easily fell into the comic roles" assigned them by television producers. The result, Clecak concluded, was the trivialization of dissent. Another critic of liberalism, the historian Christopher Lasch, drew an even broader indictment of the impact of the 1960s upon the 1970s. The counterculture's infatuation with "finding oneself" and with "alternative consciousness" ultimately contributed to a "culture of narcissism"—a rootless, self-absorbed search for the latest prepackaged life style and, more dangerously, a radically scaled-down vision of one's own connection to history and any large community.

Many of those associated with the feminist movement, which grew rapidly in the 1970s, also showed ambivalence toward the counterculture. By breaking old conventions, the counterculture helped provide space for the renewal of feminist activism. But part of the preceding Beat movement was, as Barbara Ehrenrich has pointed out, a "male revolt" hostile to family and to women. Moreover, males dominated the radical movements of the 1960s, often viewing women as primarily secretarial or sexual servants to the cause led by males. The drug culture and the sexual revolution could sometimes victimize women in the name of liberation.

The counterculture, though, had—and still has—its defenders. The historian Theodore Roszak, who first popularized the term *counterculture*, viewed dissident young people as the vanguard of a reaction against an oppressive technological society. Saturated by misdirected technology, "technocracy's children" sought a society and a level of consciousness that allowed for beauty, mystery, feeling, and love. In *The Making of a Counter-Culture* (1969), Roszak sympathetically explored the counterculture's interest in Eastern religions, Beat writers, anarchist philosophers, and mystics of all kinds. But even he warned that the middle-class rebels would have to avoid at least two dangers: losing touch with disadvantaged people, particularly nonwhites who had never enjoyed the temptations of technology; and becoming "an amusing side show" for people who confused changes in life styles with liberation. Indeed, more than Roszak would allow, elements within the counterculture itself displayed much the same commercial slickness and infatuation with technology, albeit in different forms, as the entrepreneurs on Madison Avenue. In time, hippie-style clothes, high-tech toys, and a more casual attitude toward sex became fashionable among many business and professional people; the hippie life style could blend, without much difficulty, into the dominant valves of an advanced industrial society.

1968: THE POLITICS OF CONFRONTATION

Predictably, a number of politicians launched an attack on "those dirty hippies" and "permissiveness." Ronald Reagan, for example, left Hollywood for good and pledged to "straighten out things at Berkeley" during his successful campaign for the governorship of California in 1966. Reagan and many other politicians took an increasingly hard line against the use of drugs, condemning the growing popularity of marijuana as proof of young people's disrespect for law and authority.

The 1968 presidential campaign expressed the complex tension within American society and channeled them into the political arena. As events would show, however, the electoral system offered a poor forum for resolving the deep social and cultural divisions; few national contests have produced as much bitterness and political violence as the 1968 presidential campaign.

The Fall of Lyndon Johnson

Lyndon Johnson became the first casualty. After capturing more than 60 percent of the popular vote in 1964, Johnson had celebrated his "politics of consensus." Some Republicans even worried about their party's survival. But committed to his cause in Vietnam, blamed for racial conflict, and assailed by critics of his Great Society, Johnson saw old supporters deserting him. Lyndon Johnson, one of this century's great political manipulators, became isolated; trapped in the White House by the antiwar demonstrations that followed him everywhere, LBJ spent considerable time staring at his bank of TV sets. Where had he gone wrong? Why had such a promising presidency turned into such a debacle? Johnson's standing in opinion polls steadily plummeted; his support in Congress evaporated; and dissident Democrats organized a "dump-Johnson" movement in order to do the unthinkable—deny an incumbent president his party's nomination.

At first considered hopeless, especially when Senator Robert Kennedy refused to challenge LBJ for the nomination, the dump-Johnson effort finally coalesced behind an unlikely standard-bearer, Senator Eugene McCarthy of Minnesota. An unorthodox, aloof antipolitician—detractors simply called him arrogant and lazy—McCarthy promised no great societies. His entire campaign suggested a conservative's doubts about the dreams of liberals like Lyndon Johnson. "All we want is a moderate use of intelligence," McCarthy told supporters. Gradually, the Minnesotan's low-key campaign caught fire, and a small army of college students rallied behind the only "peace candidate" in either major party. When Lyndon Johnson declined to campaign personally in the New Hampshire presidential primary, McCarthy's "quixotic children's crusade," as many in the media called it, dominated the TV screen. Meanwhile, the communists' Tet Offensive in South Vietnam and worries about the future of violent protest at home increased doubts about the president's capacity to lead the nation.

Although Eugene McCarthy actually won only 43 percent of the Democratic vote in New Hampshire's March 1968 primary, he ran well enough to refute conventional wisdom about the invincibility of an incumbent president within his own party. McCarthy also accomplished something else: He captured media attention for the anti-Johnson movement. (In some ways

McCarthy's appeal was as much anti-Johnson as it was antiwar: When asked about their second choice as a Democratic candidate, McCarthy supporters often named Alabama's hawkish governor, George C. Wallace.)

After the New Hampshire primary, Johnson's political and personal problems only increased. Within days, Robert Kennedy announced his intention to enter the race for the Democratic nomination; and, facing certain defeat by McCarthy in the Wisconsin primary, a physically exhausted Lyndon Johnson retired without a fight. On March 31, 1968, the president dramatically announced that he would not seek another term. About to be relieved of the responsibilities of the presidency, Johnson abandoned the spartan routine that his heart condition required. He resumed smoking and began to eat greater quantities of rich, fried foods. Within two years he suffered a serious heart attack; within five years he was dead.

The "New Politics" and the Election of 1968

Johnson's retreat brought forth a full-scale charge by Hubert Humphrey, LBJ's vice-president and an unsuccessful presidential contender in 1960. Humphrey enjoyed the full support of Democratic party chieftains—labor leaders such as George Meany, political bosses such as Chicago Mayor Richard Daley and Texas governor John Connally, and LBJ himself. With this backing, Humphrey could ignore the primaries and use his political muscle to line up delegates. At first, he preached "the politics of joy," but even Humphrey came to recognize the joyless political atmosphere of the 1968 election.

The unrelenting political violence of 1968 made a mockery of Humphrey's slogan. In April, Martin Luther King was gunned down in Memphis; black ghettos erupted in anger. Disorders rocked more than one hundred towns; thirty-six people died; and public officials deployed more than fifty thousand National Guard and federal troops. Many black and white radicals refused to believe that another lone gunman, this one an escaped convict named James Earl Ray, could have killed another national leader. (In 1979 a special House Committee concluded that some type of conspiracy very likely did surround King's shooting, but it provided no firm evidence.)

As Americans recovered from the shock of King's death, Eugene McCarthy and Robert Kennedy attempted to bring alienated people back into "the system." McCarthy's brand of "new politics"—a much-abused phrase that suggested no backroom deals with powerful interest groups, reliance on youthful volunteers, and straightforward political speeches—appealed to bright, politically aware college students. (Bobby Kennedy once joked that McCarthy had all the A students while he could attract only those who got grades of B or B − .) Shaving beards and donning skirts to "come clean for Gene," thousands of young people canvassed door to door and state to state with their hero. Kennedy's efforts also excited young people, but many complained that his campaign smacked too much of the "old politics." Kennedy tried to make special appeals to a diverse coalition of white ethnic voters, minorities, liberals, and even George Wallace's supporters. As he vigorously stumped Indiana, assisted by plenty of Kennedy money, reporters dubbed his campaign train the "Ruthless Cannonball."

He has the Poles in Gary,
The Blacks will fill his hall,
There are no ethnic problems on the Ruthless Cannonball.

While Humphrey rested on his safe cushion of nonprimary delegates, Kennedy and McCarthy tried to impress party leaders with their vote-getting ability. In Oregon, McCarthy became the first politician ever to defeat any Kennedy. But a Kennedy campaign was something special: An array of movie stars, musicians, athletes, university professors, and even business executives dropping everything to follow Bobby. Ignoring threats against his life, Kennedy waded into crowds wherever he went, with only a few burly friends to shield him from danger. The night of the California primary, these same supporters stood helplessly nearby as Kennedy was shot at point-blank range in the kitchen of a Los Angeles hotel. Police immediately arrested Sirhan Sirhan, a Jordanian immigrant, whom a jury later convicted of Kennedy's murder. Minutes before the shooting Kennedy had accepted congratulations for a narrow victory over McCarthy in the climactic California primary; twenty-four hours later he was dead. Although McCarthy said that he would continue to fight for the nomination, Kennedy's death took the heart out of his campaign. Humphrey had a clear path.

Meeting amid racial violence and protest in Miami (four people were killed during racial disorders there), Republicans chose a face from the past—former vice-president Richard Nixon. Although he had lost the 1960 presidential contest and had presumably retired from politics after his defeat in the California gubernatorial race of 1962, image makers proclaimed a "new Nixon." (Early in the 1968 campaign, a critic complained that "there is no new Nixon. What we have here is the old Nixon, a little older.") The dogged campaigner, whom fellow law students at Duke had called "Old Iron Butt," simply outlasted the field. Nominated on the first ballot, Nixon surprised the convention by selecting Spiro T. Agnew, the obscure governor of Maryland, as his running mate.

In his acceptance speech, the "new Nixon" suggested peaceful overtures to the Soviet Union and the People's Republic of China and pledged to give black Americans "a piece of the action in the exciting ventures of private enterprise." But the address also contained echoes of the old Nixon. He praised the "forgotten Americans, the nonshouters, the nondemonstrators"; he suggested that Americans had been "deluged" by government welfare programs that had only "reaped . . . an ugly harvest of frustrations, violence, and failure"; and he promised that his attorney general would "open a new front against crime."

The cry for law and order became stronger after the violence that accompanied the Democrats' Chicago convention. Mayor Richard Daley expected trouble. Several peace groups planned demonstrations, and the

Yippies promised a "festival of life," an answer to what they called the Democrats' "festival of death." Abbie Hoffman talked about sending ten thousand nude Yippies wading into Lake Michigan, releasing greased pigs in Chicago's crowded Loop area, and slipping LSD into the city's water supply. Mayor Daley took Hoffman's jokes seriously. Although intelligence reports indicated that the number of demonstrators would fall far below the Yippies' expectations, the mayor readied his police force and had the Illinois National Guard and the United States Army waiting for action. "If you're going to Chicago, be sure to wear armor in your hair," warned an underground newspaper editor.

After several days of skirmishes between youthful protesters and the Chicago police, serious violence erupted on the night delegates formally nominated Humphrey as the Democratic nominee for president. Police beat demonstrators, nonprotesting bystanders, and even reporters. A special commission eventually labeled the disorders a "police riot." The police, the commission concluded, had responded out of all proportion to the provocations. According to one eyewitness, "Some police pursued individuals as far as a block and beat them. . . . In many cases it appeared to me that when the police had finished beating the protesters they were pursuing, they then attacked, indiscriminately, any civilian who happened to be standing nearby. Many of these were not involved in the demonstration." But many people saw events the other way: One poll claimed that nearly 60 percent of their sample blamed the demonstrators and supported the police.

On the question of disorders at the convention and on the war issue, Hubert Humphrey found himself surrounded by squabbling Democrats. He dared not openly criticize either Mayor Daley's police or the antiwar forces. Humphrey tried to pretend that his party would pull together, but his early campaign efforts belied such optimism. Antiwar hecklers confronted the underfinanced and badly advised Humphrey at every stop, and his audiences remained small and generally unenthusiastic.

George Wallace hoped to benefit from Humphrey's troubles. Running on the American Independent ticket, the former governor of Alabama preached law and order, the slogan that black people and liberals considered merely code words for racism. Wallace's angry denials were, in a sense, correct. Race was only one of the social issues that Wallace hoped to exploit. In his standard address he contended that "there's not a dime's worth of difference" between the two major parties, denounced "pointy-headed professors" who "don't know how to park a bicycle straight," and predicted that "intellectual morons" and "theoreticians" were "going to get some of those liberal smiles knocked off their faces." Wallace cleverly linked distaste for big government with fears of the counterculture: "Our lives are being taken over by bureaucrats, and most of them have beards." As election day neared, however, many northern blue-collar workers and ethnic voters, Democrats who had been leaning toward Wallace rejoined the ranks. Aided by the pull of party loyalty, Vice-President Humphrey nearly caught Nixon.

Richard Nixon and his army of strategists watched Humphrey draw closer until the polls predicted a toss-up. Finally deciding that he would have

Antiwar protestors at the Washington State Democratic Convention of 1968. Source: *Tacoma Public Library Neg. # TPL 371.*

to untangle himself from Johnson's Vietnam policy, the vice-president announced that he favored a bombing halt as a way of speeding up the Paris peace talks. Several days before the November election, President Johnson ordered a temporary cessation of air raids over North Vietnam. These steps induced some antiwar people, including Eugene McCarthy, to announce at least grudging support of Humphrey's candidacy. But Humphrey fell about a hundred thousand votes short, and Nixon captured the presidency with only about 43 percent of the popular vote. The lonely, long-distance runner, as Garry Wills called Nixon, had finally won his big race.

Although Nixon and Humphrey had tried to identify themselves with the "new politics," their nominations, and the election of Ike's former vice-president, demonstrated the tenacity of traditional political habits and institutions. Careful study of voting behavior revealed that people most likely to cast ballots were unyoung, unpoor, unblack, and largely unsympathetic to youthful radicalism. Most voters identified cultural rebellion with ingratitude for America's material abundance; they considered left-wing politics, with its demonstrations and direct participation, socially disruptive. Those who initially wanted to cast a protest vote supported McCarthy, Kennedy, or Wallace, believing that, in their own unique ways, these three had broken with conventional politicians. With Kennedy's death, some of his discontented working-class supporters switched their allegiance to George Wallace. And after McCarthy's virtual retirement from political life following the violence of Chicago, many supporters of the new politics simply stayed home. Others reluctantly joined the other voters in choosing between two familiar candidates who stood firmly in the center of the American political spectrum.

Although historical movements rarely take sudden turns or end abruptly, many historical interpretations currently mark 1968—a year that saw massive youth protests in Germany and France as well as in the United States—as the terminal date or an important turning point for the "movement" of the 1960s. In this view, the violence of 1968 and an election among candidates Wallace, Humphrey, and Nixon underscored the organizational limits and ultimate failure of the new politics. The "good" days of the early movement were over, a judgment found in many histories and reminiscences written by people, largely males, who themselves had been radical leaders during the early 1960s. Those commentators without much sympathy for any phase of the youth politics see 1968 in an even worse light: After 1968, political naivete became fanaticism and cultural infantilism turned into simplistic barbarism. In one form or another, variations on this viewpoint have come to dominate discussions, especially after the flood of books published in 1988–1989 on the twentieth anniversary of 1968.

Seen in another way, though, the year 1968 marked neither a sudden end nor a radical turn in youth-oriented politics. The dissenting impulses of the 1960s never were nor could have been represented by a single "movement," and a single election year provides only a cloudy lens through which to view the complex social and cultural changes associated with youth-oriented radicalism. The year 1968 included many important events, but the age of protest was far from over.

SUGGESTIONS FOR FURTHER READING

The literature on the opposition movements of the 1960s is already immense—and of widely varying quality. Several "classics" of the 1960s provide good starting places: Philip Slater, *The Pursuit of Loneliness* (rev. ed., 1976); Theodore Roszak, *The Making of a Counter-Culture* (1969) and *Where the Wasteland Ends* (1972); Charles Reich, *The Greening of America* (1970). Sohnya Sayres and others, *The 60s Without Apology* (1984) and Clair and Stewart Albert, *The Sixties Papers* (1984), are useful anthologies. W. J. Rorabaugh, *Berkeley at War: The 1960s* (1989) is a model monograph.

Irwin Unger's *The Movement* (1974) is still a useful critique. Milton Viorst, *Fire in the Streets* (1981), brings to life some of the leading radical personalities. Peter Clecak, *Radical Paradoxes* (1973), and Kirkpatrick Sale, *SDS* (1972), remain valuable. On opposition to the war, see Thomas Powers, *The War at Home* (1973); Fred Halstead, *Out There* (1978); Nancy Zaroulis and Gerald Sullivan, *Who Spoke Up?* (1984) and Charles DeBenedetti, *An American Ordeal* (1990). Todd Gitlin indicts the media for speeding the fall of opposition efforts in *The Whole World Is Watching* (1980). Maurice Isserman's *If I Had a Hammer* (1987) looks at the conflict between the Old Left and the New Left. Wini Breines, *Community and Organization in the New Left, 1962–1968* (new ed., 1989), provides an important study.

The diversity of the "counterculture" is evident in Tom Wolfe, *The Electric Kool-Aid Acid Test* (1969); Morris Dickstein, *Gates of Eden* (1977); Joan Didion, *The White Album* (1979); and Charles Perry, *The Haight-Ashbury* (1985). Abe Peck covers the "underground press" in *Uncovering the Sixties* (1985), while Daniel Yankelovich tries to fathom changing social values in *The New Morality* (1974) and *New Rules* (1982).

During the heyday of Reaganism, a strong nostalgia for the early and mid-1960s began to emerge. Jim Miller, *Democracy Is in the Streets* (1987); Todd Gitlin, *The Sixties: Years of Hope, Days of Rage* (1987); Joan and Robert K. Morrison, eds., *From Camelot to Kent State: The Sixties Experience in the Words of Those Who Lived It* (1987); and Hans Konig, *Nineteen Sixty-Eight: A Personal Report* (1987), all express complex, though not uncritical, feelings of loss. In contrast, the "former radicals" who "look back" in Peter Collier and David Horowitz, eds. *Second Thoughts* (1989), have almost nothing good to say about the 1960s. Among the attempts to gain some perspective on the decade, especially the allegedly pivotal year of 1968, see Irwin and Debi Unger, *Turning Point, 1968* (1988); David Caute, *The Year of the Barricades: A Journey Through 1968* (1988); David Farber, *Chicago '68* (1988); and Douglas Knight, *Streets of Dreams: The Nature and Legacy of the 1960s* (1989).

Sara Evans, *Personal Politics: The Roots of Women's Liberation in the Civil Rights Movement and the New Left* (1979), and Alice Echols, *Daring to Be Bad: Radical Feminism in America, 1967–1975* (1989), seek to trace the emergence of a new feminism out of the male-dominated ethos of both the New Left and the counterculture and to suggest that 1968 did not represent a sudden end to insurgent movements. See also Winifred D. Wandersee, *On the Move: American Women in the 1970s* (1989) and Warren Belasco, *Appetite For Change: How the Counter-Culture Took on the Food Industry* (1990).

Chapter Eight

Protest and the Search for Power 1968–1976

THE VIOLENT YEARS, 1968–1972

Violence in Southeast Asia

Despite the years of antiwar protest and Richard Nixon's talk of a secret peace plan, the war in Vietnam continued, even accelerated, in the late 1960s. After a thorough review of war policy Nixon and his national security adviser, Henry Kissinger, made several crucial decisions. As quickly as possible the United States would turn the ground war over to the South Vietnamese and begin a gradual withdrawal of American forces while stepping up the air war. At the same time, the United States would try to enlist Soviet help in wringing concessions from Hanoi. In July 1969 the president placed his Vietnam policy within a grander design—the so-called Nixon Doctrine—pledging that the United States would continue giving military assistance to anticommunist governments in Asia but would have Asians, not Americans, do the fighting. The president was promising peace but still hoping to design the military victory that had beguiled, and eluded, his predecessors. Essentially "Vietnamization" of the war was a formula for stepping up the war while defusing domestic dissent by ending the involvement of American draftees.

Nixon looked to Henry Kissinger rather than to his cabinet to help construct his policy of Vietnamization. In fact, the foreign-policy-making process was so thoroughly centralized in the White House that Secretary of State William Rogers and Secretary of Defense Melvin Laird often remained peripheral to important decisions. Kissinger, a Harvard professor, saw world policies as a global geopolitical confrontation between Soviet and American power. According to Kissinger, America's primary duty consisted of foreclosing Soviet opportunities for expansion; conflicts anywhere in the world had to be viewed in light of how they "linked up" to the central concern of American policy. It was through his crucial concept of linkage that Kissinger justified his hopes for an early and favorable settlement in Vietnam. Kissinger hoped, he later wrote in his memoirs, to make "progress in settling the Vietnam war something of a condition for advance in areas of interest to the Soviets, such as the Middle East, trade or arms limitation."

The "secret plan" for ending the war by enticing the Soviets to pressure the North Vietnamese made at least two faulty assumptions: One, that the Soviets could easily influence Hanoi; and two, that the Soviets would be persuaded to pull their strings on America's behalf. Neither proved correct, but Kissinger continued to pursue Vietnamization.

To buy time for Vietnamization to shape South Vietnam's army into an effective force and to prepare for bringing American ground troops home, Nixon and Kissinger accelerated the conflict while still technically honoring Johnson's bombing halt over the North. They launched offensives against targets in the South and ordered full-scale combat against Cambodia. To mask this new escalation, the military once again labored to revise the English language, calling its new offensives "accelerated pacification" and "protective reaction strikes."

In May 1970 Nixon announced on national television that he had ordered an American-led invasion of Cambodia, supposedly a neutral country. In making this decision, he ignored the advice of his secretaries of state and defense and neglected to consult (or even inform) Lon Nol, America's Cambodian ally who, less than two months before, had successfully overthrown the neutralist regime of Prince Norodom Sihanouk. North Vietnamese forces had been using various parts of Cambodia as staging areas, and Pentagon strategists had long pressed the White House to clear out the sanctuaries and destroy a mythical Vietnamese guerrilla headquarters. A quick strike, it was hoped, would throw the enemy off balance and capture valuable supplies.

American troops met surprisingly little resistance in Cambodia during the April invasion and found no guerrilla headquarters, but the president's defenders nevertheless considered the maneuver a success. They claimed that it upset North Vietnam's plans and allowed the United States more time to prepare for their withdrawal. But widening the war into Cambodia ultimately had disastrous consequences. America continued to wage a secret air war in Cambodia long after the April strike, and the heavy bombing destroyed large portions of what had been a peaceful, agricultural country, creating a large refugee population and a devastating decline in food supplies. Cambodians rallied in resistance. The Khmer Rouge, the native communist guerrillas, transformed themselves from a disorganized force of 5000 in 1970 to a fierce army of 70,000 in 1975; Lon Nol found support only in the capital city. Subsequent American defeat and withdrawal would leave communist regimes in both Vietnam and Cambodia, fulfilling the domino effect the war had initially been staged to prevent.

Antiwar forces at home severely criticized the accelerating violence in Southeast Asia. Public revelations of the My Lai massacre (which had occurred in March 1968) intensified criticism of American involvement in Southeast Asia. The slowly unfolding story of what had happened in the hamlet of My Lai shocked most Americans. American troops testified to the killing of unarmed civilians, including women and children, by a company under the command of a young lieutenant named William Calley. After bungling an attempt at a cover-up, the army finally prosecuted several officers, but only Calley was convicted. A member of another unit testified to similar activities by his outfit. "I used to think my company was a bad-ass one until I started seeing others," he said. "Sometimes you thought it was just my platoon, my company, that was committing atrocious acts. . . . But what we were doing was being done all over."

The Cambodian invasion of 1970 galvanized opposition to the war, especially on college campuses. Students mounted protest marches and strikes at more than four hundred schools, and some demonstrations led to violence. Many colleges abruptly ended the spring semester early and closed their doors. The reaction to the invasion of Cambodia did produce a small tide of approval in Nixon's direction—according to one poll, the percentage of people who approved of the way the president was handling his job increased by six points—but it also hardened antiwar sentiments. Most important, the widening of the fighting into Cambodia clearly stamped the conflict as "Nixon's War."

Violence at Home

Paralleling the bloodletting in Vietnam was a violent new direction in the radical movement at home. The Weathermen—later called the Weatherpeople or the Weatherfolks in response to the feminist movement—pledged to "bring the war home to Amerika" in order to help the National Liberation Front. The Weatherpeople gained considerable attention from the media but almost no political success. Their much-publicized Four Days of Rage, an invasion of Chicago in 1969, proved a disaster. After smashing some windows, almost all of the helmeted Weatherpeople were overwhelmed, beaten bloody, and arrested by Mayor Daley's police.

After this, most of the prominent Weatherpeople went underground. Some were seeking to avoid arrest for previous activities. Some joined other desperate young people in a bombing campaign. Between September 1969 and June 1970 there were more than 170 bombings and attempted bombings on college campuses. An explosion at the University of Wisconsin killed a graduate student, and other campuses endured nonlethal attacks. Universities gradually adjusted to the threat of violence, and cautious scholars began keeping valuable materials and manuscripts at home. Bombers also struck off campuses, hitting targets such as the Bank of America, the Chase Manhattan Bank, and even the United States Congress. Three Weatherpeople blew themselves apart when their bomb factory in Greenwich Village exploded in 1970. Few of the attacks did major damage—corporation bathrooms, the easiest place to hide explosives, suffered the brunt of the onslaught—but they contributed to an increasingly ugly mood throughout the country.

President Nixon and Vice-President Agnew sanctimoniously upheld the rule of law. "You see these bums, you know, blowing up the campuses," the president grumbled after students protested (in most cases nonviolently) the invasion of Cambodia. "We cannot afford to be divided or deceived by the decadent thinking of a few young people," fumed Agnew. We could, he argued, "afford to separate them from our society—with no more regret than we should feel over discarding rotten apples from a barrel."

But more violence, in the final analysis, came from the upholders of law and order than from outgunned students and radicals. In early 1968 state troopers killed three protesting black students at Orangeburg State College in South Carolina. During a 1969 confrontation at Berkeley, state police indiscriminately dropped tear gas from helicopters and fatally shot a long-haired bystander in the back. In December of 1969 Chicago police stormed the Illinois headquarters of the Black Panthers and killed two persons. In May 1970 white police officers opened fire on a women's dormitory at Mississippi's Jackson State College, an all-black institution; two unarmed students were killed. And in the most celebrated incident, the Ohio national guard shot thirteen students, four of whom died, at Kent State.

A "Law-and-Order" Administration

On most domestic issues Richard Nixon provided no consistent leadership. Playing to the Republican party's right-wing, the president ritualistically condemned the "welfare mess" and promised to get people off relief rolls and onto work roles. But charmed and impressed by Daniel Patrick Moynihan, a Harvard professor heretofore closely allied with Democrats, Nixon also toyed with an ambitious program of welfare reform—which would have guaranteed every family a $1600 annual income—tax revision, consumer protection legislation, and environmental regulation. Indeed, a number of important legislative measures, including environmental protection and health-and-safety laws, were passed during Nixon's years in office. Similarly, welfare-state expenditures actually grew during Nixon's presidency, a testimony to the residual strength of liberalism in Congress and in federal bureaucracies, pressure from insurgent groups, and Nixon's own lack of any overall vision of domestic matters.

Nixon was far more interested in foreign than domestic affairs. And when he and his close advisers did gaze inward, they generally focused upon efforts aimed at punishing their "enemies" and rewarding their "friends" than at actually changing the basic assumptions of the welfare state, a clear goal of the conservative Republicans who would come to Washington with Ronald Reagan in 1980. In the end, Nixon appeared to believe more was to be gained—for his political ambitions, his psychological need for confrontation, or both—from battling a host of different enemies than from tackling substantive policy issues.

Ironically for an administration in which most of the top officials ended up facing criminal charges, the dominant domestic thrust of the Nixon years remained a drive for "law and order." Youth and nonwhite insurgency movements were singled out as special targets. To many Americans, the young antiwar protesters seemed a band of troublemakers. After the killings at Kent State, public opinion polls showed that most people believed that the National Guard had fired on the unarmed students in self-defense; Nixon and Agnew continued their tough talk; and Attorney General John Mitchell strengthened the Justice Department's internal security division. Moreover, as subsequent investigations would reveal, the White House, the FBI, and the CIA all continued—or intensified—various illegal activities against domestic radicals.

The FBI, for example, did not limit itself to surveillance of groups espousing violence; it also worked to infiltrate and harass groups and individuals who favored significant, but peaceful, social change. In one celebrated case, the bureau circulated vicious rumors about the personal life of a prominent actress who had ties to the Black Panthers. Similarly, some of the FBI's undercover agents operated as *agent provocateurs* and actually urged violent action by protesters. Commenting on the FBI's notorious COINTELPRO operation—which extended from 1956 to 1971 and was cancelled only after stolen FBI documents revealed its existence—a committee of the House of Representatives made a sweeping indictment: "Careers were ruined, friendships severed, reputations sullied, businesses bankrupted and, in some cases, lives endangered."

While conducting or condoning massive lawbreaking by the national surveillance bureaucracy, the Nixon administration was also mobilizing the legal system against dissidents. In the most celebrated political prosecution since the 1940s, the Chicago conspiracy trial of 1969, Attorney General Mitchell pressed for indictments against eight leading radicals. (Mitchell's predecessor, Ramsey Clark, had decided not to prosecute, because of insufficient evidence.) The government charged the group—which included Tom Hayden, Bobby Seale, Abbie Hoffman, and Jerry Rubin—with conspiracy and with crossing state lines to encourage violence at the 1968 Democratic convention. Some of the defendants viewed the affair as a countercultural "happening" rather than a legal battle, and the defense never mounted a coherent counterattack. At the end of the trial Judge Julius Hoffman unexpectedly cited all of the defendants for various actions in contempt of court. Concluding the sorry affair, the jury rendered a compromise verdict: It acquitted all the defendants of the more serious conspiracy charge but convicted the most famous—including Yippies Rubin and Hoffman—of crossing state lines to incite a riot. After a lengthy appeal process, all of the defendants escaped jail, but the Chicago conspiracy trial hardly cast much credit on the American legal system.

Other such trials—including prosecutions of antiwar priests Philip and Daniel Berrigan, of Bobby Seale, and of various lesser-known radicals—produced few convictions, but they did help to focus public attention on the political "criminals in the streets." Simply by filing charges, the Nixon administration and state officials encouraged public fears of the radical "menace" and increased the disarray of the left.

The Violence Wanes

Meanwhile, Richard Nixon continued to pose as the president who would listen to the "forgotten American." From 1969 to early 1972 Nixon and Agnew plied "middle Americans" with one theme: A small group of New Left "hooligans," aided and abetted by "radical liberals" within the Democratic party, threatened the country's stability. For two years Agnew assailed the "biased liberal" media, which "slandered" the president; the "nattering nabobs of negativism," who scorned traditional American values; the "curled-lip boys in the eastern ivory towers," who thumbed their noses at ordinary people; and those renegade professionals such as Dr. Benjamin Spock, who encouraged the "growing spirit of permissiveness." As the off-year elections of 1970 neared, Agnew stepped up his attacks.

Still, the Republicans made few gains in the 1970 elections. The GOP did add a couple of Republicans to the Senate but dropped about a dozen seats in the House and lost no fewer than eleven governorships. The Democrats, though badly divided and somewhat demoralized, remained the majority party. Nixon's political strategist consequently abandoned grand theories about "an emerging Republican majority" and began to plan a 1972 campaign that divorced the president, as much as possible, from the rest of the Republican ticket. Nixon's image makers left all the invective to a slightly more subdued Agnew, organized more subtle campaign tactics for 1972, and accentuated the president's role in foreign affairs.

The passions of the 1960s slowly seeped from domestic politics. By beginning to reduce U.S. ground forces in Vietnam, promising to end the military draft, and helping to lower the voting age to eighteen, the Nixon administration removed three highly emotional issues from the immediate political agenda. Although many other questions remained, especially the conflict in Southeast Asia itself, they no longer brought massive numbers of people into the streets.

Youth-oriented politics, for example, lost its prominent position in the mass media. Seeking new sources of inspiration and fresh recruits, a few reckless radicals saw prison inmates as the new vanguard of revolution. This desperate turn—toward the most powerless group in society, and one heavily infiltrated by police informers—proved suicidal. George Jackson, who became a radical hero after publication of some of his prison letters, was gunned down (assassinated, insisted his supporters) during an alleged escape from San Quentin in 1973. That same year, a tiny group of white radicals joined with an escaped African-American prisoner to form the Symbionese Liberation Army, or SLA. The kidnapping of Patricia Hearst, daughter of a prominent newspaper publisher, instantly converted members of the SLA into celebrities; finally, in the spring of 1974, six members of the group were killed in a shoot-out with the Los Angeles police, which was carried live on TV. Patty Hearst was freed but later stood trial for complicity with her SLA captors.

Although a few other young people, claiming inspiration from the 1960s, dabbled in similarly suicidal activities, the vast majority of social activists adopted new, nonviolent strategies in the early 1970s. Having discovered no magical shortcuts to social transformation, some drifted away from all movements; but, while the ups and downs of Richard Nixon dominated the national political stage during the early 1970s, many other young activists worked, quietly in the wings, for significant social change.

THE SEARCH FOR POWER, 1968–1976

Although the Nixon administration's constant fears were undoubtedly overstated, dissent did spread widely throughout American society. In the early 1970s a number of different groups were demanding more power for their own special constituencies. Few achieved stunning victories, but they all laid the groundwork for what they expected would be new gains in the future.

Black Power

The late 1960s and early 1970s saw African-American politics moving in many different directions. Following his murder, Martin Luther King's SCLC lost prestige, especially when its "Poor People's March" of 1968 proved a complete disaster. Dr. King's unfinished project, this "march" was more than a single-day event: It sought to make an inter-racial group of poor people an ongoing presence in Washington and to lobby Congress and the Nixon administration for new social legislation. But its tent encampment became waterlogged in torrential spring rains, and the inhabitants split into squabbling factions. Nixon's administration expelled the few remaining activists, bringing a dismal end to the era of mass civil rights demonstrations.

Taking a different tack, a broad coalition of African-American activists formed the National Black Political Assembly in 1972. More than ten thousand people met in Gary, Indiana, to hammer out a "Black Agenda." A militant statement that upset integrationists, it charged that the "crises we face as black people . . . are the natural end-product of a society built on the twin foundations of white racism and white capitalism." In retrospect, the Gary meeting marked the high point of black power unity; within months, deep fissures developed within the Black Political Assembly as Marxists tilted with liberals, integrationists with cultural nationalists. And while these activists debated theories of cultural and political change, the African-American scholar Manning Marable has argued, the mass of workers, students, and the unemployed lost interest in this bold effort to create a nationwide political structure for African-Americans.

Nonetheless, African-American politics changed significantly. The continued migration of people to northern cities (together with the flight of many whites) ensured the election of greater numbers of African-American political leaders. In 1955, for instance, only a couple of districts of New York City and Chicago sent black representatives to Congress; by 1972, fifteen African-Americans held seats in the House of Representatives. A number of cities—including Cleveland, Gary, and Newark—elected African-American mayors, and several northern states, especially Michigan and New York, claimed growing numbers of black officials at all levels of government.

But new African-American officeholders brought only minor policy changes. Cities with black-elected officials also generally had large (and largely poor) African-American populations; their urban problems certainly involved, but also transcended, racial issues. No more than their white predecessors, African-American politicians were not miracle workers. And they faced, once in power, a particularly difficult problem: Should they target the majority of new programs directly for poor neighborhoods or should they work with local whites and thereby gain access to public and private funds for rebuilding the entire urban infrastructure? Skillful (or lucky) African-American politicians, such as Coleman Young in Detroit, seemed able to satisfy conflicting pressures, but others (such as Kenneth Gibson in Newark) found themselves ensnarled in competing demands.

Their efforts to reach out to powerful interest groups, in order to obtain private and public funds for general urban projects, did not always satisfy the specific desires of their black constituency. In Detroit, for example, leaders from poor black neighborhoods charged that Mayor Coleman Young (elected in 1973) catered to the corporate and political elites' desire to rebuild the Motor City's business center while generally ignoring the plight of Detroit's poorest black residents. Young countered that Detroit's citizens desperately needed a viable business environment and that his policies addressed the needs of the entire population. In local communities, cynicism about all politicians, black as well as white, set in. Despite the black power movement, for example, the percentage of northern blacks who bothered to register and to vote actually declined between 1964 and 1972.

Meanwhile, the Nixon administration moved cautiously and obliquely on racial questions. Gaining only five of every one hundred votes cast by African-Americans in 1968 and doing no better in 1972, Nixon had the bulk of his political capital invested elsewhere. Although he took a strong stand against school busing, even appearing on national television in 1972 to seek a moratorium on this method of achieving integration, he generally followed a circumspect course on racial issues. Daniel Patrick Moynihan, a former official in the Kennedy administration and Nixon's own domestic Democrat, urged "benign neglect"—a policy of scaling down the level of promises as a means of generating less frustration among African-Americans over the slow pace of change.

Moynihan's proposal, whatever its merit as a public policy position, did represent a shrewd appraisal of the nation's ambiguous record on racial progress. Change on both the economic and the political fronts was occurring, but the immediate results were seldom dramatic. Aided by favorable rulings from the Supreme Court and by pressure from Democratic holdovers in HEW, a number of young blacks were finding greater educational and economic opportunities. On the issue of education, a majority of the Supreme Court gradually moved beyond a narrow reading of *Brown* v. *Board of Education* and held that the Constitution demanded that schools be "racially mixed." Although the Court did not apply this principle in every case, its new rulings generally required considerable busing of children from their old neighborhood school districts to other schools in order to provide "racial balance." Officials in HEW, citing the small numbers of nonwhites and women in the professions, began to press graduate and professional schools to take "affirmative action" and recruit a student body that was not overwhelmingly white and male. College-educated blacks stood to gain from such pressure, but many universities hesitated to over-emphasize their affirmative action programs, which were often denounced for establishing quotas and for denigrating merit. Working-class blacks encountered more obstacles, especially from labor unions whose largely white memberships considered the government's efforts to increase minority employment a direct attack on their traditional seniority systems. In 1970, for example, only 3.3 percent of the nation's sheet-metal workers and 1.7 percent of its tool and die makers were black.

The Nixon administration gave greatest priority to economic issues. It promised to help find better jobs for African-Americans who already possessed marketable skills and to promote more opportunities for "black capitalists." In these areas some gains were made. The number of banks owned by African-Americans, for example, more than doubled between 1970 and 1975; a similar expansion occurred in the small-business sector, especially with "mom and pop" stores. The administration did urge graduate and professional schools to take "affirmative action" and recruit student bodies that contained more minorities, especially African-Americans. Citing gains such as these, Attorney General John Mitchell advised African-Americans to "watch what we do, not what we say."

But many critics denounced what the Nixon administration did as well as what it said. Bishop Stephen Spottswood of the NAACP accused the administration of adopting racist policies to attract the "white backlash" vote; the head of the U.S. Civil Rights Commission denounced its reluctance to enforce existing civil rights measures; and Leon Panetta, head of the Civil

Rights Division within the Department of Health, Education and Welfare (HEW), resigned in protest over Nixon's opposition to school busing as a means of integrating public schools.

In many areas, Nixon's record did look bad. The administration did little to help register African-American voters in the South; its promises to push integration of federal housing programs went almost nowhere; and it even failed to provide adequate funding for its own pet project, "black capitalism." On a broader front, the gap between black and white incomes grew wider during the Nixon years.

Meanwhile, the Voting Rights Act of 1965 (renewed in 1970) and pressure from black groups gradually produced some tangible results in the South. In the election of 1970 more than a hundred black candidates gained office in the South; by the end of that year more than seven hundred black people held political office in the southern states. At the same time, black voters gained more leverage in contests involving only white candidates. Openly seeking the support of blacks, many white candidates moderated their stands on racial issues.

Such gains, however, did not automatically bring significant changes to the South. In many heavily black counties and towns, black candidates still failed to gain office. More important, even the triumph of black politicians could not solve longstanding social and economic problems. Changing the skin color of mayors and county officials did not rejuvenate those rural areas plagued with limited resources and antiquated public services. Even the most energetic black officials often found it difficult to run all the bureaucratic roadblocks and obtain state or federal funds for their communities. By 1973, ten years had passed since Martin Luther King shared his dream during the March on Washington; despite some changes during that decade, King's vision still remained a dream.

Brown Power

Although the Black Power movement captured the most media attention, other groups also displayed new cultural pride and growing political militancy. Mexican-Americans, living principally in the Southwest and in northern communities close to migrant farming jobs, grew in numbers and began to develop political power.

From the New Deal of the 1930s through the 1950s, leaders in Mexican-American communities had sought to promote equality in legal rights and integration into the political mainstream. Proud of their Mexican origins and cultural traditions, they envisioned fitting into a pluralist society in which cultural difference could be maintained while barriers of discrimination eroded. Gaining strength from the broader civil rights movement of the 1950s, middle-class organizations such as the League of United Latin American Citizens (LULAC) and the Unity League forced desegregation of some public facilities and schools, worked against discrimination in housing and

employment, and helped elect the first local Mexican-American officeholders in the Southwest. Political mobilization of Mexican-Americans in El Paso,
Texas, who comprised one-half of that city's total population, swept Raymond L. Telles into office as the first Mexican-American mayor in 1957. In
the same period, the more militant working-class organization, ANMA,
backed drives for labor union organizing and protested the mass deporta-
tion of Mexicans under the McCarran Act before it became a casualty of FBI
surveillance and harassment of the cold war years.

The limited gains and gradualist strategies of the 1940s and 1950s,
however, seemed scarcely to dent structures of socioeconomic disadvantage.
During the 1960s the average Mexican-American child had only a sev-
enth-grade education; nearly nine of every ten dropped out of Texas high
schools before graduation. Many young people had to leave school to help
support their families. As one teacher put it, "Our kids don't drop out; they
are pushed out by poverty." The tradition of maintaining a Spanish-based
culture and the proximity of Mexican cultural institutions also stigmatized
Mexican-Americans. In some California school districts students could be
expelled for speaking Spanish, even in the playground. Bilingualism, a
quality highly valued among middle-class white children, often became a
badge of inferiority for Mexican-Americans. Standing on the edge of two
cultures, Mexican-Americans suffered all of the consequences of marginali-
ty: low-wages, political powerlessness, inadequate housing, and limited access to services.

By the late 1960s, a new generation of young leaders, impatient with
the legal and political strategies of the 1950s, launched militant mass movements designed to lift economic status and to create a positive cultural
identity. Some demanded more aggressive mobilization on behalf of political and economic goals; others advocated separation from the dominant
society.

César Chávez launched a drive to raise wages among Mexican-American farm workers. Chávez, who had grown up in California migrant camps
during the late 1930s, recalled his family's first grape-picking job: "Each
payday the contractor said he couldn't pay us because the winery hadn't paid
him yet. At the end of the seventh week we went to the contractor's house
and it was empty—he owed us for seven week's pay. . . . We were desperate."
Chávez never forgot his people's poverty, and when the federal government's *bracero* (farm worker) program ended in 1964 he began to unionize
workers in the grape fields. With the source of new, cheap labor from
Mexico diminished, unionization had a chance. The outlook grew even
brighter when Chávez's United Farm Workers Union (UFW) attracted support from the powerful American Federation of Labor. During the grape
pickers' strike in Delano, California, in 1965, Walter Reuther of the United
Auto Workers joined Chávez on the picket lines, carrying a sign reading
HUELGA ("STRIKE") and reminiscing about his own organizing fights
during the 1930s. Robert Kennedy also visited the scene and became the
UFW's most influential political supporter. But the growers held out, always

finding enough hungry and jobless people to replace the strikers. Finally, Chávez adopted the technique that would make him famous—the nationwide boycott. Dramatizing his personal commitment, Chávez went on a lengthy fast, an act that damaged his frail health.

Chávez's appeal to boycott California grapes captured widespread sympathy among liberals and radicals during the mid-1960s. For over a year, millions of Americans refused to buy grapes (the army bought them in great quantities to send to Vietnam, however), and growers finally signed with the UFW. Chávez, always a favorite of the media, became the first Mexican-American to appear on the cover of *Time* magazine, and many reporters hailed him as a Spanish-speaking Martin Luther King. When lettuce growers signed what Chávez considered "sweetheart contracts" with the Teamsters Union, he appealed to Americans to boycott lettuce. By the early 1970s, however, the novelty of boycotts had worn off, and Chávez's victories grew fewer and fewer.

While Chávez worked to improve economic conditions among field workers, a militant Chicano student movement demanded and promoted educational change. In East Los Angeles in 1968, 10,000 high school students participated in a "Blow Out," a strike dramatizing educational racism. Similar student strikes spread throughout the Southwest. On college campuses, radicalized students successfully formed Chicano Studies programs at some universities and made new contributions to Mexican-American history and literature. *El Grito* and *Aztlan*, the first national Chicano studies journals, and Quinto Sol Publications, the first independent Mexican-American publishing house, provided sympathetic forums for new Chicano writers and scholars.

Student militancy fed new political movements. A charismatic minister in New Mexico, Reies Lopez Tijerina, attempted to organize a separatist movement and reopen the Mexican-American War of 1846–1848. His organization, the Federal Alliance of Land Grants, reclaimed southwestern land, water, and grazing rights that whites had usurped over the previous hundred years. In 1967 he declared the area an independent republic. Guerrilla bands supporting Tijerina formed in northern New Mexico in the late 1960s and seized control of a portion of Kit Carson National Forest. When authorities arrested some of his followers, other disciples of Tijerina raided the courthouse in Tierra Amarilla to free them. The desperate action, which killed one deputy, catapulted Tijerina into the national news and caused widespread fear among Anglos in the area. Rumors swept New Mexico that Cuban-trained guerrillas were hiding in the mountains, and the National Guard patrolled the area for a time.

José Angel Gutiérrez's political party, La Raza Unida, directed dissent into politics. In 1970 La Raza captured a majority of seats on the school board in Crystal City, Texas, and began to remold the educational system according to the needs of the Spanish-speaking population. Soon La Raza gained control of all other political offices in Crystal City and turned the town into a showcase of Chicano government, hoping to spread the party's popularity into barrios throughout the Southwest. Throughout the decade, Chicanos, like blacks, made substantial gains in terms of political office-holding.

Despite the rising level of Chicano militancy, officials on the national level devoted little serious attention to the problems of Mexican-Americans. In 1969 Senator Joseph Montoya of New Mexico introduced a bill to extend the life of the President's Inter-Agency Committee on Mexican-American Affairs, a group that studied Chicano problems. The bill passed the Senate and went to the House, where it was "lost." After months of delay searchers finally found the bill, misfiled in the Foreign Affairs Committee. The movements led by Chávez, Tijerina, and La Raza declined rather rapidly, weakened by both internal division and by external repression, including FBI surveillance, infiltration, and mass arrests.

Still, the political militancy and cultural pride of these years helped nurture major political gains for Mexican-Americans in the future: by 1988, some 3360 Latino officials held elected office, mostly in areas where the militant Chicano movements of the late 1960s had been strongest.

Red Power

"Red power" did not really break into the national news until a cold November morning in 1969 when a group of militant Native Americans seized Alcatraz Island in San Francisco Bay. Hundreds of Indian supporters soon joined them, demanding that the government convert the island into an Indian cultural center and appropriate funds for a Thunderbird University. Few white people took the Indians' proposals seriously. For many Indians, nevertheless, the occupation had a symbolic significance. It was an important step in the effort to create a pan-Indian cultural consciousness. The Indians on Alcatraz represented tribes throughout the United States and Alcatraz provided a particularly appropriate symbol: Its uninhabitable buildings, bad water and sanitation, and certain unemployment resembled conditions on most Indian reservations.

The vast majority of Indians missed out on the affluence of postwar America. Two-and-a-half decades after World War II, the per-capita income of Indians was 60 percent less than that of whites; Indian life expectancy was only forty-seven years; half of all Indian children never completed high school; and the unemployment rate for Indians was 40 percent (on most reservations it exceeded 50 percent). But statistics told only a small part of what it meant to be a native of America. Discrimination against Indians was everywhere. La Nada Means, one of the original occupiers of Alcatraz, remembered the "meanness of the small towns around the reservation. Blackfoot, Pocatello—they all had signs in the store windows to keep Indians out. . . . There were Indian stalls in the public bathrooms; Indians weren't served in a lot of the restaurants; and we just naturally all sat in the balcony of the theaters." What were the effects of such treatment? "It becomes part of the way you look at yourself." she explained.

After Alcatraz Indian activists became even more militant. Ojibwas in the Minnesota-St. Paul area organized the American Indian Movement (AIM). In 1973 two AIM leaders, Russell Means and Dennis Banks, began protesting the disparity in law enforcement for Indians and whites. In Custer, South Dakota, officials charged a white with second-degree manslaughter for fatally stabbing an Indian, while in nearby Rapid City an Indian accused of killing a white woman was held for murder without bail. Means and Banks led protests in both cities, and the hundreds of Indian demonstrators eventually clashed with police. AIM then seized a trading post at Wounded Knee, South Dakota, the place where the Seventh Cavalry had crushed the last substantial pan-Indian resistance movement in the 1890s. AIM leaders believed that this small community on the Pine Ridge Reservation offered an appropriate place for launching a cultural-political revival.

AIM's bold tactics split the Indian community at Pine Ridge. Some condemned AIM's members as outside agitators who brought physical destruction to an Indian town and repudiated Indian ways by attacking tribal elders. Others, including many older traditionalists, sympathized with AIM's opposition to tribal leaders, criticizing them for corruption and for a cozy relationship with the Bureau of Indian Affairs.

Federal marshals finally cleared Wounded Knee, but AIM then shifted its focus into the courts. Indicted on various counts, Banks and Means began a spectacular trial in St. Paul, first trying to have United States treaties with Indians (they contended the government had systematically violated them) admitted into evidence on their behalf. After a nine-month trial the presiding judge dismissed the indictments and charged the government prosecutors with serious misconduct. By the mid-1970s other Indians throughout the country were launching legal challenges and threatening direct action to redress grievances. Although militant tactics did not gain support from the entire Indian community, red power, like black power, had a far-reaching impact. It promoted a new pride in Indian culture, a fresh concern with preserving an ancient heritage, and a stronger determination to use the courts to make whites live up to past promises.

Woman Power

A new women's movement became an increasingly important part of the social ferment of the 1960s and 1970s. Public rhetoric of the 1950s had emphasized domestic roles for women. In 1955 Adlai Stevenson, the two-time Democratic candidate for president, told graduates of a prominent women's college that their job in politics should be to use the "humble role of housewife" to influence their husbands and sons. Eminent male psychologists of the era warned that mental disorders could result from a woman's failure to accept passive, "feminine" characteristics, and they portrayed those who advocated broadening acceptable social roles for women as maladjusted and neurotic. Popular magazines and programs for women also emphasized channeling self-expression in so-called "natural" directions—toward cooking, childrearing, and interior decorating.

During the 1960s, however, the ideology of domesticity increasingly clashed with women's experiences and, eventually, with a growing feminist consciousness. The number of women working outside the home rose dramatically; a growing percentage of young women remained single much longer than had their sisters during the 1950s; divorce rates increased; the number of female-headed households grew; women, especially African-American women, played significant roles in the early civil rights movement; and the birth-control pill contributed to changes in sexual relationships.

In 1963 Betty Friedan published *The Feminine Mystique*, an influential critique of the sex-role conditioning that Friedan believed channeled women into positions of inferiority. From dolls and dainty ruffles through teenage dating conventions to myths of married bliss as a happy dependent, women were confined within a mystique that prevented them from developing their full potential as human beings. According to Friedan, women should be able to move beyond the domestic sphere without suffering social stigma and should have options for self-fulfillment equal to those accorded men. Friedan's book touched a nerve, particularly among white middle-class women whose lives were most bound within postwar expectations of domesticity.

Organizing followed. In 1966 Friedan and other women founded the National Organization for Women (NOW). Modeled on civil rights organizations, NOW campaigned against institutions that practiced sex discrimination, lobbied for child-care centers, and publicized women's causes through the media. NOW created local chapters and eventually adopted, from other feminist groups, the idea of "consciousness-raising." Consciousness-raising sessions encouraged small groups of women to vent grievances; to question prevailing constructions of gender; and, perhaps most important, to explore the larger political dimensions of their own personal lives. Consciousness-raising, feminists hoped, would enable women to examine social arrangements and draw the collective strength in order to make changes in society and their everyday lives.

The Civil Rights Act of 1964, enacted mainly to assist the struggle for racial equality, offered a new legal tool for women, and women's organizations lobbied hard for its passage. The act prohibited discrimination on the basis of sex as well as on race; some Southern representatives had pushed for a provision on sexual equality, hoping that this might diminish the bill's chances for passage. Using this new Civil Rights Act, women's groups attacked a host of discriminatory practices. Newspapers could no longer run "want ads" that distinguished between men's and women's work, and the federal government's requirement of equal pay for equal work was strengthened. By the late 1960s, the government mandated that corporations or institutions receiving federal funds adopt nondiscriminatory hiring practices and, in the early 1970s, pressed for "affirmative action" as a means to recruit more women and minority-group applications into those schools or jobs in which there were smaller percentages of women than in the larger population.

The antiwar and New Left movements of the late 1960s also contributed to a new brand of radical feminism. Both movements developed sociopolitical critiques that fed the growing feminist consciousness. Moreover, in organizing against racial injustice and the Vietnam War, women realized their own second-class status, even within supposedly radical movements. Men generally monopolized the podia and the media spotlights, relegating women to lesser roles. In the Black Power movement, militancy sometimes intertwined with assertions of male dominance; within organizations such as SDS, the white male leadership initially saw little contradiction in expecting women to accept secondary roles. While participating in movements committed to social change, many women came to realize, for the first time, the extent of gender discrimination. As a result, struggles for women's liberation developed within older insurgency movements: Chicana groups coalesced within the Farm Worker's movement in the West; African-American women expressed and organized around an ethic of "black feminism"; and white women also discovered that "sisterhood is powerful."

By the early 1970s, feminism became a broad, but by no means unified, movement; class, race, and ethnicity divided women even as gender united them. Consisting largely of middle-class professional women, NOW sought legal equality through the legislatures and the courts. Political radicals—such as Jane Alpert, who became a fugitive from justice after getting caught up in several bombing incidents—attacked the same capitalist system in which members of NOW wanted to work. Cultural radicals assailed marriage, a social arrangement that they considered inherently sexist and exploitative. A new generation of African-American writers, including Alice Walker and Toni Morrison, gave voice to the traditions of black women. And groups of women from all racial and ethnic backgrounds built new institutions to serve needs that male-dominated structures had long ignored: rape-crisis centers, battered women's shelters, women's health collectives, women's studies programs in colleges and universities, and support groups for clerical workers combatting sexual harassment in the workplace. New periodicals such as *MS* and more scholarly journals such as *Feminist Studies* (1972) and *Signs* (1975) provided forums for feminist ideas.

As feminism expanded its base, counter-organizations of women who recoiled against the "women's libbers" also began to appear. Resenting implications that they were ignorant, useless, and exploited, some housewives rallied around older values. These women claimed that motherhood and devotion to their husbands should continue to be the hallmarks of true femininity.

One of the most bitter battles pitting women against women came over the long-proposed Equal Rights Amendment to the Constitution. The amendment, granting equal rights specifically to women, passed Congress in early 1972 and was quickly ratified by more than half of the states. But the necessary approval from three quarters of the states did not come, and the amendment's progress stalled. NOW lobbied intensely on its behalf, but vigorous opposition from people such as archconservative Phyllis Schlafly and organizations such as the Christian Crusade more than counterbalanced NOW's efforts. Opponents charged that the amendment would not only undermine the stability of the traditional family but that its effect on alimony, protective labor laws, and eligibility for military service would positively harm women themselves. In response to such arguments and to the growing identification between the political right and antifeminism, the Republican party reversed a position it had held for the past forty years and dropped support of the ERA from its 1980 platform. The ERA was never ratified.

Abortion became an even more controversial issue. In *Roe v. Wade* (1973), the Supreme Court upheld a pregnant Texas woman's claim that her state's criminal abortion law abridged her personal privacy by denying her the right to seek a medically safe abortion. After this decision, abortions could be legally and more safely obtained by most women during the first trimester of pregnancy. But people who supported a woman's right to make her own reproductive choices quickly realized that *Roe* v. *Wade* was an ambiguous victory. Most immediately, it fueled a powerful backlash in the form of the "right-to-life" crusade.

The right-to-life movement—which drew much of its support from traditionalist Catholics, fundamentalist Protestants, and ultraconservative political groups—denounced abortion as legalized murder and championed the "rights of the unborn." Calling their crusade "pro-family," it bitterly condemned many social changes of the 1960s and 1970s, especially those related to achieving greater gender equality. Abortion rights advocates countercharged that anti-abortion activists usually ignored most other questions involving family or right-to-life issues. A powerful element in the New Right coalitions that were emerging in the 1970s, pro-life groups often favored a militaristic foreign policy and the death penalty, and they generally opposed social programs such as subsidized child-care and sex education that might offer alternatives to abortion. As public debates became more acrimonious, politicians found that abortion could overshadow all other issues, even in local elections. The right-to-life crusade, like that against ratification of the ERA, gained strength throughout the 1970s.

By mid-decade, women's roles were clearly undergoing significant changes. Women working outside the home became the norm, and gender barriers were toppled in nearly every occupation and profession. On the other hand, not all changes were positive ones. Greater employment opportunities by no means brought equality at the pay window: The median income for women who worked full time was less than 60 percent of the median income for men. (The disparity actually grew larger during the 1960s and 1970s; the ratio had been 63 percent in 1956). In addition, most men continued to expect certain supposedly male prerogatives. On the average, for example, husbands of working wives did only about one-fourth of all work around the house, creating a "double day" for women who were employed outside their homes. Changes in gender roles also seemed to bring a dangerous anti-female backlash; domestic violence against women appeared on the rise (or, as feminist consciousness grew, this crime was more often reported to public authorities); rates of divorce also increased, a trend that often meant a drastically reduced living standard for newly single women. Similarly, with large numbers of unmarried women trapped in low-paying jobs or on welfare, some analysts highlighted "the feminization of poverty" as one of the major legacies of the 1970s.

Still, the late 1960s and the 1970s did see major social changes for women. As a force for transformation, even radical feminism exerted an impact, especially on college campuses where faculty and administrators became more sensitive than ever before to practices and attitudes considered "sexist." Similar developments were evident everywhere, from the Girl Scouts' new concern for female autonomy, to the growing admission of women into the ministry of mainline Protestant churches, to the gender integration of previously all-male bastions such as Rotary Clubs and Chambers of Commerce. Although much remained to be done, even in the area of defining basic goals, the everyday lives of millions of women were becoming fundamentally different from those that their mothers had experienced only a generation earlier.

Ethnic Power

During the 1960s the crusades of women, blacks, and other nonwhite minorities tended to dominate the discussion of social problems by the media and by academicians. By the early 1970s, however, it had become evident that other people believed that they too needed more visibility and more power. Spokespeople for white ethnics complained that liberal reformers were too anxious to advance others, especially African-Americans, at their expense. Despite optimistic theories about the emergence of a "postindustrial" society and despite many years of faith in the fabled melting pot, ethnicity remained an important reality in American life.

In some ways the assertiveness of white ethnics represented a complicated response to the black movement. White ethnics, like proponents of black pride, extolled the traditional values of their cultures and emphasized the deep significance of the old country to them and to their children. The melting pot had only singed the people whom Michael Novak, a Catholic philosopher of Slovak background, called the "unmeltable ethnics." Efforts at "Americanization" had never extended into the private realm, into the close-knit, family-oriented communities of the white ethnics. As a result, large numbers of ethnic families devoted much of their leisure time to social and cultural activities that expressed pride in their Old World pasts. Thus, the new ethnicity was an old phenomenon; the novelty came in the greater pride and the increased self-confidence with which younger Polish-Americans, Slovak-Americans, and other "unmelted ethnics" defended their cultural heritage and their present way of life.

The new directions in the black movement also had much to do with the surfacing of the new ethnicity in the late 1960s and early 1970s. Deeply rooted in clearly identified neighborhoods, ethnic groups felt threatened by the influx of black newcomers, many of them from the South, into northern industrial cities. Many ethnics also felt challenged when nonwhite minorities pushed for greater employment opportunities. Ethnic workers, for instance, regarded hard-won union seniority systems as forms of social insurance and were not ready to sacrifice them for "affirmative action." Their resentment only increased when white and black integrationists labeled ethnic groups barriers to social progress.

The ethnic awakening, though, represented more than a white backlash. Although there were many points of conflict between blacks and white ethnics, there were also, as the 1970s would reveal, equally important common interests. Poor schools, decaying transit facilities, inflation, and all the other problems of the 1970s affected most urbanites. Even more important, the new assertiveness among blacks and the "unmelted ethnics" could be traced back to the high-tech, corporate-dominated society that the United States had become. There was a recognition by many white ethnic and black leaders that dominant elites had long ignored their interests and their cultures.

Despite generally rising real wages, for example, workers felt that they were not doing as well as they should be. Working-class families complained that their neighborhoods had been destroyed by urban-renewal projects, their streets overrun by criminals, their savings and paychecks undermined by inflation, their take-home pay cut by rising taxes, and their sons shipped to Vietnam. Many of these grievances were authentic. The small increase in real income, for example, never quite covered all the new expenses. In 1968 an urban worker with two children, according to figures from the Bureau of Labor Statistics, needed almost $10,000 a year to live at "a moderate but adequate standard of living." Yet even well-paid workers made less than $8000, and more than 60 percent of white middle-class families required two or more breadwinners to boost their living standard into the "moderate" range. Only through the miracle of installment buying and the growing number of working women who provided families with a second paycheck, could most families maintain middle-class status; in 1969 the nation's total installment debt reached almost $90 billion.

The tremendous popular response to the television version of Alex Haley's *Roots* and to the film *Rocky* suggested the depth of dissatisfaction. Haley's tale about the tenacity of the black family experience was not exactly the story of Polish-American or Irish-American "roots." Yet the dominant theme *was* the same: the search for links to the past and a sense of stability in a time of change. If blacks found their special heroes in Haley's characters, many white ethnics found theirs in *Rocky*. Never patronizing the working-class culture of Philadelphia's Italian-American neighborhoods, the popular motion picture—as opposed to its formulaic sequels—depicted the ethnic's version of the American dream—a decent place to live; a life of understandable scale; and, above all, respect for one's own accomplishments.

THE YEARS OF PROTEST, 1963–1976:
AN AMBIGUOUS LEGACY

The years between 1968 and 1976, during which Richard Nixon and Gerald Ford occupied the White House, witnessed the continuation, not the repudiation, of movements begun during the 1960s. Even after Nixon's 1968 election, radical change still seemed possible; indeed, sometimes, as one believer in the promise of the 1960s later recalled, it appeared that "everything was possible."

By mid-1970s, however, the new politics of the previous decade and many of the insurgency movements no longer provided the driving forces in American political culture. Once so hopeful of rapid, almost instantaneous change, many veterans of the various movements gradually wore down from too many battles. The more radical ones always had to consider the danger—a very real one, as members of the Black Panthers and the American Indian Movement found out—of governmental actions, both legal and illegal, against them and their friends. Writing after the deaths of two black students, killed during protests at Southern University in 1973, the black poet June Jordan confessed,

> *I'm tired*
> *and you're tired*
> *and everybody's goddam tired*
> *tired*
> *students tired*
> *Liberals tired*
> *Revolutionaries tired . . .**

Moreover, the search for power and the struggles for change produced fragmentation as well as community. As feminists and black activists discovered, new strategies and tactics could lead to confrontations not only simply with defenders of the status quo but also with both liberals, who still supported gradualist social change, and "sisters" and "brothers" who disagreed upon where to take the next steps toward some significantly different future. The gap between what insurgents believed needed to be done and what could be accomplished rarely seemed to be closing.

But the sense of exhaustion, deep as it ran among veterans of the movements, proved only one of the legacies from the years of protest. Looking back on the period from 1963 to 1976, other broad themes emerge.

*Reprinted by permission.

First, most of the various movements seeking greater power and social change left important legacies. Civil rights laws, abolition of the military draft, withdrawal of United States troops from Vietnam, some less restrictive drug laws, changes in college curricula and social life were some of the more immediate changes traceable to the movements begun in the 1960s. If one takes a longer view of their impact, the insurgents created the basis for ongoing activity during the late 1970s and into the 1980s by feminist groups, advocates of gay and lesbian rights, environmental groups, community-based self-help organizations, and a variety of other organizations and impulses that took their original inspiration from the years of protest.

A second legacy of the years from 1963 to 1976 was the gradual exhaustion, as June Jordan suggested, of the welfare-state liberalism of the Fair Deal, the New Frontier, and the Great Society. The search for power by people who felt postwar liberals had done too little, too slowly, contributed to welfare-liberalism's decay. On the one hand, the years of protest cost centrist liberals like LBJ much of what they had expected would be their natural constituency among those young people and nonwhite minorities who came to identify welfare liberalism with a corrupt status quo. On the other hand, when liberals like Johnson or George McGovern tried to move cautiously leftward, hoping to catch up with at least some of the various movements, they risked losing many people who justifiably feared that they would shoulder the tax burden for larger welfare-state programs. Both radicals and liberals, argued spokespeople for the New Right, had lost touch with the nation's "real majority." In this sense, many of those to the right and those to the left of welfare liberalism agreed: It represented an outdated approach to social and economic problems.

Thus, another legacy of the years of protest gradually emerged: a new conservative movement, symbolized by Ronald Reagan and his attacks upon the welfare state. The turbulent years between 1963 and 1976 threw up all kinds of unusual political figures, most of whom enjoyed instant media attention and then suffered almost equally rapid obscurity. Most political pundits predicted a similarly brief career for Ronald Reagan, who emerged in 1964, during the Goldwater campaign. Despite the conventional wisdom, heard from 1965 until 1980, that "Reagan is too old," he capitalized upon resentment against radicals and against the liberal welfare-state to become almost the only prominent political figure from the years of protest to retain his position during the 1980s. Reagan's curious career says a great deal about the ambiguous legacy of the years between 1963 and 1976.

SUGGESTIONS FOR FURTHER READING

On the escalation of violence in Southeast Asia, see Seymour Hersh, *Cover-Up* (1972); William Shawcross, *Sideshow* (1979); and Karl D. Jackson, *Cambodia, 1975–1978: Rendevous with Death* (1989).

One can get a sense of the mood at home from *The Age of Paranoia* (1972), a selection of stories from *Rolling Stone* magazine and from Joseph Kellner and James Muneves, *The Kent State Coverup* (1980).

For a general theory of insurgency during these years, see Ira Katznelson's *City Trenches* (1981). See also Michael Reich, *Racial Inequality* (1981); Rufus Brown, Dale Rogers Marshall, and David Tabb, *Protest Is Not Enough: The Struggle of Blacks and Hispanics for Equality in Urban Politics* (1984); Peter Mathiessen, *In the Spirit of Crazy Horse* (1983); George Lipsitz, *A Life in the Struggle: Ivory Perry and the Culture of Opposition* (1988) and Frank Parker, *Black Votes Count* (1990).

The complexity of ethnic issues may be gleaned from Michael Novak, *Rise of the Unmeltable Ethnics* (1973); Richard Kirckus, *Pursuing the American Dream* (1976); Patricia Zavella, *Women's Work and Chicano Families: Cannery Workers of the Santa Clara Valley* (1987); William Julius Wilson, *The Declining Significance of Race: Blacks and Changing American Institutions* (1978) and *The Truly Disadvantaged: The Inner City, the Underclass, and Public Policy* (1987); and Carlos Muñoz, Jr., *Youth Identity and Power: The Chicano Movement* (1989).

Chapter Nine

The Oversized Society: Life During the 1960s and 1970s

The post-1960 era was a time of giantism and excess. Lyndon Johnson, the extravagant Texan who dominated the middle of the 1960s, symbolized the change: He drove too fast; he threw gargantuan barbecues; and in one well-publicized incident he pulled his dog's ears until the puppy yelped. Restraint seemed a quality of the past. The era throbbed with raw power and extremes. American involvement in Vietnam seemed to escalate uncontrollably; both Johnson and Nixon roared at their critics; huge business conglomerates formed; rock singers grew old before they turned thirty; football replaced baseball as the national sport. The 1970 census reported that three of every ten homes had more than one television set and that only three of a hundred had no TV at all. The post office, assisted by its new Zip Code numbers and electronic equipment, delivered a yearly average of four hundred pieces of mail to every man, woman, and child. Book publishers issued more than 35,000 titles annually, double the number put out just ten years earlier. The 1980 census and other surveys showed jumps in scale that were just as staggering. According to one study, the average American threw away four pounds of garbage per day, and the nationwide total amounted to 150 million tons a year—enough refuse to fill three lines of garbage trucks extending from New York to Los Angeles and enough potential energy to light the United States for an entire year.

Growth did not necessarily bring satisfaction. To many people the scale of life had become nearly incomprehensible. Who could understand a trillion-dollar economy, trace lines of responsibility through the sprawling federal bureaucracy, or gain redress from an impersonal, computerized corporation? Summing up the misgivings of many, the journalist Kirkpatrick Sale argued in 1980 that American life had come to exceed any meaningful "human scale."

THE ECONOMY: A GATHERING OF GIANTS

The Military-Industrial Complex

In his farewell speech of 1961, President Dwight D. Eisenhower warned of a permanent government-supported weapons industry. No longer, he explained, did Americans mobilize civilian industries for war and reconvert them after the peace. Cold war pressures had kept the economy on a perpetual war footing and had created "a permanent armaments industry of vast proportions." The old general warned that "we annually spend on military security more than the net income of all United States corporations," and he feared that the military-industrial complex held the "potential for the disastrous rise of misplaced power."

The military-industrial complex grew even larger during the Vietnam War era. This national defense structure consisted, at the top, of politicians, military people, business contractors, and university researchers, and, at the bottom, of workers in defense industries. All of these groups were mutually dependent. Government grants for research and development constituted a significant portion of many university budgets; huge corporations, such as General Dynamics and Lockheed, depended almost exclusively on government contracts; and by 1967 the salaries of nearly 3 million people came from defense-related work. But the government was beneficiary as well as benefactor: Without this complex of research, industry, and manpower, policymakers could not have pursued their idea of national security, which in postwar years required large-scale military capabilities.

The interests of the military-industrial complex cohered perfectly; the system demanded ever-larger expenditures, always rationalized in patriotic language. If the air force wanted a new plane, Boeing Aircraft wanted a lucrative contract and the people of the Pacific Northwest wanted more jobs. Taxpayers who shouldered the bill had little control over spiraling costs, for few could evaluate the need for a new weapons system. Sophisticated weaponry mocked the concept of democratic policy-making. This defense complex ran counter to other old values as well. In 1971 Congress took the then unprecedented action of extending governmental loans to a private corporation—Lockheed, a leading defense contractor—in order to save it from bankruptcy. How could Americans honestly extol the virtues of free enterprise and a free-market economy when the Pentagon directed the largest planned economic system outside the Soviet Union?

The end of the Vietnam War brought little decrease in military production. So important had continued prosperity for defense industries become that the Nixon administration assiduously sought new customers abroad. During the 1970s American arms sales to foreigners boomed, providing one of the few bright spots in a dreary picture of deteriorating trade balances. There were always customers for arms—always friends, such as the Shah of Iran and the generals in Brazil, eager to beef up their military establishments. Between 1972 and 1978 the Shah purchased nearly $20 billion worth of military equipment from the United States. For America, arms sales supposedly brought two blessings—profits and the development of strongly militarized allies who could police their particular region and relieve the United States of direct involvement in the maintenance of the status quo.

The main drawback to arms sales was the rising level of violence throughout the world, as countries in Southeast Asia, the Middle East, Latin America, and finally Africa began to engage in mini-arms races. As sophisticated weaponry saturated the world, the toll of death and destruction from regional rivalries and civil war increased immeasurably. But this appalling development went scarcely noticed by the American public. Even President Jimmy Carter, who had promised in his 1976 campaign to curtail America's role as a merchant of death and encourage human rights abroad, proved unwilling to accept the consequences of canceled contracts, reduced exports, and discontented allies. The flow of arms sales under the Carter administration continued unabated, changing not its volume but only its channels. After the Shah's ouster in 1979, for example, the huge amounts of advanced weaponry formerly sold to Iran found buyers in Israel, Egypt, and elsewhere. And in January 1980 Carter gave the go-ahead for production of America's first armament manufactured solely for export—the FX fighter plane.

Brisk military spending also continued at home. One might have expected that a period marked by the end of conflict in Vietnam and by arms limitation (SALT) talks with the Soviets would have de-emphasized the arms race, but the reverse was true. Expenditures in Vietnam had delayed modernization, and the military had accumulated a backlog on its wish list. The lengthy SALT negotiations, which produced an interim agreement called SALT I in 1972 and the more comprehensive accord, SALT II, in 1979, actually inflamed military rivalry as both sides hurried to develop new weapons that could be traded off for concessions from the other side.

Government research money accelerated new developments that spilled out of the defense sector and transformed American life. The 1960s initiated an age based upon computers and vast communications networks. The electronics industry became a chief beneficiary of well-funded research, and most sectors of the economy entered the "computer revolution." Everything from police records to life-support systems in hospitals to office typewriters were plugged into computers. File cabinets eased toward obsolescence, while "information managers" and "word processors" replaced old-fashioned bureaucrats and secretaries.

The space program—which depended upon the interrelationship of university research, government funding, and industrial production—was also a child of this new age. Shortly after the Soviet Union launched its first Sputnik satellite in 1957, Congress created the National Aeronautics and Space Administration (NASA), and in 1961 President Kennedy committed the nation to landing a man on the moon by 1970. The space program, often compared to the Manhattan Project, which developed the atomic bomb during World War II, organized scientific and technical bureaucracies into a crash effort to surpass the Soviet Union in space exploration.

Critics of the program's expense called it a "moon-doggle" and compared it to ancient Egypt's pyramids—a feat of much grandeur but little practicality. They pointed to the trading advances Japan was making by directing its research and development efforts into products that would do well in foreign markets. The space program, they argued, directed American specialization into channels ultimately detrimental to its balance of trade.

To counter such charges NASA mobilized its information managers. It projected a utilitarian image, stressing the spin-offs of space research for civilians, such as heart pacemakers and miniature electronic components. NASA officials also liked to compare their feats to that of Charles Lindbergh in 1927. (Lindbergh celebrated his solo flight across the Atlantic as a union of man and machine in a book entitled *We*; the original astronauts issued a ghost-written account of their adventures called *We Seven*.) But Lindy's flight rested largely upon private effort and a few financial backers; the Mercury and Apollo programs, products of government-managed technology, relied upon thousands of people in aerospace industries, "operation teams," and recovery forces. Even the tiny Mercury program required nearly two hundred managers.

Despite its wide publicity, enormous pool of employees, and spectacular technological achievements, the space program seldom attracted broad popular enthusiasm. After the much-celebrated moon walks, NASA's other activities attracted little attention. But NASA's programs continued to grow. Satellites brought a quiet revolution in international communications, increasing America's worldwide dominance over radio and television transmission. And joining satellite technology with weapons research spurred an arms race in space, a race characterized by bizarre, deadly instruments and enormous costs.

The Great Business Boom

During the 1960s, the huge infusion of government money into the economy, together with a rising level of consumer spending, brought rapid business expansion and consolidation. Growth seemed to be the key to survival, and the fastest way to expand was to merge with or purchase other firms. In 1968, large corporations acquired ten times greater assets than the amount that had changed hands in 1960. This growth of huge enterprises further centralized economic power. By the late 1960s the two hundred largest United States companies controlled 58 percent of all manufacturing assets in the nation.

New companies most often were not purchased by competitors in the same field but were absorbed by business empires that managed a wide variety of unrelated industries. Financial daredevils could no longer legally corner the market in any one product (horizontal monopoly) or establish control over all the steps of production in the manufacture of any one item (vertical monopoly). Modern entrepreneurs, however, pioneered conglomerates, businesses that minimized overall risk by diversifying holdings. Gulf and Western and Transamerica Corporation, two of the wonder children of the 1960s, acquired companies as fast as they could find them; they owned Hollywood studios, auto parts distributorships, land development corporations, insurance companies, and sports arenas.

The secret of conglomerate growth lay in the acquisition of investment institutions, such as insurance companies. These businesses dealt in capital rather than in goods and could funnel investment money directly into the conglomerate's coffers. With one subsidiary borrowing from another, conglomerates could internally finance their expansion. International Telephone and Telegraph (ITT), in an out-of-court antitrust settlement in 1971, was willing to sell two of its well-known properties, Levitt Construction and Avis Rent-A-Car, in return for government permission to purchase Hartford Fire Insurance Company. Later investigations suggested a link between the Justice Department's willingness to settle with ITT and the company's contributions to the Nixon reelection campaign of 1972.

Under pressure to grow rapidly, some businesses fell into shady dealings and unsound financial practices. The 1960s were spiced with the kinds of abuses associated with other periods of full-throttle expansion: bribed officials, defective products, defrauded consumers, and ineffective government regulations. But Americans of the 1960s did little on a small scale, and, true to form, one of the most daring frauds of all time hit the business world. A relatively new California insurance company, Equity Funding Corporation, built a phenomenal growth record on the basis of more than $2 billion worth of phony insurance policies and more than $120 million in nonexistent assets. Caught up in the southern California boom mentality, officials systematically fabricated two-thirds of their firm's policies, sending its insurance in force soaring from $54 million in 1967 to $615 billion just five years later. Government auditors never caught the fraud because they did not check the computers; an associate finally exposed the scheme in 1973. The Equity Funding scandal, the first great computer crime, was a "simple perversion of a simple computer system," one data processor at Equity Funding later commented. The *Wall Street Journal* headlined the revelations with a warning: "Crooks and Computers Are an Effective Team." Computer-assisted fraud quickly became a major problem of corporate life.

As American enterprise expanded at home, it also moved into other lands at a pace that astonished and alarmed many foreigners. A variety of motives led American business to establish operations in foreign lands: cheaper labor, lower interest rates, favorable tax laws, proximity to new markets and raw materials. Whatever the precise constellation of motives in particular cases, the net result was an unparalleled outflow of investment dollars. IBM, for example, provided 70 percent of all computers in the noncommunist world and maintained research labs in most of the developed nations; Standard Oil of New Jersey drilled and distributed oil throughout the globe; Pepsi-Cola became a universal refreshment, admitted even into the Soviet Union.

The financial power of these multinational companies often exceeded that of the nation in which they operated. One official for the American Agency for International Development reported in the late 1960s that if the gross national products of nations were ranked with the gross annual sales of corporations, half of the top hundred would be corporations and two thirds of these would be American-based. Devaluation of the dollar in 1971 slowed the flight of American enterprise abroad, and other multinational competitors—especially Japanese companies—began to challenge Americans, but problems between American firms with a global reach and smaller nations persisted.

Rapid business growth and new technological discoveries changed the way Americans lived. Natural materials, such as wood, wool, cotton, and natural rubber gave way to artificial substitutes—plastics, acrylic fibers, and synthetic rubber. In 1968 the quantity of synthetic fibers surpassed the output of natural fibers. All kinds of new products flooded the marketplace. During the 1960s drug and grocery stores stocked six thousand new products every year; the rate for the introduction of new items nearly doubled during the 1970s. More than half the items stocked by supermarkets in the 1970s did not even exist in 1960, and nearly half of the products available in 1960 had been withdrawn from the marketplace a decade later. Stiff competition for the buyer's dollar often made packaging and advertising more important than a product's content. Critics of the highly competitive breakfast food industry, for example, claimed that the quality of some products was so low that the flashy packages had more nutritional value than the overprocessed grain inside. And cereals with solid nutritional content often contained excessive amounts of sugar. The variety of new products grew so rapidly that finding an unused brand name could be a problem. Some large companies set their computers to work providing printouts of letter combinations that sounded attractive—Exxon and Pringles were just two of the results.

Entrepreneurs devised new methods to market these products. After 1960, independently owned, locally operated shops found their customers turning to large chain or franchise operations that offered greater volume at lower prices. What McDonald's did for hamburgers, Holiday Inn did for travel, K-Mart for retailing, and 7-Eleven stores for neighborhood groceries. Every city of any size had a "miracle mile" or a "strip" nearly identical to that of every other: a string of discount houses, supermarkets, and fast-food chains. Shopping became easier when the Bank of America introduced BankAmerica (renamed Visa). This new credit card, quickly imitated by New York banks, tempted customers to spend and borrow more, channeled large amounts of consumer purchasing through a few large banks, and threatened to make currency nearly superfluous.

For some companies the uncertainties of the 1970s ended the great business boom. Giants, such as the Penn Central railroad, Franklin National Bank, and W. T. Grant, slid into bankruptcy. One of America's largest employers, Chrysler, survived, but only with the aid of federally guaranteed loans. Bethlehem Steel posted large deficits, and U.S. Steel announced the closing of sixteen plants in thirteen cities, signaling the fact that the American steel industry, which had let its domestic plants run down while investing heavily abroad, was no longer competitive in the world market.

But if many of the old industrial-age companies fared poorly, the other sectors boomed. Demand accelerated for consultants of all sorts; cable television became a major industry; industrial-aircraft manufacture flourished; and sporting-goods and leisure companies chalked up large gains. (In 1979 American joggers spent $400 million on running shoes and warm-up suits alone.) Perfection of the silicon chip, a tiny microprocessor that for $10 could do the work of a $100,000 computer, revolutionized electronics, opening the way for new products, such as computerized cash registers and video games. Challenging supermarkets as the source for "family meals," fast-food chains also continued their growth. McDonald's, always the front-runner, erected four thousand new outlets during the 1970s.

As inflation pushed interest rates well into two-digit numbers, the world of finance began to experience a revolution. The stock market languished during the 1970s, and many brokers diversified their services so that people could easily put their money in a variety of investments. Investors began speculating in "futures" or in gold and silver; international bullion prices rose more than 1000 percent during the decade. Inflation and economic uncertainty called into question the steady investment practices of the past and made the game of high finance more complex and much more risky.

Energy and Ecology

Galloping growth oftentimes trampled the environment. To achieve a high living standard, people used the country's water, air, minerals, and timber as if they were unlimited, and they purchased more and more resources from foreign lands. In 1970, one expert calculated, Americans constituted less than 6 percent of the human race but used 40 percent of the resources consumed worldwide each year and produced 50 percent of the physical pollution.

Cheap energy had been one basic ingredient in the postwar economic growth, and its use multiplied at an astonishing rate. Gasoline consumption rose from 1 billion barrels in 1950 to 2.25 billion barrels in 1971; production of electricity increased 500 percent between 1950 and 1971. By 1979 the United States was using 18.4 million barrels of oil a day, of which 8.2 billion were imported; the United States was consuming nearly 30 percent of all the oil produced in the world.

New products were partly to blame. Aluminum, for example, an excellent substitute for steel and tin in certain cases, was dubbed "congealed electricity" because of the enormous amount of energy required to produce it. The United States processed twenty times more aluminum in 1971 than it had before World War II, and each year production figures climbed higher. Aluminum beer cans, aluminum pipe, aluminum siding, all treasured for their light weight and noncorrosiveness, contributed to the pressure on the environment.

Where would Americans find the energy required to fuel their economy in the future? The question became more urgent after the Organization of Petroleum Exporting Countries (OPEC) embargoed oil in 1973 and sent prices skyrocketing. For the rest of the decade, OPEC prices increased and Middle Eastern turmoil ended the days of cheap energy. In January 1971 the average price of a barrel of OPEC oil was $1.80; by the end of the 1970s it was $20.00 and going up.

Advocates of unrestricted domestic development of energy sources had some answers. Increased strip mining and relaxation of environmental regulations would enhance the nation's ability to use its enormous coal deposits. Accelerated oil drilling in offshore beds would bring new supplies hitherto blocked by environmental safeguards. Development of atomic power plants and strip mining for uranium fuel would increase America's energy self-sufficiency. And production of "synfuels," liquid fuels made through a high-technology process from deposits of coal and oil shale, might also make effective use of native resources.

Environmental groups questioned many of these plans, and their organized strength grew steadily throughout the 1970s. In April 1970 environmentalists held Earth Day, a carnival extravaganza of booths and speakers designed to spawn the same kind of nationwide concerns that civil rights and antiwar causes had generated during the 1960s. Subsequently, scientists, such as Barry Commoner, author of *The Closing Circle*, became popular on the college lecture circuit. Commoner warned that, beyond a certain point, damage to ecological systems was irreversible, and that we were rapidly approaching, if we had not already reached, that critical moment. The obsession with careless material growth, he argued, had strained the environment to the breaking point. Commoner and others popularized the word *ecology*, the natural balance necessary to sustain life on this planet, and tried to put distance between the new environmental movement and the "Don't Be a Litterbug!" and "beautification" campaigns of the past.

In the early 1970s, halting construction of the Alaska pipeline became a *cause celebre* among environmentalists, who claimed that an oil pipeline would upset the ecology of the frozen tundra and adversely affect plants and animals. For several years groups such as the Sierra Club and the Friends of the Earth successfully blocked the pipeline, but the energy crisis of 1973, produced by the boycott of the United States by Middle Eastern oil suppliers, brought rapid congressional approval for construction. The Alaska pipeline, together with relaxation of various environmental regulations, showed how quickly many people might dismiss ecological considerations when faced with energy shortages. Meanwhile, business pressure groups and political conservatives tried to make environmentalism a dirty word. Affluent environmentalists, it was charged, opposed the kind of economic development that would allow middle-class Americans to maintain their present living standard and poorer citizens to improve their lives.

Environmentalists and industrialists continually clashed over the issue of pollution. The rising material standards that people thought would enhance their comfort bore price tags—brownish skies, strangely colored rivers, drying lakes, aggravated respiratory problems, and a sharply rising cancer rate. Urban areas suffered most visibly in the 1960s; breathing New York's air for a day, one study reported, was the equivalent of smoking four packs of cigarettes. Throughout the nation, once sparkling trout streams turned into sickly trickles of industrial waste. Strip mining, which had doubled during the 1960s, raised the specter of permanent destruction of land.

Industrialists, of course, did not favor dead lakes, wasted land, toxic subsoil, and unhealthy air. But charged with the duty of running their companies at a profit, they did not take the long-range view of many environmentalists. Most wished to postpone or to compromise environmental concern in order to keep their businesses profitable, and they often had the support of their workers and anyone else dependent upon their products. Environmentalists, it was charged were impractical; it was impossible to live in a risk-free society. Industrialists and their supporters emphasized two other points: Stringent regulations would put an even greater stress on America's apparently dwindling energy reserves by making it difficult to use high-pollution fuels, such as coal, and the cost of meeting tough environmental standards would make domestic industry uncompetitive with foreign enterprises.

Trying to steer a course between environmental hazards and tolerable costs was the government's Environmental Protection Agency (EPA). Established in 1970, it became the government's largest regulatory body, employing 10,000 people and striving to enforce the new statutes enacted by Congress. The new environmental legislation of the 1970s aimed at limiting the use of pesticides, protecting endangered species, insuring occupational safety, controlling strip mining practices, and establishing maximum levels of emission of certain chemical and bacteriological pollutants into the air and water. Predictably, the EPA came under sharp attack from both industrialists and environmentalists: Industry charged it with obstructionism; environmentalists assailed its laxity. But the EPA's efforts did improve safety in the workplace, dissipated much of the urban smog of the 1960s, and cleaned up at least the surface of many of the nation's waterways.

With visible pollutants and some gross violations of nature under greater control by the late 1970s, even graver problems emerged. The higher smokestacks that had helped eliminate smog merely elevated pollutants, spread them over wider areas, and altered their chemical composition. The resultant "acid rain," which threatened cropland throughout the country, constituted a less visible but more serious hazard than smog. Safe disposal of toxic wastes presented another significant problem. In the early 1980s people began to discover that many industries had for years haphazardly dumped toxic chemical wastes. These substances, some of which were capable of promoting genetic defects and cancer, sometimes even became landfill for housing projects, as was the case at Love Canal in upstate New York. Unlike the pollution problems of the past, those of the oversized society tended to be invisible; their toxic efforts were more long-term and were not immediately apparent. Any increased rate in environmentally caused cancer, for example, might take twenty years to detect. The 1970s

Air pollution, a major urban problem in the 1960s, prompted the passage of new federal antipollution regulations. Here, an official from the Tacoma, Washington, health department is measuring air pollution from the roof of the public library. Source: *Tacoma Public Library, Trueblood Collection #884.*

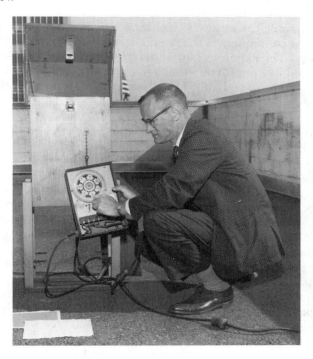

may have been an "environmental decade" of new concern and legislation, yet the environmental problems bequeathed to the 1980s seemed more complex than previous ones.

Toward the end of the 1970s, environmental groups increasingly focused on the issue of nuclear power. Ralph Nader and others argued that atomic power plants presented unacceptable risks, and the "antinuke" movement received a boost from the popularity of a film about a nuclear meltdown—*The China Syndrome* (1978). And just when the power industry was laughing at the implausibility of the movie, a real-life accident in the spring of 1979 raised fears about nuclear energy to new heights.

A malfunction in the nuclear reactor at Three Mile Island, near Harrisburg, Pennsylvania, touched off a near disaster. Residents living near the facility evacuated their homes, and the confusion and conflicting reports during the several days of crisis ballooned public doubts about technicians' abilities to handle this deadly new technology. According to power-company supporters, the Three Mile Island accident proved that the ultimate disaster, a total meltdown, could be avoided and that even a fairly serious accident could result in no loss of life. Critics, however, pointed out the lack of established safety procedures, highlighted the escape of radiation into the surrounding atmosphere and water, and calculated the huge costs of clean-up. The official reports of a special presidential commission and of the Nuclear Regulatory Commission (NRC) came down hard on the power industry. The NRC's investigation concluded that without "fundamental changes" in the nuclear industry "similar accidents—perhaps with the potentially serious consequences that were avoided at Three Mile Island—are likely to recur." The expenses of new designs, more elaborate safety procedures, and possibly even further damage suits exploded claims that nuclear energy would be cheap and safe. The all-out rush to switch to nuclear energy sources slowed and then stopped.

By the late 1970s most people agreed that they should meet the energy crisis with some sort of common action. But what? Environmentalists favored federally assisted crash programs to encourage decentralized production of power through solar, geothermal, or wind-generated systems. Ralph Nader and Barry Commoner pressed the argument that the energy debate, in fact, involved fundamental issues of economic control: It pitted decentralized, "democratic" energy sources against those that the utility and oil companies could continue to monopolize and run from a centralized facility. Supporters of the owner industry, however, considered solar, geothermal, and wind power to be marginal sources at best, unable to satisfy the nation's voracious appetite for energy. They urged Washington to cut the red tape of environmental regulations and open some long-delayed offshore oil developments, and they continued to tout coal, synfuels, and atomic power.

Everyone, though, stressed conservation: Tax breaks encouraged home weatherization, utility companies "advertised" for wise use, and the American people responded to higher prices. Consumption of crude oil fell from 7.15 million barrels in 1979 to 6.8 million in 1980. Buying habits or life styles were not significantly scaled back, but the meteoric rise in energy use since World War II did level off.

Land and Real Estate Hustlers

A great land boom that began in the mid-1960s added to environmentalists' concerns. Huge land development corporations began subdividing tracts at an alarming rate, focusing their efforts on the sunbelt states of Florida, California, New Mexico, and Arizona but also operating in northern recreational states, such as Colorado and Maine. The National Association of Home Builders estimated that Americans built ninety thousand *second* homes in 1971, although the *overall* number of homes constructed that year was lower than it had been a decade earlier. But these fishing huts, mountain cabins, seaside bungalows, and future retirement villas represented only a fragment of the land that had been cut into parcels and put up for sale as potential homesites; 97 percent of the land sold remained close to its original state, with no improvements or structures. In the late 1960s, it seemed, more affluent Americans just wanted to own a piece of land, whether they intended to build on it immediately or not.

TABLE 9-1   Population Decline of the Industrial Northeast, Rise of the Sunbelt*

OLD INDUSTRIAL CENTERS	1970	1980	% CHANGE
New York	9,897,000	9,060,000	−8%
Chicago	6,975,000	7,032,000	+1
Philadelphia	4,824,000	4,696,000	−3
Detroit	4,200,000	4,342,000	+3
Boston	3,849,000	3,848,000	—
Pittsburgh	2,401,000	2,261,000	−6
Cleveland	2,064,000	1,893,000	−8
Buffalo	1,349,000	1,240,000	−8
RISE OF SUNBELT			
Dallas-Fort Worth	2,318,000	2,961,000	+28%
Houston	1,985,000	2,887,000	+45
Atlanta	1,390,000	2,004,000	+44
San Diego	1,358,000	1,858,000	+37
Miami	1,268,000	1,574,000	+24
Tampa-St. Petersburg	1,013,000	1,552,000	+53
Phoenix	971,000	1,505,000	+55
Fort Lauderdale-Hollywood, Fla.	620,000	1,005,000	+62

*In response to these demographic trends, public policymakers debated their proper course of action. In 1980 a special presidential commission recommended that the national government allow demographic trends to run their course and that it should take no dramatic action to bail out older industrial centers.

Source: U.S. Census Bureau.

Colorado Land. An undeveloped development in Colorado. Source: *Bill Wunsch, The Denver Post.*

Why this obsession with land buying? One reason was that the 1960s provided a perfect climate for a land boom. The new affluence brought second homes within the reach of millions; faster automobiles and new interstate highways made more distant vacation homes practical; increased leisure time and earlier retirement raised the demand for recreation. And in a decade of economic growth it was easy to appeal to people's spirit of adventure, to convince them that they could afford the monthly payments and that land was always a good investment. One company's sales pitch asked, "Do you know any big rich man who doesn't own real estate? . . . Wouldn't it be wise to buy land somewhere—anywhere—before prices get out of reach?" Land hustlers rolled out (and usually overstated) forecasts of population growth and made land ownership seemed like a vanishing luxury.

As soon as entrepreneurs discovered how easily they could sell land, "development" corporations sprang up everywhere. Some created attractive planned communities with good sanitary facilities, nearby employment opportunities, and luxurious recreation areas. But too many others simply bought large tacts of cheap land and resold it in expensive lot-sized packages. A development company in Florida, for example, purchased some swampy land for $180 an acre and quickly resold it for $640 an acre. To make this enormous profit, the company did not drain the land, build roads, plan sanitation facilities, or construct major buildings. It merely hired a high-pressure sales force, ran advertisements around the country, and gave the supposed community a fancy name. Word of such profits turned subdividing into a national craze, and most conglomerate enterprises quickly created land development subsidiaries. By the early 1970s developers in California were buying fifty thousand to one hundred thousand acres a year; subdivided land near Albuquerque, New Mexico, was slated to hold a population four times the size of Baltimore; and plots for sale in Colorado would have increased the state's population five ties over. In North Carolina, a real estate entrepreneur and a former lawyer were charged with mail fraud after allegedly trying to sell over 60,000 acres of the Great Smoky Mountain National Park.

During the 1970s the land boom abruptly expanded to where most demographers of the 1960s would have considered the least likely place of all—the nation's central cities. The 1970s bred near-perfect conditions for a reversal in urban fortunes. Rising gas prices mounted a frontal assault on commuting; the large baby boom generation strained the housing market; widespread cultural nostalgia helped generate interest in the renovation of old houses; a temporary decline in crime rate boosted the image of cities. New pollution standards made urban air bearable again, and cities also benefited from the demise of some dirty, industrial-age jobs and the rise of clean, service occupations. By 1980 the largest single employer in "steel city"—Pittsburgh—was not U.S. Steel but the University of Pittsburgh. Although New York City and Cleveland hit the headlines for walking the tightrope of bankruptcy in the 1970s, many more urban centers found that federal funds temporarily gave them a surplus. In 1969 few cities received more than 10 percent of their general revenue in the form of federal money; by 1980 many cities received over 50 percent in federal funds.

Such conditions produced urban revitalization in some sections of most American cities. Developers once devoted to mapping out suburban shopping centers began selling designs for urban malls. In "rescued" neighborhoods, renovators attacked any edifice with a brick facade still standing, and prices shot up as speculators quickly acquired an interest in promoting historical preservation. Condominiums attracted a generation of busy young professionals who wanted the advantages of home ownership without the disadvantages of single-home upkeep.

This "gentrification"—the return of the gentry class to the inner city—had its flip side. Revitalization was, after all, highly selective. "Old towns" of new-old cobblestone streets sprouted where architecture was interesting and sound. But the rise in rents drove the poor out of the best of their neighborhoods and left them in the worst. And where did people in need of inexpensive housing go? Moving to a more run-down neighborhood only increased the general demand for housing and mercilessly drove up prices for everyone. Speculators began to realize that even nonrenovated areas experienced a boom in prices and brought easy profits. For the poor, then, the inner-city renewal of the 1970s was often something to oppose and organize against. It brought not only rising prices but physical disruption, dispersion of older communities, and a growth in homelessness among the poor. But most city officials were slow to grapple with the adverse results of "gentrification"; they were delighted by the new activity, and they kept busy joining public and private capital in new development projects that were aimed at their most affluent residents and the highly courted "tourist trade."

AN OUT-SIZED CULTURE

The Publishing Industry

The book publishing industry, once the comfortable preserve of gentlemen-publishers and small booksellers, underwent considerable growth and change after 1960. By the mid-1970s, the number of bookstores in the United States had surpassed, for the first time since the early days of the cinema, the number of movie theaters, and the yearly revenues of the publishing industry outstriped those of Hollywood. Americans bought twice as many books each year as movie tickets. Although small bookstores still held their fascination, especially for browsers, most people shopped in streamlined book supermarkets. Large-scale operations, such as the spectacularly successful B. Dalton chain, dominated sales figures. Using their own computerized systems, book supermarkets stocked relatively few titles, primarily mass-market paperbacks and hardbacks from the best-seller lists, and aimed for a brisk, steady turnover. In fact, a large order from a chain operation could ensure a book's place on the best-seller list. Such a sales system threatened the survival of many small bookstores and made it more difficult for readers to find shops willing to stock, or even order, volumes that lacked mass appeal.

Many would-be authors complained that a similar trend toward concentration in the publishing industry limited opportunities for new literary talents. As a consequence of the general consolidation of American business, most American publishers became subsidiaries of large corporations, often "communications groups" that included newspapers, electronic media, and records. The results, according to media analysts, were not always pleasant. First, publishing executives were anxious to show superiors in the corporate hierarchy that books, like other products, could generate sizable profits. The easiest way to do this, of course, was to publish only those volumes likely to find a mass readership and avoid more esoteric titles. Critics, such as Noam Chomsky, warned that the consolidation of the publishing industry raised the threat of a powerful new censorship of unorthodox styles and ideas.

A fierce critic of American foreign policy, Chomsky charged that a subsidiary of Warner Communications suppressed one of his studies because corporate executives considered the book unpatriotic. Although the company fulfilled its commitment to print the book, the conglomerate failed to promote or even distribute it. Ultimately, it was republished and distributed by a small cooperative in Boston. The Chomsky-Warner affair defied simple analysis. Some observers ridiculed the suggestion that Chomsky had been censored. His book, after all, had never been the subject of government pressure, and it *had* been published—twice—and eventually marketed. Yet the incident remained troubling. In an age of relatively inexpensive photo-duplication techniques, publication of a book was often a minor task. In an age of mass communication networks, distribution and promotion were more crucial. If authors wished to publish their own books or to work with smaller presses, they found themselves at a great disadvantage in reaching a wide audience. Was the denial of access to the channels of mass distribution a new form of corporate censorship that could impede the flow of dissenting views?

With the trend toward "McDonaldization" in publishing, authors discovered that their ability to market their works might be more important than their ability to write them. Some publishers conceded that, before making a final commitment to publish a book, they considered the author's potential charm on television talk shows. The publisher of the best-selling *Your Erroneous Zones* recalled that he had been more enthusiastic about the television personality of the author, Dr. Wayne Dyer, than about his book. The tie-in between book publishing and the electronic media grew even closer as the communications groups began to "package" expensive media products. The ultimate in commercialized "art" might span the entire communications spectrum: a network TV mini-series for the domestic market; a theatrical movie for distribution overseas; a record album of the sound track; and a mass-market paperback for drugstore racks and large bookstore chains.

Many veterans of the literary establishment condemned such trends. Publishing, they conceded, had never been a purely philanthropic enterprise, but never had it been so crassly commercial. The metamorphosis of the highly prestigious National Book Awards—prizes selected by prominent literary critics and by celebrated authors—into the American Book Awards—which were to be chosen by committees that included mass-market publishers and individuals from the bookstore chains—symbolized the new developments.

Similar trends toward consolidation and commercialization affected American journalism. Continuing a pattern that had been evident for more than half a century, the American newspaper business became increasingly concentrated. By 1980 only readers in the largest cities could turn to competing daily papers. While financial pressures forced some papers to fold, including the widely acclaimed *Chicago Daily News*, many more, especially in smaller cities, became the property of large newspaper chains. For those who could afford the new computerized technology, journalism was more profitable than ever. Although not all chains imposed a single editorial policy upon their papers, there could be no doubt that fewer and fewer hands wielded the power of the press. Because of such concentration, critics of the media complained, journalists became too complacent; lacking competition, they also lacked incentive to dig out fresh material on local affairs. Reluctance to probe into the dark corners of municipal life, it was further charged, reflected the close, interlocking relationships between newspapers and powerful local interests.

Critics of the media also denounced "celebrity journalism." Recognizing that most Americans relied upon television as their primary source of information, afternoon newspapers increasingly emphasized "soft" features on popular culture, living styles, and prominent personalities. Readers in

New York City were treated to the most spectacular example of this change when Australian news magnate Rupert Murdoch purchased the *New York Post* and converted it into an updated version of the old tabloids of the 1920s. Celebrity journalism also spawned "personality magazines," including the very successful *People*. Devoted almost entirely to the rise and fall of celebrities and distributed only at magazine counters and on supermarket racks, *People*—Time, Incorporated's answer to the *National Enquirer* and the *Midnight Globe*—spawned several clones, and the trend toward celebrity journalism reached its logical conclusion when the media began to cover its own celebrities—in a short-lived publication appropriately entitled *Media People*.

Although the catch phrases "consolidation" and "celebrification" accurately summarized the dominant trends in publishing in the 1960s and 1970s, there were other forces at work. Despite the growth of publishing conglomerates, many smaller houses did prosper on the fringes of the industry. Many publishers, regardless of size, remained committed to bringing out specialized works, even if they did not seem to be candidates for the best-seller lists or for TV mini-series. Meanwhile, the fragmentation of cold war orthodoxies was reflected in the magazine publishing business. Many of the magazines that had sought a "general" family-oriented readership— such as *Look*, the *Saturday Evening Post, Life*, and *Harpers*—either folded completely or underwent drastic overhauls. More specialized journals—such as the *National Review* on the political right and *The Nation* on the left— gained in circulation and prestige. Even in the newspaper business, diversity survived. Most of the "underground" papers of the 1960s, including the famous *Berkeley Barb*, ultimately failed, but alternative journalism survived in the form of community-based newspapers. The going was always rough for these publications, but many journalists, especially younger ones who could not find other jobs in a glutted market, were willing to make the sacrifices. Finally, the growing amount of criticism directed at the publishing industry by media-watching publications such as the *Columbia Journalism Review* offered a healthy contrast to the smug complacency that had prevailed during the cold war era.

The Motion Picture Industry

Significant changes also affected the motion picture industry during the 1960s and 1970s. For more than four decades, filmmaking and the huge Hollywood movie factories had been synonymous. Using their sprawling back lots and deploying vast armies of contract players and stars, the major studios steadily nourished the dreams of millions of moviegoers. Young men dueled alongside Errol Flynn or Clark Gable, and women floated through the glamorous world of Barbara Stanwyck or Lana Turner. But during the 1960s the giant studios came upon bad days. Challenged by television and victimized by urban decay, which frightened many people away from the old downtown movie palaces, Hollywood's film moguls watched box office receipts decline steadily. Seeking to reduce production costs and to bring new realism to the screen, many filmmakers abandoned the Hollywood sets completely and shot entirely on location, often outside the United States. At the same time, many of the old stars either died or retired; others, such as Rock Hudson and Elizabeth Taylor, suddenly discovered that their names alone no longer guaranteed a film's financial success.

During the late 1960s and early 1970s, filmmakers tried to reach out to new audiences, especially young people, with films that were very different from the classics of Hollywood's studio era. Consciously working against Hollywood's standard pro-military frame, Stanley Kubrick populated the national-defense establishment with morons and lunatics in *Dr. Strangelove* (1963); he later explored the mystical science fiction of Arthur C. Clark in *2001* (1968) and looked at the issues of violence and behavior modification in *A Clockwork Orange* (1972). While traditionalists denounced new films such as these, movie executives recognized that only a handful of films aimed at the old "family audience" still made any money. The box-office success of Dennis Hopper's *Easy Rider* (1969), a cheaply made film about two hippies who used a drug sale to finance a motorcycle trip across the southwestern United States, interwove many themes of the "new Hollywood"—social criticism, sex, and violence—and inspired a number of (much less successful) films about the counterculture, including the documentary *Woodstock* (1970). Meanwhile, several African-American directors offered a series of pictures, derided by critics as "blaxploitation" films, set in violence-filled, corporate-controlled, inner-city neighborhoods, the kinds of places through which Gene Kelly had danced in films of the 1940s.

Perhaps the most interesting series of films to span the late 1960s and the entire decade of the 1970s focused on loneliness and alienation in an oversized society of overgrown institutions and increasingly powerless individuals. At the same time, many of these films also rebelled against the old genres, the tight forms—such as the gangster movie or the western film— that had marked Hollywood's classic studio system. Robert Altman's *M*A*S*H* (1970) mocked the standard war picture, while his *McCabe and Mrs. Miller* (1968) and *Buffalo Bill and the Indians* (1976) debunked the myths upon which Hollywood's western films had long been based. In *The Long Goodbye* (1973), Altman turned Philip Marlowe, the independent detective hero made famous by Humphrey Bogart in *film noirs* of the 1940s, into a confused loser, a patsy who could not even find his own cat. Going even further, Francis Ford Coppola's *The Conversation* (1974) offered a chilling and almost despairing view of a culture based upon surveillance.

Although many of these films gained more support from critics than ticket-buyers, Coppola in particular attracted huge audiences with his Godfather sagas, films that reworked the gangster genre while also exploring the theme of alienation. These two films, especially *Godfather II* (1974), presented a deeply pessimistic critique of American society and American history. The only refuge the film offers is the tightknit, patriarchal family, a place of apparent warmth and safety, lorded over by a tough, but protective, godfather. Inexorably, though, the godfather's business as a crime boss—which also blends into his other business and political connections—corrupts the family circle. One by one, family members fall. At the end, in the America of the 1970s, the new godfather is left alone: isolated, lonely, alienated, an outcast from both society and his own family.

Toward the end of the 1970s, this cinema of loneliness and alienation lost touch with popular tastes. Altman's only commercial success came with *M*A*S*H* at the beginning of the decade, and Coppola's ambitious plans to create his own studio collapsed under his own lack of box-office hits. Taking its place was a new cycle of motion pictures from film-school graduates who had reverentially studied Hollywood's traditional myths. Steven Spielberg updated the monster genre with his blockbuster *Jaws* (1977), and George Lucas surpassed Spielberg's epic with *Star Wars*, a film that owed most of its images and situations to familiar Hollywood genres—especially to the war film and the western—as well as to the graphics of video games. In contrast to previous films of the 1960s and 1970s, *Star Wars* seemed to make militarism seem fun once more.

Although some critics decried the emphasis on giant blockbusters such as *Star Wars*, a trend necessitated by rising marketing costs, film culture in many ways grew stronger than it had ever been before. Increased popular attention to film styles and themes, for example, reflected the popularization of more sophisticated types of cinematic criticism. During the 1970s most urban areas supported "retrospective houses"—commercial theaters that specialized in previously released classics—and theaters that emphasized foreign movies and the type of thoughtful films once dismissed as noncommercial "art" movies. And even as Hollywood's revenues declined in relation to those of television (or even the record and book publishing industries), more people were coming to take the motion picture itself more seriously. The study of film, both Hollywood's products and documentary works, became a part of most university and many high school curricula during the 1970s. Journals devoted to criticism, theory, and film history proliferated as more and more people came to appreciate the subtle, complex connection between the world of the movies and everyday life.

Sports

Sports also reinforced the expansive trends in American life. There were more fans, more teams, and more television coverage. At the beginning of the 1960s big-league baseball still dominated the sports scene, and the two major leagues expanded into new cities during the 1960s and 1970s. But despite its growth, the national pastime lost ground to other spectator sports, particularly to the faster-moving, more violent games of football, basketball (a noncontact sport only in theory), and ice hockey. Pro football's Super Bowl replaced baseball's World Series as sports' most talked-about annual attraction. Cities competed vigorously for almost any type of professional franchise; lucrative television contracts and generous tax write-offs made ownership of a team especially alluring to wealthy business people.

Always seeking new forms of competition to sell, promoters aggressively marketed golf tournaments (women's as well as men's), imported soccer, tried (unsuccessfully) team competition in tennis, and even formed "major leagues" for slow-pitch softball and volleyball. Similarly, the growing popularity of women's sorts produced a short-lived women's professional basketball league and superstar status for women's tennis and golf. Predictions that the energy shortage was ending America's love affair with the automobile did not cool sports fans' ardor for all types of auto racing. The Indianapolis 500 rivaled the Super Bowl as sports' biggest one-day event, and President Jimmy Carter's favorite spectator sport, stock-car racing, retained its great popularity in the South.

Even professional boxing, once considered on the ropes because of the taint of fixed matches and the declining supply of "hungry" fighters, staged a vigorous comeback. The dominant figure was Muhammad Ali, the three-time heavyweight champion of the world. Ali modestly claimed that he was the best-known person on the planet, and there seemed little reason to doubt him. Certainly, he made boxing a worldwide enterprise. In 1964 he made his first title defense before a handful of people in a hockey rink in Lewiston, Maine; fifteen years later, he could boast that he had fought before millions of people from Malaysia to Zaire. Ali noted accurately that governments, and not simply promoters, bid for his services. Ali's success in the ring, however, was tempered by a dramatic decline in his personal health, a condition some physicians blamed on his long career.

Sports figures remained society's special heroes. Some, like football's Jim Brown, retired in favor of full-time acting; while others, such as O. J. Simpson and Joe Namath, found it more profitable to hop back and forth between stadium and sound stage. Many sports celebrities discovered that business ventures could handsomely supplement their athletic contracts. During the heady 1960s, some even challenged Colonel Sanders and McDonald's in the highly risky franchise food business, but most contented themselves with a safer course—product endorsements. After breaking Babe Ruth's lifetime home run record, Hank Aaron signed a $5 million contract with Magnavox.

Inevitably, politicians tried to tap the glamor that surrounded big-time sports celebrities. Richard Nixon assiduously cultivated his image as the nation's number-one sports fan. (He even contributed a trick play to the 1972 Super Bowl; perhaps an evil omen, the play lost thirteen yards.) During presidential campaigns candidates rushed to sign up prominent athletes for their campaign squads, and a former pro football star, Jack Kemp, rivaled a former college benchwarmer, Ronald Reagan, as the hero of conservative Republicans.

Most of the professional team sports went through considerable turmoil during the 1960s and 1970s. Players achieved at least partial emancipation from the once dictatorial control of their "owners." Professional athletes had long complained that they received a disproportionately small share of the profits, but through the 1950s the laws applying to sports stood fully on the side of capital. A new generation of athletes, armed with union advisers and spurred on by the sight of burgeoning sports revenues, changed this. Hockey, basketball, and football players made some gains when rival leagues began to bid for their services in the late 1960s and early 1970s, but not until the mid-1970s were their victories, and new breakthroughs by baseball players, written into law. In 1970 baseball's owners narrowly escaped defeat when the Supreme Court, after considerable internal squabbling, finally voted five to three to reject a suit challenging the national pastime's reserve clause as the basis of a form of involuntary servitude. The owners' victory was short-lived.

By 1980 other legal decision had given athletes in all major sports the freedom to "play out their options" to their old team and to auction off their services as "free agents" in the marketplace. The result was hefty inflation in the entire salary structure of professional sports. In 1979 Nolan Ryan, owner of baseball's fastest fast ball, became a million-dollar-a-year player when he switched his allegiance from Gene Autry (the cowboy-star owner of the California Angels) to the Lone Ranger (the old cowboy hero who symbolized the home state of Ryan's new team, Houston). Although some fans grumbled—especially when highly paid players failed to deliver—most owners found that steadily rising revenues and generous tax breaks could generally cover the new salaries.

Sports and legal questions became intertwined with issues relating to gender. Sports critics condemned big-time sports for promoting sexism—pointing, for example, to the emphasis on female "cheerleading" squads that resembled Las Vegas chorus lines—and urged inclusion of more women into the world of athletics. Colleges and universities, mandated by law to achieve "equality" in sports activities, faced especially difficult decisions about how to finance and promote women's sports. Should women's basketball, volleyball, and track, for instance, be restructured along the same lines as big-time men's activities, with full-ride scholarships and all the accompanying problems? Or was it preferable for women's sports to adopt different models? In sports where professionalism prevailed, such as tennis and golf, the trend was unabashedly toward emulating the male model: Prize money, endorsement contracts, and media coverage for women all steadily escalated after the mid-1970s.

The growing commercialization of big-time sports, even at the collegiate level, also provoked lively debate. Traditionalists continued to defend amateur sports as character-building enterprises, and some social observers joined fans in celebrating the vicarious thrill of watching highly skilled professionals perform their special magic. Reflecting upon the improvisational moves of basketball players like Julius Irving ("Dr. J."), Michael Novak compared the game to jazz. But other observers, including former football players, such as Dave Meggyesy and Peter Gent, took a more critical approach. Summarizing this trend toward more iconoclastic sports journalism, Robert Lipsyte condemned Americans' infatuation with "Sportsworld, an amorphous infrastructure that acts to contain our energies, divert our passions, and socialize us for work or war or depression."

Writing in a different vein, Christopher Lasch argued that the real tragedy of recent years had been the "trivialization" of athletic contests into debased, prepackaged spectacles. The nearly criminal violence in professional hockey, Lasch suggested, resulted from the extension of the game to areas without any authentic ice-hockey tradition: Unaware of the subtle aspects of the game, most fans could react only to mayhem and bloodletting. A cult of violence was clearly evident in professional boxing and wrestling. Boxing's resurgence was accompanied by a rash of ring fatalities, signs of careless matchmaking, inadequate medical supervision, and complacent officiating. Though the mayhem in professional wrestling was obviously feigned, scenarios became much more violent than they had been in the "golden days" of the 1950s: Wrestlers routinely promised to maim or cripple opponents, and promoters eagerly pushed spectacles featuring cages, chains, crowbars, and all manners of theoretically lethal weaponry.

Television

The key to the rejuvenation of boxing, and the *sine qua non* for almost every other sport, was television. At the beginning of the 1970s professional football invaded Monday night's prime-time schedule and, to the surprise of most sports and media experts, ran away with the ratings contest. Two years later, even before a terrorist attack upon Israeli athletes gave the 1972 summer Olympic Games new political significance, the Munich Olympics

The care and feeding of complex media equipment became part of everyday life in the "oversized society." Source: *National and Peel Collection, Minnesota Historical Society.*

confirmed the drawing power of sports, including previously obscure ones such as women's gymnastics. By 1980 the air time devoted to sports by the three major networks had more than doubled. The reason was simple. Sports brought "good numbers"—high ratings; good numbers produced another set of happy figures—increased advertising revenues; and together, the two sets of numbers translated into greater corporate profits for ABC, CBS, and NBC. Between 1970 and 1975 the percentage of NBC's advertising take that came from sports nearly doubled. And higher television revenues *from* sports inevitably meant higher payments *to* sports for the privilege of carrying events on television. In 1976 the rights to telecast the Montreal Olympics cost ABC $25 million; four years later, the same network paid more than $200 million dollars more for rights to the 1984 summer games.

This symbiotic relationship between sports and television helped to solidify TV's position as the most popular of the popular arts. First of all, TV remained popular in terms of its ability to attract mass audiences, not only in the United States but throughout most of the world. According to a study completed in the mid-1970s, nearly half of the population ranked watching television—as opposed to watching motion pictures, reading, playing cards, talking with friends, or any other activity—as their favorite pastime. Surveys also showed that people were spending more and more time with their sets: In 1961 respondents indicated that they watched television slightly more than two hours a day; by 1974 the figure had jumped to more than three hours per day. By the time a child graduated from high school, it was estimated, he or she had spent more time with television sets than with a twelve-year supply of schoolteachers.

Network TV's content was shaped by its broad-based audience. Throughout the 1950s some people had hoped that TV would somehow emphasize "serious" programming, such as symphony concerts, sophisticated dramas, and in-depth news analyses. At the same time, when some prominent sponsors underwrote entire shows, corporate image-makers often considered critical acclaim as important as mass audiences, if not more so. But when television changed its sponsorship base, so that the 30-second, individually sold commercial became the key element in network programming, the number and type of people tuned to a particular show became all important, to both sponsors and programmers. Few advertisers wanted to buy time on a program with small audiences or on one with a viewership composed largely of older people with small disposable incomes. Television programmers came to focus more and more on the bottom line: They were in the business of attracting the largest possible segment of the American population and then reselling this audience to corporate sponsors at the highest possible rates.

Faced with the almost impossible task of predicting what a diverse audience might want to watch, network executives increasingly came to rely on a relatively small group of programmers and upon tried-and-tested formulas. People who had developed and packaged one successful show gained an inside track. During the 1960s and 1970s, for example, Aaron Spelling became a prolific presence in network television. Beginning with

The Mod Squad, a program about youthful crimefighters who supposedly expressed the countercultural values of the 1960s-youth generation, Spelling developed a string of "crime" series that ended with *Hart to Hart*, a show that featured a wealthy couple who flaunted all the up-scale consumer values of the late 1970s. Every one of his shows hit the top twenty-five for at least one year, and Spelling, who called his programs "mind candy," epitomized the successful television *auteur*. He offered viewers predictable plots, simplistic characters, lush scenery, and reassuring endings; he provided ABC with consistently high ratings; and he left himself with a backlist of series that could be sold for syndication outside of prime time.

Despite the increasingly narrower range of programming during the 1960s and 1970s, some shows did break familiar genres and molds. CBS's *Sixty Minutes*, the first "television magazine," eventually entered the Nielsen's top-ten ranking. *The Mary Tyler Moore Show*, a variety of programs by Norman Lear (including *All in the Family*), and *M*A*S*H* won plaudits for bending hackneyed television formulas. With the emphasis these programs gave to character development and ensemble playing—rather than focusing upon a show's headliners or weekly guest stars—viewers could find a continuity missing from most television shows. With Hollywood's film archives almost depleted, TV executives also began to produce their own made-for-TV films and longer "mini-series," including the much-discussed *Roots* in 1977. Meanwhile, television comedy broke new ground in the 1970s with *Saturday Night Live* and *SCTV*, two ensemble shows that specialized in satire directed not only at political and social events but at the TV medium itself.

By the 1970s viewers could also select a highbrow alternative to network television, though few actually did so. Public television, authorized by Congress in 1967 and expanded (with the help of corporate and foundation grants) in the 1970s, attracted only about 5 percent of the viewing audience for its most popular adult shows. (Children's programs, such as *Sesame Street* and *Mr. Rogers' Neighborhood* did considerably better.) But the public broadcasting bureaucracy still produced considerable controversy. In 1972 Richard Nixon tried to block public television's appropriations because of the allegedly left-liberal bias of its public affairs offerings. Private broadcasting interests complained bitterly about the steadily increasing federal subsidies. Public television's most popular programs, critics liked to point out, were purchased from British television rather than produced by PBS' own staff. Finally, noting the large number of programs bankrolled by oil companies, some wags claimed that PBS stood for the Petroleum Broadcasting System, not the Public Broadcasting System.

Most people who touted television's potential ignored both the networks and PBS; instead, they claimed that new technologies unveiled in the 1970s seemed the best hope for innovation and greater diversity. "Minicams" and new videotape equipment greatly increased television's mobility and the speed with which it could send images back to viewers. The new communications satellites allowed live transmissions from most parts of the world. Introduction of cable television systems gave millions of subscribers new options, including channels reserved for "public access" programming.

Public access channels, supporters claimed, would finally give citizens a real chance to explore the limits of media; even the instant arrival of X-rated television in some cities did not cool the enthusiasm for future break-throughs. The arrival of videotape machines allowed more affluent viewers to record programs for replay at their convenience, an important step toward breaking the tyranny of the network schedules.

Popular Music

Many pop-music stars surpassed television personalities and sports figures in popularity and wealth. Performers received huge fees for concert appearances and staggering royalties from album sales. Some of the super-stars of the 1960s—Janis Joplin, Jimi Hendrix, and Jim Morrison, for example—lived at a frantic pace, spending money wildly while killing their talent and ultimately themselves with drugs and alcohol. When Morrison succumbed to a heart attack at twenty-seven, physicians reported that his internal organs resembled those of a person in his fifties. Other stars dis-played more concern about their health and their financial balance sheets. Bob Dylan, the Beatles, and James Brown became multimillionaires. Even the Grateful Dead, the group most closely associated with San Francisco's original hippie movement, eventually concentrated upon cash flows and tax write-offs as much as upon musical arrangements. In 1973 the business magazine *Forbes* estimated that at least fifty rock superstars earned between $2 million and $6 million a year. "The idea all along," explained Alice Cooper, "was to make $1 million. Otherwise the struggle wouldn't have been worth it." As one study put it, "Rock and Roll was here to pay."

In addition to obtaining great financial rewards, rock musicians finally gained serious critical attention. The success of the Beatles and Dylan helped rock music escape its juvenile image in the 1960s, and both rock and folk-rock became widely accepted as serious forms of artistic expression. The poetic lyrics of Dylan and Paul Simon reflected the frustrated dreams of restless youth, their concern about the "sounds of silence" ("people talking without listening"), and their outrage against the persistence of social injus-tice. Young composers blended various types of musical styles into the rock idiom. Traditional folk music, black blues, jazz, and country-western music all influenced trends in the progressive rock of the 1960s.

Throughout the 1960s, rock music constantly intersected with political and cultural events, offering a kind of running commentary on each new turn in the youth movement. In 1966, for instance, the Beatles released both their much-celebrated psychedelic album, *Sgt. Pepper's Lonely Heart's Club Band*, and John Lennon's "All You Need Is Love." Juxtaposed with the intense outpouring of feeling against United States involvement in Vietnam, violence in black ghettos, and the rising fervor of the youthful New Left, the Beatles appeared to be urging young people to take a break from politics and immerse themselves in the pleasures of the counterculture. As if in reply, Bob Dylan's *John Wesley Harding* avoided psychedelic trappings and adopted a philosophical-religious tone, with songs like "All Along the Watchtower" and "I Dreamed I Saw St. Augustine." The following year, as the political atmosphere became more explosive, the Rolling Stones issued "Street Fighting Man," a new rock anthem that expressed both anger at the political establishment and a deep ambivalence about the role of rock-and-roll millionaires in the so-called youth revolution.

The Stones' *Sympathy for the Devil* (1968) presaged the music of the 1970s, which replaced songs of community and hope with ones of individualism and decadence. In contrast to the communal spirit of the late 1960s, much of the music of the 1970s highlighted the cult of rock stars as "lonely isolated artists," people set apart from the larger community, except from those consumption communities expected to buy singles, albums, and T-shirts. Beset by personal and artistic difficulties, the preeminent symbol of the rock community, the Beatles, released their final collaborative album in 1970. By then, the high-tech, decibel-breaking sound of heavy metal contrasted vividly with folk-rock anthems of the sixties. Designed largely for audiences of working-class males, who gathered in cavernous urban auditoriums, heavy metal seemed calculated to drown out all sense of feeling and to mimic the screeching noise of industrial society. Heavy metal groups, such as Kiss, also explored another popular theme of the 1970s-style rock: decadence. Rock "artists" of various persuasions became symbols of spiritual exhaustion and the single-minded pursuit of pleasure. Alert to changing consumer trends, the Rolling Stones easily slipped from a revolutionary stance to a calculated pose of decadence.

At the same time, the entrepreneurs of "pop music," seeking a cleaner image, began to distance their products from rock-and-roll. The big business of making and distributing music was returning to a kind of pre-rock standardization. Recording companies, which surpassed the Hollywood film industry in yearly revenues during the 1970s, emphasized expanding their incomes. Competition among record executives, who were expected to anticipate not only the next new musical fad but also the following one, encouraged corruption and discouraged innovation. The major labels, which were generally owned by giant multinational firms, were more than eager to package the latest trend, subsidizing journalistic puffs for the rock magazines and concert tours for the latest products of their hit-making machinery; they were more reluctant to underwrite significant new directions in music.

A similar situation prevailed in the radio industry. The expansion of FM stations during the 1960s and early 1970s broke the tyranny of the old Top-40 playlist. Formats became freer; the range of music expanded; and local and regional artists could usually get their recordings on the air. By 1980, though, radio-programming services had again narrowed the musical spectrum. Relying upon sophisticated survey data, programming services carefully packaged each minute of air time, eliminated the discretion of disc jockeys, and emphasized the music that their data said would appeal to their clients' desired audience. They ignored artists and musical styles that did not fit "the program." Local talents lost out to national recording stars, and individuals on the smaller record labels lost out to artists being promoted heavily by the majors.

Corporate domination also affected African-American music. During the 1960s, James Brown became a symbol of both independent "black capitalism" and cultural innovation. "The hardest working man in show business" broke rock and rhythm and blues molds to feature soul music and, its later variant, funk. And from the late 1960s through the mid-1970s, Aretha Franklin, with her gospel-inspired readings of soul, broke through the male-dominated genres that had epitomized rock. Brown, Franklin, and the various artists who recorded for Stax, a small record label based in the South, all tried to avoid the kind of accommodation that many African-Americans associated with the Detroit-based Motown sound. But the money that could be made from soul and from African-American consumers of it eventually attracted the attention of both the Harvard Business School—which did a study for CBS in 1971—and the major record labels. By 1976, Stax had been absorbed into CBS, and other multi-media conglomerates were working to assimilate soul into various "cross-over" forms, such as disco.

Meanwhile, country and country-rock music, especially in the early 1970s, suddenly became a national, increasingly corporate-based, phenomenon. Even before Jimmy Carter, Georgia's little-known governor, set out to gain a nationwide following, the music associated with the honky-tonks of Dixie swept over the northern states. During the 1950s and even much of the 1960s, northerners who wanted to hear country music on their radios had to wait until evening when they could pick up high-beaming stations from the Deep South. By the 1970s, though, every metropolitan area had several country music stations, and many country artists were "crossing over" to the pop and rock stations. Singers such as Kris Kristofferson, Dolly Parton, and Willie Nelson (the first country artist to win a platinum record, symbolic of sales of one million albums) became nationwide celebrities with television and movie careers.

The appeal of country music was difficult to explain. Some people claimed that they liked its simplicity and honesty, its stories of broken hearts and faded loves—"Your Cheatin' Heart Will Tell on You." Others seemed attracted by its nostalgic overtones, its celebration of rural life and simple virtues—"My Heroes Have Always Been Cowboys." But perhaps in the oversized 1970s, country music's deeply rooted quality, its sense of limits, and its acceptance of failure, articulated a southern idea that came home to the rest of the nation.

Give Me That Old-Time Religion/
Give Me That Big-Time Religion

During the 1950s some observers happily claimed that Americans were becoming an increasingly religious people. Church membership climbed steadily; President Eisenhower spread "piety along the Potomac"; and the Reverend Norman Vincent Peale's popular *Power of Positive Thinking* seemed to carry faith and optimism to Protestants throughout the land. In 1955 the sociologist Will Herberg noted that the Judeo-Christian religious tradition was merging with American ideas to produce a consensus on deep-seated values among Protestants, Catholics, and Jews. A few skeptics warned that church attendance did not necessarily measure religious commitment and charged that churches emphasized form over substance, fund-raising over worship. But if the religious messages were vacuous, at least the sanctuaries were full. Most churchgoers seemed content with the way things were.

Churches, however, did not escape the broad turmoil of the 1960s— the bureaucratization, the splits over social issues, and the disenchantment of the young. By the end of the decade established churches had been wracked by factionalism, had lost membership, and were challenged by newer sects and evangelical movements.

During the 1960s the merger movement became almost as fashionable in religion as in business. Mainstream Protestant denominations seemed preoccupied with consolidation and centralization. Lutherans, Methodists, and Congregationalists each approved important mergers arranged by their national decision-making bodies and accepted by most local congregations. Greater centralization crept into other functions as well. More and more, national church boards set church policy, raised funds, budgeted money, and directed missionary and social efforts. The umbrella organization for Protestant churches, the National Council of Churches, revamped its structure in mid-decade to further the centralized direction of policy. But the interjection of national-level decisions into affairs of local churches often created dissension within individual congregations.

When national church bodies, which were fairly liberal politically, began to express themselves on controversial issues, such as civil rights and the war in Vietnam, factional disputes in local congregations became severe. Many people wanted their church to remain detached from social issues, as it had in the 1950s; others pressed for it to be even more active in protest against injustice and inhumanity. The split over the role of the church was basic, and it was bitter. Many religious leaders walked a tightrope, fearing that a lean toward either side might cost them part of their congregation. Lack of a clear identity drove many people out of the church and into agnosticism or noninstitutionalized personal religion. According to surveys conducted by the Gallup organization, there was a marked decline in church attendance during the 1960s; this drop was most evident in the "mainline" denominations.

The Catholic Church had to contend not only with social issues—Catholics were bitterly divided between deep-seated conservatism and the "Catholic Left radicalism" of priests such as Daniel and Philip Berrigan—but also with the even more explosive matter of church policy. The Second Vatican Council of 1962–1965 ushered in a reformist period by substituting English for Latin in the liturgy. Subsequently, demands accelerated for greater changes. While traditionalists looked on in horror, some Catholics pressed for liberalization of rules concerning priestly celibacy, the role of women in the church, and birth control.

American Jews confronted a problem even more baffling than divisions over doctrine and social policy: how to maintain an ethnic and religious identity. Large numbers of young people failed to understand or follow their Hebrew school lessons; many married gentiles. In fact, the majority of American Jews, while still identifying themselves as part of a Jewish ethnic group, belonged to no synagogue or temple. Economic success within the Jewish community and the decline of overt anti-Semitism, ironically, actually posed serious challenges for the Jewish faith.

Discontent within established churches and general social turmoil benefited new movements and faiths. Evangelical spirit swept the country, turning revivalists such as Billy Graham, Oral Roberts, and Billy James Hargis into the heads of multimillion-dollar enterprises. Although their religious organizations became huge bureaucracies relying upon mass media and the latest advertising techniques, their evangelism attracted people through its appeal to personal religion and past virtues. Evangelical fundamentalism provided an anchor for many Americans who felt buffeted by change.

Some popular preachers, such as Hargis and Carl McIntire, closely linked Christianity, anticommunism, and ultra-right-wing politics. Hargis charged that equal rights for women would bring the nation to the brink of hell, and his organization carried on a well-funded campaign against feminist causes. McIntire joined Hargis in an attack on the environmentalist movement. He charged, "It has been thought that the great emphasis upon ecology was a diversionary tactic to turn people's minds away from . . . what the Communists are doing throughout the world to take over. But now it is seen to be even deeper than that; it involved the rejection of Christianity."

While Hargis and McIntire occupied the far right, Oral Roberts and Billy Graham became important establishment figures. Roberts financed his own university in Oklahoma and used the school's successful basketball team as a promotional device. (During one stretch the squad lost only 19 of 134 games.) He also built a huge television empire, which rivaled that of the acknowledged king of evangelists, Billy Graham. Still, Graham continued to be the most revered fundamentalist leader. He took his crusades around the world, preaching to crowds of over a hundred thousand people, and he became an important spiritual counselor to President Nixon, often leading prayer breakfasts at the White House. Year after year he stayed near the top of the list of "most admired Americans."

During the 1960s new religious movements sprang up, particularly among the young. The Bahai faith built several breathtaking and expensive structures in the United States and gained numerous converts; members of the Hare Krishna sect, with their shaved heads and robes, appeared in larger cities; "Jesus freaks" replaced political agitators on some college campuses; the Children of God and other communal cult groups attracted middle-class youth who were willing to renounce their families and adopt a new life and loyalty. Religiosity took on other dimensions as well. Americans became fascinated with spiritualism, mysticism, and transcendental mediation. Bookstores expanded their sections on religion and the occult, and the success of *The Exorcist* indicated that such subjects had wide appeal to moviegoers. Many people of all ages and political persuasions, it seemed, were seeking refuge from a bureaucratic, centralized, and oversized society.

Many of the religious trends of the 1960s continued through the 1970s. Although attendance at Catholic masses leveled off after the declines of the 1960s, mainline Protestant and Jewish congregations continued to lose members. At the same time, all of the major denominations still struggled to heal internal divisions, especially those involving the role of women in the church. By the 1970s feminists in major religions argued that women were entitled to participate more fully in nearly all phases of spiritual life. The Roman Catholic Church reaffirmed its opposition to such changes—including papal bans on female priests and on artificial methods of birth control—but most Protestant denominations agreed to modify at least some patriarchal practices. The situation in Judaism was complicated by the division between the Orthodox, Conservative, and Reform movements. While Conservative and Reform congregations changed some traditional rituals and doctrines, the Orthodox movement, the only wing of Judaism to gain members in the 1970s, held firm. Finally, the evangelical revival of the 1960s gained momentum in the 1970s. Even though mainline Protestant denominations lost members, the total number of Protestants attending church remained constant because of the growth of evangelical congregations.

The growth of evangelicalism and religious fundamentalism could be measured in watts, in dollars, and in political power—as well as in the number of people actually attending churches. Radio and television ministries remained central forces in this surge; Billy Graham and Oral Roberts were joined by hundreds of other media preachers. Among the most prominent were Robert Schuller, who preached an updated, California version of Norman Vincent Peale's *Power of Positive Thinking*; Jerry Falwell, a family-oriented fundamentalist in the Oral Roberts mold; and dynamic, gospel-singing Jimmy Lee Swaggart, a cousin of country-rockers Jerry Lee Lewis and Mickey Gilley. In an even less traditional vein, Pat Robertson, a former corporate lawyer turned evangelist, hosted the *700 Club*, a born-again Christian version of the familiar TV talk show.

Although the three TV networks refused to sell any of their prime time to religious broadcasters, the media preachers used their burgeoning bank accounts to purchase time from local stations and even to establish their own networks. Robertson's Christian Broadcasting Network (CBN) boasted of its own satellite system and of its ability to reach hundreds of stations and cable-TV systems on an around-the-clock basis. By the end of the 1970s there were more than fourteen hundred radio stations and thirty TV outlets that specialized in religious broadcasts; every week they were joined by another radio station and every month by another television station.

By the late 1970s some of the more prominent preachers had entered the political world. While many people lost faith in established institutions, especially the national government and the public school systems, evangelical and fundamentalist religious groups attracted new converts and gathered political strength. Both Pat Robertson and Jerry Falwell, for example, promised to lead their followers, and the nation, out of the wilderness by joining with political figures on the right. Falwell's political lobby, the Moral Majority, campaigned against homosexuals, federal involvement in education, and the Equal Rights Amendment for women. The Moral Majority also ran workshops and seminars for religious politicos and issued a "morality rating" for members of Congress. By the end of the 1970s an alliance between the right wing of the GOP and the ultraconservative religious groups was clearly evident: The 1980 Republican platform promised to tear down the signs of an oversized government and to put the nation back on proper moral footing by, among other things, appointing as federal judges only those individuals who opposed abortion laws.

At the same time, the religious cults condemned by both the Moral Majority and hard-line ministers continued to flourish. These groups, like the evangelicals, seemed to gain support as a result of continued popular doubts about many social institutions. A powerful cult, the Unification Church, was headed by South Korea's Sun Myung Moon, a staunch anticommunist with ties to the South Korean CIA. Using sophisticated behavior modification methods to gain followers and corporate management techniques to handle the church's growing wealth, the "Moonies" gave thousands of young people a new sense of community. Moon's church also gained the endorsement of prominent supporters, including some conservative academics who shared Moon's political outlook. Moon's sect pushed right-wing politics, laissez-faire capitalism, and a hard-line anticommunist foreign policy. From 1969 to 1974 it funneled a considerable amount of money—much of it coming from young Moonies selling flowers—to various groups supporting Richard Nixon. Such activities finally provoked several federal investigations and a jail sentence for Moon himself.

A crusade against cults gained considerable attention when 918 members of the People's Temple cult died in a mass-suicide ritual in Guyana in 1978. Led by a charismatic and increasingly paranoid preacher, the Reverend Jim Jones, the People's Temple appealed to the very poor, to those who could find no secure place in the oversized society. Loosely aligned with the political left, Jones offered the promise of both religious salvation and social progress. He gained thousands of followers, especially among poor African-Americans in the San Francisco Bay area, and many of them moved with him to South America. Though concerned about very different issues, Jones and his followers ultimately reached a conclusion similar to that of the conservative evangelicals and fundamentalists on the far right: The United States was a flawed society. Lacking the financial resources and political clout of the religious right, the most desperate members of the People's Temple believed they could save themselves and their families only through flight—from this country and, finally, from life itself.

The Education Labyrinth

Pressure from the baby boom generation and demands of a rapidly expanding economy initially brought enormous changes to America's educational establishment in the postwar era. Thousands of new schools had to be built and equipped, and many corporations stood ready to sell the latest in instructional devices. Under Lyndon Johnson's Great Society programs, federal funds became available for expanding and upgrading education. Almost every suburban classroom had its arsenal of audiovisual equipment and supply of "teaching packages" containing all kinds of material to help students understand a particular topic or concept. Most of the new techniques sought to involve students as active participants rather than as passive listeners. In some schools, architects eliminated walls, creating an open and airy environment in which students would, it was hoped, become more expressive.

The educational revolution involved course content as well as teaching techniques. The "new math" and the "new English" substituted analysis and understanding for traditional categories and extensive memorization; the "new social studies" emphasized personal evaluation of documents and "values clarification" exercises rather than regurgitation of names and dates. Under pressure from women's organizations and minority groups, most schools replaced the white middle-class characters of Dick and Jane. At its best, the educational revolution promised to produce individuals who could think, evaluate, and make critical judgments. At their worst, changes in method outstripped changes in educational personnel, and many older teachers found themselves confused and resentful. New approaches that worked in a laboratory school did not always succeed in the average classroom. Brighter pupils easily adapted to the new math, but slower students graduated without the basic skills needed to balance a checkbook. After more than a decade of experimentation, critics of the new techniques contended that "Johnny still can't read, and he can't add, either."

During the 1960s one answer to the failure of traditional classrooms was to offer education outside the school system. Some parents who disliked the "authoritarianism" of traditional public schools sent their children to experimental "free schools." In response to criticism of education for minority children (such as Jonathan Kozol's *Death at an Early Age*), some reformers attempted to use the free-school concept in ghetto areas. Head Start, a key Great Society program, attempted to provide educational experiences for poor and minority preschoolers so that they could enter kindergarten on a par with more "privileged" middle-class children. Educational television also helped preschoolers and reached dropouts, adults and school-aged youngsters with educational material ranging from United States history to language instruction to guitar playing. Public television developed the most successful venture in children's shows—*Sesame Street*. Colorful and fast-moving, *Sesame Street* had its viewers reciting numbers, letters, and difficult words (some in Spanish) before they entered kindergarten. Although *Sesame Street* captivated both parents and children, traditionalists disliked the program's flashy style and rapid cuts.

Many schools experienced rapid changes in their student bodies during the 1960s. Especially in rural areas, public officials worked to consolidate small schools into better-equipped large ones. As a result, the size of educational institutions increased dramatically. In 1950 there were over 86,000 school systems in the country, averaging about 300 students each; by 1965 there were fewer than 30,000 systems, averaging 1400 students each. Most children no longer knew all their classmates or teachers, and many students rode buses to school. The undeniable educational gains of consolidation came at the expense of nearby facilities and a feeling of community.

As long as school buses assisted consolidation of small schools they were generally welcomed as symbols of educational progress, but when courts began to order busing to fulfill another educational function—racial integration—many people began to view them as part of a sinister plot. In the late 1960s, and early 1970s, busing provided the focus of discussion on civil rights questions. Using buses to achieve racial balance raised complicated social, legal, and educational problems. Even some minority-group parents denounced forced integration, fearing that their children would lose traditional cultural values in white-dominated schools. They called for community control, rather than forced integration of the schools.

The baby boom generation also strained institutions of higher education during the 1960s. Universities contended not only with the natural population increase but also with a rising percentage of youth who chose to go to college. In 1955 only 27 percent of college-aged people attended schools; by 1965 the figure had risen to 40 percent. The flood of new students stemmed from postwar affluence, government-assistance programs, the desire of many young men to avoid the draft by staying in school, and a huge influx of young women. Graduate schools also boomed. By the mid-1960s there were about a quarter of a million full-time graduate students, three of five receiving some form of financial support. Half of all the Ph.D. degrees granted in the United States between 1861 and 1970 were earned in the 1960s. A researcher writing in 1971 accurately predicted that "we have created a graduate education and research establishment in American universities that is about 30 to 50 percent larger than we shall effectively use in the 1970s and early 1980s."

The debates of the 1960s—over the size and structure of schools, over philosophies and techniques of instruction, and over the content and the rigor of the curriculum—became more bitter and complex during the 1970s. First, the declining birth rate of the 1960s finally caught up with education: For the first time in several decades students were not crowding the education labyrinth. Already faced with rising costs and declining revenues, school officials responded at the primary and secondary levels by consolidating some schools and closing down others. Even without busing for racial balance, neighborhood schools would not be nearly as close to most people's homes as they had been during the 1950s and 1960s.

Although colleges and universities also began to face the necessity of contraction, they enjoyed greater flexibility than primary and secondary schools. They, unlike the lower-level schools, could create students. Increasingly, colleges and universities sought "the nontraditional student." Foreign students and "adult scholars"—individuals (especially women) slightly or considerably older than the traditional eighteen to twenty-two age group—became obvious targets. Four-year institutions also began to compete more actively with two-year colleges for students. And, of course, colleges and universities vied with one another to attract a steady number of students from an ever-shrinking pool of high school graduates. Admissions offices became "recruiting centers," relying upon consultants to provide their college with an attractive image and an effective set of recruiting tools. A number of smaller colleges gave up and closed their doors during the 1970s, and even the most successful institutions became highly conscious of costs during the 1970s.

In contrast with the generally flush 1960s, all levels of education confronted economic problems during the 1970s. Even Harvard and Yale, well-endowed private institutions that attracted large sums of federal money, worried about their ability to maintain, let alone expand, their programs. Public schools, which had to depend upon tax dollars, faced growing popular protests against higher property taxes and new school-revenue bonds. As a result, many school districts throughout the country were forced to slash educational staff, instructional programs, and extracurricular activities. The problem was most serious in large cities, where shrinking tax bases and rapidly escalating costs added to difficulties produced by reluctant taxpayers.

But the problems of American education transcended issues of revenue and taxation. There were more subtle forces contributing to what appeared to be a growing backlash against a strong commitment to education of the young. Put simply, more and more people saw public schools, especially in urban areas, as educational and social failures. In some schools, traditional discipline problems—truancy, smoking in rest rooms, scuffles on the playground—seemed trivial when compared with the everyday reality of hard drugs and violent attacks on both teachers and students. At the same time, educational results, as measured by standardized tests, steadily dropped. (To be fair to urban schools, the decline was a nationwide phenomenon: Between 1966 and 1976 the average score on the verbal portion of the SAT test dropped from 467 to 429.) The hope that school integration would introduce children to a heterogeneous environment began to fade as more affluent families, minority as well as white, left for the suburbs or sent their children to private schools. The vast majority of urban public schools came to serve primarily children from poor families. In Pasadena, California, for example, more than 35 percent of white parents removed their children from public schools after court-enforced busing went into effect; nationwide, it was estimated, 40 percent of middle-class African-American parents sent their children to private schools.

Meanwhile, at all levels, people debated familiar, yet central, questions: What should students learn? And how should they be taught? In response to the continuation of trends begun during the late 1960s, which tried to open up new subject areas and introduce more flexible methods of instruction, a strong "back-to-basics" movement emerged. At the post-secondary level, traditionalists began to regroup and to seek a rollback of changes they believed were eroding educational excellence. A movement to reinstitute requirements, to establish "core" curriculums (or at least "core" courses), and to contain the spread of programs in areas such as women's and minority studies slowly took shape.

Similar debates engulfed the primary and secondary educational systems. Writing at the end of the 1960s in *Teaching as a Subversive Activity*, Neil Postman had gained instant visibility for popularizing the ideal of individualized, open schools. A decade later, in *Teaching as a Conserving Activity*, Postman retained faith in individualized learning, but he also stressed the importance of creating an educational atmosphere that emphasized group cooperation and social order. He advocated dress codes so that students would recognize schools as places of "dignity and a special kind of learning"—places different from other parts of the burgeoning youth culture. In a small but highly dramatic way, Postman's change of emphasis reflected the dilemmas of trying to educate youth in an oversized society.

SUGGESTIONS FOR FURTHER READING

Changes in the scale of social and economic institutions are analyzed, from varying perspectives, in W. Lloyd Warner, *The Emergent American Society* (1967); Arthur Selwyn Miller, *The Modern Corporate State* (1976); Morris Janowitz, *The Last Half-Century* (1978); Christopher Lasch, *The Culture of Narcissism* (1978); Kirkpatrick Sale, *Human Scale* (1980); and Theodore Lowi, *The End of Liberalism* (rev. ed., 1979); John Tirman, ed., *The Militarization of High Tech* (1984); Donald Worster, *Rivers of Empire* (1985); Louis Galambos, *The New American State: Bureaucracies and Policies Since World War II* (1987); and Paul Kennedy, *The Rise and Fall of the Great Powers* (1988).

On economic issues, see Seymour Melman, *Pentagon Capitalism* (1970); Richard J. Barnet and Ronald Muller, *Global Reach* (1974); Samuel Bowles, David M. Gordon, and Thomas Weisskopf, *Beyond the Wasteland* (1983); Charles P. Kindleberger, *Multinational Excursions* (1984); Lester Thurow, *Dangerous Currents* (1984); the relevant sections of Lewis Mandell, *The Credit Card Industry: A History* (1990); and David Vogel, *Fluctuating Fortunes* (1988).

On environmental issues, see Rachel Carson, *The Silent Spring* (1962); Barry Commoner, *The Closing Circle* (1971); Amory Lovins, *Soft Energy Paths* (1977); Richard J. Barnet, *The Lean Years* (1980); Michael Brown, *Laying*

Waste (1980); Donald Worster's *Rivers of Empire* (1985); Samuel P. Hays, *Beauty, Health, and Permanence* (1987); Joseph Morone and Edward Wood- house, *The Demise of Nuclear Energy? Lessons for Democratic Control of Technology* (1989); and the relevant sections of Anna Bramwell, *Ecology in the Twentieth Century (1989)*.

On education, see the conflicting interpretations in the following: Herbert Gintis and Samuel Bowles; *Schooling in Capitalist America* (1976); Hugh Davis Graham, *Uncertain Triumph: Federalist Education Policy in the Kennedy and Johnson Years* (1984); Ira Katznelson and Margaret Weir, *Schooling for All* (1985); Lois Weis, ed., *Class, Race, and Gender in American Education* (1988); and Alan Bloom, *The Closing of the American Mind* (1988).

On mass culture, see Robert Lipsyte, *Sportsworld* (1975); Geoffrey Stokes, *Star-Making Machinery* (1976); Edwin Cady, *The Big Game* (1978); Peter Guralnick, *Lost Highways* (1979); Robert Sklar, *Prime-Time America* (1980); Greil Marcus, *Mystery Train* (rev. ed., 1990); Stuart and Elizabeth Ewen, *Channels of Desire* (1982); Ben Bagdikian, *The Media Monopoly* (1983); Jon Weiner, *Come Together: John Lennon and His Time* (1984); Herbert Schiller, *Who Knows? Information in the Age of the Fortune 500* (1984) and *Culture, Inc: The Corporate Takeover of American Expression* (1989); Robert Kolker, *Cinema of Loneliness* (rev. ed., 1988); Todd Gitlin, *Inside Prime Time* (1985); Benjamin Rader, *In Its Own Image: How Television Has Transformed Sports* (1985); Helen Baehr and Gillian Dyer, eds., *Boxed In: Women and Television* (1987); Mark Crispin Miller, *Boxed-In: The Culture of TV* (1988); and Michael Ryan and Douglas Kellner, *Camera Political: Politics and Ideology in Contemporary Hollywood Cinema* (1988).

On big-time religion see Marshall Frady, *Billy Graham* (1979); David Harrell, *All Things Are Possible* (1974), *Oral Roberts* (1985), and *Pat Robertson* (1987); Charles Shepard, *Forgiven: The Rise and Fall of Jim Bakker and the PTL* (1989); and Randall Balmer, *Mine Eyes Have Seen the Glory: A Journey into the Evangelical Subculture of America* (1989).

Chapter Ten

The Politics of the 1970s

DOMESTIC POLITICS UNDER THREE PRESIDENTS

Richard Nixon promised a law-and-order administration and political calm; instead, his reckless and lawless presidency produced even more political turbulence in addition to a constitutional crisis that Nixon himself never seemed fully to understand. The president's tight circle of advisers—especially his "Berlin Wall" of John Ehrlichman and H. R. (Bob) Haldeman—shielded him from dissenting views and reinforced his worst instincts, especially a fondness for seeing politics in highly personal terms. Nixon seemed to enjoy tilting at political enemies, so it was not surprising that his White House would have its own semiofficial "enemies list" and order illegal surveillance of people whom the president deemed dangerous to the nation. Only after it was too late did Nixon even begin to recognize the depths of his "Watergate problems."

Even after Richard Nixon's forced resignation in 1974, the nation's political culture, including popular attitudes toward public policy and the entire governmental structure, appeared unsettled. Both of Nixon's successors in the 1970s, Gerald Ford and Jimmy Carter, came to the same realization as their ousted predecessor: The presidency, though obviously an office of great power, could not always command. Belying the idea that the nation was saddled with an "imperial presidency," the chief executives of the 1970s constantly confronted the limits of their effective power. The presidency, like other political institutions, remained hamstrung by ongoing controversies about the proper role of government and by continuing struggles among institutions and individuals. The 1970s, then, did not signal an end to the political battles of the 1960s but, rather, a continuation of attempts to define the nation's role in the world and the meaning of equality.

Politics in a Media Age

George McGovern, an apostle of the "new politics" of the late 1960s, captured the 1972 Democratic nomination for president. Working with activists who wanted to move their party dramatically leftward and capitalizing upon changes in the party rules, which were enacted after the chaos at the 1968 Chicago convention, the McGovern campaign skillfully lined up delegates in the nonprimary states. Meanwhile, in those states that did hold primaries, the South Dakota senator outlasted more centrist candidates, notably Edmund Muskie and Hubert Humphrey. Overall, though, McGovern won only a handful of popular-vote primaries.

By the time Democratic delegates gathered in Miami for their 1972 convention, a number of familiar faces, including Mayor Richard Daley of Chicago, were absent. Outmaneuvered by McGovern's strategists, many Democratic regulars watched the convention on TV. The Miami gathering, complained one veteran labor leader who disliked the "new politics," contained too many women, too many long-haired young men, and too few cigars. McGovern easily captured the nomination on the first ballot, but a number of old-line Democrats, such as Chicago's Daley and labor's George Meany, were less than enthusiastic and gave McGovern only tepid support or left him to stumble on by himself.

And stumble he did. McGovern was soon forced to jettison his running mate, Senator Thomas Eagleton of Missouri, when it was revealed that Eagleton had undergone electric-shock treatment for nervous exhaustion. Worse, several prominent Democrats (including Edward Kennedy) declined to become Eagleton's replacement. McGovern eventually did find a partner (Sargent Shriver, a brother-in-law of Ted Kennedy and LBJ's ambassador to France), but he could never get large numbers of voters to accept his theme of "Come Home, America." His central issue, a speedy withdrawal from Vietnam, angered those who endorsed Nixon's call for an "honorable" peace, and McGovern failed to convert his reformist stands on domestic issues into popular support. Calls for higher taxes on large inheritances and for "demogrants" of $1000 to every citizen, for example, appeared to alienate some traditionally Democratic voters without attracting significant numbers of new supporters.

The Nixon reelection campaign, on the other hand, enjoyed plenty of support, much of it in the form of illegal financial contributions from large corporations. While importuning potential donors, Nixon's "bagmen" warned of the antibusiness tone of a McGovern administration and hinted at

Richard Nixon and Family. In the happy days of his presidency Richard Nixon relaxes with his wife, Pat; his daughters, Julie and Tricia; and his son-in-law, David Eisenhower. In his final days, Nixon retreated into a closed circle of his family and a few close friends. Source: *National Archives.*

the advantages contributors would gain from a second Nixon administration. Not even the arrest, in mid-June of 1972, of the "Watergate burglars"—political spies with close ties to the Republican campaign and to the White House itself—could slow Richard Nixon's reelection drive. Ronald Ziegler, the president's press secretary, quickly dismissed this illegal entry into Democratic party headquarters, by people who had links to the CIA and FBI and who were equipped with sophisticated wiretapping equipment, as a "third-rate burglary." Ziegler was soon forced to retract this statement, but the media gave the Watergate break-in little attention during the 1972 campaign. Certainly it had no discernible effect on Nixon's or McGovern's political fortunes. The McGovern-Shriver ticket carried only one state, Massachusetts, and the District of Columbia. Richard Nixon, dismissed only six years earlier as a political has-been, climaxed his comeback by capturing nearly 61 percent of the popular vote and all but a handful of the electoral ballots.

Subsequent analysis of voter statistics only confirmed what was apparent in November 1972: The electorate perceived George McGovern as being far outside the political mainstream, while Richard Nixon managed to occupy a broad centrist position, as LBJ had done against Barry Goldwater in 1964. In some ways such a view was accurate. On a number of issues McGovern did stand to the left of Fair Deal–Great Society liberalism. Yet McGovern's basic position hardly qualified as a radical one; he did not lean as far to the left in 1972 as Goldwater had to the right in 1964.

Although McGovern, like Goldwater, sometimes failed to explain his position as clearly as he might have, the mass media utterly failed to break through the protective shield around the Committee to Re-Elect the President. The problem, it should be emphasized, was not that most members of the press secretly favored Nixon, nor was it that Nixon and his aides skillfully managed events. The basic difficulties transcended "dirty tricks" and Madison Avenue tactics. As close observers of the media noted, the settled rules of "objective" reporting tended to work in favor of the incumbent, who relied upon traditional themes, and against his challenger, who tried to interject new issues and to attack Nixon's performance as chief of state. It seemed a revolutionary departure, for example, when NBC reported that Nixon was distorting McGovern's positions on defense expenditures, welfare policies, and changes in the tax laws. For most of the campaign, the "boys on the bus" (as *Rolling Stone's* Timothy Crouse called the press corps) reported statements by Nixon or by his press secretary at face value. Thus, McGovern generally "alleged" while the president and his supporters "announced." This dominant media perspective proved particularly helpful to Nixon—and damaging to McGovern—when the administration was "announcing" the impending "end" of the war in Vietnam or "denying" charges about Watergate and other alleged "dirty tricks" by the Nixon forces.

Most of the investigative reporting about Watergate came from a single newspaper, the *Washington Post*, and from two individuals, the *Post's* Bob Woodward and Carl Bernstein. Even these reporters, persistent as they were, uncovered little new material about the Nixon administration by themselves. In developing their much-celebrated stories on Watergate, Woodward and Bernstein had to rely upon "Deep Throat," a still-unidentified informant (or perhaps several informants) within the government bureaucracy.

Although the media may not have initially played the dramatic role pictured by journalists themselves or by the film *All the President's Men*, it ultimately became a force in Watergate politics. If the press lacked the power and resources to discover many dark secrets by itself, journalists could give widespread coverage to the taint of scandal spreading around the Nixon administration. Using information developed by federal prosecutors and relying upon leaks by anti-Nixon sources within the vast federal bureaucracy, some members of the press finally assumed an aggressive, adversary relationship toward the administration. For their part, Nixon and his close advisers, who had been castigating the press for several years, issued vague hints about reprisals against "irresponsible" journalists.

Threats against the media by the Nixon administration represented only part of an increasingly desperate "game plan" being diagrammed in the Oval Office. As transcripts of tape conversations between the president and his aides later revealed, Richard Nixon found that he could not halt, or even slow, the leaks to the press about the "underside" of his administration. In the late summer of 1973 rumors of wrongdoing began to envelop Nixon's vice-president, and in October Spiro T. Agnew pleaded no contest to charges of accepting kickbacks. With Agnew forced to resign in disgrace, Nixon chose Gerald Ford, the Republican's minority leader in the House, as his new vice-president. The man who held the office generally considered to be the most powerful in the world discovered his inability to control events or even employees of his own executive branch.

The Underside of the Nixon Administration: Leaks and Plumbers

Many of Nixon's Watergate troubles stemmed from his own fears about the reliability and loyalty of various governmental agencies and officials. The Watergate burglary team, it appears, first took shape from efforts to provide the White House with its own covert intelligence unit. As early as the summer of 1970, the so-called Huston Plan proposed reorganizing covert activities in order to improve the administration's ability to coordinate the use of wiretaps, mail covers, and "surreptitious entries" (that is, burglaries). Although Nixon secretly approved the outlines of such a plan, this idea for directing covert activities from the White House alarmed the established arms of the nation's "secret government," the CIA and the FBI. Claiming that the Huston Plan threatened serious violations of civil liberties, J. Edgar Hoover offered especially strong resistance, and the president was forced to drop the idea.

While the White House began to leak information to the press critical of the aging FBI director, it also looked for ways of restarting the Huston initiative. Top officials finally decided to use the issue of drugs as a cover for creation of a secret strike force, controlled from the White House, that could bypass agencies allegedly "infested" with Democrats. G. Gordon Liddy, a former FBI agent, played a key part in formulating plans for a new antidrug squad within the Treasury Department. Once operational, the unit could undertake covert work against Nixon's enemies and draw upon the talents and resources of the national government. And if things went wrong, claims that the unit was fighting the drug menace could be used as a justification for its covert activities. Members of the administration began planning a mass-media crusade against drugs, and a presidential declaration of a national "heroin emergency" was slated for late June of 1971. But on June 13, the *New York Times* began to publish excerpts from the *Pentagon Papers*, a hitherto secret history of America's involvement in Vietnam.

Enraged at the appearance of this classified report, which had been prepared by the Defense Department during the Johnson administration, Nixon's inner circle shifted their attention from drugs to security "leaks." His antidrug speech was canceled, and the national heroin emergency was never declared. Instead, the administration mobilized to stop further publication of the *Pentagon Papers* and to plug the leaks within its own executive branch. Almost immediately, it obtained a court injunction that barred further publication of the *Pentagon Papers*. Responding to this unprecedented use of a prior restraint—censorship in its classic form—the *New York Times* appealed to the United States Supreme Court. By a vote of six to three the justices lifted the injunction, holding that the First Amendment barred prior restraints in instances such as this. Although many people, particularly in the media, celebrated this as a victory for "open government," the administration was already mounting a much more extensive, and more covert, crusade for executive secrecy.

Using personnel already assembled for the antidrug crusade, the White House formed its own leak-stopping crew, the self-styled "Plumbers." The group soon included Gordon Liddy, E. Howard Hunt (a former CIA agent), and several Cuban exiles with close ties to the CIA. After it became known that Dr. Daniel Ellsberg, a former analyst for the Defense Department and for the Rand Corporation, bore primary responsibility for leaking the *Pentagon Papers*, the Plumbers began a campaign to harass and discredit him, including a burglary of the office of Ellsberg's psychiatrist. The secret strike team conducted similar activities against other "enemies" of the White House. This group, with the significant addition of James McCord, another former CIA operative, formed the nucleus of the group that made the badly bungled entry into Democratic headquarters at the Watergate.

Nixon's defenders have consistently contended that these kinds of activities did not start with Watergate. Indeed, careful studies relying upon official documents obtained under the Freedom of Information Act have shown that the development of secret government preceded the presidency of Richard Nixon. John Kennedy, for instance, took a particular interest in expanding the executive's covert capacities, both overseas and at home, and Robert Kennedy, his attorney general, gave the FBI nearly carte blanche in wiretapping and bugging operations.

The Nixon administration did, however, significantly expand the scope and purpose of covert activities. During Lyndon Johnson's second term, for example, successive attorneys general had moved to limit FBI wiretaps, and the number of taps declined from 233 in 1965 to only 9 in 1968. The next year, though, Nixon and his attorney general, John Mitchell, claimed that the chief executive could order wiretaps, without having to obtain a court order, upon any group or individual considered a threat to "national security." (In 1972 the United States Supreme Court held that presidents could not order, on their own authority, electronic surveillance of purely domestic organizations.) Reports on some of these taps, such as ones on government employees and on several journalists suspected of having sources inside the Nixon administration, were forwarded not only to officials concerned with "national security" but also to Nixon's primary political strategist, Bob Haldeman.

Haldeman's involvement in the earliest wiretaps established the pattern that would lead to Nixon's downfall: the attempt to centralize power within the president's inner circle. As the historian Garry Wills has noted,

Nixon and his close aides operated a kind of counterinsurgency presidency. Seeing themselves as the lonely defenders of the American way, the Nixonites waged war not only against the New Left but also the very same establishment that the protesters often attacked—the mainstream press, J. Edgar Hoover's FBI, and even the CIA. In the end Nixon became ensnarled in his own clumsy effort to create a secret government, one that could spy on both the people in the streets and on various elites in Washington.

The same concern for centralizing control within the White House affected the conduct of foreign relations. Nixon and Henry Kissinger, his national security adviser, saw the official foreign policy agencies—including the departments of state and defense and the CIA—as oftentimes uninformed and as consistently unimaginative. Worse, Nixon and Kissinger believed, these branches of government were filled with individuals who would obstruct presidential initiatives or, as in the case of Daniel Ellsberg, leak sensitive and secret material to the press. As a result of their fears and their desire for greater White House power, Nixon and Kissinger began to conduct their own secret foreign policy—secret from the American people and from other government officials as well. Their decision in 1970 to begin heavy bombing of neutral Cambodia, for example, deliberately bypassed high officials in the state and defense departments.

Nixon's Last Battle

In the end, Nixon's secret war in Cambodia—like his other attempts to bring foreign and domestic "dirty tricks" under the control of the White House—became public knowledge and then part of the legal case against the president and members of his administration. Despite various attempts to "cut off" the trail of criminality—at the Watergate burglars, then at high officials within the Committee to Re-Elect the President, and finally at top-ranking members of the White House staff—Nixon's pursuers pressed on. In May 1973 a special Senate committee headed by North Carolina's Sam Ervin began televised hearings into charges of misconduct during the last presidential election. Ervin, who liked to call himself a simple "country lawyer," quickly became a media celebrity, and his folksy image contributed to the panel's public credibility. Throughout the summer of 1973 witness after witness offered tantalizing hints about involvement by the White House in a series of unseemly activities. Even Senator Howard Baker of Tennessee, a Republican loyalist, came to ask a familiar question: "What did the president know and when did he know it?" Then, in mid-July, the answer to this query suddenly had a most unlikely source of verification—Richard Milhaus Nixon.

"Nixon Bugged Himself!" proclaimed newspaper headlines. Apparently called to testify about relatively minor issues, an obscure White House official named Alexander Butterfield revealed that Nixon had secretly taped the bulk of his presidential conversations and his phone calls. These tapes promised the "smoking pistol" that Nixon's defenders had challenged his accusers to produce. The Ervin Committee and the special Watergate prosecutor, Archibald Cox of Harvard Law School, immediately sought access to the tapes. Claiming an absolute "executive privilege," Nixon flatly refused.

Ringed by lethal strands of audio tape, Richard Nixon vainly struggled to survive the Watergate fight. Although some advisers urged him to destroy the tapes, Nixon tried to battle free, while still clutching the damning evidence. A veteran political club-fighter who trusted his ability to survive any scrap, the president bobbed and weaved and occasionally even tried to counterpunch. But his opponents had the heavier weapons. In October 1973 a desperate attempt to knock out the special Watergate prosecutor backfired: The dramatic dismissal of Archibald Cox, for his refusal to accept Nixon's formula for limited access to nine crucial tapes, only led to the departure of Elliot Richardson and William Ruckelshaus, two of the most respected figures remaining in the Nixon administration, and to the arrival of another prosecutor, Leon Jaworski. It also forced Nixon to surrender the tapes, one of which contained an 18½-minute gap that was later found to have been the result of deliberate erasing.

The "Saturday Night Massacre," as the firing of Cox was called, represented Nixon's last real attempt to take the offensive. Slowly the president retreated, trying to stave off impeachment. By early 1974, after a grand jury indicted seven of his top aides, Nixon could do little more than continue his personal cover-up, hoping that his opponents would run out of energy and that he could somehow avoid being indicted by a grand jury or impeached by Congress.

Increasingly, the fight pitted a badly confused Nixon, comforted in the final days of his presidency only by his immediate family and a handful of loyal aides, against the combined power of the other branches of the national government. Nixon tried one last desperate gamble: He released his own edited version of forty-two taped conversations that were being sought by Jaworski and by the House Judiciary Committee. The bowdlerized transcripts, often sanitized by the phrase "expletive deleted," only raised new doubts about the president's honesty and his competence. More important, the Nixon tapes failed to satisfy either the House committee or Jaworski; both sought additional tapes and transcripts.

Nixon's defenders in Congress and his lawyers before the Supreme Court had no better luck than their chief. By early summer the issue was not whether the House Judiciary Committee would support Nixon's impeachment but how many Republicans would join the Democratic majority and how many articles of impeachment they would vote against the president. On the other side of Capitol Hill, the Supreme Court, which had expedited the appeal of Nixon's refusal to honor a subpoena for additional tapes, voted unanimously to reject the president's sweeping claim that tapes needed for a criminal investigation were protected by "executive privilege."

At nearly the same time, the House Judiciary Committee completed its deliberations on articles of impeachment. On July 27, 1974, three days after

Nixon's rebuff by the Supreme Court, the committee passed, by a margin of twenty-seven to eleven, the first article of impeachment against the president. It charged Richard Nixon with obstruction of justice for his efforts to impede the investigation of Watergate. Subsequently, the committee voted two other articles. One charged Nixon with abuse of presidential power by trying to use agencies, such as the IRS and the FBI, for partisan purposes, and the other charged him with violating his constitutional duty to enforce the law by refusing to turn over subpoenaed tapes. (Significantly, the committee rejected an article that would have cited Nixon for his secret bombing of Cambodia.)

Although Nixon remained publicly committed to a floor fight in the House and to a last-ditch battle in the Senate, the president's shrinking entourage was working to ease him out of office. While waiting for the Supreme Court to hand down its decision on Nixon's tapes, a presidential aide finally found, in these same tapes, the elusive "smoking pistol." The tape of a conversation between Nixon and Haldeman on June 23, 1972, was unequivocal: The president had plotted from the very beginning to use the CIA to halt investigation of the Watergate break-in on the spurious grounds of national security. The tape contained proof, in clear language, that the president himself had orchestrated the cover-up, had conspired to obstruct justice, and had been systematically lying about his role.

In late July and early August, aides to Nixon and to Vice-President Gerald Ford began cautiously discussing plans for terminating the Nixon administration and inaugurating a Ford presidency. Unyielding to the end, Nixon insisted that the conversation between Haldeman and himself contained no fatal admissions. But his new chief of staff, General Alexander Haig, flatly contradicted this claim and went ahead with plans for the transition to a new presidency. Once the transcript of the June 23 meeting became public, most of Nixon's remaining supporters vanished. Finally, Richard Nixon gave up his lonely battle and surrendered. On August 9 he resigned, and Gerald Ford became the nation's first nonelected president.

Stagflation

The Watergate scandal paralyzed the national government just when complex economic problems required new policies. Richard Nixon faced two alarming new economic trends—"stagflation," a concurrence of recession and inflation; and a growing deficit in the United States balance of payments.

Conventional economic wisdom held that inflation resulted from an "overheated" economy in which demand far exceeded supply; dampening demand by inducing a mild recession would thus reduce inflation. In attacking inflation early in his presidency, Nixon acquiesced to policies that in order to slow spending raised interest rates and brought more unemployment. The recession came. Skyrocketing interest rates nearly ended residential construction, forced barely solvent businesses such as the Penn Central

Railroad into bankruptcy, brought a decline in industrial production, and raised unemployment to 6 percent. Yet, contrary to expectations, prices continued to gallop forward. Big business and big labor continued to layer higher wages and higher costs upon an economy now slumping into recession. By 1971 pundits were speaking of "Nixonomics"—a new economic condition of stagflation in which unemployment and the spiral of inflation crept upward simultaneously.

After experimenting unsuccessfully with these anti-inflation measures, Nixon decided that inflationary prosperity was better than an economic slowdown that might, as it had done in 1960, jeopardize his next presidential campaign. He began devising policies to correct the recession he had earlier induced. After telling a startled group of journalists, "I am now a Keynesian," Nixon took up that favorite tactic of liberal Democrats, deficit spending financed by government borrowing. This dramatic about-face prompted a television commentator to quip, "It's a little like a Christian crusader saying 'All things considered, I think Mohammed was right!' " But antirecession spending scarcely dented unemployment, and, under renewed stimulus, prices spurted ahead even faster. Measures taken against either inflation or unemployment seemed only to make the other problem more severe. Some advisers within and without the administration began to advocate an across-the-board governmental imposed freeze on wages, prices, and interest rates as the only sure way to hold down inflation, but Nixon shied away from "artificial controls which could only foul things up."

Worrisome foreign-trade statistics soon caused the president to change his mind once again. For eighty years the United States had exported far more than it imported, but after World War II huge military expenditures and corporate overseas investment created deficits in the balance of payments. The country paid some of this debt with gold; by 1972 America's prewar hoard of bullion had shrunk by half, to $10 billion. For the rest, foreign creditors accepted paper dollars, pleased with the stimulating effect of this large new source of capital that could be used for domestic investment. By 1970, however, the Vietnam War had brought ever larger deficits, and inflation had crippled America's ability to sell its high-priced goods abroad. More and more paper flooded Europe's money markets, inevitably jolting prices. United States Treasury officials, hoping to avoid devaluation of the dollar—an act that would undermine the dollar's position as the preeminent international currency—quickly urged England, West Germany, and Japan to revalue their currencies upward to discourage American buying. Only the Germans complied. Then, at the end of June 1971, the Commerce Department announced a trade deficit, the first since 1890. As fears rose about the nation's solvency, speculators attacked the United States dollar, dumping vast amounts on world currency exchanges to avoid the losses that would result from a widely expected devaluation of the dollar.

After a hurried meeting with his financial advisers at Camp David in August 1971, Nixon dramatically responded to the international monetary crisis and to the larger problems—including inflation and the new trade deficit—that fueled it. First, the United States ceased to value the dollar in terms of gold. Instead, American currency would "float" on the exchanges, supply and demand determining its worth. Second, a 10 percent tariff surcharge was instituted, which significantly reduced imports into America. Nixon later removed the surcharge in return for obtaining new world monetary agreements. The new arrangement terminated the system of fixed exchange rates established in the Bretton Woods Conference of 1944, and it reduced the dollar's position as the most privileged medium of international exchange. The dollar became just another currency whose value fluctuated. By substantially altering the system of international exchange, Nixon had given Americans more room to manipulate currency values in the fight against the trade deficit, but he had also led the United States and the world into the uncharted waters of floating exchange rates, a system that had proved perilous and destabilizing in the 1930s.

Nixon's advisers also plotted a new antiinflation program for the domestic economy. The president froze wages and prices for ninety days, an interim measure called Phase I, while he worked on a comprehensive program to attack inflation and the trade deficit. On November 15, 1971, the White House announced its new program, Phase II. This plan cut government spending (slashing $5 billion from foreign aid and the federal civil service) but focused far more on stimulating business through a tax credit aimed at promoting modernization of American enterprise. To stimulate the crucial automobile industry, Congress repealed the 7 percent excise tax on American-made cars. Such measures ensured higher profits for business and, together with the certainty that Nixon would not risk retrenchment in an election year, perked up the sluggish economy. Consumer spending increased, and public confidence blossomed in the spring of 1972. Meanwhile, the new Cost-of-Living Council attacked inflation by banning wage hikes of more than 5.5 percent and supposedly limiting retail-price increases to 2.5 percent. Though inflation continued, especially in the uncontrolled food and farm commodity markets, public confidence improved enough for Nixon to defuse the economic issue during the 1972 campaign.

Nixon's tactics were thus to give the economy a mild stimulus while holding down inflation through government controls. The strategy lasted just long enough to aid Nixon's reelection. Once settled in his second term, Nixon replaced Phase II price ceilings with voluntary restraints. Predictably, consumer prices shot upward, compensating for the time they had spent under controls. Within six months, Treasury Secretary George Shultz candidly admitted, "Phase II is a failure." So, in midsummer Nixon again froze prices, this time for sixty days, while his advisers again debated alternatives. Finally, in April 1974 Nixon again reversed course, canceling all government restraints. Convinced that "artificial bureaucracies" could never substitute for the "free" marketplace, Nixon was unwilling to take steps more drastic than economic controls that were just voluntary or temporary. When it became clear, in 1974, that such mild controls did not work, Nixon—now immersed in Watergate difficulties—effectively abandoned any coherent strategy for dealing with stagflation.

The effectiveness of Nixon's mercurial economic strategies was not helped by the deadlock between the executive and congressional branches. Nixon's economic programs—especially his determination to cut federal spending for social welfare—provoked growing hostility between the White House and the Democrat-controlled Congress. In 1973 the president vetoed nine major bills, even education and antipollution measures. He also calmly announced that he would impound funds, rather than spend them, if Congress overrode his decisions, an action that congressional opponents (and later the courts) condemned as unconstitutional. Growing personal hostilities and policy differences, aggravated by Watergate, brought the two branches of government into an adversarial relationship in which nothing was accomplished.

When Nixon left office, economists, like members of Congress, continued to debate what had gone wrong. Had government controls been too severe or insufficient? Should government spending have been cut to curtail inflation or increased to combat recession? Meanwhile, inflation continued at an annual rate of nearly 10 percent while unemployment hovered at just under 6 percent, a recession rate. After a five-year battle against stagflation and trade deficits, the economic situation was worse than ever, and inflation had become endemic. All of Nixon's remedies had failed, though economists and politicians differed sharply in their diagnoses of the precise reasons for their failure. All could agree that inconsistencies of approach and scatter-gun solutions had seriously aggravated problems.

The Ford Presidency: The Wounds Remain

The Nixon presidency, coming so soon after the political traumas of the late 1960s, appeared to raise new doubts about the nation's political system. Although defenders of the postwar order, such as the semiofficial presidential chronicler Theodore White, hastened to see Nixon's fall as proof that "the system worked," less sanguine observers pointed out that the long Watergate battle showed the inflexibility of the constitutional system and that the affair reached a timely conclusion only because of Nixon's telltale tapes. Moreover, might not Watergate represent only one more episode in the seamy history of America's "secret state"? According to this interpretation, Watergate grew out of a long power struggle involving several government bureaucracies and various political and economic elites opposed to the Nixon administration. Investigative reporters, for example, have suggested that Woodard and Bernstein's "Deep Throat" could have been a CIA operative who had "infiltrated" the White House and that one of the Watergate burglars, James McCord, may have deliberately sabotaged the ill-fated operation at Democratic headquarters.

For many ordinary voters Watergate appeared to be yet another example of political corruption in Washington. Although millions of people did retain their faith that the political system worked, a majority of those eligible to vote displayed considerably more cynicism about politics and about the

President Gerald Ford, whose brief post-Watergate presidency was filled with more symbols than substance, throws out the ceremonial first pitch. Source: *Gerald R. Ford Library.*

individuals who sought public office. According to public-opinion polls, popular confidence in government officials had been declining throughout the 1960s, the years of Vietnam, and this slide continued both during and after the Watergate period (see Table 10–1). In the presidential election of 1972, only 56 percent of those eligible to cast ballots did so; in 1976 the turnout decreased once again, this time to 54 percent.

Gerald Ford later praised his brief presidency as a time for healing, but during the years 1974–1976 old political wounds continued to fester, and new ones appeared almost daily. Popular doubts about how the system really worked were only increased—or simply confirmed—when Ford offered Nixon an unconditional pardon, an act that shielded the former president from prosecution and contributed significantly to Ford's defeat in the 1976 presidential race. Moreover, the Ford years brought new revelations about illegal, or at least questionable, activities that had been undertaken since World War II by the FBI, by successive presidents, and by the CIA.

The CIA was already deeply divided by its involvement in Watergate politics and by serious internal power struggles, and the agency could no longer keep its own secrets. Former agents, such as John Marks and Philip Agee, wrote best-selling exposés of their old "company," and aggressive

TABLE 10-1   Levels of Confidence in People Running Key Institutions, 1973*

Percentage of Respondents Expressing
Various Levels of Confidence
As far as the people in charge of running——— are concerned, would you say you have a great deal of confidence, only some confidence, or hardly any confidence at all in them?

INSTITUTIONS	HIGH	MEDIUM	LOW
Major companies	29%	44%	20%
Organized religion	36	35	22
Higher education institutions	44	37	15
U.S. Senate	30	48	18
Organized labor	20	41	32
The press	30	45	21
U.S. House of Representatives	29	49	15
Medicine	57	31	10
Television news	41	43	14
Local tax assessment	19	40	30
U.S. Supreme Court	33	40	21
Local government	28	49	19
State highway systems	34	43	17
Local public schools	39	36	18
State government	24	55	17
Local police department	44	36	18
Executive branch of federal government	19	39	34
Local United Fund	35	35	20
Local trash collection	52	27	12
The military	40	35	19
The White House	18	36	41
Law firms	24	49	20

*Opinion polls revealed significant public distrust, during the Watergate era, of many major institutions; political pundits talked of a "crisis of confidence," especially in light of the low ratings given to the White House and to Congress.

Source: U.S. Congress, Senate, Committee on Government Operations, Confidence and Concern: Citizens View American Government, 93rd Cong., 1st Sess., 1973.

reporters exploited leaks within the agency itself. A series of stories told of various CIA domestic spying operations, apparently clear violations of the agency's mandate to operate only overseas. Ironically, Gerald Ford, who gained notoriety for his personal clumsiness—including a history of stumbling in and out of helicopters and of careening down ski slopes—ineptly blurted out the clandestine government's most explosive secrets: Before a group of *New York Times* executives, Ford revealed the CIA's involvement in attempts to assassinate foreign leaders, including Cuba's Fidel Castro. Although the *Times* itself sat on the story, Ford's gaffe soon reached reporters who were not bound by the president's claim that his remarks to the *Times* executives were off the record.

Even before the story about assassination plots broke, President Ford had created a special commission, headed by his newly appointed vice-president, Nelson Rockefeller, to look into allegations of domestic spying by the

CIA. In time, committees in both the House and the Senate heard testimony about a wide range of CIA "dirty tricks"—drug-testing projects on unsuspecting subjects, mail covers on private citizens, efforts to "destabilize" the economies of "hostile" nations, and several bizarre plots to murder foreign leaders. Although cynics doubted that the whole story had been told, the hearings did fuel the long process, begun by dissenting scholars and journalists during the 1960s, of rewriting the simplistic history of the cold war era. Testimony before several congressional committees, especially the lengthy record compiled by Frank Church's Senate panel, left no doubt that intelligence officials sometimes considered constitutional and legal restraints mere annoyances, paper restrictions that were to be ignored whenever it seemed convenient to do so.

Ford's greatest annoyance may have been the revelations of past misdeeds that undercut the public's faith in government. His most pressing problem, however, was the economy. Like Nixon, Ford aimed his economic remedies alternately at inflation and then recession, and they ended up producing worse cases of both.

During the first weeks of his presidency Ford targeted inflation, rather than unemployment, as the nation's most serious economic problem. The White House organized a belt-tightening campaign against rising prices that Ford called WIN ("Whip Inflation Now"). WIN was accompanied by buttons and ballyhoo, but its primary achievement was to nudge the country into its worst recession since the 1930s. Consumer demand dropped precipitously, especially in the crucial automobile industry, where higher sticker prices and worries about the availability of gasoline frightened off potential buyers. Triggered by large layoffs in Detroit, unemployment quickly spread. Slackening demand closed more and more factories, which in turn further reduced demand.

Faced with a jobless rate averaging 12 or 13 percent and with falling production almost everywhere, the president reversed course within a few months. In late 1974, now focusing on jobs and trying to cure recession, Ford projected a budget deficit of some $60 billion and asked Congress for a tax cut. This heavily inflationary plan was designed to increase retail spending and to create a demand for manufactured goods. After several months of politicking, Capitol Hill finally passed an act that rebated some taxes already paid in 1974, reduced the withholding rate, and provided tax credits for the purchasers of new homes. Government also forced down interest rates to around 8 percent. Taken together, these measures prompted a modest economic revival during the summer of 1975. Inflation, however, also resumed, once again rising toward double-digit rates. The economy seemed to oscillate between recession and inflation, both worsening with each swing, and both undermining America's economic position internationally.

While economics bedeviled Americans, other issues widened the gap that had opened between president and Congress during the Nixon years. Afraid that dependence on Arab oil might weaken American foreign policy, Ford wanted to raise the price of domestic gasoline by boosting federal taxes and ending all price controls on oil. The marketplace would "ration" gasoline and, in effect, force down consumption. Democrats in Congress countered that Ford's approach would only accelerate inflation and unfairly hurt poor people, while giving oil companies windfall profits.

Other factors complicated an easy resolution of the differences between the president and Congress. In the 1974 elections voters had sent many younger, more liberal Democratic representatives to Capitol Hill. These new legislators, together with some of their more experienced colleagues, recoiled at some of the business-as-usual politics of logrolling. By early 1975 they had ousted several powerful committee chairs who had long blocked liberal legislation. Then too, many legislators saw an opportunity in the Watergate scandals to reassert their prerogatives. This feisty, heavily Democratic Congress outlined its own energy program. But Ford vetoed bills that would have maintained price controls and allocated funds for mass transit, while publicly denouncing governmental gasoline rationing as unworkable. Lacking unified leadership—more than ten Democratic senators, for example, were maneuvering for their party's 1976 presidential nomination—Congress enacted laws to improve gasoline mileage in American cars and increased taxes on "gas guzzlers." The absence of any coherent response to the nation's economic and energy problems illustrated the drift that beset public-policy making in the 1970s.

Jimmy Carter: "Compassion and Competency?"

James Earl Carter, soon to be known around the globe as Jimmy, capitalized upon popular disenchantment with runaway intelligence agencies, political corruption, political insiders, and economic disarray. Emphasizing his rural roots, his born-again Christianity, and his lifelong distance from Washington, the naval-commander-turned-peanut-farmer promised voters that he would never sail a crooked ship of state. Beginning the 1976 race for the White House in 1973, the former governor of Georgia presented himself both as a plain person of the people—"a Southerner and an American . . . a farmer . . . a father and a husband, a Christian"— and as a skillful technocrat—"an engineer . . . a planner . . . a nuclear physicist." These diverse talents, he suggested, made him the ideal person to answer the "two basic and generic questions" facing the nation: "Can our government be honest, decent, open, fair, and compassionate? Can our government be competent?" Thus, Carter campaigned for the Democratic nomination and then against Gerald Ford for the presidency as an honest, neopopulist manager, someone who could balance both the nation's moral accounts and its national budget. He avoided strong stands on difficult issues—such as the government's role in defining social justice or in attacking inequality—and tried simply to project a straightforward, down-home image.

Carter's meteoric rise was aided not only by his own ability to project a multifaceted image but by his staff's ability to operate in the new political climate of the 1970s. Popular disillusionment during the Vietnam and Watergate eras had contributed to a decline in party loyalty and in voter

Criticized for drowning in day-to-day details while president, Jimmy Carter gradually won wide acclaim for his continued public service after leaving office. Source: *Jimmy Carter Library.*

turnout, and the upheavels of the late 1960s and early 1970s had brought significant changes in the ways in which the two national parties, especially the Democrats, selected delegates to their national conventions. By 1976 local party machines and prominent party leaders had lost considerable clout. Carter's strategists realized that they could appeal directly to party activists, either in person or through the media, and make an end run around traditional party stalwarts. Thus, Carter outmaneuvered more established Democrats, most of whom could not match his energy (holding no political office, Carter could devote full time to campaigning) or his shrewd, young campaign staff.

Another outsider with plenty of time to run for office, California's former governor Ronald Reagan, almost snatched the GOP nod away from Gerald Ford, who was even less exciting as a candidate than as a president. Had Reagan only started his charge a little sooner or had the GOP's primary process been as "democratized" as that of the Democrats, Reagan might have pushed aside Ford and captured the Republican nomination in 1976.

Taken together, the new political climate and the new political ground rules made Carter's ultimate victory over Ford difficult to interpret. On the one hand, the election of 1976 can be seen as less "democratic" than other recent presidential elections since large numbers of voters apparently found neither of the major candidates acceptable. Less than 25 percent of the total electorate cast their ballots for Jimmy Carter in November. But viewed in a different way, Carter's victory may be seen as the triumph of new "democratic" trends and the erosion of elitist patterns. Those party activists who did participate, especially in the Democratic primaries, saw their votes counting for more than they had in previous elections. In 1968, it should be remembered, Lyndon Johnson could virtually hand the nomination over to Hubert Humphrey, and in 1972 George McGovern could gain the nomination by winning only eight presidential primaries. In contrast, Jimmy Carter had to survive nearly four years of caucus battles and primary fights—what one journalist aptly labeled a political marathon—before he could even claim the nomination. Thus, Carter's electoral triumph owed relatively little to the traditional power brokers and a good deal to the "new politics" of the late 1960s.

But once anointed by the voters, Jimmy Carter still needed to convince powerful interest groups of his capacity to lead. Events of the late 1960s and early 1970s had affected the rules by which candidate Carter captured the presidential sweepstakes, but they did not greatly change the larger political and constitutional structure, the one in which President Carter had to operate. As critical observers noted, the nation's postwar constitutional system was dominated by powerful vested-interest groups. This system produced very valuable rewards for the organized—including tax deductions, government subsidies, and lucrative public contracts—but gave the unorganized largely the leftovers. Lyndon Johnson's Great Society sought to extend the boundaries of the welfare state, but it made little effort to change the basic distribution of power. Well-organized elites tended to view the relatively unknown Carter, and his rhetoric about populist democracy, as a possible threat to a political-constitutional system that seemed already under siege. Many of Carter's difficulties as president, then, grew out of the unorthodox route by which he had come to the White House and his self-proclaimed status as an "outsider."

From the very outset, Carter struggled to win the support of powerful elites, to triumph in what might be seen as a second presidential "election." His much-publicized ties with the Trilateral Commission—a group of business leaders and academics who favored closer cooperation among the world's industrial democracies and more comprehensive economic planning by the national government—helped relatively little. Carter selected several of his new inner circle, including his first secretary of the treasury (Michael Blumenthal) and his national security adviser (Zbigniew Brzezinski), from the commission's membership. But Carter, more than other recent presidents, underwent lengthy scrutiny by important corporation executives, prominent bankers, and other leaders of powerful institutions and interests. Carter's problems were complicated by the fact that he had to work with a Congress filled with incumbents who had close working arrangements with the very interests that distrusted the new president. Carter owed his position to his direct appeal to a shrinking electorate, while traditional interest groups, based upon geography and economic self-interest, retained much influence in Congress.

Given this structural situation, then, it was not surprising that Jimmy Carter soon found himself under sharp attack for his allegedly weak leadership, political naiveté, and inability to understand the complexities of power in Washington. Yet Carter's situation was not unique: All three presidents who preceded him—Johnson, Nixon, and Ford—faced similar problems. In part, such difficulties stemmed from the tremendous expectations placed upon the office and the person who held it. The presidency had become the focus of the national political life, but no president possessed the power, formal or informal, to deal with the problems of a system undergoing severe stress.

Overseas, both Jimmy Carter and the nation had to confront a world order in which American power and influence simply could not be used as they had been in the past. At home, the sluggish economy and growing awareness of social inequality produced a political culture significantly different from that of the first two decades of the postwar years. The problems of the Carter years can be understood only against the backdrop of these significant foreign and domestic developments, changes that began to occur even before Jimmy Carter began his dash for the White House.

NIXON, KISSINGER, AND WORLD POLITICS

The "Three-Dimensional Game"

Henry Kissinger, Nixon's national security adviser until February 1973 and thereafter his secretary of state, viewed himself as a master of geopolitical strategy. He talked of detente with the Soviets, but his later memoirs make it clear that his detente was not a policy of passivity, acceptance, or compromise. Instead, it involved "a firm application of psychological and physical restraints and determined resistance to challenge." It was a beefed-up form of containment. Detente, according to Kissinger, was *realpolitik*—political realism exercised forcefully, unrelentingly, and with a great variety of political, economic, and psychological methods.

Arranging America's geopolitical cards to maximum advantage involved introducing a new player—China. Triangular diplomacy might put maximum pressure on the Soviets and gain substantial advantages for the United States, as each of the bitter communist rivals courted America's support. Throughout the Nixon-Kissinger years, Americans negotiated with the Soviets and opened channels to China in what Kissinger called a "three-dimensional game" of diplomacy.

After 1969, the Soviet Union and the United States intermittently discussed nuclear arms control—proposals to regulate future growth, not to scrap existing military hardware. In 1969 both powers pledged not to build underwater installations and agreed to begin strategic arms limitation talks (SALT) in April 1970. Such negotiations required intense bargaining over intricate technical issues as well as over broad questions of strategic balance.

Yet after mid-1971, when the United States formally accepted the principle of nuclear parity, diplomats made rapid progress.

Reassured by the progress of SALT, the Nixon administration took up a more visible but even less familiar task, relations with China. Small courtesies started a chain reaction. Nixon spoke of "the People's Republic," not Red China, and told journalists of his desire to visit "that vast, unknown land." Nervous about their ancient enemy, Russia, and about Japan's surging economy, Chinese leaders reopened Sino-American talks through both countries' ambassadors in Warsaw. Nixon eased trade restrictions against China in early 1971, and the Chinese reciprocated with an invitation for a ping-pong tournament. Then in July Kissinger made a secret trip to Peking to arrange a presidential visit for 1972. The announcement of Nixon's trip startled both liberals and conservatives in the United States and refashioned world politics. The United Nations admitted the People's Republic three months later, rejecting the American two-China proposal, which was designed to preserve membership for Jiang Jie-Shi's regime on Taiwan.

On February 21, 1972, one of America's most celebrated anticommunists traveled to Peking to shake hands and bow gently with Mao Zedong, the world's archetypal anticapitalist. President and First Lady walked atop the Great Wall, mingled with communist dignitaries, and ate a twenty-two course state dinner. But public goodwill, carefully televised, could not dissolve long-standing animosities. Four days of negotiations with Premier Zhou Enlai produced primarily a list of postponements. The United States agreed that Taiwan's future was "an internal matter," but China pledged to deal with Taiwan "peacefully." Nixon reminded Chinese leaders of America's friendship with Japan, and Zhou broached the subject of "Tokyo's militarism." Mao voiced sympathy for "the people's struggle" in Indochina; Kissinger responded with references to "self-determination" and America's "eventual withdrawal." Though the new contacts went on—especially scientific exchanges, token shipments of grain from the United States, and relaxation of trade and travel restrictions—movement toward compromise on fundamental differences remained slow.

The prospect of Sino-American detente apparently pushed the Soviet Union into some technical concessions at SALT and toward an invitation, eagerly accepted, for Nixon to visit Moscow in the spring of 1972. There, Nixon and Soviet leader Leonid Brezhnev initialed arms control treaties called SALT I. SALT I terminated development of antiballistic systems (ABMs), defensive shields that American scientists had deemed exorbitantly expensive and probably technologically impractical anyway. It also capped the number of nuclear missiles that each side could own, although the Americans and later the Soviets quickly expanded their stocks of MIRV missiles containing multiple warheads on each missile. Thus, both sides could abide by the treaty yet still expand their numbers of deliverable weapons. The United States had a two to one lead in total warheads. SALT I's actual results did little to cool the arms race, but the treaty did provide the experience of and precedent for arms control negotiations. A year later Brezhnev visited the United States, and Nixon returned to Moscow in mid-1974. The momentum of detente continued and seemed to prove the advantages of triangular diplomacy.

As the Watergate scandals unfolded, Nixon increasingly sought redemption by stressing his international accomplishments. His personal diplomacy with China and Russia rated high in domestic opinion polls, and Kissinger was the only prominent member of Nixon's inner circle who emerged unscathed from the Watergate scandals.

The War in Southeast Asia

Despite the popularity of detente, the war in Vietnam still threatened the president's reputation and sapped America's strength. Nixon angrily told the nation that the United States would not "become a pitiful, helpless giant."

In 1971 Nixon continued negotiations in Paris while widening the war into Cambodia and Laos. Cambodia's neutral government of Prince Norodom Sihanouk fell to a U.S.-backed, right-wing general, Lon Nol, in 1970, and the Nixon administration, taking advantage of the coup, decided to invade to "clean out" communist supply camps. As American bombing and destruction in Cambodia proceeded, amidst an outcry of antiwar protest at home, Nixon also ordered attacks in Laos. In both countries North Vietnamese counterattacked, and the American invaders were routed. In Laos terrified South Vietnamese troops dangled from helicopter skids trying to escape; American advisers reported wholesale desertions.

In Paris, several months of secret diplomacy between Kissinger and North Vietnam's Le Duc Tho stalled. Leaders in Hanoi, encouraged by their adversary's misadventures in Laos and Cambodia and already planning their own military offensive, insisted that Thieu and his followers must go. For its part, however, the Nixon administration saw Nguyen Van Thieu's presidency as the symbol of South Vietnam's self-determination. Slow bargaining against the luxurious setting of Parisian restaurants and elegant townhouses could not unravel the basic puzzle: If Thieu stayed on, the war would go on; without Thieu and his political organization the country would easily fall under communist control, for the NLF was its best-organized opposition force.

Both sides stepped up their search for a military solution. In late March 1972 North Vietnam attacked along a broad front, capturing An Loc, a gateway city only thirty miles from Saigon. Thieu's troops fell back on all fronts, and American air power failed to check the communist ground advance. With many in the Pentagon again predicting humiliating defeat, Nixon resumed bombing raids in North Vietnam and Cambodia and ordered the navy to mine North Vietnam's harbors, a risky move that Lyndon Johnson had carefully avoided because of the possibility of damaging Russian or Chinese ships and triggering superpower conflict. With this new escalation, few military targets remained untouched, and civilian casualties and numbers of refugees mounted.

The violent spring and the upcoming American elections at first spurred more diplomacy. Several weeks before the end of the 1972 presidential campaign, Kissinger announced another cease-fire. "Peace," he said, "is at hand." But as so often in the past, American leaders still believed that their sophisticated military technology could force a quick victory. In mid-December 1972, Nixon ordered an armada of B-52s to attack North Vietnam twenty-four hours a day "until they are ready to negotiate." Despite heavy losses, American bombers attacked North Vietnam's factories, ruined rice fields, and destroyed schools, hospitals, and other civilian facilities. This so-called Christmas attack was the heaviest aerial bombing in history. It caused an international uproar and a determination among antiwar members of Congress to end America's involvement in the Vietnam conflict.

The Christmas bombing marked the last desperate gasp of the American effort. In January 1973 the United States and North Vietnam signed the Paris Peace Accords, ending formal hostilities. Washington promised to withdraw its remaining 50,000 troops, dismantle its military installations, and deactivate mines in North Vietnam's harbors. No foreign troops were to remain in Laos or Cambodia, but Hanoi's forces could stay "in place" within South Vietnam. North Vietnam agreed to release American prisoners of war and to cooperate in national elections in the South. But the accords did not bring peace, only a slow withdrawal of U.S. troops. The war between the communist North and Thieu's dictatorship dragged on, 48,000 soldiers dying during the first eighteen months of the "cease-fire." By the summer of 1974 war had again returned to most of Indochina.

Meanwhile, Hanoi's almost legendary general, Nyguyen Giap, was organizing a coordinated assault by all his forces for the spring of 1975. Disintegration and demoralization in the South aided his plans. Thieu arrested opponents, banned opposition political parties, and closed down most newspapers. To consolidate his military position and possibly frighten the United States into sending more hardware, Thieu suddenly withdrew his armies from the three northernmost provinces of South Vietnam. But the planned retreat turned into a disorganized rout when Giap's troops took the opportunity to attack. Deprived of American air support, the dispirited South Vietnamese troops raced southward, pillaging their own villages as they went. The North Vietnamese followed, scarcely having to fight, while hundreds of thousands of civilian refugees crowded highways. Only at the gateway to Saigon itself, the provincial capital of Xuan Loc, did the South Vietnamese army make a stand. But Thieu's regime collapsed, and the communists overwhelmed the city in less than a week. On May 1 North Vietnamese and NLF forces entered Saigon, while the last American officials were frantically escaping from the United States embassy by helicopter.

Face-saving maneuvers followed. Military airlifts flew over 100,000 South Vietnamese, mostly those closely identified with the United States, to new homes in America. Meanwhile, Kissinger and the new president Gerald Ford tried to block the diplomatic and psychological consequences of the communist victory. Quietly reassuring allies in Western Europe, the secretary of state denied that his country would yield to "neoisolationists" at home. The administration also successfully countered congressional efforts to reduce the numbers of American soldiers stationed overseas and to pare military spending. To regain an image of diplomatic initiative, Kissinger gave a green light to a CIA project to supply and bankroll friendly forces in the Angolan civil war. (America's secret intervention in Angola prompted large-scale Soviet and Cuban aid to the other side; when Congress discovered and terminated this CIA adventure in Africa, the Soviet-backed faction came to power.)

In Cambodia, Lon Nol's U.S.-backed regime had succumbed to communist Khmer Rouge forces under Pol Pot. In late May 1975 the new Khmer Rouge regime seized an American merchant vessel, the *Mayaguez*, and imprisoned its crew for allegedly carrying contraband within Cambodia's territorial waters. President Ford, determined to flex American muscles and recoup his sagging popularity at home, dispatched a naval task force and some two thousand marines to rescue the thirty-nine man crew. Critics denounced the gunboat diplomacy that cost America thirty-eight dead and fifty wounded, but most Americans supported their president. Clearly, although the communist victory in Vietnam may have marked the limits of American power, the Ford administration still wanted to show worldwide reach.

The long struggle in Vietnam proved more costly than anyone had imagined. It provoked bitter divisions at home and ended the consensus of the post–World War II period. It also raised a preoccupation with secrecy within the government. The Watergate scandals and the revelations of CIA activities gave mere glimpses into the "secret government" that had grown during the war. At the international level, the war strained the American balance of payments and built up pressure on the dollar. Defeat hurt the credibility of American commitments abroad, chipping away still more at the dollar's strength. Through Vietnam, Americans discovered the consequences of power used unwisely.

For many years, Americans seemed to want to forget their defeat. The idea that a small Asian nation could have, after a ten-year struggle, forced the retreat of the United States, a country at the pinnacle of its power, seemed almost beyond comprehension. Unlike the returning veterans of World War II, for example, Vietnam veterans were often shunned and their needs ignored. Even the government that had ordered them into combat tried to dodge its responsibility for the Agent Orange-related disorders that afflicted many veterans. Agent Orange was a deadly defoliant used to level the jungles in Vietnam. After a long court battle, during which it was revealed that Dow Chemical Company and government officials had known in advance about the chemical's hazards, the government set aside a compensatory fund. But the amount was small in comparison to the number of veterans afflicted, and many chose not to join in the settlement at all because they perceived it as deficient.

If slightly submerged for a time, however, domestic division over the war and important nagging questions remained. Slowly, interest in the Vietnam war rekindled and, within a few years, a battle over how to interpret "the lessons" of the struggle emerged. Not surprisingly, evaluations of the war tended to reflect the positions held at the time of the struggle.

Hawks continued to present the case that the war could have been won. Some blamed the lack of a government-censored media and claimed that journalists had drained the American people of a will to persevere. Some complained that the "war was lost in Washington" by "the politicians" who would not commit themselves to the military measures necessary for victory. Some blamed the antiwar movement and argued that defeat took place "in the streets of America." Most hawks argued that the military itself was not at fault but was the victim of a nonsupportive domestic milieu. But even within military ranks subtleties developed. One analyst propounded the novel thesis that the war was lost because the military emphasized counterinsurgency tactics rather than the kind of conventional warfare in which America excelled.

Wartime doubters and dissenters expanded their case that the war was "in the wrong place, at the wrong time, for the wrong reason." Vietnam held little strategic importance for the United States, and American leaders had mistakenly made the land into a symbol of American honor. The North, most argued, waged a "people's war" while Americans came to be seen as foreign invaders, the inheritors of a colonialist tradition. Even some segments in the military bolstered these arguments, demonstrating that "victory" could have no operational meaning in a struggle that required the destruction of a land and its people in order to win.

Interestingly, amid the welter of arguments on all sides emerged a central point of agreement: In Vietnam, the ends had not matched the means. Military leaders warned that they would never again become the tools of a "no-win" policy, and most Americans wanted no more engagements that demanded expenditure of lives and treasure for hazy goals and problematic national interest. In short, American governments ought more carefully to weigh gains against costs and not simply assume omnipotence; no one wanted "another Vietnam."

The Middle East and Latin America

As Americans disentangled themselves from Southeast Asia, the Middle East exploded in war. In the fall of 1973, on the Jewish holy day of Yom Kippur, Egyptian and Syrian armies attacked Israel. With United States diplomatic support and large donations from American Jews, the Israelis first weathered the assault and then drove deeply into Arab territories. Anxious to defuse Arab-Israeli hostilities, Kissinger argued that the United States could best help Israel by negotiating with its enemies, not fighting them. He launched nearly two years of dramatic "shuttle diplomacy," which eventually achieved a tentative settlement: Israel would pull back from part of the Sinai, and the United States would grant military aid to both Israel and Egypt. Best of all, according to Kissinger, his shuttle diplomacy eased the Soviets out of the picture altogether. In March 1976, President Sadat even canceled the Soviet's rights to use Egyptian ports.

Kissinger's efforts to jockey for geopolitical advantage and reduce Soviet influence throughout the world translated into a simple formula: Support "friends" and punish "enemies." In pursuing this policy, Kissinger did not worry much about the character of his friends' internal policies. Kissinger's realpolitik held that as long as these countries provided a regional bulwark and were hospitable to American economic interests, issues of morality were beside the point. Kissinger's grand design for world stability through regional policemen aligned American's global interests with some of the most oppressive dictators in the world: Shah Reza Pahlevi in Iran, Park Chung-Hee in South Korea, Ferdinand Marcos in the Philippines, and the military leaders of Brazil. In Africa, Kissinger's "tar-baby" report of 1969 concluded that black African insurgent movements were not "realistic or supportable" alternatives. The Nixon-Kissinger policy was therefore to continue to look primarily to South Africa (which received 40 percent of United States investments in Africa) and European colonialists to provide stability in the region and to form close ties with the military regime in oil-rich Nigeria.

America's military assistance and military-training programs fed these dictatorships. Private foreign sales of American arms also skyrocketed, reaching $10 billion by the end of the Nixon presidency. Arms sales ameliorated America's serious balance-of-payments problems and contributed short-term stability, but they incubated more military dictatorships. In Latin America during the Nixon years, for example, countries in the "southern cone"—Uruguay, Chile, Argentina—experienced coups that interrupted traditions of stable, civilian democracy and brought brutal, U.S.-backed military dictatorships to power.

The case of Chile demonstrated the punitive measures the United States could employ against a regime that tried to pull out of its sphere of influence. In 1970 Salvador Allende, a Marxist, was elected president of Chile, a country with a strong tradition of civilian government and an apolitical military establishment. Greatly alarmed by Allende's campaign pledges to nationalize American-owned copper companies and move the country toward socialism. Nixon and Kissinger met with CIA chief Richard Helms, who emerged from the Oval Office with these notes:

One in 10 chance perhaps, but save Chile!
worth spending
not concerned risks involved
no involvement of Embassy
$10,000,000 available, more if necessary
full-time job—best men we have
game plan
make the economy scream
48 hours for plan of action

With an unlimited budget and full authority for any maneuver to "save Chile" from its elected ruler, the CIA first attempted to arrange a military coup to prevent Allende from taking office. This plan ran against the Chilean military's traditions and thus, at that point, failed. CIA encouragement did, however, lead to the assassination of one of Chile's most respected generals, a man who persistently opposed a military takeover. Next, Helms urged an economic offensive: The government ceased its aid to Chile; the World Bank cooperated by dropping Chile's credit rating; private banks suspended loans; and International Telephone and Telegraph (ITT) and American copper companies, which Allende had nationalized, worked tirelessly to promote his downfall. As chaos overtook the Chilean economy (Chile had huge foreign debts because of the large loans extended under JFK's Alliance for Progress), CIA dollars helped finance a trucker's strike that brought distribution to a halt. Shortages mounted, and the middle class increasingly blamed Allende. In 1973 the military finally decided to intervene. The leaders of the coup killed President Allende and thousands of his supporters and installed a regime so oppressive and barbaric in its use of torture that it quickly became an embarrassment to many in the United States government. Over Kissinger's protest, Congress subsequently suspended aid. And after the new Chilean government managed to assassinate Allende's former ambassador to the United States, right on the streets of Washington, D.C., relations between the two countries broke down almost completely—at least on an official level. On a private level, however, United States enterprise and investments again flooded Chile, attracted by the ironfisted stability.

FOREIGN AFFAIRS UNDER JIMMY CARTER

The Human Rights Policy

The Kissinger-Nixon-Ford years saw breakthroughs, such as the opening of a dialogue with China, but the government's willingness to shrug off glaring violations of human rights by many of its allies provoked growing outrage abroad as well as at home. Jimmy Carter's promise, as a presidential candidate, to encourage respect for human rights in international affairs won him popularity. Forming alliances with hated despots, Carter argued, was neither morally right nor strategically sensible: Opposition to terror and despotism in many countries had, under Kissinger's policy, become identified with opposition to United States influence. Once America abandoned its image as a benevolent power, Carter claimed, it lost its major strength in international affairs and its most powerful weapon in the cold war.

The human rights policy proved difficult to effect. President Carter appointed a full-time officer to oversee implementation of the policy, supported the weighing of human rights records in the granting of foreign aid, and stopped America's role as a supplier of instruments of torture. But rapid changes could not help but affect America's global position. In fact, Carter quickly assured many of America's dictator-allies that United States national security commitments would continue to take precedence over their internal conduct. Thus, governments, such as those in Iran, South Korea, and the Philippines felt few punitive measures under the new human rights policy, but they did feel increasing pressure to ease up on flagrant violations. Countries less strategically exposed, such as Chile and Argentina, felt the new administration's disapproval much more dramatically.

As Carter's critics had predicted, the human rights policy gave heart to popular liberation movements in several countries and brought dilemmas to Carter's policymakers. The contradiction between the emphasis on human rights and the previous geopolitics of Henry Kissinger surfaced most notably in Nicaragua and Iran. In these countries popular uprisings swept the hated regimes of Anastasio Somoza and Shah Reza Pahlevi out of power in 1979. Despite severe pressure from domestic Republican allies of both regimes, the Carter administration, after a few attempts at compromise solutions, did not intervene to save the despots. After so many years of profiting from a close alliance with dictators in both countries, however, the United States should not have expected the new governments to be particularly friendly. In Nicaragua the new regime headed by the revolutionary Sandinista movement increasingly adopted a Marxist orientation antagonistic to the United States. In Iran, Carter faced an even more difficult situation that ultimately proved to be his administration's undoing.

After Shah Pahlevi's ouster in Iran, a long-exiled religious leader, the Ayatollah Khomeini, established an Islamic Republic dedicated to wiping out the influences of Americanization. In late 1979 a group of Islamic revolutionaries entered the compound of the American embassy and seized about sixty Americans. The Iranian government demanded custody of the shah, who had been admitted into the United States to undergo medical treatment for cancer, in exchange for the release of the hostages. Khomeini also talked of gaining possession of the shah's personal fortune and of placing some of the American hostages on trial for spying, using evidence captured in the embassy takeover. Despite the shah's departure from the United States and various attempts at mediation, U.S.–Iranian relations worsened. Iran cut off oil shipments to the United States; the American government froze Iranian assets, instituted full economic pressure against the ayatollah's regime, and attempted—against the advice of Secretary of State Cyrus Vance—an unsuccessful military mission to rescue the hostages. In this climate of extreme tension, even the shah's death in the summer of 1980 did not bring swift release of the hostages. Finally, in a frantic round of diplomacy in the closing days of the Carter administration, freedom for the hostages was exchanged for complex economic settlements, but relations between the two countries remained poor.

At home, Carter came under immense criticism. Many Americans across the country tied yellow ribbons to trees to symbolize the hostages' plight. One television network began a nightly news program called *America Held Hostage*. In the wake of Vietnam, the Iranian crisis seemed one more example of American weakness, and Jimmy Carter got the blame.

Despite difficulties, President Carter's human rights emphasis re-dressed the previous draft of American policy toward alliances with repres-sive, unpopular regimes. It encouraged the forces of democratization that would sweep Latin America in the late 1970s and 1980s, especially the return to civilian rule in Ecuador, Peru, Brazil, Argentina, and Uruguay. And Carter also engineered rapprochement with black Africa. United Nations ambassador Andrew Young, a black veteran of civil rights struggles in the South, gained African trust as had few high-ranking Americans before him. Although Young was forced to resign in 1979 after he lied to the State Department about engaging in talks with representatives of the Palestine Liberation Organization (PLO), a group with which the State Department had forbade dealings, the new look in African policy continued anyway. For example, President Carter stood strongly behind British efforts to force the white-minority government in Rhodesia (Zimbabwe) to effect a peaceful transition to black rule, a transition that signaled the end of an important bastion of white rule in Africa. If the Carter presidency seemed a particular-ly unsettled period in American foreign policy, the difficulties can be traced, in part, to earlier alliances with oppressive tyrants and unpopular regimes.

The Fruits of Negotiation

Unlike the human rights policy, many of Carter's major negotiating achievements—those in Panama, the Middle East, and China—built upon the initiatives of his Republican predecessors.

In September 1977 the United States and Panama signed two treaties covering the ownership, operation, and defense of the Panama Canal. United States control over the Canal Zone, a strip of 550 square miles slicing through the middle of Panama, had caused bitter resentment for years and brought serious riots in 1964. Denounced in Latin America and throughout the Third World for still holding this land acquired in the days of territo-ry-grabbing imperialism, the United States under President Johnson com-mitted itself to the negotiation of a new treaty. Talks took place over the next thirteen years. After heated debate and a full application of presidential leverage, the Senate ratified the new treaties in 1978. Under their terms, the Canal Zone ceased to exist, and Panama assumed general jurisdiction; the United States retained primary responsibility for operating and defending the canal until the year 2000 but with ever increasing Panamanian participa-tion; and Panama agreed that the canal should be permanently neu-tral—open to all vessels with no discrimination on tolls. In addition, Panama would receive a share of canal revenues and a substantial commitment of American loans (not grants).

Although critics charged that the treaties represented a rollback of America's strength, the Carter administration stressed that the increasingly obsolete canal was no longer the economic and strategic lifeline it had once been. Moreover, ratification would deflate anti-American sentiment in Latin America, a goal of growing importance to Carter's negotiators as Mexico, Ecuador, and Peru were discovering new fields of petroleum.

Fresh from the battle over the Panama treaties, President Carter turned his full attention to the Middle East. Kissinger's efforts at shuttle diplomacy between Tel Aviv and Cairo had stalled after the breakthrough of partial Israeli withdrawal from the Sinai Peninsula in 1975. But Egypt's president, Anwar Sadat, surprised the world by traveling to Jerusalem. Sadat's visit to Israel indicated the economic exhaustion that ongoing confrontation had brought to both Egypt and Israel. The time again seemed right for progress. For thirteen days in 1978, Carter, Israeli Prime Minister Menachem Begin, and Anwar Sadat remained in near isolation at the presidential retreat at Camp David, Maryland. When they emerged, they issued for television audiences an emotional three-way statement that outlined the beginnings of a negotiating process, subsequently ratified by treaty.

The Camp David agreements provided only a framework, not the substance, of a settlement. The most difficult issue—the future of the West Bank and Gaza—remained unresolved. Israel categorically forbade any official participation by the Palestine Liberation Organization in the negotiations, even though the PLO was the major representative of the Arab Palestinians in the West Bank and Gaza. The PLO and most Arab states charged that Sadat had negotiated matters that were not his to negotiate. The split within the Arab world widened as Israeli-Egyptian divisions narrowed. Some domestic critics, observing that the exclusion of the PLO and the antagonism of other Arabs made substantial solutions even more difficult than before, wondered whether Carter, Begin, and Sadat had created the illusion of settlement to raise their images at home. But optimists argued that the importance of the 1979 peace treaty lay in the momentum of negotiation. Clearly, the Egyptian-Israeli peace firmly established United States hegemony and eliminated Soviet influence in Egypt. Carter, like Nixon, dangled the large carrot of American aid and increased arms sales in order to keep the appearance of negotiations alive.

Carter's diplomacy with China had less ambiguous results. On January 1, 1979, the United States and the People's Republic of China established formal relations, and over the next year they signed a number of cultural, scientific, and economic agreements. A joint economic committee cochaired by the secretary of the treasury, worked to enhance trade, and the United States zoomed up to fourth place among China's trading partners. In January 1980 Defense Secretary Harold Brown's trip to China (coinciding handily with the Soviet invasion of Afghanistan) signaled the opening of a military relationship as well. The new technocrats who succeeded to Chinese leadership after the death of Mao were bent upon accelerating modernization by borrowing from the capitalist West, and the lure of the China market once again enthralled the American business community.

Renewing the Cold War

Toward the end of 1979 the counselor for the department of state summarized the general view that had initially guided the Carter administration's foreign policy worldwide: "It is not a sign of weakness to recognize that we alone cannot dictate events elsewhere. It is rather a sign of American maturity in a complex world." More negotiation, more compromise, and greater attention to human rights marked Carter's early foreign policy.

External events and political pressures at home gradually led Carter to revise his foreign policy emphasis. By 1978 policymakers talked more of larger military spending and cold war dangers. Then in December 1979 the Soviet Union invaded Afganistan. The Soviet action, the first armed Soviet invasion since the incursion into Czechoslovakia in 1968, probably reflected the Soviets' fear of a unified Islamic movement and their desire to solidify their shaky sphere of influence. Coming at a time when Americans were exceedingly nervous about the security of Middle Eastern oil supplies due to the Iranian revolution, the Soviet invasion touched off feverish cold war rhetoric reminiscent of the 1950s.

Critics of Carter's foreign policy leaped to their election-year podiums, denounced America's presumed weakness, and clamored for a response. The Carter administration warned Americans that "overreaction" was as dangerous as "underreaction" but announced reprisals against the Soviets. Carter ordered a halt to exports of grain and high technology to the Soviet Union, began to arm Pakistan, publicly highlighted the secretary of defense's trip to China, organized a boycott of the Olympic Games held in Moscow in the summer of 1980, withdrew the SALT treaty from the Senate, and reinstituted registration for a military draft. Despite such measures—the strongest response possible short of some type of military action—more and more Americans began to charge that Carter had presided over an erosion of American power that had opened the way for the Soviet invasion of Afghanistan. Neoconservative groups such as the Committee on the Present Danger constructed a litany of signs of America's weakness: the shah's ouster in Iran, the Soviet-Cuban presence in Africa, the growing power of Soviet-aligned Vietnam in Southeast Asia, and the revolutionary ferment in the Caribbean. The promise of resurgent American power became the theme of Ronald Reagan's presidential campaign of 1980, as public opinion polls showed that 82 percent disapproved of Carter's handling of foreign policy.

Carter knew the political perils of soft-line diplomacy. Afghanistan, he claimed, had shattered his previous illusions about Soviet behavior, and he promised to lead the nation in more forceful directions. A rift became increasingly apparent between Secretary of State Vance, who believed in detente and the negotiating process, and National Security Adviser Brzezinski, a hardliner with a bipolar view of world politics who deeply distrusted the Soviets. After Carter ordered his ill-fated military mission to rescue the hostages in Iran (whose lengthening captivity had become a major political liability), the secretary of state resigned his post. Vance indicated that he was out of sympathy not only with what he considered a rash and risky military incursion into Iran but with the new confrontation policy in general. But with Republicans goading the administration about a weak defense, Carter complemented cold war rhetoric with promises to revitalize America's strategic posture. He began refurbishing military bases throughout the world and beefing up American military capabilities in critical areas, such as the Indian Ocean and the Caribbean; he increased defense spending and promised more emphasis on new high-technology weapon systems (satellites and lasers); and he strongly backed the controversial and costly MX missile system. His advisers even began to blur the traditional distinctions between "nuclear" and "conventional" military action, leaving the Russians to speculate publicly that Americans no longer considered "limited" nuclear strikes unthinkable.

Although the new cold warriors drew alarming pictures of an expansionist Soviet Union, the Soviets were themselves feeling embattled. Suffering major economic problems, threatened by growing dissent at home, and wary of a resurgent and hostile China, Soviet leaders also faced a decline in geopolitical power. Kissinger and Carter had both outmaneuvered the Soviets in the Middle East and effectively excluded them from influence in that area. Signs of discontent in Eastern Europe—especially the successful strike by Polish workers in August 1980—highlighted strains even within the Warsaw Pact.

If both American and Russian leaders felt increasingly insecure about their global roles in the early 1980s, it was because the rest of the world was struggling to avoid the tight grip of bipolar alliances and to build new power blocs. OPEC; the movement of "nonaligned nations"; the Committee of 77, which represented the Southern Hemisphere in the so-called North-South debate; the new power of Islam; the rising economic power of Japan; and a variety of regional pacts all illustrated the growing intricacy of world politics. Yet, as in the era of the first cold war, the leaders of the superpowers appeared tempted to resort to a simplistic bipolar analysis to explain away the complexities of neutralist or nationalist aspirations.

THE NEW EGALITARIANISM

The Meaning of Equality

Perhaps the most perplexing issue facing the nation in the 1970s was its commitment to equality. Nearly all of the Republic's sacred documents—including the Declaration of Independence and the Constitution's Fourteenth Amendment—affirmed the idea of equality. Yet one of the undeniable themes in the nation's history had been the persistence of inequality—political, legal, and economic. Even in the late 1960s, as the need for the Voting Rights Acts of 1965 and 1970 confirmed, many African-Americans in the South still lacked the same political rights as whites.

The search for greater equality during the 1960s and 1970s revealed some fundamental differences over the meaning of equality and over the desirability of making it a key national goal. As the nation approached and then passed the bicentennial of its birth, debates about equality became more heated. In the late 1970s, polarization over the issue of equality, though less visible than a decade before, was no less intense, especially in journalistic and academic circles.

Throughout most of the nation's history, "equality" seemed to mean "equality of opportunity," the chance for every citizen to join in the race for individual success. The sweetest victories and the largest rewards, it was assumed, should still go to those who ran the swiftest. But everyone should have a chance to get to the starting line, and no one should have to jump hurdles while their more fortunate competitors sailed along an obstacle-free track. Yet even equality of opportunity, though much celebrated, remained a dream for many people. The race-for-success ethos had worked as well as it had, it might be argued, because so many people never really got into the contest at all. Women, African-Americans, ethnic minorities, gay people—these and other groups carried "handicaps" that prevented them from even getting to the starting blocks. The famous blues singer Big Bill Broonzy summarized the way many black people saw the great American race:

> If you're White, you're all right,
> If you're Brown, stick around,
> But if you're black, O' brother,
> Get back! Get back! Get Back!*

Many of the political and legal battles of the 1960s and of the 1970s aimed at preventing people from being "moved back," at rehandicapping the race, and at removing old hurdles. Thus, the demands of the civil rights movement involved elimination of various obstacles, such as segregation laws and discriminatory hiring practices, that prevented African-Americans from entering the gates of national institutions. Similarly, women's groups channeled their energies toward passage of the Equal Rights Amendment, an attempt to end discrimination through legal and constitutional change.

While the struggle to eliminate obstacles to equality of opportunity was still proceeding, the victories in this area began to change the perspective of many activists. As they looked at the race-for-success ideal, these "new egalitarians" began to argue that efforts to allow everyone to enter the race and to remove the old system of hurdles were not enough. Renewed commitment to the principle of equality of opportunity would not likely change the fact that only a few people were leading the race for economic success, that many people were bunched in the middle of the pack, and that a sizable portion had fallen permanently behind. In the distribution of both income and wealth, the United States in 1980 remained a very unequal society: At the top of the scale, 5 percent of the population received 20 percent of the nation's income and owned more than 50 percent of its wealth; the lowest 20 percent, in stark contrast, gained 3 percent of the income and held less than .5 percent of the wealth. According to the new egalitarians, such inequality of condition and of results meant that there were all sorts of subtle and hidden handicaps in the system. If the United States were to be a truly

*Source: Carrousel France.

egalitarian society, there must be vigorous and affirmative action to achieve greater "equality of condition" rather than simply a spurious equality of opportunity.

In the late 1960s and especially the early 1970s, the agenda of egalitarianism changed. Not only should African-American students be protected from discriminatory procedures that barred them from educational institutions, the new egalitarians argued, but there should be "affirmative action" programs to ensure their admittance and their graduation. In the area of employment, proponents of affirmative action urged programs to ensure that women and minority applicants were not simply interviewed but were then hired and promoted on an "equal" basis. Proof of substantial progress was increasingly measured by comparing the percentage of women and minorities in educational or business institutions with their percentage of the total population, a process that opponents condemned as inevitably leading to the institution of quotas.

The quest for greater equality of condition involved more than pressure for affirmative action programs in educational and corporate institutions. Looking at the gross inequality of wealth and income, many egalitarians argued that the nation must confront the issue of income redistribution. After surveying the problem in *Inequality* (1971) and resurveying it in *Who Gets Ahead?* (1979), the sociologist Christopher Jencks claimed that social science data showed that attempts to equalize people's "personal characteristics," especially their educational backgrounds, was an "unpromising way of equalizing incomes." If people truly wanted a more equal economic order, Jencks concluded, efforts to "redistribute income itself" offered the "most effective strategy."

But as George McGovern discovered during his ill-fated presidential campaign, redistributive proposals were difficult to sell to voters. Although many of Richard Nixon's "forgotten Americans" would have benefited from McGovern's proposed changes in inheritance laws, for example, most voters saw his ideas as too radical. "They must think they're all going to win a lottery," complained McGovern. In fact, many people viewed redistribution as hostile to their interests. It seemed to strike at the deeply rooted commitment to "propertarianism" and at the faith that no matter now unjust the general economic system might appear something would turn up for them. (Public opinion polls taken in the late 1970s revealed a similar phenomenon: People expressed considerable pessimism about the general economic situation but a striking optimism about their own prospects.)

Yet the movement for equality spread, and some of the new egalitarians went beyond purely economic issues to argue that everyone should have an equal opportunity to enjoy, without risking penalties, their chosen style of life. Some of the most bitter battles in the struggle for equality were fought over the issue of homosexuality. During the late 1960s and throughout the 1970s more and more homosexuals "came out of the closet" and joined a growing "gay rights" movement. Gay rights activists first wanted acknowledgment of their right to privacy, their right to satisfy their own sexual preferences with other consenting adults. Increasingly, they also demanded that gay and lesbian people be treated, in their public roles, no different than heterosexuals. The gay rights movement pushed for state and municipal laws ending traditional patterns of discrimination and sought greater police protection against physical abuse. Although the gay rights movement won significant support, especially from civil liberties elites, it also produced a considerable backlash among those who feared the spread of what they considered an immoral way of life.

Efforts to create greater equality for women also raised controversy. Here, it was the American family, the bedrock of the social order, that became the issue. Proposals to expand government funding for day-care centers—necessities for most women who wanted both children and a job—angered those who claimed that the state should stay out of private matters and those who argued that more day-care facilities would only upset an already unstable family structure. In addition, most employers displayed little enthusiasm for ideas such as flexible work hours and job sharing, arrangements that could benefit both men and women who wanted families and careers.

The New Right

Fervent opposition to the new egalitarianism helped unify the new conservative coalition of the 1970s. Although some commentators had predicted that the "Goldwater caper" of 1964 signaled conservatism's imminent collapse, right-leaning leaders inside and outside the GOP smoothly regrouped their forces. As conservatives gained new visibility and greater self-confidence, a New Right emerged as an important political force.

Several things distinguished this New Right from the conservative movement of the 1940s and 1950s. First, conservatives now gained broad popular support, especially through their alliance with rapidly growing evangelical religious groups. Conservatives, who had once had to search for roots in the distant past, could now join the religious right in rallying around contemporary institutions such as the American family. (For the emergence of the religious right see Chapter 9.) In addition, conservatives mastered the latest media and organizational techniques. Conservative speakers, such as William F. Buckley and Milton Friedman, became skilled television performers, and conservative fund-raisers mounted highly sophisticated direct-mail appeals for donations. Following the lead of Goldwater's 1964 campaign, conservative political strategists were oftentimes more innovative than their opponents on the political left. Although many members of the GOP had opposed the changes in campaign-financed laws that grew out of Watergate, Republican-oriented pressure groups on the right skillfully used loopholes in the new measures, especially the provision allowing unlimited spending by independent "political action committees"—PACS.

The New Right also enjoyed a livelier and broader intellectual base than the conservatism of the 1950s. During the 1970s, an informal conservative coalition benefited from a steady flow of prominent refugees, particularly East Coast intellectuals, from the cold war liberalism of the "vital center." Some of these "neoconservatives" settled into research positions at well-funded, right-leaning think tanks (such as the American Enterprise Institution in Washington); others occupied newly funded chairs and programs at universities and smaller colleges; and most wrote for a variety of lively scholarly and popular journals.

Neoconservatives blended the old with the new. Espousing a more cautious and extremely nervous version of the old anticommunist liberalism that had been forged during the early postwar era, neoconservatives denounced familiar enemies, especially international communism, Marxism, domestic radicalism, and mass culture. Their favorite causes—such as political gradualism, enlightened capitalism, economic growth, and high culture— also had been the bedrock of their ideology during the period of Truman's Fair Deal. But the leftward drift of liberalism and the emergence of a new cultural and political radicalism during the 1960s propelled many neoconservatives toward the New Right during the 1970s. Norman Podhoretz, editor of *Commentary* magazine, proudly pointed out that he had published Paul Goodman in the early 1960s and had only broken ranks after realizing the "sinister" implications of that decade. The counterculture, Podhoretz claimed, was winning, and sober intellectuals had to take a firm stand against "irrational" ideas and "dangerous" values.

Critical of what they considered a cowardly appeasement of communism overseas and a soft-headed tolerance of cultural and political radicalism at home, chastened liberals like Podhoretz, Irving Kristol, Daniel Bell, and Nathan Glazer formed the intellectual core of neoconservatism. In addition to their own numerous publications, they helped to popularize some of the more conservative social science literature, especially the work of Edward Banfield and James Q. Wilson. The resulting battles between the neoconservatives' set of academic "experts" and those of the left were fierce. Many of the leading neoconservative theorists possessed backgrounds in both academia and journalism, and they combined these talents to produce sprightly polemics for *Commentary* and more scholarly pieces for *The Public Interest*, an influential periodical edited by Kristol and Glazer.

Although neoconservatives found the United States—indeed, Western civilization—entering a period of profound crisis, the specter of the new egalitarianism frightened them almost as much as did the Soviet Union. Some neoconservatives were disturbed by the new efforts to achieve the traditional goal of equality of opportunity, at least when such equality was sought by militant feminists, cultural radicals, and gays. Irving Kristol and the political scientist Walter Berns, for example endorsed more vigorous censorship of cultural materials, and Ernest van den Haag warned that the new militancy of gays threatened traditional values based on heterosexuality.

The attack on the new egalitarianism, however, centered on what neoconservatives denounced as "equality of outcomes." Nathan Glazer condemned affirmative action as an insidious form of reverse discrimination, a doctrine that discriminated not simply against white males but against all people of true merit. When applied to African-Americans, the political scientist Robert Sasseen argued, affirmative action really affirmed an "arrogant contempt" for blacks: It disguised a "paternalistic policy" that consigned its purported beneficiaries to "perpetual inferiority" and to a life as "special wards of the state." Midge Dector denounced militant feminism as a revolutionary attack on motherhood, as a sign of deep-seated self hatred, and as the manifestation of the "desperately nihilistic idea" that there were no "necessary differences between the sexes." Irving Kristol blamed most of the controversy over equality on "an intelligensia" that despised liberal capitalism and "that is so guilt-ridden at being implicated in the life of the society that it is inclined to find even collective suicide preferable to the status quo."

The National Government and the Riddle of Equality

The struggle over the meaning of equality was not, of course, limited to rhetorical clashes. The egalitarian currents of the 1960s and 1970s, as wary neoconservatives recognized, touched most areas of public life, especially educational and corporate institutions. Did affirmative action programs that set aside a specified number of classroom seats or jobs for certain minorities constitute reverse discrimination against others who claimed they were more deserving of the places on the basis of their individual merit? Should, for instance, African-Americans or Latinos be admitted to a law school, while whites with higher test scores were rejected? (Such questions became especially difficult and emotional when the persons rejected came from ethnic groups, such as Jewish and Italian-Americans, who had once suffered from discrimination themselves.)

The controversy over affirmative action and reverse discrimination raged throughout the 1970s, and the United States Supreme Court finally entered the lists. In the much-discussed *Bakke* case of 1978, a deeply divided Court struck down a plan that set aside a certain quota of seats at a California medical school for "minority" applicants. But, more significantly, a majority of justices also indicated that they were not willing to invalidate all affirmative action programs. The Court upheld a private affirmative action plan, devised by Kaiser Aluminum in order to upgrade the positions of minority workers, and approved a congressional requirement that 10 percent of all contracts awarded under a public works program go to "minority business enterprises."

Affirmative action was just one of many issues related to the economic policies of the 1970s. Following the retirement of Lyndon Johnson, no president gave the issue of economic inequality much attention. Richard

Nixon and his domestic strategists offered the poorest one-fourth of the population "benign neglect," while they courted the "forgotten American"—middle-class and lower-middle class citizens who worked hard and paid more than their share of taxes. Nixon also promised to slash national welfare expenditures and to inaugurate revenue sharing, a plan to dispense federal money in the form of discretionary block grants rather than as a part of prepackaged, nondiscretionary programs from Washington. The idea, part of Nixon's broader concept of a "new federalism," was supposed to encourage decentralization of authority in both planning and administration and to revitalize state and local government.

Not unexpectedly, reality lagged behind rhetoric. Although Nixon shut down Johnson's Office of Economic Opportunity and never did emphasize spending for social welfare, many of the Great Society's programs already enjoyed strong support from many members of Congress and from a variety of interest groups. As a result, expenditures for social welfare, measured as a percentage of the GNP, actually continued to rise under Nixon and then under Gerald Ford. By this standard, the growth was faster under two Republican presidents than under Lyndon Johnson, though these funds still failed to alleviate deeply rooted inequalities. Meanwhile, Nixon's promise to the "forgotten American" went largely unfulfilled as soaring inflation rates eroded most workers' real income.

President Jimmy Carter seemed most interested in procedures and planning than in broad policy arguments or political philosophy. Carter's first proposals for national action sounded no clarion calls for social justice but stressed managerial and technical issues—reorganization of the executive branch, streamlining of existing welfare programs, and new budget procedures. When confronted by energy problems, Carter did talk about energy as "the moral equivalent of war," but his "wartime" strategy followed rather conventional paths. Most important, the Carter administration's plans assumed that the old liberal *deus ex machina*—economic growth—could be restored and could provide, as it had in the past, a means of avoiding a direct confrontation with the problem of inequality. If, through the magic of new energy-producing technologies, the economic pie could once again expand, even the smallest slices would be bigger.

The Carter administration, however, was no more successful than the Nixon or Ford administrations in promoting real economic growth. Throughout the 1970s, under Republicans and Democrats, the American economy failed to perform as well as it had done in the 1960s—or even in the 1940s and 1950s. Although the United States still produced more than any other nation, the gap narrowed as America's economic productivity—its output per worker—grew more slowly than that of other industrial nations. Even Britain and Italy, countries with serious economic problems, could boast of higher productivity rates than the United States. At the same time that productivity languished, inflation flourished. The inflation rate for 1979 stood at nearly 14 percent, and the monthly rate for early 1980, when figured on a yearly basis, ran as high as 20 percent. According to one study, a family of four that had earned $13,200 in 1970 would have required an income of more than $25,000 to maintain the same standard of living in 1980. Although the salaries of most upper-income professionals kept pace with inflation, most American workers suffered a decline in their real income.

The nation's economic difficulties contributed to the unsettled political climate. In 1976 Jimmy Carter exploited the popular distrust of political institutions; as president, he became the victim, rather than the beneficiary, of popular cynicism about government. And in charting his political course he had to deal with a party structure that was undergoing constant shifts and sags. Just as the Goldwater defeat had proved only a temporary setback for the Republicans in the 1960s, Watergate marked merely a momentary downturn for the GOP in the 1970s. While the Republican party regrouped behind Ronald Reagan and its refurbished right wing, the Democratic party splintered into even more factions than it had in the late 1960s. Carter and his strategists successfully built their own electoral machine, but many Democrats, especially social activists, expressed little enthusiasm for Carter's domestic policies.

Even if he had been blessed with only political assets and no liabilities, Jimmy Carter would still have found it difficult to discover easy answers to the nation's economic woes. On economic questions there seemed no "conventional wisdom" to which Carter—or any president—could turn. The economist–social critic Herman Daly, for example, spoke for many advocates of the "small-is-beautiful" approach when he urged abandoning the old goal of economic growth in favor of a "steady-state economy," one that aimed at "sufficient wealth efficiently maintained and allocated, and equitably distributed—not maximum production." Other social critics also advocated major departures from the old liberal economic formulas. After surveying the growing pressures on the supplies of resources in the United States and in other nations, Richard J. Barnet predicted the onset of "the lean years." He urged greater government planning, reliance upon "soft" rather than "hard" energy technologies (solar energy in preference to nuclear energy, for example), and greater democratization of the national and international marketplaces. The socialist writer Michael Harrington joined Barnet in condemning the misuse of power by the giant multinational corporations. In the age of monopoly capitalism, Harrington argued, unemployment, inflation, and a stagnant economy grew out of decisions first made in corporate board rooms and then accepted by political leaders. America's economic ills, Harrington contended, reflected underlying structural problems, conditions rooted in the very nature of an oversized capitalist economy.

Other observers offered a much different analysis. According to neoconservative theoreticians such as Irving Kristol, traditional economists such as Milton Friedman, and representatives of large business corporations, economic problems could be traced back to the national government's interference in the marketplace and to "crushing" levels of taxation, especially upon businesses. They blamed huge government deficits, unnecessary environmental restraints, ill-advised safety regulations, and the general burden of governmental-required paperwork for stifling economic growth. (As the economist Lester Thurow pointed out, though, those countries with higher productivity *all* had much *more* governmental regulation than the United States.) These conservative writers promised no easy solutions, but they urged massive government deregulation and substantial tax cuts, measures calculated to stimulate the "supply side," that is the productive infrastructure of the economy. They also called for tighter control over the money supply and a sharp reduction of government borrowing to finance deficits which, they claimed, deprived private business of necessary loans for research and expansion. They insisted that their proposals were good not only for business but for all citizens. Conservatives did not ignore the issue of greater economic justice for the poor and for various minority groups; but the problems of the poor could only be solved, they argued, through the unleashing of American capitalism.

Even the more conventional liberal economists, to whom Carter ultimately turned, offered him a variety of approaches to the key problems of productivity and inflation. Although the president endorsed the Humphrey-Hawkins bill, which pledged that the White House would reduce unemployment to 4 percent by 1982, his economic advisers focused on fighting inflation. First, they bowed toward the arguments of the deregulators and sought to lower prices by ending federal regulatory structures, such as those in the transportation industry, that supposedly raised prices. And though the Carter administration rejected a thoroughgoing system of wage and price controls, it announced voluntary wage and price guidelines. Finally, Carter and his economic aides pursued a policy of tightening credit (thus raising interest rates) and of "cooling down" the economy. Carter's monetary policies did drive down the inflation rate—though it still hovered near double-digit levels—but they also generated rising unemployment and increased social tension. By the summer of 1980 the nation had slid into one of the worst recessions since the 1930s.

The Election of 1980

Lacking a broad base of political support and much experience in government, Carter seemed confused in his approach to domestic affairs. As Nixon had done with his "Berlin Wall," Carter ducked behind a small group of fellow Georgians, skillful political tacticians without any broad vision of national priorities. Confidence in Carter's performance, as measured by various public opinion surveys, steadily plummeted. By the time of the Democratic convention in August 1980, only 23 percent of the Gallup Poll's sample thought he was doing a good job. Carter's showing was even more dismal than that of Harry Truman during his final months in office or of Richard Nixon during the dog days of Watergate.

Yet Carter amazed most political pundits and recaptured the Democratic nomination. As the nation's commander in chief, he ironically gained support as a result of his own foreign policy problems. With Iranians occupying the American embassy in Teheran and the Soviets invading

Afghanistan, many Democrats rallied around their leader, even when his policies—such as admitting the Shah of Iran into the United States—had contributed to some of the problems. Carter also benefited from the liabilities of his major Democratic rival, Senator Edward Kennedy of Massachusetts. Although Kennedy enjoyed generally favorable coverage before he declared for the presidency—and after his capitulation to Carter—his vulnerabilities, especially his own personal problems, dominated the media while he was an active candidate. Many Democrats, pollsters discovered, distrusted Kennedy more than they disliked Carter. Even many who saw the president as something of a bumbler still considered him a decent and honest man. Finally, Carter effectively (ruthlessly, claimed the Kennedy camp) used federal patronage to build local ties. Although the White House lacked clear strategies for meeting domestic ills, it did dispense federal grants, both large and small, to Democratic mayors and governors. Thus, the Democratic National Convention of 1980 produced a curious result: Delegates warmly applauded the person they had rejected for the presidency, Edward Kennedy (and incorporated many of his proposals into their party's platform), but unenthusiastically renominated a candidate, Jimmy Carter, who seemed a sure loser in November.

Election day proved a disaster for Jimmy Carter and a serious setback for the Democratic party. The GOP's ticket of Ronald Reagan and George Bush carried 44 states, including most of those in Carter's native South, and captured 486 electoral votes. (Independent candidate John Anderson gained enough of the popular vote, 7 percent, to qualify for federal funds but failed to win any electoral votes.) Post-election analyses revealed that Reagan and Bush had cut into almost all of the traditionally Democratic voting blocs, especially union members, Jews, and white ethnic voters. According to one survey, 25 percent of those Democrats who voted supported Reagan. The oldest person ever elected to the presidency—Reagan was only a few months short of seventy on November 4, 1980—the former Governor of California even outpolled Carter among voters under thirty years of age.

At the same time, Reagan's Republican party showed that it had recovered from Richard Nixon and Watergate. The GOP gained twelve Senate seats and took control of the upper house of Congress for the first time since 1954. A number of prominent Democratic liberals—including George McGovern—were turned out of the Senate. Although the Democrats managed to hold onto the House of Representatives, the GOP still picked up thirty-three seats in the lower house. In many other ways, however, the presidential result represented more of a repudiation of Jimmy Carter than an affirmation of Ronald Reagan. Nearly half of the eligible voters did not vote for any presidential candidate, so that Reagan's 51 percent of the popular vote gave him the support of little more than one quarter of the potential electorate.

Reagan and his inner circle of wealthy advisers came to Washington in order to reverse the domestic political trends that had dominated the postwar political era. In contrast to Carter, for example, Reagan pledged not to reorganize governmental agencies but to dismantle at least some of them.

His secretary of interior promised he would not even listen to environmental "extremists," and Budget Director David Stockman suggested that most governmental welfare programs should be eliminated. The "new egalitarianism," Reagan's conservative supporters hoped, would be a thing of the past.

A master of political symbols, Ronald Reagan won rave reviews for presidential image-making. The lavish inaugural proceedings, generously sprinkled with designer gowns, rented limousines, and Reagan's old Hollywood friends, recalled the early days of the Kennedy administration; Reagan's speeches, which called for rebuilding "the American dream" and for overcoming fears of new approaches, suggested the self-confident optimism of Franklin Roosevelt; and the president's narrow escape from an assassin's bullet, only a few months after taking office, placed him in the fearless western mold of John Wayne, a pop culture hero often invoked by Reagan himself.

ASSESSING THE 1970s

Despite numerous attempts to offer a comprehensive historical vision of the 1970s, scholars have come to emphasize very different facets of this complex decade. To some, it exuded a spirit of aimlessness in both public and private life. In a much-debated report prepared for the Trilateral Commission, the political scientist Samuel Huntington linked this spirit to a "failure of leadership" that ultimately stemmed from "an excess of democracy." The egalitarian demands of the late 1960s and the 1970s, in this neoconservative analysis, overburdened both the political and economic systems.

Other observers also detected a sense of aimlessness but drew different conclusions from those drawn by Huntington. Finding a proliferation of "personal-growth" therapies, a spirit of self-absorption, and an apparent retreat from social concern among young people, Tom Wolfe (in a generally positive analysis) called the 1970s the "me decade." Pointing to similar trends, but interpreting the theme in a much less positive way, the historian Christopher Lasch saw the 1970s dominated by a "culture of narcissism."

Yet even Lasch, one of the decade's bitterest critics, could find other facets to the 1970s, including a remarkable growth of local, community-based self-help movements. Looking back upon the "splendid decade," William Braden of the *Chicago Sun-Times* called the 1970s a time of "grass-roots revival." In small ways, often far from the glare of the national media, the "me decade" may have produced as much, if not more, ferment for social change as the 1960s. In one sense, the social initiatives of the 1970s avoided the tactics of the 1960s, especially the penchant for substituting mass-mediated political spectacles for grass-roots organizing. Yet, in another way, social movements of the 1970s tried to build upon impulses of the 1960s, such as the community-action programs of the Great Society.

Great Society programs had encouraged ordinary citizens to participate in community projects. Some of these efforts, such as attempts to gain community control of neighborhood schools, failed to topple oversized and centralized bureaucracies. But other local efforts met with limited, sometimes even striking, success. Local arts programs contributed to a grass-roots cultural revival reminiscent of the 1930s. Neighborhood clinics, legal-aid offices, and recreational and counseling services became regular features of everyday life during the 1970s. Meanwhile, community organizing, a strategy pioneered by Saul Alinsky's school for "radicals" in Chicago, developed broader goals and spread to other parts of the country and ideological spectra.

The nature of the 1970s, as well as the legacy of the 1960s, also encouraged the emphasis on grass-roots, self-help efforts. In a dialectical process, the growth of outsized institutions in an age of economic instability encouraged local counter-responses. In a trend thoroughly representative of the decade's complex reaction to oversized institutions, small "group homes," in which people with disabilities could be helped in a community and family setting, came to offer alternatives to the large and costly mental health facilities of the oversized medical establishment.

Many different groups participated in the decade's grass-roots approach to social change. Many African-Americans, for example, found it difficult to maintain, let alone expand upon, the economic gains of the late 1960s and early 1970s. In 1978 there were twice as many blacks out of work as a decade earlier. The same year, the median income of African-Americans stood at only 55 percent of the median income of whites, the same percentage as in 1965, the year LBJ unveiled his Great Society. The concentration of poor blacks in decaying parts of central cities became even more intensive: By the late 1970s more than half of the nation's black population lived in the oldest, shabbiest portions of the inner cities. Meanwhile, the national black organizations and their white allies found it difficult to get significant new help from the federal government. Consequently, many concluded that the most effective strategy involved a return to their own communities and a renewed effort to develop new institutions and a spirit of self-help. Jesse Jackson, the controversial leader of Operation PUSH, headed one such movement in Chicago; Detroit became another city in which local organizations grew significantly; and a black-owned news service provided an alternative community network for small African-American newspapers across the country.

Members of other ethnic groups adopted similar strategies. During the late 1970s increased immigration (both legal and illegal) and high birth rates swelled the Hispanic population—largely Mexican-American and Puerto Rican—to about 6 percent of the nation's total. Without significant help from Washington or from local governments, many Hispanics turned to community-based institutions. César Chavéz continued to be the most charismatic Mexican-American leader, especially in rural areas. But others, such as Ernie Cortes of Los Angeles' United Neighborhood Organizations, worked to organize urban communities, often relying upon the resources and personnel of the Catholic Church. Native American leaders also eased away from dramatic clashes with white authorities, placing a new emphasis on self-sufficiency.

Efforts at local organizing were not limited to nonwhite minorities. Confronted with rampant inflation and with the continued surge of urban-development projects into their communities, the "unmeltable" white ethnics mobilized. In ethnic neighborhoods as well as in other parts of cities and suburbs there was a significant growth of local neighborhood associations. According to one estimate, there were literally millions of such organizations. Many rural areas experienced similar examples of new grass-roots organizations. In Minnesota and Wisconsin, for example, farmers joined with city folk to protest the spread of nuclear power plants and the proliferation of high-voltage power lines.

Moreover, ferment went beyond ethnicity and geography. Older Americans, one of the country's fastest-growing minorities, banded together to make "gray power" a reality. Feminist groups formed collectives that attempted to restructure everything from women's health care to literary forms to small business organization. Some blue-collar workers organized to demand more control over their job sites. Recognizing that new technologies might threaten not only their jobs but also their health, advocates of "workplace democracy" challenged claims about "corporate responsibility" and distrusted government inspectors who supposedly oversaw health and safety standards. In a few cases, groups of workers became owners, taking over plants that were being abandoned by large corporations and running them as worker-community ventures. Consumer-cooperatives also flourished. In response to pressure from cooperative supporters, Congress created in 1978 the National Consumer Cooperative Bank a special institution that could provide loans to this new form of grass-roots enterprise.

What was the larger significance of all these self-help, grass-roots movements? Given the political fragmentation of the 1970s, many answers were close at hand. Advocates of local activism saw such movements as tangible signs of a "new citizenship." At the backyard and neighborhood levels, people seemed ready and willing to reassert control over their lives and challenge big government, big business, and other established institutions of power. Such movements, their celebrants proclaimed, heralded the birth of new forms of community and a "new populist" spirit.

Other analysts and even participants in such movements were not so sanguine. They worried that individual organizations tended to focus upon single issues and to ignore a larger vision of the entire nation's future. The successful effort by the gray-power lobby to extend the mandatory retirement age to seventy, for instance, only seemed to place another hurdle in the paths of women and minority workers. And pressures to raise Social Security benefits for the elderly resulted in Congress placing new tax burdens on younger wage-earners. Some political observers complained that "single issue" pressure groups only further fragmented the political process and delayed formulation of general policies aimed at a broad socioeconomic reconstruction. And, finally, even many people associated with these new efforts remained suspicious about linking up with other grass-roots organizations. In the western states, Native American groups hesitated to cooperate with ranchers and farmers—longtime enemies—in a common stand on environmental and energy issues. Similarly, organizations of blacks and white ethnics traditionally drew a good deal of their individual energies from antagonistic rather than from cooperative relationships.

The highly publicized taxpayer revolts of the late 1970s highlighted the ambiguous nature of this new localism. On the one hand, the tax revolt seemed to confirm fears about the dangers of single-issue activism. Gaining momentum after Californians enacted Proposition 13 (a 1978 measure that cut state property taxes in half) and marching behind neopopulist attacks on big government, tax-cut leaders sold a seemingly simple proposal that had complex consequences, especially to poor people who faced cutbacks in public services. On the other hand, studies of tax-revolt movements showed that rank-and-file rebels were not mean-spirited or selfish. Using the democratic process to fight what they considered inequitably apportioned taxes and unresponsive governmental bureaucracies, these taxpayers did not want low taxes as much as they wanted more equitable rates. They wanted better, not less, government. They still accepted the broad outlines of the postwar welfare state and endorsed government programs to meet "real" social needs.

Yet, in the context of the fragmented politics of the 1970s much of the neopopulist tax-cutting failed to translate into any broader idea of community. Indeed, Ronald Reagan, with his individualistic vision of a new capitalism, seemed a major beneficiary of the impulse toward localism and self-help. Distrust of government institutions, especially at the national level, gave the Reagan administration an opening to argue against extending, and even for dismantling, social welfare programs. Although many social activists continued to see community organizing and grass-roots action as the best path toward social change, the ascendancy of Reaganism at the national level would change the ways in which political and social issues would be defined in the 1980s.

SUGGESTIONS FOR FURTHER READING

Garry Wills's book *Nixon Agonistes* (rev. ed., 1980) is a good single-volume introduction to Richard M. Nixon and his place in postwar political culture. More recent entries in the Nixon bookshelf include Bruce Odes, ed., *From the President: Richard Nixon's Secret Files* (1989); Stephen Ambrose, *Nixon: The Triumph of a Politician, 1962—1972* (1989); and Herbert Parmet, *Richard Nixon and His America* (1990).

On Watergate and the broader ethos of secret government, see Peter Schrag, *Test of Loyalty* (1974); Theodore White, *Breach of Faith* (1975); Athan Theoharis, *Spying on Americans* (1978); Frank J. Donner, *The Age of Surveillance* (1980); L. H. LaRue, *Political Discourse; A Case Study of the Watergate*

Affair (1988); and Stanley I. Kutler's *The Wars of Watergate* (1990) on the constitutional dimensions of Watergate.

On international issues during Nixon's presidency and the rest of the 1970s, see Paul Sigmond, *The Overthrow of Allende* (1977); John Stockwell, *In Search of Enemies* (1979); Walter LeFeber, *The Panama Canal* (1979); Barry Rubin, *Paved With Good Intentions: The American Experience with Iran* (1980); Franz Shurmann, *The Foreign Politics of Richard Nixon* (1987); Penny Lernoux, *Cry of the People* (1980); Gaddis Smith, *Morality, Reason, and Power: American Diplomacy in the Carter Years* (1986); Raymond Garthoff, *Detente and Confrontation: American-Soviet Relations from Nixon to Reagan* (1985); and Garry Sick, *All Fall Down: America's Tragic Encounter with Iran* (1986).

On the political culture of the 1970s, see Peter Caroll, *It Seemed Like Nothing Happened* (1983), a general history of the entire decade; Harry C. Boyte, *The Backyard Revolution* (1980); Thomas Ferguson and Joel Rogers, *The Hidden Election* (1981); Walter Dean Burnham, *The Current Crisis in American Politics* (1982); Martin P. Wattenberg, *The Decline of American Political Parties* (1984); Gillian Peele, *Revival and Reaction: The Right in Contemporary America* (1984); Theodore Lowi, *The Personal President* (1985); Mark E. Kann, *Middle-Class Radicalism in Santa Monica* (1986); and Thomas Ferguson and Joel Rogers, *Right Turn: The Decline of the Democrats and the Future of American Politics* (1987).

Betty Glad's *Jimmy Carter* (1980) is a highly critical work, while Carter's own reminiscences are entitled *Keeping Faith* (1982). See also Charles O. Jones, *The Trusteeship Presidency: Jimmy Carter and the United States Congress* (1988); and Erwin Hargrove, *Jimmy Carter as President* 1989).

On the complex issues raised by the new equality debate, see Christopher Jencks, *Who Gets Ahead* (1979); Paul Blumberg, *Inequality in an Age of Decline* (1980); Lars Osberg, *Economic Inequality in the United States* (1984); Philip Green, *Retrieving Democracy* (1985); Charles Harr, *Fairness and Justice Law in the Service of Equality* (1987); Jay MacLeod, *Ain't No Makin' It: Leveled Aspirations in a Low-Income Neighborhood* (1987); Peter L. Berger, *Capitalism and Equality in America* (1987); Nathan Glazer, *Affirmative Discrimination: Ethnic Inequality and Public Policy* (rev. ed., 1987); Kenneth L. Karst, *Belonging to America: Equal Citizenship and the Constitution* (1989); Sara Evans and Barbara J. Nelson, *Wage Justice: Comparable Worth and the Paradox of Technocratic Reform* (1989); Irving Solomon, *Feminism and Black Activism in Contemporary America* (1989); and Karen Hansen and Ilene Philipson, eds., *Women, Class, and the Feminist Imagination* (1990).

Chapter Eleven

Nostalgia and Nostrums: The United States In the 1980s

In his 1952 dystopian novel *Player Piano*, Kurt Vonnegut imagined a governmental system run by faceless technicians and presided over and legitimated by a movie-actor president. Media politics, he seemed to predict, would merge with democratic forms until the myth-making functions of electoral campaigns had wholly separated "politics" from "governance." Less than thirty years later the United States did have a screen star as its chief of state, and Ronald Reagan promised that his presidency would inaugurate a new "conservative" era in American life, comparable to the "liberal" era ushered in by Franklin Roosevelt's New Deal.

Whatever his limitations in Hollywood, Reagan became a skilled political performer; his old screen charm bloomed into a quality that had been lacking during the Nixon-Ford-Carter years—presidential charisma. After Nixon's perpetual five o'clock shadow, Ford's stumbling, and Carter's furrowed brow, Reagan brought many Americans, and the media, a welcome change: an easy smile, rugged good looks, quick one-liners. Even frequent misstatements of fact in press conferences, incredible gaffes, evidence of corruption by close associates, and policies with clearly adverse consequences failed to dent his image. Reagan, Representative Patricia Schroeder commented, was a "Teflon-coated president"—nothing stuck to him. Reagan instinctively knew how to tap into many popular dreams and national myths; this "great communicator" knew how to use the media. His was a presidency of symbolism, and—in that sense—perhaps did represent a new age in American politics in which specific information and coherent ideas were less important than a general, cheerful, reassuring image.

One set of images upon which Reagan skillfully drew stemmed from the early days of the cold war. The Soviets, he warned, operated an "evil empire." Reagan's world was populated by good guys ("freedom fighters") and bad guys (communists, except the Chinese, and "terrorists," a new category of villains that emerged in the 1980s). He designed foreign policies with all the subtlety of a child's Saturday morning cartoon show.

In domestic policy, Reagan's symbols, ironically, often contradicted the reality emerging from his policies. He often recalled a folksy, Norman Rockwell-style America of small towns, limited government, hardworking people, and old-fashioned morality. Yet his farm policies brought a rural crisis that threatened to shut down Main Street; he led an attack upon labor unions, affirmative action, and assistance to the working poor; and he increased government spending to bring on soaring deficits. Reagan's politics and his appeal largely rested upon nostalgia for a small-scale past, but his policies accelerated the giantism that had come to characterize American life in the 1960s and 1970s.

The Reagan years were ones of paradox: While the president's policies encouraged the concentration of power (and thus the feelings of powerlessness) in everyday life, he himself tapped the yearnings for simpler times in which "the people," not governmental bureaucrats, were in control. It was revealing that, after eight years of living in the White House and presiding over rampaging budget deficits, Reagan could still rouse his supporters by denouncing "the big spenders in Washington."

SOCIOPOLITICAL CONFLICT IN THE 1980S

Plebiscitary Politics

Admirers credited Ronald Reagan with sparking a movement that promised to take both society and politics "back to the future." Certainly, he did help rekindle faith in national institutions and capabilities. But even though he attracted millions of votes and dominated the political culture of the 1980s, controversy swirls around the precise nature and legacy of the "Reagan Revolution."

Supporters depicted Reagan's successive electoral victories as seminal postwar events. In this view, his 1980 defeat of Jimmy Carter and 1984 drubbing of Walter Mondale, self-proclaimed heir of Hubert Humphrey, signaled the end of the welfare-state liberalism that had been associated with Humphrey, Harry Truman, Lyndon Johnson, and the dominant wing of the Democratic party.

Yet, upon closer examination, the idea of any political "revolution" seems suspect. First, the appeal of welfare-state liberalism had been waning since the late 1960s; except for Social Security, primarily a program for the elderly, most welfare-state initiatives never enjoyed broad or deep support among the electorate. And after governmental regulations of the late 1960s and early 1970s, such as environmental and consumer protection laws, impinged upon business decision making, a corporate-sponsored counterattack began to tap a deep antigovernment sentiment, especially among people who felt pressed by both taxes and inflation.

Though a Democrat, Jimmy Carter had also drawn strength from this backlash and anticipated some of Reagan's anti-Washington stance. When he began running for the White House in 1974, it should be recalled, Carter campaigned as an outsider who would bring small-town virtues and common sense to the wicked national capital. His bid, in fact, drew support from Pat Robertson and Jerry Falwell, prominent members of the Reagan coalition during the 1980s. In some ways, Reagan's domestic stance simply refined and extended Carter's anti-establishment populism.

Mondale's ill-advised attempt to revive the old Democratic vision contributed to Reagan's lopsided 1984 reelection victory. In this sense, the presidential contest of 1984 featured two candidates who looked backward, toward different perspectives of an older, pre-1970 America. While Mondale recalled the welfare-liberalism of Humphrey and Johnson, Reagan promised the kind of prosperity and international power associated with Harry Truman, Dwight Eisenhower, and John Kennedy. Against the backdrop of economic recovery, an unprecedented peacetime military buildup, and political apathy, more voters bought Reagan's nostalgic vision than bought Mondale's.

Presidential elections, however, do not simply turn on imagery, let alone on clashes between well-defined and coherent programs. Increasingly, presidential sweepstakes have become "yes or no plebiscites" on the personalities of the candidates. In large part, the post-1960s disarray in party alignments and emergence of high-tech, mass-mediated campaigns targeted at independent and swing voters encouraged plebiscitary presidential elections. The 1972 campaign, when Richard Nixon's strategist distanced his reelection effort from the Republican party, provided the model.

As both a challenger and an incumbent, Ronald Reagan primarily ran as Ronald Reagan and only secondarily as a Republican with a coherent philosophy and concrete program. In 1980, his victory depended upon the strong "no" vote against Jimmy Carter, the highly unpopular incumbent; in 1984, Reagan gained both millions of "yes" votes for his personal performance and millions of "no" votes against Mondale, who seemed a decent-enough person but a dull, uninspiring personality. Going against political tradition, Reagan's landslide 1984 victory failed to carry his party; the GOP gained only fourteen seats in the House—remaining the minority party there—and actually lost two seats in the Senate. Finally, claims that the 1984 reelection validated any Reagan agenda must explain why exit polls suggest that 20 percent of those who voted for the president in 1984 had "serious" doubts about his domestic policies and that another 20 percent did not care much about any issues at all.

The peculiar nature of his own support, especially among the New Right, intensified Reagan's need for plebiscitary, rather than issue-oriented, elections. If the postwar Democratic party splintered over questions of race and culture, the post-1976 Republican party was divided by issues of religion and culture. Activists from the New Right, especially those from fundamentalist and evangelical religious groups with Democratic heritages, lacked deep loyalties to the GOP and, oftentimes, to Reagan himself. With ties to large corporate interests and his Hollywood background—which privately inclined him to more flexible attitudes on social-cultural-religious issues such as AIDS and abortion than many of his supporters—Ronald Reagan was never the New Right's favorite; he simply seemed the most conservative political figure with the best chance to win the White House. Despite an alliance with the New Right, Reagan's independent campaigns and his ambiguity on a variety of issues again suggested that he led no mass social or political movement. Some of the most vocal leaders of the New Right, such as North Carolina's Jesse Helms, continually criticized Reagan's policies as insufficiently conservative, especially on issues such as abortion and prayer in school.

On a variety of other questions, Reagan also tested the faith of many of his supporters. What held Reagan's political coalition together, apart from his personal charm and tough rhetoric on foreign policy, were the familiar denunciations of welfare-state programs. Repeated calls for "getting government off our backs" and for lowering tax rates carried a broad, somewhat nostalgic, appeal. But when it came to pushing specific proposals through Congress or implementing policy via the federal bureaucracy, the Reagan administration achieved relatively little of the New Right's cultural agenda, and it trimmed, rather than completely dismantled, most domestic programs. Moreover, from a cultural standpoint, the White House looked more often to the lavish life styles of Hollywood and corporate board rooms than to the small-town culture of traditional conservatives and the New Right. To the extent that a loosely imagined set of preferences and prejudices amounted to a political and economic program, Reaganism envisioned a high-tech, fast-living, big-corporate style of neocapitalism fundamentally at odds with the Main Street values of many old-style Republicans and the New Right.

Reaganomics: The Boom

Reagan's economic advisers promised to stimulate the most "efficient" and "productive" segments of the economy. According to the theory of "supply-side" economics, government policies should target producers, giving them incentives to save and invest, thereby increasing the supply of goods available for consumers and decreasing the inflationary pressures of the 1960s and 1970s. In addition, deregulation of the economy (which actually began in the airline industry during the Carter years) and revision of tax rates (an idea first embraced by the Kennedy administration) became centerpieces of Reaganomics.

Reaganomics initially seemed a disaster as the nation slid into its worst recession since the 1930s. The official unemployment rate soared to nearly 11 percent; industrial output plummeted; businesses, especially family-run farms in the Midwest, failed at alarming rates; the nation's GNP actually declined (or, in the language of economics, "grew at a negative rate"); its balance of trade deficit reached record highs as did the federal government's budget shortfall. In the third year of Reagan's presidency, the budget deficit topped the $200 billion mark, while the accumulated national debt broke the trillion-dollar barrier. Although Reagan had promised balanced budgets, his economic advisers downplayed the deficit and other gloomy statistics; they confidently predicted that, once inefficient producers had been wrung out of the economy and labor costs had been pushed down, supply-side economics would produce both a recovery and a more competitive economy.

Indeed, by late 1982, some economic indicators were beginning to turn around, and the promised "Reagan boom" seemed at hand. Budget deficits remained high, and Congress finally enacted the Gramm-Rudman-Hollings Act of 1985, which tried to legislate automatic budget cuts. But, in light of the general economic growth, even many of Reagan's severest critics thought deficits were an issue that should be ignored; balancing budgets could mean a return to recession just when recovery was underway. Deficits, after all, provided economic stimulation and helped avert hard choices about spending.

Most economic indicators improved dramatically during the mid-1980s. By 1987 the Dow Jones Industrial Average stood at more than 2700, an all-time high. Even the "Black Monday" crash of October 19, 1987, which saw the Dow Jones set another record by plummeting 508 points in a single day, failed to dampen either general confidence in the Reagan boom or the stock market; economic expansion continued, and Wall Street fought back from Black Monday. By the end of Reagan's presidency the Dow Jones average again topped the 2700 level.

Pundits created a new symbol for the success of Reaganomics: *Newsweek* dubbed 1984 the "Year of the Yuppies"—young, upwardly mobile, urban professionals who, supposedly, had been hippies during the 1960s. Allegedly marking the end of that decade's idealism, these aging baby boomers were represented, especially in films such as *The Big Chill* and *Wall Street*, as consumption-hungry profit-maximizers, crass materialists with no time for moral and social issues. In addition to seeking a career in "the fast lane," the stereotyped Yuppies focused on health spas, cholesterol levels, foreign-car dealerships, fern bars, trendy restaurants, and clothing boutiques. And as part of their general ethic of "wanting it all," according to one canard, calculating Yuppies even sweated themselves "into shape" for eating; in this way, they could enjoy the best in wine and food without having to suffer the usual drawbacks.

Advertisers certainly believed in the Yuppie. Racks of new "life style" magazines featured vacation, decorating, fashion, and cooking tips for the upwardly mobile. Even Yuppie children became targets, as Saturday morning TV schedules aggressively pushed products, such as "Gobots" and "Transformers," disguised as cartoon shows. Just as suburbanites had once symbolized the affluent culture of the 1950s, the Yuppie became a central symbol of Reaganomics: At their 1988 National Convention, Democrats were encouraged to express contempt for eight years of Reagan by buying buttons that said "Die Yuppie Scum."

The Reagan era also brought a new culture of extravagance (rather than one of mere 'Yuppie affluence). How could the very wealthy, who basked in the glow of Reaganism, hope to burn off their extra money? The media offered role models. *Lives of the Rich and Famous* showed TV viewers how movie stars and corporate moguls lived in elegance. A young business tycoon from New York City became both an omnipresent media celebrity and a consumer product himself; an office tower, a gambling casino, an airline, an apartment palace, an autobiography, and even a board game all carried the name of Donald Trump. Malcom Forbes, publisher of the financial magazine bearing his name, rivaled Trump, especially when he motorcycled with Hollywood stars, threw a multimillion dollar birthday bash for himself in Morocco, and published *Forbes'* annual tally of the nation's richest 400 individuals, a counterpart to *Fortune* magazine's more traditional list of the top 500 corporations. Supermarket tabloids splashed the comings and goings of Trump and Forbes across their front pages; being a tycoon again seemed in fashion.

Many people—not simply Yuppies, the very wealthy, and large corporations—participated. Family-owned businesses thrived: At the end of the 1980s, one-third of the Fortune 500 companies were family-owned, and 60 percent of the nation's GNP was generated by family businesses. The percentage of women working outside their homes steadily increased, and members of ethnic minorities with marketable skills found improving job prospects. Some evidence even suggested that general economic prosperity, as Reagan's supporters had predicted, trickled down and benefited the poor. During the early 1980s, before the full impact of the drug epidemic, the violent crime rate in urban neighborhoods declined, while the percentage of African-Americans graduating from urban high schools increased. Celebrants of Reaganomics conceded that this expansion had not been "perfect," but they deemed its problems easily manageable.

Reaganomics: The Bitter Legacy

Critics thought otherwise and worried about the legacy of eight years of neocapitalist economics. Labor unions lost much of whatever countervailing clout they once possessed. Reagan's successful 1981 crushing of PATCO, the union representing air traffic controllers, set the tone. New conservative appointees to the National Labor Relations Board (NLRB) gave this national regulatory agency a decidedly anti-union tilt, and the federal courts, constantly restocked with Reagan-nominated judges, also showed little inclination to support organized labor. Meanwhile, the decline of the nation's old industrial infrastructure inevitably eroded the labor movement's traditional base, and organizers made slow progress in unionizing the growing service sector. By 1990, barely 15 percent of workers belonged to a union. The famed job expansion under Reagan had produced disproportionate numbers of nonunionized, low-paying service jobs.

Critics of Reaganism also worried about the nation's corporate structure. Much of the new wealth of the 1980s, for example, rested on a decade of corporate mergers, many of which were financed by "junk bonds," securities without the kind of backing required of more traditional commercial paper. The junk-bond craze of the 1980s, in fact, barely survived Reagan's presidency. Ivan Boesky, one of the decade's most celebrated merger-moguls, plea-bargained a reduced jail term by agreeing to testify against other leading financial figures. Allegations of massive fraud, including insider stock market trading, rocked the entire merger-mania culture. And in 1990, the giant financial institution of Drexel Burnham Lambert—which had specialized in arranging corporate mergers by floating junk bonds—declared bankruptcy. According to the gloomiest financial analyses, the worst, in the form of severely depreciating values for junk bonds, was yet to come.

Meanwhile, the savings-and-loan industry, which had apparently prospered after relaxation of government regulation in the early 1980s, also barely staggered into the 1990s. Many S&Ls overindulged on junk bonds and high-risk real estate schemes; others squandered money in old-fashioned ways, such as fancy living by owners and top management. Whatever an institution's particular poison, the entire industry—and the taxpayers who had to rescue it—faced tough times. According to one estimate, the government bailout plan for S&L, hastily enacted in 1989, threatened to cost the average taxpayer $3000 over the course of the 1990s.

Even this massive rescue operation failed to stem the tide of failures. The official list of savings institutions judged "sick," "ailing," or simply insolvent grew steadily. By the early 1990s, following a decade of reduced economic involvement by Washington, the S&L bailout ironically made the United States government the single largest operator of financial institutions in the country. And, given the amount of junk bonds that shaky S&Ls owned, the federal government also stood to become the largest holder of these questionable securities.

The Legacy of the 1980s on Everyday Life

Insolvency was not simply a problem for the savings and loan industry. During the 1980s, corporations, family businesses, and private citizens all came to depend more heavily than ever before on borrowed money; businesses relied upon complex debt-restructuring deals, while ordinary consumers counted on their credit cards. The explosion of credit allowed

Ronald Reagan's presidency built upon his image as a movie hero, particularly playing upon western themes. Source: *National Archives.*

Americans to run up record levels of personal indebtedness. In the 1970s, the average citizen spent 65 percent of his or her income, after purchasing necessities, on paying the interest charges on borrowed money; by the end of the 1980s, the comparable figure going to debt service reached 90 percent! Bankruptcy proceedings, not surprisingly, also soared; ordinary people and former wheeler-dealers, such as the flamboyant Texan John Connelly, had to concede that their personal boom had ended.

Moreover, even the everyday life of the fabled Yuppie was not all fern bars and BMWs. Free-spending Yuppies undoubtedly existed, but they hardly represented the way of life of most baby boomers or young professionals. Less than 5 percent of the baby-boom generation earned enough— or could borrow enough—to live affluently; more than half of the baby boomers actually made under $20,000 a year. Even for young professionals on the rise, everyday life meant long work schedules and complex juggling of family responsibilities. According to one analysis, many young professionals suffered from deep fears about whether or not they could continue to prosper and from nagging insecurities about whether or not their sacrifices were even justified. Such pressures and doubts bore down especially hard on women trying to crack male-dominated professions. The use of the term *Yuppie* as an epithet, one suspects, was sometimes employed to disparage and discourage young women who were struggling to follow nontraditional career paths.

Considerable evidence suggests that many young professionals, especially women, never held the political conservative values widely attributed to Yuppies. Although immersed in private issues, such as raising families and finding meaningful work, young professionals also worried about social questions such as abortion, day-care services, foreign policy, and the environment. And on issues such as government support for day-care, comparable pay for women, and aid to the *contras*, opinion studies suggested that so-called Yuppies seemed no more, and probably less, inclined toward conservative positions than other people.

While most young professionals found upward mobility difficult, many other people found their economic status stagnating or slipping during the 1980s. Although severe inflationary pressures subsided, the average worker's take-home pay, according to Labor Department statistics, actually declined slightly during the Reagan boom. Between 1978 and 1988 the average wage rose to over $9 per hour, but, when adjusted for inflation, it slipped against the real cost of living. Women's wages continued to lag behind those of men, minorities behind those of whites. As a consequence of dominant wage structures, many young working-class people, even families with two incomes, could not enter the home-buying market; for the first time since World War II, the percentage of people owning their homes began to drop.

The decade also saw significant transfers of wealth toward the already wealthy. According to careful studies of pre-tax income shares, between 1980 and 1985 the annual income portion going to the richest 20 percent of the population increased by about $44 billion, while the remaining 80 percent saw their share decrease by about the same amount. At the end of the 1980s, even the staunchly conservative *Business Week* magazine marked the growing income gap and shrinking middle class as a potentially serious national problem.

Many forces contributed to the growing inequality in income distribution. The flood of the young, baby-boom generation into the work force, together with the rising percentage of working women, swelled demand for entry-level jobs, even at lower wages. But critics could also assign at least part of the blame to Reaganomics. Reductions in tax rates, for instance, primarily benefited the top-income levels; according to one study, the wealthiest 1 percent of the population watched their taxes decrease by 25 percent during the 1980s, while those in the bottom 40 percent saw virtually no tax relief.

Similarly, cutbacks and spending reductions for social programs, part of the effort to "get government off people's backs," took their toll. Programs for public employment and job training, which had never been extensive, were trimmed back in the 1980s. And the disappearance of jobs in the declining industrial-manufacturing sector meant that many people, newcomers as well as workers who had been laid off, lacked the special knowledge and credentials to compete for high-paying jobs in other areas. In the early 1970s, for example, young workers with a high-school diploma still earned 86 percent of what the college-educated received; by the late 1980s, the percentage had dropped to about 65 percent.

The ethnic dimensions of this disparity were heightened by the declining number of African-American and Latino children, raised in middle- and low-income families, who were enrolled in college. At a time when high-school completion rates were increasing, the percentage of low-income African-Americans who went on to college dropped by nearly 10 percent during the early and mid-1980s; the comparable figure for Latinos fell by about 7 percent. After 1986, data showed an increase in the total number of African-Americans enrolled in colleges and universities, a figure that largely reflected increased enrollment by middle-class students at private institutions. Meanwhile, college-completion rates for other groups, especially Asian-Americans, rose during the entire decade.

The "Invisible" Legacy of the 1980s: Social Issues

The 1980s seemed to glorify acquisition of wealth even as it brought increasing desperation to the lives of the nation's poor. Variously labeled as the "underclass," the "truly disadvantaged," and the "persistently poor," millions of people could only glimpse the Reagan boom from afar. Throughout the decade, city streets filled with homeless people. Some suffered either from drug dependency or mental disorders—"deinstitutionalization" of the mentally impaired, a "reform" of the 1970s, oftentimes substituted bus and subway stations for state hospitals. But many others, including entire families, had simply been pushed out of the job or housing markets into the streets and into temporary shelters. Of the more than 30 million people officially classified as "poor," more than one-third, 13 million, were children; nearly a half million children were estimated to be among the homeless.

Although homeless people became a familiar part of urban streets, the 1980s also recalled Michael Harrington's earlier observations about the invisibility of poverty-related problems in an affluent society. Only some spectacular event, such as the March 1990 fire in which eighty-seven Caribbean and Latin American residents of New York City perished at an unlicensed social club, seemed to focus the mainstream media's attention on everyday social and economic issues. In contrast to media stereotypes, for example, many of the desperately poor did not live in identifiable, poverty-dominated ghettoes but could be found scattered throughout different communities, the most segregated of which were defined by ethnicity or by age. Similarly, nostalgic stereotypes of rural life continued to conceal harsh realities. The rural poor, in fact, found it more difficult to escape poverty than their urban counterparts. Although some experts hoped that the worst of the problems—farm foreclosures, bank failures, and personal despair—were receding toward the end of the 1980s, the fact that many farm families relied on food stamps and surplus commodities remained one of the grim ironies of the decade.

Both scholarly studies and muckraking magazines told even bleaker stories. A general, twenty-year follow-up to the Kerner Commission Report, entitled *Quiet Riots*, charged that "unemployment, poverty, social disorganization, segregation, family disintegration, housing and school deterioration, and crime" were greater problems in 1988 than they had been in 1968. Welfare benefits, which had risen during the 1960s and early 1970s, leveled off and then declined; when adjusted for inflation, the average welfare recipient suffered a cut of about 25 percent in the value of payments and food stamps during the 1980s.

The quality of social services aimed at the poor also dropped. One specialized study, which tracked African-American men during the early 1980s (before AIDS and crack-cocaine presumably made life much worse), found that "black men in Harlem were less likely to reach the age of 65 than men in Bangladesh," one of the poorest countries in the world. The nation's infant mortality rate remained higher than any industrial country, while New York City's rate (which had been declining in the 1960s and 1970s) actually rose during the 1980s, an increase that public health experts attributed to inadequate health- and social-service facilities and to soaring crack use among poor women.

The "feminization of poverty" was another trend of the 1980s. According to some studies, one-half of people living in poverty also lived in families headed by women. While studies by conservative social scientists, especially Charles Murray's *Losing Ground*, blamed the welfare system, particularly AFDC payments, for encouraging women to stay on welfare rather than to look for work, other analyses highlighted structural and psychological explanations. The absence of both well-paying, entry-level jobs and positive role models made reliance on declining welfare payments seem many poor women's best alternative. As one mother who wanted employment explained, "I get so nervous and scared going out looking for a job . . . I never know how to talk." And welfare, unlike most low-wage jobs, provided coverage of basic health care needs, an essential consideration especially for women with small children.

People across the political spectrum agreed that the welfare system needed reform so that it did not perpetuate women's poverty and dependency but could, instead, assist women in gaining employment skills. The Family Support Act, passed in 1988, required states to implement some form of "workfare," new employment requirements for women on welfare. At best, "workfare" reforms might assist women in attaining job skills and make provision for childcare and health care needs. At worse, "workfare" might become another program that stigmatized its participants as lazy or "bad." Dominant cultural institutions sent poor women very mixed messages: The "good" mother, so many cultural images still implied, stayed home with her young children. Clearly a major challenge for those favoring welfare reform involved designing work requirements that were not punitive but constructively geared to promoting greater self-sufficiency. Questions about how social and employment policies should deal with gender issues received relatively little attention in either public-policy or mass-mediated discussions.

The "Visible" Legacy: Drugs, AIDS, and Abortion

Unlike the class and gender questions, some social issues did attract extensive media attention. Both Ronald Reagan and his successor, George Bush, pledged all-out wars against drug dealers and drug use. Nancy Reagan headed a much-publicized, but largely ineffectual, campaign to get potential drug users to "Just Say No." Bush appointed tough-talking William Bennett, who had been Reagan's spokesperson on higher education, as a "drug czar" and charged him with stopping the flow of illegal drugs into the country and confronting the violent gangs that distributed them. Yet only a few blocks from the White House, drug dealers continued to peddle their wares, relatively free from official interdiction of any kind; no community, including small towns and wealthy suburbs, escaped drug dealers and problems of substance abuse.

Similarly, rich and poor alike faced a deadly new threat, AIDS. Acquired immune deficiency syndrome actually designated several types of invariably fatal viruses that were usually sexually transmitted. Throughout the decade, both the unknown and the celebrated died from AIDS; Hollywood's Rock Hudson, *Gunsmoke's* Amanda Blake ("Miss Kitty"), the Old Right's Roy Cohn, the New Right's Terry Dolan, and the fashion world's Halston were a few of the prominent people who succumbed.

Everything about AIDS seemed controversial. Initially, the disease primarily affected homosexual males, and this may have inclined socially conservative public officials to downplay efforts to fight, or even to publicize, its spread. Similarly, association of AIDS with people from Africa and the Caribbean encouraged both misinformation and prejudice. Even scientists pursuing a cure became embroiled in nasty disputes over how AIDS was spread, which people were at greatest risk, and what team of scientists deserved the credit (and the money) for isolating its probable viral source. Meanwhile, activists complained that Washington was moving far too slowly to develop and license drugs that promised at least some relief from the ravages of AIDS.

Faced with intransigence and delay, gay and lesbian activists mounted self-help measures. Charging the Reagan administration with kowtowing to the New Right, by initially dismissing AIDS as a "special-interest" issue, gay leaders urged "safe sex" and monogamous relationships. Homosexuals continued, however, to oppose the kinds of sexual strictures favored by the New

Right. Although right-wing libertarians opposed any governmental inter-ference with gay and lesbian life styles, most religious conservatives de-nounced homosexuality as sinful and urged use of criminal penalties, a stance that received the blessing of the United States Supreme Court in *Bowers* v. *Hardwick*. Reagan's own Surgeon General, Dr. C. Everett Koop, enraged the New Right by acknowledging the reality of sexual relationships outside the bounds of heterosexual marriages and promoting condoms as sensible precautions against the spread of sexually transmitted diseases.

The politics of AIDS was overshadowed by the furor over abortion. Here, New Right activists continued to preach a simple message: The gov-ernment must say "no" to abortions, save in exceptional cases such as rape, incest, or some life-threatening danger to a pregnant woman. Although opinion polls suggested that most people favored legal abortions under more flexible regulations, the anti-abortion forces pressed their case through both direct action, including the kind of civil disobedience pio-neered by the civil rights movement of the 1950s and 1960s, and more conventional political activities.

The anti-abortion, or "pro-life," coalition increasingly hoped that the Supreme Court would overturn the 1973 *Roe* v. *Wade* decision. In the fall of 1987, "pro-choice" forces joined with civil-liberties groups in successfully blocking Reagan's confirmation of Robert H. Bork, an outspoken opponent of liberal activism by the Court, to the High Bench. By a 58–42 margin, the Senate rejected the nomination of Bork, who many expected would provide the crucial vote needed to overturn *Roe* v. *Wade*. Reagan lost another nomi-nee, who withdrew after revelations of pot smoking during his law-professor days; but he finally obtained, rather easily, confirmation of Anthony Kenne-dy, a quiet Californian who was probably more of a Reagan-style conserva-tive than Bork was.

Justice Kennedy did, in fact, provide a key anti-abortion vote in the *Webster* case, a 1989 decision that further politicized the abortion issue. Here, by a 5–4 margin, the Supreme Court upheld a Missouri statute that severely limited women's access to legal abortions, thus opening the door for further state restrictions. But Justice Sandra Day O'Connor, another Reagan ap-pointee, refused to join the four-justice bloc ready to overturn *Roe* v. *Wade*. As a result, both pro-choice and pro-life forces mobilized, all across the country and even in United States territories such as Guam, for state-by-state legislative and court battles over the abortion issue. Meanwhile, gaining access to safe and legal abortions—became more difficult than it had been in several decades.

THE NEW COLD WAR

During the campaign of 1980, Ronald Reagan portrayed Jimmy Carter as a weak leader presiding over the erosion of American power abroad. Reagan promised to "restore" respect for the United States by aggressively confronting the Soviet's "evil empire" in every part of the world. Returning to the rhetoric and assumptions of the cold war, in which the world was simplistically viewed as a bipolar battleground between the forces of good and evil, Reagan's early foreign policy stressed unilateralism, militarism, and crusading anticommunism. During his first term, the president launched a massive military buildup, abandoned détente with the Soviets, dragged his foot on arms control negotiations, installed new missiles throughout Europe, pulled out of the United Nations Educational, Scientific, and Cultural Organization (UNESCO), beefed up the CIA, sent troops to Lebanon and Grenada, funded a mercenary army to fight the Marxist government of Nicaragra, and publicly provided "covert" funds for anti-Marxist troops in Angola and Afghanistan. Reagan seemed to tap a latent desire, after the nation's defeat in Vietnam, to assert American power aggressively and globally.

A massive military buildup, unprecedented in peacetime, became the dominant feature of the Reagan presidency. Huge new expenditures, accompanied as they were by tax cuts, tripled the national debt, increased the government's share of the GNP to over 25 percent, and transformed the United States from the world's principal creditor into its largest debtor. Critics charged that such large deficits undermined the nation's economic health, but Reagan requested deeper and deeper cuts in domestic social programs to alleviate the deficits. He refused to acknowledge what his first budget director, David Stockman, discovered: that reduction of social spending could never come close to bridging the tremendous gap between military buildup and tax cuts.

In Reagan's vision, activism by the federal government was appropriate in the area of military protection, not social welfare. The "Reagan revolution," which the president aspired to implant deeply in American life, required curtailing the government's domestic regulatory and welfare functions while its main enterprise became expansion and management of the national-security sector. The administration aimed at enlarging both nuclear and conventional capacity. It ordered more of the highly controversial MX missiles and B-1 bombers and enlarged its force of old-fashioned Trident submarines. Over grass-roots protests throughout Europe, America's NATO allies succumbed to Reagan's pressure and deployed American-made Pershing II and cruise missiles in Western Europe. Billions of dollars went into the military payroll and for modernization of equipment and bases. And billions more simply bought waste and corruption. Congressional investigations revealed gross abuses and mismanagement in the military-industrial sector: They found both massive (and sometimes deliberate) cost-overruns by large contractors and small-time price gouging, including cases in which suppliers charged the Pentagon hundreds of dollars for common, inexpensive hardware-store items.

During his first term, Reagan used arms control talks primarily to help fuel this massive buildup. As a candidate, Reagan condemned Carter's SALT II accords, which Congress never ratified but which both the United States and the USSR unofficially observed. As president, he opened new negotiations, which he relabeled START (Strategic Arms Reduction Talks), and then argued that only enlarged military budgets and an arms buildup could produce successful negotiations. But arms control proved politically popular at home, and a rapidly growing movement, which urged a "freeze" on nuclear weapons, blasted the administration for its apparent opposition to slowing the arms race.

Carrying military competition to outer space became the most important—and most controversial—part of Reagan's military agenda. In 1984, after several private meetings with Dr. Edward Teller, the "father of the H-bomb," Reagan surprised even close advisers by proposing a "Strategic Defense Initiative" (SDI), a space-based system that would supposedly shield the United States from incoming warheads. Widely called "Star Wars," SDI would theoretically provide more protection than the traditional policy of deterrence through "mutual assured destruction" (MAD).

Controversy over SDI mounted, as scientists and politicians calculated its staggering costs (perhaps a trillion dollars!) and weighed its practicality. Many scientists warned that the computer software to operate a comprehensive space defense could never be made reliable. The dependability of advanced space technology became an even larger issue after the spring of 1986, when the space shuttle *Challenger*—whose mid-morning launch enjoyed well-publicized, live television coverage—exploded in midair, killing all seven of its crew. Moreover, some strategic analysts pointed out that a missile defense system would only prompt the other side to build more technologically elaborate missiles, thereby greatly escalating the arms race without improving national security. SDI also divided the scientific community; some scientists pledged to accept no contracts for government work on SDI while others welcomed the new pipeline of lucrative contracts. Though incredibly costly and probably impractical, the SDI proposal, which was quietly scrapped after Reagan left office, managed to dominate foreign policy and budget debates for several years, and it loomed as a major obstacle to arms reduction agreements with the Soviets.

The militancy with which the Reagan administration pursued its new cold war policies contributed to the intensity of longstanding conflicts in the Middle East, Africa, and Latin America. In these areas, historic racial, ethnic and religious divisions, as well as economic hardship associated with the foreign debt crisis, underlay political turmoil. But Reagan's hard-line advisers formulated policy through a prism in which every setback for United States influence meant an advance for the Soviets. In many ways, though, the USSR was itself increasingly beleaguered: It was bogged down in a brutal, unpopular, and costly war in Afghanistan; it was challenged by the popularity of Poland's anti-Soviet Solidarity movement; it was saddled with the expensive aid still being supplied to Cuba; and it was straining to maintain its superpower status on the basis of a staggering, stagnant economy. Still, Reagan's picture of the Soviet Union as a nation making aggressive gains worldwide provided the backdrop for assertive, militaristic policies by the United States.

It was in Lebanon that the Reagan administration first showed its readiness to deploy military power. In 1982, Israeli forces invaded Lebanon in order to destroy and disperse the Palestine Liberation Organization (PLO). Lebanese Moslems, allied with Syria and backed by the Soviet Union, fought both the Lebanese Christians and the Israeli occupiers. After arranging Israeli withdrawal, the Reagan administration dispatched 1600 American troops as part of a multinational force. But Moslem fighters renewed the struggle, now against troops from the United States. After 241 American troops were killed by a suicide commando mission in October 1983, domestic criticism of Reagan's Lebanese policy mounted. American military presence had aggravated, not lessened, violence and factionalism in Lebanon. Early in 1984, an election year, American troops withdrew, and Syria consolidated its influence over Lebanon. The Reagan administration's plan to limit Syrian gains and stabilize Lebanon through military power proved an unmitigated failure.

Moreover, the perception among Arabs that America's policy in the Middle East was almost identical to Israel's brought additional problems. Some Palestinian groups, fragmented and further radicalized after their expulsion from Lebanon, stepped up the use of terrorism and found support in Libyan leader Muammar Qaddafi. As Qaddafi railed against Zionism and the United States, Reagan denounced the Libyan leader as a terrorist and a "flake." In the spring of 1986 Reagan ordered the bombing of Libya, as part of a broader plan to eliminate Qaddafi from the scene. Bombs did considerable damage and killed Qaddafi's daughter, but his government survived. In the meantime, negotiations to end the spiraling bloodshed among Israel and its neighbors—by moving toward some resolution on the Palestinian problem—stalled.

Violence elsewhere in the Middle East mounted, as Iran and Iraq engaged in a prolonged and devastating war, and militant Islamic groups seized a number of hostages from Western countries they viewed as enemies. Publicly refusing to negotiate for hostages, for fear of encouraging more kidnappings, America's policy in the Middle East continued to drift throughout Reagan's presidency.

Consequently, the president's advisers sought to find easier, less risky places to assert military power. In counterpoint to the misapplication of force in Lebanon, Reagan scored a popular victory by invading the tiny Caribbean island of Grenada in October 1983. Justified as necessary to safeguard American medical students, who were allegedly endangered by a leftist, revolutionary regime, the invasion really aimed at overthrowing an unfriendly government that looked to Castro's Cuba for inspiration and material support. The task was quickly accomplished, though later assessments by military specialists uncovered major flaws in the Grenada invasion; only a Pentagon-imposed blackout on news coverage delayed reports of unnecessary casualties, bungled intelligence-gathering, and uncoordinated battle strategies. But Reagan's popularity soared. Many people seemed eager to forgive the Lebanese fiasco and to bask in what the administration proclaimed as a clear-cut military success closer to home.

In Africa, Reagan's anticommunist crusade brought a stepped-up commitment to rebels seeking to overthrow the Marxist government in

Angola and a more sympathetic policy toward white leaders who were determined to maintain apartheid in South Africa. The Reagan administration sided with the South African government in denouncing the African National Congress (ANC) as communists, even though it represented the oldest black political organization in South Africa and enjoyed widespread support internationally and within the black community in South Africa. Reagan's assistant secretary of state for African affairs labeled his South African policy "constructive engagement," arguing that American support for the white South African government would promote change in its racial policies faster than punitive measures.

Constructive engagement brought the administration into growing conflict with many black African leaders and sparked mounting dissatisfaction at home. South African Anglican Bishop Desmond Tutu, winner of the Nobel Peace Prize in 1984, charged that Reagan's sympathy toward white South Africans significantly worsened the situation for blacks and called for a change. Meanwhile, grass-roots street protests throughout the United States, smaller-scale versions of the civil rights and antiwar protests of the 1960s, pushed Congress and then the president into adopting at least some limited economic sanctions against South Africa. In 1985 an executive order curtailed loans to the South African government, prohibited importation of South African gold coins, banned most transfers of nuclear technology, and forbade export of some computers.

The Reagan administration centered its anticommunist crusade against Nicaragua. Determined to oust Nicaragua's Sandinista government—because of its Marxist leanings, its pro-Cuban stance, and its desire to shed historical dependence on the United States—Reagan's Latin American policy experts employed the by-now classic techniques of covert action: an economic offensive induced shortages and discontent; a propaganda campaign portrayed the Nicaraguan government as nothing but a Soviet or Cuban client; and support and training for a counterrevolutionary army, called the *contras*, kept the Nicaraguan government under siege. Meanwhile, the United States expanded its military pressence in neighboring Honduras and conducted ominous, massive "training exercises" throughout the Caribbean area, clearly threatening invasion of Nicaragua.

Congressional opposition and adverse public opinion, however, restrained the president. Domestic opposition intensified after revelations that the United States had mined Nicaraguan harbors (technically an act of war) without congressional assent. And the United States suffered a blow to its international prestige when the World Court confirmed Nicaragua's charges that American aggression violated international codes of conduct (the Reagan administration denied that the court had any jurisdiction in the matter). In 1984 Congress cut off military (though not humanitarian) aid to the *contras*, after considering the mounting evidence of their terrorist tactics and corruption.

Undeterred, Reagan's policymakers redoubled their efforts. They stepped up economic destabilization measures against Nicaragua and secretly pressed foreign governments and ultraconservative millionaires to fund the *contras'* military efforts. In 1986 the fund-raising effort took a bizarre turn: Lt.-Col. Oliver North, an aide in the office of the National Security Adviser who was directing the secret fund-raising and arms-supplying effort to the *contras*, offered to sell weapons to Iran both in exchange for release of American hostages in the Middle East and to gain funds that could be then diverted to the *contras*. The head of the CIA, the national security adviser, and other top officials apparently knew of the scheme; in effect, an inexperienced, oftentimes ineffectual young officer received broad authority to run his own foreign policy. Oddly, it was Reagan's close adviser and attorney general, Edwin Meese, who, at a news conference, inadvertently revealed the peculiar connection between North's Iran and *contra* projects.

When news of the Iran-*contra* scandal hit the front pages, Reagan's Watergate seemed at hand. (The media dubbed it "Irangate.") For a variety of reasons, the revelations of the affair, gradually emerging in televised congressional hearings during the summer of 1987, deeply discredited Reagan's foreign policy. First, North's plan violated the spirit of the congressional ban against military aid to the *contras*. Second, it contradicted Reagan's strong public stands both against negotiating with terrorists for hostages and against providing Iran with military assistance in its ongoing war with Iraq. The Reagan administration seemed to be carrying out policies directly contrary to its public posture. Third, the whole approach to foreign policy raised serious questions about presidential leadership. As details of the scandal emerged, the president first seemed to deny knowledge of the deals but then accepted responsibility without seeming to comprehend the legal ramifications and policy contradictions.

Although Col. North enjoyed a brief run as a kind of folk hero, the image of Reagan's presidency suffered. Throughout lengthy investigations—by Congress, by a presidential panel, and by a special prosecutor—the public increasingly glimpsed an administration that was fragmented, excessively secretive, and even lawless. North and National Security Adviser John Poindexter, among a number of others, were convicted on criminal charges related to the affair. The former movie star turned "Teflon president" suddenly looked old, confused and barely in charge. More and more people questioned the wisdom of his policies.

SUDDEN THAW

During the last year and a half of the Reagan presidency, the new cold war, which the president had stoked with inflamed rhetoric and hard-line policies, suddenly thawed to a point that approached meltdown. In a dramatic irony, the Reagan presidency reversed course and took unprecedented steps toward détente.

In 1987, the administration that had launched the biggest military buildup in history signed a major arms control treaty. A year earlier, at a summit conference in Reykjavik, Iceland, the first summit of the Reagan presidency, the Soviets had advanced the surprising proposal that both countries cut their nuclear weapons by half. Negotiations over such dramatic cuts, however, stalled over the issue of SDI, Reagan's pet project that the Soviets wanted to end. Finally, in December 1987 a treaty reducing Intermediate Range Missile Forces (IMF) was approved at a summit held in Washington, D.C. The IMF only slightly altered overall strategic balances, but the agreement was unprecedented in its political and symbolic significance. Both sides agreed to eliminate short- and medium-range missiles from Europe (including those that the early Reagan administration had pushed so hard to install) and approved on-site verification procedures, safeguards the Soviets had previously resisted. IMF signalled a major shift away from the arms race of the cold war.

What triggered this sudden thaw? For both countries, the reasons were much the same: grass-roots pressure to redirect government priorities; top leaders who began to take a more pragmatic, less ideological, approach to policy; and urgent domestic economic problems.

In the United States during 1987, several trends jolted the Reagan administration into its foreign policy reorientation. Grass-roots concern over nuclear weapons had grown rapidly, and politicians were becoming increasingly sensitive to popular fears about superpower conflict. As foreign policy anxieties mounted, the Irangate scandal dramatized the excesses of secret government and the dangers of a heavily ideological, do-anything-necessary attitude.

Moreover, new advisers gained Reagan's ear. By the end of 1987, many of the officials who had shaped policy in the early Reagan years—among them William Casey in the CIA, Caspar Weinberger and Richard Perle at the Defense Department, John Poindexter and Oliver North in the office of the National Security Adviser—were no longer in the administration. New appointees, such as Howard Baker and Frank Carlucci, were less committed to anticommunist crusading and less beholden to the ultra-right wing of the Republican party, which had been so influential in the early Reagan years.

Perhaps most importantly, economic problems got the attention of business and policy elites and shook public confidence in the consequences of Reaganomics. Nearly everyone agreed that both the yawning budget deficit and the adverse balance of trade could portend a national security threat greater than communism: the threat of long-term economic decline. Academic publications and the public press trumpeted dire warnings about the end of the "American age." A scholarly history book, *Rise and Fall of the Great Powers* by Paul Kennedy, shot to the top of the best-seller list and helped popularize the theory of "imperial overreach." Historically, heavy military spending had caused the decay of powerful nations, and this seemed to be the fate awaiting the United States in the late twentieth century. The *New York Times Magazine*, in an issue that featured Paul Kennedy and other prophets of America's decline, pictured the United States as a aged, balding eagle, supported by a cane. Such economic worries, combined with the Democratic victories in the 1986 elections, eroded congressional support for such weapons systems as SDI, allowing the Soviets to negotiate arms limitation without insisting on formal assurances of SDI's termination. As the public and policy elites became increasingly concerned over the deficit and trade balance, support for détente and arms control became more evident.

Changes in the Soviet Union also set the context for reduced tensions. Mikhail Gorbachev came to power in the USSR as part of a younger generation committed to major structural transformations in the communist system. Announcing policies of *glasnost* (a more open society) and *perestroika* (economic restructuring and liberalization) at home, Gorbachev also championed arms control and détente abroad. His initiatives brought him sympathetic coverage from the world press. As the image of "Gorby" as a forward-looking international leader blossomed, the Reagan administration seemed more and more a captive of the old and dangerous cold war thinking.

Gorbachev, of course, was as much the result of changes in the Soviet Union as their cause. By the late 1980s, the Soviet economy was in chaos, environmental damage was alarming, and the system simply could no longer afford the expense of maintaining the cold war and managing an increasingly restive empire. In Eastern Europe, deteriorating economic conditions and the advancing age of the Soviet-allied leadership portended a coming crisis for communist regimes. The Soviet's attempt to impose a client government on Afghanistan proved so costly and unpopular that Gorbachev finally withdrew Soviet troops, and the USSR's other international commitments also came under reconsideration. Moreover, Gorbachev and his reformist advisers realized that the economic integration of Western Europe, projected for 1992, would leave the Soviet Union and its communist allies falling farther and farther behind in economic development. Restructuring (*glasnost* and *perestroika*) needed to begin immediately, or the USSR's economic and imperial decline might be irreversible.

Leaders in both the United States and the Soviet Union finally acknowledged that the world was no longer bipolar. The robust economies in Japan and Germany, the projected integration of Western Europe, and rapid development in "Pacific rim" areas such as Korea and Southeast Asia began to reshape geopolitical and strategic thinking. The idea of a U.S.–Soviet cold war became an outmoded construct in a rapidly changing world order; and domestic and foreign policies had to make adjustments. Governments seemed to chase transformations as much as they led them.

The Election of 1988

The turnabout in foreign policy, occurring shortly before the presidential election of 1988, removed many issues from the center of political debate. The Reagan legacy seemed to fit on every side of foreign policy issues, and the Democrats lacked firm ground. Most Democrats neither wanted nor were able to outflank Reagan in cold war crusading. Yet with the progress on arms control and the mellowing of the Soviet threat, the Reagan administration could also claim credit for détente and a safer world. Both George Bush and Democratic nominee Michael Dukakis, the governor of Massachusetts, tried simultaneously to project "toughness" in foreign policy yet to endorse the easing of the cold war.

The presidential election of 1988 resembled other recent contests: It turned more on the personalities and the symbols identified with the individual candidates than on policy differences. Dukakis, an uninspiring campaigner in the Walter Mondale mold, cautiously talked about reversing the Reagan animus against social programs but offered no startling new proposals of his own; rather, he primarily presented himself as a "competent" economic manager who could bring the "Massachusetts miracle" to Washington. While stressing his years as Reagan's loyal vice-president, especially his emphasis on voluntarism (symbolized by the image of "a thousand points of light"), Bush also promised a "kinder, gentler America." The controversial selection of J. Danforth (Dan) Quayle, an inexperienced and apparently uninformed senator from Indiana, as his running mate gave Bush only momentary problems. Advised by tough, young GOP strategists, such as Lee Atwater (the first head of any major party who could play the electric guitar), Bush's media managers portrayed Dukakis as big on taxes, soft on crime, and the captive of special interests (such as pro-choice forces and Dukakis's former rival Jesse Jackson). Their candidate, in contrast, pledged no new taxes and stressed his reverence for national symbols, particularly the "right to bear arms" and the Pledge of Allegiance to the flag.

Pundits differed on the meaning of Bush's comfortable—426 electoral votes to 112, 40 states to 10—victory over Dukakis in November. Noting that most Democrats, including liberals closely identified with social issues, had fared much better than Dukakis, supporters of Jesse Jackson faulted the Democrat's tepid campaign strategy; an aggressive, left-leaning effort, in their analysis, would have ignited the imagination of millions of nonvoters who, then, could have carried a progressive Democrat into the White House. Even analysts on the political left doubted this interpretation. According to most surveys, nonvoters tended to see issues in about the same way as those who did cast ballots; thus, any effort to mobilize the "disenfranchised" risked a further backlash against a national Democratic party that was already too closely identified with cultural issues of the 1970s. The traditional, middle- and working-class Democrats, in the opinion of most observers, continued to vote for their party's state and congressional candidates but also continued to distrust their presidential candidates. According to some analysts, Bush's victory suggested that Republicans would retain the White House for at least several elections to come; others insisted that the bland Dukakis had come close to winning a number of key states, thus showing that a better candidate could reverse recent GOP victories in the presidential sweepstakes.

All pundits, however, agreed on one thing: Increasing reliance on big money from political action committees (PACs) and on television meant that national politics tilted decisively toward incumbents and away from two-party competition. In 1988, virtually every member of Congress who ran for reelection emerged victorious, and fifty-eight members who ran unopposed still collected $14 million in PAC campaign funds. Meanwhile, more than 80 percent of all congressional winners polled at least 60 percent of the vote, suggesting that only a small minority of races involved real two-party competition. In this context, George Bush, the first sitting vice-president to go on to the White House since Martin van Buren in 1836, looked forward to enjoying an eight-year stay at 1600 Pennsylvania Avenue.

The Summer of 1989

Bush hardly settled into the Oval Office before a chain of dramatic events reshaped international affairs. For at least two years it had been obvious that the cold war order was about to unravel, but no one anywhere could have predicted the rapidity of change that began in the summer of 1989.

In late 1988 Mikhail Gorbachev had, in effect, renounced Leonid Breshnev's doctrine forbidding any nation from renouncing communism. "Freedom of choice is a universal principle," Gorbachev declared. And Eastern Europeans quickly tested his words. Poland ousted its communist government in favor of a new one based upon the popular, noncommunist labor movement Solidarity. East Germans dismantled the Berlin Wall, forced their communist government to resign, and moved quickly toward reunification with West Germany. Czechoslovakians, Hungarians, Romanians, and Bulgarians all mounted massive street demonstrations, tossed out their communist rulers, and then struggled to establish new systems with market economies and parliamentary governments. A few months before, winds of liberalization had swept China, but the Chinese government abruptly halted the movement, killing thousands of student protestors in Tianemen Square in Beijing and tightening its grip over social and economic life. Such repression, though, did not come in Eastern Europe; there, most countries enjoyed a fairly peaceful transfer of power.

Americans seemed dazzled by the pace of events. "No one was expecting the Eastern bloc to go out of business in a month," one State Department official exclaimed. "It's as though there is a fire, and we are chasing the trucks to the scene." Some saw opportunities: McDonald's quickly opened restaurants in Budapest and then in Moscow; *Playboy* became the first American magazine sold in Hungary.

The abatement of the cold war reverberated in events throughout the world. In Africa, tensions in some trouble spots had already eased. Long-negotiated settlements finally brought independence to Namibia and the beginning of withdrawal of Cuban troops from Angola, both areas in which cold war tensions had exacerbated and prolonged disputes. Early in 1990, the South African government recognized the African National Congress, the black nationalist group it had long labeled as communist, and freed its most prominent leader, Nelson Mandela. Another startling thaw came in

Nicaragua, where the Sandinista government, which the United States had long tried to undermine, held a free election and was voted out of power. The new government and the Sandinistas both talked of trying to work toward national reconciliation. Clashing interests and ideologies remained in all of these places, but confrontation—at least in public rhetoric—went out of fashion.

As the Soviet leaders became increasingly preoccupied with internal matters, including movements toward independence or automony in the Baltic states and other regions of their far-flung empire, the Bush administration began to shape a new foreign policy for a post-cold war world. The Secretary of defense projected a slowed pace of defense spending, and members of Congress began to talk hopefully about a "peace dividend." Still, if the Soviet threat seemed to be diminishing, Bush's policymakers pointed to new foreign dangers, particularly the importation of drugs and the power of foreign drug cartels. The military, once skeptical of playing a role in the so-called war against drugs, became more intrigued with its possible new mission as its budgets, no longer automatically buoyed by the waters of the cold war, came under challenge.

The Bush administration did turn to the military for the opening salvo in its antidrug campaign. Bush ordered the invasion of Panama, the installation of a government friendly to the United States, and the arrest and extradition of the Panamanian dictator, General Manuel Noriega. The Reagan administration had previously indicted Noriega on drug trafficking charges and tried vainly to force him out of power through economic coercion. Although Reagan's tactics nearly destroyed the Panamanian economy, Noriega only tightened his own political grip and denounced Yankee meddling. Despite fears that Noriega, who had once worked closely with the CIA, might embarrass the United States by exposing intelligence secrets, the Bush administration decided on military action against the general. Not only did American intervention in Panama gain Bush wide popularity at home and reestablish a friendly government with which to complete the gradual transference of the Canal to Panama, but it seemed a warning of strong action to other drug dealers in the hemisphere.

Other U.S. military actions against drugs, such as an attempt to blockade the coast of Colombia in order to interdict drug shipments and to support aerial destruction of coca fields in Peru, became increasingly controversial. Drug-exporting countries urged the United States to pay attention to the laws of supply and demand: to reduce consumption at home and to become more attuned to incentives that might cause coca producers to shift to other cash crops. As tension rose, however, new domestically produced synthetic drugs grew in popularity. The futility of going after the producers of drugs and blaming foreign nations for an alarming domestic trend became manifest.

Besides drugs, another candidate for successor to the cold war was the environment. No less a figure than George Kennan, the so-called father of the cold war containment doctrine, now ranked environmental degradation as the most pressing threat to national security during the 1990s.

Environmental dangers stemmed from many different causes. Scientists documented deterioration in the life-protecting ozone layer. Human practices that made desert out of productive land spread famine in Africa and elsewhere. Rain forests, which are needed to clean and produce oxygen for a healthy planet, suffered accelerating destruction. Water systems and animal habitats came under attack from acid rain and chemical poisons. Perhaps most ominously, experts debated whether or not the planet was beginning to experience the onset of the dreaded "greenhouse effect"—a global warming caused by the heat from industrial processes—that could alter climate patterns and dramatically disrupt the daily lives of every person on earth.

It was in this context that Earth Day II, the twentieth anniversary of what had been a small, consciousness-raising festival held in 1970, became an elaborate global event in April 1990. In one sense, Earth Day II offered the kind of star-studded spectacle that increasingly marked mass-mediated culture: Hollywood and rock music stars were the headliners.

International drug cartels and environmental hazards, however, were quickly overshadowed as the most pressing of post-cold war problems when, in August of 1990, Iraq launched a surprise invasion of Kuwait. The Middle Eastern tinderbox—a volatile mix of oil politics, colonial legacies, Arab-Israeli hatreds, Palestinian grievances, disparities between rich and poor—heated up and quickly assumed global proportions.

Iraq's leader Saddam Hussein saw the invasion of Kuwait as part of his broader ambition to raise the market price of oil and to establish Iraqi leadership over the Arab world. Kuwait, he argued, had been historically part of Iraqi territory. The United States, together with most of the rest of the world including other Arab countries of Egypt and Syria, quickly denounced the invasion. As Iraqi troops menacingly amassed near the border of Saudi Arabia, the United Nations voted in favor of economic sanctions against Iraq. Mounting the nation's biggest mobilization since World War II, President Bush rushed American military power to protect Saudi Arabia and cut off supplies to Iraq. The day-to-day headlines of Saddam Hussein and President Bush exchanging insults strikingly revealed the obsolesence of cold war patterns and the emergence of new international divisions.

THE CULTURE OF THE 1980s

The Culture of Nostalgia

Culture remained an arena for political and social battles during the 1980s. Nostalgia for products and images from the 1940s, 1950s, and early 1960s—a trend commonly associated with Reaganism—dominated mass culture. The popular board game *Trivial Pursuit* rewarded players for remembering the kind of shirts worn by the Beach Boys or the name of Ann

Margaret's first motion picture; a special set of questions for baby boomers focused entirely on cold war nostalgia. Meanwhile, two of the decade's most popular new TV programs, *Family Ties* and *The Cosby Show*, offered updated, upbeat versions of the family sitcom of the 1950s.

Overall, the major TV networks reprised the past. Programs with innovative story lines and production techniques, such as *The Lou Grant Show* and *Hill Street Blues*, received cancellation notices or retreated to safer formats. The hottest "new" network products of the early and mid-1980s, prime-time soap operas such as *Dallas* and *Dynasty*, merely adapted a familiar daytime format to nighttime viewing. By the 1990s, programmers for the three major networks seemed running out of both ideas and viewers, as surveys showed people tuning them out in order to watch on their own VCRs or cable television.

Cable television itself relied heavily upon familiar formats. ESPN, for example, initially pioneered all-sports programming by introducing viewers to unfamiliar TV fare, such as Australian-rules football and table tennis; but by 1990, ESPN largely beamed a steady diet of boxing, football, baseball, and basketball. The "premium" cable channels, such as HBO and Showtime, did underwrite some original productions, and Nickelodeon developed new programs for children. But even these channels primarily reran older products, drawn from TV and Hollywood, in order to fill their time slots. *Leave It to Beaver, I Love Lucy, Father Knows Best*, and other black-and-white artifacts from the 1950s became cable-TV staples. Similarly, Ted Turner's new cable channel, TNT, drew upon his company's vast holdings of Hollywood films. (Although TNT allowed film buffs to see many long-neglected treasures of early Hollywood, Turner also enraged traditionalists by striking new, colorized prints of many classic pictures in order to update them for contemporary viewing tastes.)

Meanwhile, back in Hollywood, classical motion-picture genres, which had begun their comeback in the late 1970s, continued to thrive. George Lucas and Steven Spielberg, blockbuster filmmakers who had been raised on TV and the film fare of the 1950s, lovingly recalled their youth with expensive epics about monsters, rock-and-roll, alien empires, and powerful heroes. In two of the three *Indiana Jones* thrillers, the Lucas-Spielberg hero even fought those most familiar of cinema villains, Adolph Hitler's Nazis.

Nostalgia meant big business for male heroics. Sylvester Stallone's "Rocky," a clubfighting journeyman in his film debut, went upscale in the 1980s, eventually winning the "heavyweight championship"; by *Rocky IV*, he even joined Ronald Reagan's fight against the "evil empire" and battled a communist superman—right on Soviet soil. Stallone's simplistic patriotism also garnered huge box-office revenues in his cycle of *Rambo* films, violence-filled epics featuring an embittered Vietnam vet. Though Stallone himself had missed the real Vietnam, his Nautilus-tuned character announced that defeat in Indochina—which *Rambo's* version of history attributed to journalists and cowardly politicians—could be avenged by a properly motivated, unencumbered super hero. "Rambo" joined an entire platoon of heavily muscled, tight-lipped vigilantees who created so much celluloid havoc that Hollywood devised a whole new rating category, PG-13, for films in which macho avengers violently blasted their villains.

With the increase in movie mayhem, women's roles generally fared badly. Although pictures aimed at specialized audiences (such as John Sayles's *Liana* and Yvonne Ranier's *The Man Who Envied Women*) might feature strong female characters and feminist themes, major distributors considered "women's films" risky ventures. Hollywood's moguls preferred women who stood by their men and stood up for traditional values, as they did in *Tender Mercies* and *Country*. Women who stepped out of narrowly drawn gender lines risked becoming the butt of cruel jokes—or worse. An antifeminist backlash was unmistakable in the new genre of "slasher" films: Women were not only sex objects but also potential victims for sadistic knife-and-chain-saw artists. Mainstream films were not exempt. Box-office successes such as *Jagged Edge* and *Fatal Attraction* carried strongly antifeminist undercurrents; similarly, the blockbuster *Batman* featured the casual brutalization of women by Jack Nicholson's anti-hero, "the Joker."

Successful, mass-market films that touched upon women's liberation generally soft-pedaled their messages. The highly publicized *Lives and Loves of a She-Devil*, though adopted from a celebrated feminist novel and featuring two strong women stars (Meryl Streep and Rosanne Barr), attracted only bad reviews and sparse audiences. In contrast, Jane Fonda's *9 to 5* leavened its feminist politics with fantastical and slapstick humor. *Tootsie*, in some ways the most successful "feminist" film hit of the 1980s, cast Dustin Hoffman in the picture's titled "female" role.

Much, though certainly not all, popular music also revolved around nostalgia and male fantasies. All across the country, radio stations switched to "oldies" formulas; in larger markets, every decade from the 1940s to the 1970s could claim at least one spot on the radio dial. Risking once again the hazards of "the road," aging rock superstars mounted new nationwide, and even international, tours. The Who and the Rolling Stones attracted the most attention and money, but many other middle-aged men, now sans drugs and young groupies, retraced paths of former glories. The top-selling African-American artist of the 1980s, Michael Jackson, bet much of his personal fortune on nostalgia when he purchased the rights to most of the Beatles' tunes. Many of his own songs expressed a kind of Peter Pan-ish retreat from social concerns into childlike innocence. And Jackson also joined millions of other people in making visits to Disneyland, the Magic Kingdom of the 1950s, a favorite pastime.

Reworking the Past

But looking backward could also take peculiar twists, not all of which meant nostalgia for the pre-Vietnam era. The music critic Nelson George, for example, coined the term "retroneuvo" to characterize pop music that borrowed, often very consciously, from the past in order to create fresh new sounds; retroneuvo, according to George, appreciated, rather than simply reprised, the postwar musical heritage. At their best, Prince and even Michael Jackson wove numerous musical traditions in exciting and novel productions.

Steven Spielberg's original *Back to the Future* (1985) captured some of the retroneuvo spirit. Here, Marty McFly, a young man trapped in a dull and strife-torn family, is hurled, by errant technology, back to the pre-rock-and-roll 1950s. There, he finds his mother-to-be is attracted to him, rather than to his nerdy father-to-be. After "inventing" rock music, punching out the local hoods, and uniting his parents-to-be, Marty (played by Michael J. Fox of *Family Ties*) scrambles back to "the future," the 1980s of Ronald Reagan. Having placed an imprint upon the past, Marty finds the present remade: Because of *his* intervention, "history" will be transformed for the better.

Different people found very different messages in *Back to the Future*. Reagan quickly invoked its fascination with high-technology, borrowing a line from the movie for his 1986 State of the Union address: "Where we're going, we don't need roads." The president's critics found another Reagan-like message in the film—an ability to imagine that technology and simple optimism can solve complex, deeply rooted problems. Yet, in other ways, *Back to the Future* also expressed disquietude about both the present and the past that Reaganesque culture celebrated. Rather than simply offering an escapist trip to the 1950s, it also suggested a deeply felt desire for a significantly different present and implied that past mistakes, especially those made during the immediate postwar era, had helped to produce the dilemmas of the 1980s.

People found other, more complex examples of creatively reworking the past in cultural products identified as "postmodern." An ill-defined but important cultural style that began to take shape in the 1970s, the postmodernism of the 1980s and early 1990s enthusiastically embraced forms from the past. Especially attracted by mass culture, postmodernists admittedly recalled the familiar, but in new and unusual ways. Postmodern architects, for example, rejected the so-called international school, with its sleek, straight-lined, steel-and-glass skyscrapers. Ridiculing these "glass boxes" as soulless and pretentious monuments to industrial and cultural elites, postmodernists celebrated the architecture of the ordinary, including highway billboards, Las Vegas casinos, and almost anything with elaborate ornamentation. In the AT&T building in New York City, for instance, the architect Philip Johnson turned away from his internationalist past and designed a novel structure that resembled a nineteenth-century grandfather clock, topped by something that recalled Chippendale furniture of the eighteenth century.

Both approving and hostile critics agreed that postmodernists self-consciously blurred and often parodied traditional cultural forms. Postmodern culture delighted in transgressing old boundaries, such as those between mass and elite culture or between fiction and history. Woody Allen's *Zelig* (1983), for example, blended grainy film footage from the 1920s with new (though perfectly matched) scenes from the 1980s and created a pseudo-documentary about a fictional celebrity whom historians had supposedly forgotten. This approach encouraged viewers to imagine they were seeing Allen's character playing baseball with Babe Ruth and talking literature with F. Scott Fitzgerald. This postmodernist parody rejected both the conservative nostalgia of Reaganism and the liberal commitment to the sanctity of accurate historical documentation.

Some critics even proclaimed the arrival of postmodern TV, with shows that reworked, generally in clever parodies, earlier network texts. The first TV hit of the 1990s, *The Simpsons*, offered a cartoon version of a strife-ridden, off-center family. Recalling *Father Knows Best* and classic cartoon families such as *The Flintstones*, this show found a spot on a rival "fourth network," Fox Broadcasting. Ridiculing, while it was recycling, traditional sitcom motifs, *The Simpsons*—and its even more controversial Fox network counterpart *Married with Children*—offered an alternative to the carefully sanitized and thoroughly predictable mainstream fare of the 1980s and early 1990s. In both *Married with Children* and *The Simpsons*, conflict could not always be contained and order did not always prevail; yet these fictional families still expressed a sense of love and solidarity in the most troubled of times.

Other postmodernists went much farther in their search for new cultural forms. Some artists used the types of copying machines found in any college library or print shop to create new works of "art." Others used computers and even fax machines, rather than the traditional brushes and easel, to "paint" their images. Simultaneously stretching traditional artistic boundaries and mocking the repetitive culture of advanced capitalism, such productions parodied the classic TV commercial that asked viewers to decide, "Is it live? Or is it Memorex?"

Cultural Conflict in the 1980s

During the 1980s, some products of mass culture challenged Ronald Reagan's claims of a steadily improving quality of life. In the era of TV satellites, for example, the alliance between music and social activism assumed new forms, as in the Live-Aid concert for African famine relief and several Farm-Aid productions on behalf of rural people in the United States.

Although these high-tech spectacles triggered relatively little controversy, other cultural trends prompted considerable debate. Emerging on the fringes of the popular music industry in New York City during the early 1980s, "rap" became the most controversial new music of the decade. It graphically expressed the contradictory emotions of young African-Americans, especially males. Some songs, for example, rivaled heavy metal music in their misogynistic lyrics; other rap anthems angered Jewish-American groups; and some rappers infuriated law enforcement officials by their "bad attitude"—a term denoting everything from clothing styles to "obscene" language to social outlook—and by the violence that occasionally accompanied rap performances. Rap's admirers, by contrast, emphasized its energy and its connection to everyday experiences and generally neglected social problems; many rap artists, recalling the politics of Black Power, went beyond songs about sex, drugs, and violence to produce ethnically assertive lyrics such as "Proud to Be Black" and "Fight the Power." Rap music underscored the complex cultural conflicts of the 1980s.

Despite the dominant nostalgia, the nation's culture *was* changing, especially as the result of a new wave of immigration. After forty-five years of decline, immigration had been steadily rising in the post–World War II decades; but in the 1980s, the number of immigrants not only expanded dramatically but the countries of origin also changed. Immigrants from Asia, principally Vietnamese and Cambodians, comprised nearly half of the total, while newcomers from Latin America and the Caribbean constituted the next largest groups. Settling in specific areas—such as southeast Florida, Los Angeles, Texas, New York City, and the San Francisco Bay area—the new immigrants quickly made their cultural imprints.

Newcomers from Latin America, for example, joined a Latino minority that was already expanding much faster than the nation's non-Latino population. At that rate, before the second decade of the twenty-first century, Latinos would surpass African-Americans as the largest ethnic minority in the United States. Of course, the broad category of Latino actually blanketed a number of different ethnic groups, each of which brought diverse cultural influences, ranging from salsa music to several new cable-TV networks, during the 1980s. Political attitudes also varied markedly, from arch-conservative, anticommunist refugees from Castro's Cuba to radical heirs of Chicano militancy of the 1970s. But while popular music, journalism, and television all felt the impact of Spanish-language products, the decade also witnessed signs of a cultural backlash. In the face of vibrant and growing Spanish-language cultures, a number of states proclaimed English as their official language and attempted to roll back movements for bilingual education.

Even when new cultural forms, such as salsa and rap, achieved commercial success, other controversies erupted. Spike Lee's movie *Do the Right Thing*, for example, sparked bitter debates, especially since its cinematic images of racially divided, violence-filled neighborhoods paralleled non-cinematic conflicts in cities such as New York, Miami, and Boston. Although his fans saw this young African-American writer-director as doing no more—though no less—than exploring the widely acknowledged problems of racism and poverty, conservative critics claimed *Do the Right Thing* advocated violence as a solution for social and racial ills. Hollywood's Academy Awards completely bypassed Lee's critically acclaimed film, while naming *Driving Miss Daisy*—a picture with politically safer messages about an elderly southern white woman and her African-American chauffeur—as the best motion picture of 1989. In a similar vein, the controversial, postmodern documentary *Roger and Me*, also ignored in the Academy Awards, angered powerful economic interests and cultural patrons with its anti-General Motors message.

The Mass Culture Debate Revisited

The question of how to deal with controversial cultural products cut across many different media and political alliances. Pornography, explicit works that represented the ambiguous legacy of the sexual revolution of the 1960s and 1970s, exemplified many of the dilemmas. What kinds of expression, for example, even qualified as pornographic? To some, the fact that works could get exhibited on some art-gallery's walls, rather than on magazine racks, did not mean that they might not still be pornographic. The sexually explicit and homoerotic photographs of Robert Mapplethorpe, for instance, prompted widespread controversy in several major cities. A heated debate over public funding of the arts resulted from cancellation of a Mapplethorpe exhibition at the prestigious Cochrane Gallery in Washington, D.C. Although a few leaders of the artistic community sympathized with the Cochrane's fear of jeopardizing funding with such contested subject matter, most condemned the gallery for allegedly caving into "censorship" and the political sensibilities of the New Right.

Other types of sexually explicit products, such as commercially distributed magazines, books, and videos, prompted different types of controversies and political alignments. Angered by a rising tide of violence against women, a powerful wing of the feminist coalition blamed pornographic materials for helping to incite the epidemic. Most pornography, they charged, had little to do with encouraging a healthy eroticism and everything to do with exploiting, degrading, and endangering women. In spearheading legal campaigns against pornography, the "anti-porn feminists" saw themselves acting upon a longstanding conviction that the personal and the political could not be separated. Similarly, some veterans of the countercultural 1960s, who now were raising families in urban neighborhoods, also supported the padlocking of businesses that dealt in sexually explicit materials; cleaning out peep-shows and magazine racks seemed part of a larger crusade to rekindle a spirit of neighborhood uplift and community building.

The anti-pornography movement confronted an equally diverse opposition. Making cultural judgments that accorded with those of the New Right instinctively unsettled many in the artistic community. Rallying around the banner of free expression, they joined civil libertarian groups (such as the ACLU) in condemning anti-pornography initiatives as violations of constitutional guarantees. Many of these people and groups had been struggling, since the early cold war era, to expand First Amendment rights, and they feared that lowering any legal barrier against censorship would only embolden cultural and political know-nothings. The anti-pornography movement also troubled many feminists: Was not this new censorship, even though framed in terms of protecting women, part of a broader crusade to revive small-town, Main Street values, including older notions about the "proper" roles into which women should be contained?

Similarly complicated debates swirled around other cultural products, especially rock music. Even before the furor over rap, a campaign to censor rock lyrics, led by the spouse of a United States senator, gathered momentum; worried about governmental intervention, the major record labels rejected the pleas of free-speech advocates and adopted a system of warning labels for songs with images of violence or sex.

MTV, the twenty-four-hour-per-day pop-rock cable network, also stirred controversy. MTV obviously raised the stakes for people in the music business: A hit video came to be almost as important as a gold record, a platinum album, and movie soundtrack. With the stakes so high, critics charged that MTV favored style over substance, featured established groups rather than newcomers, promoted white artists over black ones, and served up anti-female images only slightly less objectionable than those in porno and slasher films.

Despite such criticism, MTV steadily gained revenues and critical attention. Its many admirers quickly credited MTV with spreading a postmodern visual aesthetic that extended the power of rock music with multifaceted media imagery; this thesis gained support with the instant popularity of *Miami Vice*, an otherwise thoroughly familiar detective series that adopted MTV's video style. Buoyed by this critical attention, MTV self-consciously featured "postmodern video" and enticed prominent filmmakers to take rock-video jobs. Some of these products, such as Genesis's anti-Reagan classic "Land of Confusion," offered pointed, anti-establishment viewpoints. And the videos of Madonna, which both recalled and transcended the Marilyn Monroe imagery of the 1950s, sparked debates among religious leaders and feminists as well as among music critics. With all of its contradictory looks, MTV could charm even the most mainstream of people: Its rock-video-inspired reprise of the 1980s even earned MTV a prestigious award for journalistic excellence.

The Culture of Sleaze

Nostalgia for the culture of the late 1940s and early 1950s, ironically, paralleled revival of one of the least desirable aspects of that earlier era—widespread corruption or, at the very least, the perception that corruption flourished nearly everywhere. As the Reagan administration was preparing to leave office, a widely respected Republican rhetorically asked, "For God's sake, are we not entitled to hope that the next administration will be a little less sleazy?" Indeed, the "sleaze factor" appeared oozing into many areas of American life in the 1980s.

Political culture seemed to reek of it. More than a hundred members of Ronald Reagan's administration were either convicted of crimes or cited for ethical violations by various government watchdog bodies. Several top-ranking officeholders, including two cabinet officers, resigned while under fire. The department of Housing and Urban Development (HUD), another scandal-tainted cabinet office, paid outrageously large "consulting" fees to prominent Republicans and channeled scarce housing and redevelopment funds into a series of questionable projects. Meanwhile, appointees in the

Pentagon pleaded guilty to accepting bribes, and investigative journalists claimed that Reagan's $2.2 trillion worth of defense expenditures included huge cost overruns on faulty products and unnecessary expenditures for vastly overpriced spare parts.

Reagan's Democratic adversaries also had their troubles. During the 1988 presidential primaries, candidate Gary Hart challenged journalists to scrutinize his personal life: "If anybody wants to put a tail on me, go ahead. They'd be very bored." Quite the contrary. Apparently shadowing his every move, journalists discovered Hart, who campaigned as a "family man," sailing off the Florida coast and sneaking around Washington with "another woman." Although some traditionalists thought such scandal-hunting overstepped the longstanding maxim that the private foibles of political figures were not "news," journalists rushed to find new sleaze. Several prominent Democrats, including House Speaker Jim Wright, were forced to leave office in the wake of stories, pressed by both journalists and Republican activists, about questionable financial dealings.

Powerful religious figures also had their problems. Reverend Jimmy Swaggart, head of a vast television and religious-publishing empire fell into disgrace and (even worse for an evangelical preacher) media oblivion, when a rival minister revealed Swaggart's patronage of prostitutes. Oral Roberts, a longtime leader of the electronic church, confronted falling TV ratings and declining revenues after a tacky campaign in which he claimed that the Lord might strike him down if donors failed to fill his coffers. And perhaps in the biggest sleaze spectacle of the 1980s, Jim and Tammy Bakker lost their religious theme park, television network, and personal fortune when a sex and money-skimming scandal enveloped their "ministry"; after an angst-filled trial, Jim Bakker received a lengthy jail sentence.

The culture of sleaze also became big business. CBS's *60 Minutes* used stories about scams and schemes to reach Neilsen's top ten, while ABC's *Nightline* received its highest-ever ratings when it featured an interview of the Bakkers. By the mid-1980s, imitators of *60 Minutes* flooded TV's syndicated market, peddling stories and formats considered too sleazy to meet network standards. One popular cultural form, professional wrestling, also thrived on sleaze: Treachery and double-dealing were required behavior, and one night's hero could become the following evening's villain. (Although the cartoonish Hulk Hogan seemed immune, even the once-lovable Andre the Giant joined the sleazy "family" of Bobby ("the Brain") Heenan in the 1980s.) Meanwhile, supposedly legitimate sports wallowed in scandal as sports pages detailed allegations of players betting on games, accounts of heavy (often illegal and sometimes fatal) drug use, and even of fixed games and point shaving. By comparison, the sports scandals of the late 1940s and early 1950s seemed minor-league affairs.

Two of the biggest non-sports heroes of 1980s failed to escape taint during the 1990s. One of the former decade's central icons, Donald Trump, became tabloid fodder when tales of his marital and financial troubles became public. Similarly, Ronald Reagan's Teflon coating began to become stained by sleaze. The Gipper, most people continued to believe, was person-ally innocent of sleazy behavior; but political observers suspected that he had paid too little attention to the sleazy people and events connected with his presidency. Reportedly, for example, Reagan once mistook Samuel Pierce, head of scandal-ridden HUD, for a big-city mayor. Reagan seemed similarly oblivious to mounting evidence of corruption in the savings and loan indus-try. Even many admirers expressed sadness when the ex-president traded upon the glamour of his former office to obtain a seven-figure fee for several speeches in Japan. After Reagan had been out of office a year, opinion polls showed his approval rating below that of another former president, Jimmy Carter, the person whom Reagan had handily out-polled only a decade earlier.

Retrospective

The 1980s, like all the other mileposts in the postwar era, offered as much ambiguity as clarity: a time of prosperity and poverty, a period of official peace and expensive preparations for war, a politics dominated by a septuagenerian president and a culture still indebted to the youth move-ment of the 1960s, a society teeming with images both of nostalgia and a high-tech future.

Any point in time is a culmination of previous trends, but the 1980s, more than most, seemed a summary decade. The population of the United States was, after all, aging. The median age had risen from seventeen in 1968 to thirty-seven by 1987. The largest bulk of the population remembered, often nostalgically, the 1950s; it matured through the searing experiences of the 1960s and early 1970s; it reached the 1980s wondering about ultimate direction, both personal and social. American life in the 1980s seemed to thrash around in memories, mixing nostalgia, old causes and divisions, and "lessons" from various pasts with high hopes and desperate dreams about the future. The World War II generation—which had felt such a high degree of national consensus—was about to pass from the scene. What new agendas would be set? What new visions would inspire? The future, as always, would be what people could make of it.

SUGGESTIONS FOR FURTHER READING

A good place to begin looking at the 1980s is in the census data; see Andrew Hacker, ed., *US* (1983); and for a controversial, though provocative, inter-pretation of the nation's place in the world, see Paul Kennedy, *The Rise and Fall of the Great Powers* (1988).

Attempts to understand Ronald Reagan include Lou Cannon, *Reagan* (1982); Robert Dallek, *Ronald Reagan and the Politics of Symbolism* (1984); Michael Rogin, *Ronald Reagan the Movie* (1987); Garry Wills, *Reagan's Ameri-*

ca: Innocents at Home (1987); Sidney Blumenthal, *Our Long National Day-dream: A Political Pageant of the Reagan Era* (1988); Jane Mayer and Doyle McManus, *Landslide: The Unmaking of a President, 1984–1988* (1988), and Kevin Phillips, *The Politics of Rich and Poor* (1970).

Attempts to assess the broad impact of the Reagan years include Sidney Blumenthal and Thomas Byrne Edsall, eds., *The Reagan Legacy* (1988); Ryan J. Barilleaux, *The Post-Modern Presidency: The Office After Ronald Reagan* (1988); Kathleen Hall Jamieson and David S. Birdsell, *Presidential Debates: The Challenge of Creating an Informed Electorate* (1988); William F. Grover, *The President as Prisoner: A Structural Critique of the Carter and Reagan Years* (1989); Richard O. Curry, *Freedom at Risk* (1989); John Kenneth White, *The New Politics of Old Values* (2nd ed., 1990); and Harold H. Koh, *The National Security Constitution: Sharing Power After the Iran-Contra Affair* (1990).

Economic policies are the subject of Michael Boskin, *Too Many Promises: The Uncertain Future of Social Security* (1986); William Greider, *Secrets of the Temple* (1987); James Tobin and Murray Weidenbaum, eds., *Two Revolutions in Economic Policy: The First Economic Reports of Presidents Kennedy and Reagan* (1988); Martin Anderson, *Revolution* (1988); Dennis Swann, *The Retreat of the State: Deregulation and Privatization in the UK and the US* (1988); Roger E. Meiners and Bruce Yandle, *Regulation and the Reagan Era* (1989); James K. Galbraith, *Balancing Acts: Technology, Finance, and the American Future* (1989); and Kenneth R. Hoover, *Conservative Capitalism in Britain and the United States: A Critical Appraisal* (1989).

Foreign policies are discussed in Walter LaFeber, *Inevitable Revolutions: The United States in Central America* (1983); Strobe Talbot, *Deadly Gambits: The Reagan Administration and the Stalemate in Nuclear Arms Control* (1984); Thomas Walker, ed., *Reagan versus the Sandinistas* (1987); Kenneth Oye and others, eds., *Eagle Resurgent? The Reagan Era in American Foreign Policy* (1987); James A. Bill, *The Eagle and the Lion: The Tragedy of American-Iranian Relations* (1988); Morris H. Morley, ed., *Crisis and Confrontation: Ronald Reagan's Foreign Policy* (1988); Roy Gutman, *Banana Diplomacy: The Making of American Policy in Nicaragua, 1981–1987* (1988); H. Bruce Franklin, *War Stars: The Superweapon and the American Imagination* (1988); Coral Bell, *The Reagan Paradox: American Foreign Policy in the 1980s* (1989); and William E. Brock and Robert D. Hormats, eds., *The Global Economy; America's Role in the Decade Ahead* (1990).

Other issues of the Reagan presidency include Elder Witt, *A Different Justice: Reagan and the Supreme Court* (1986); and C. Brant Short, *Ronald Reagan and the Public Lands: America's Conservation Debate, 1979–1984* (1989).

On social issues of the 1980s, many of the works cited at the end of Chapters 8 and 9 remain relevant. In addition, see Robert Bellah and others, *Habits of the Heart: Individualism & Commitment in American Life* (1984); Mark Friedberger, *Shake-Out: Iowa Farm Families in the 1980s* (1989); Valerie O'Conner Sutter, *The Indochinese Refugee Dilemma* (1989); Randy Shilts, *And the Band Played On: Politics, People, and the AIDS Epidemic* (1988); Fred Harris and Roger W. Wilkins, eds., *Quiet Riots: Race and Poverty in the United States:*

The Kerner Report Twenty Years Later (1989); James Coates, *Armed and Dangerous: The Rise of the Survivalist Right* (1989); Luciano Mangiafico, *Contemporary American Immigrants: Patterns of Filipino, Korean, and Chinese Settlement in the United States* (1988); William Julius Wilson, *The Ghetto Underclass* (1989); Barbara Ehrenreich, *Fear of Falling: The Inner Life of the Middle-Class* (1989); and Neil Miller, *In Search of Gay America: Women and Men in a Time of Change* (1989).

On postmodernism, see Charles Jencks, *Post-Modernism: The New Classicism in Art and Architecture* (1987); E. Ann Kaplan, *Rocking Around the Clock: Music Television, Postmodernism, and Consumer Culture* (1987); Linda Hutcheon, *A Poetics of Postmodernism* (1987); David Harvey, *The Condition of Postmodernism* (1989); and Linda J. Nicholson, ed., *Feminism/Postmodernism* (1990).

Index